직독직해로 읽는

크리스마스 캐럴
A Christmas Carol

직독직해로 읽는

크리스마스 캐럴
A Christmas Carol

개정판 1쇄 발행 2020년 10월 30일
초판 1쇄 발행   2011년 10월 20일

원작	찰스 디킨스
역주	더 콜링(김정희, 박윤수, 이혜련)
디자인	DX
일러스트	정은수
발행인	조경아
발행처	랭귀지북스
주소	서울시 마포구 포은로2나길 31 벨라비스타 208호
전화	02.406.0047　　**팩스**　02.406.0042
이메일	languagebooks@hanmail.net
MP3 다운로드	blog.naver.com/languagebook
등록번호	101-90-85278　　**등록일자**　2008년 7월 10일
ISBN	979-11-5635-144-3 (13740)
가격	13,000원

ⓒ LanguageBooks 2011

「이 도서의 국립중앙도서관 출판예정도서목록(CIP)은 서지정보유통지원시스템 홈페이지(http://seoji.nl.go.kr)와
국가자료공동목록시스템(http://www.nl.go.kr/kolisnet)에서 이용하실 수 있습니다.(CIP제어번호: CIP2020043676)」

직독직해로 읽는

크리스마스 캐럴
A Christmas Carol

찰스 디킨스 원작
더 콜링 역주

Language Books

머리말

"어렸을 때 누구나 갖고 있던 세계명작 한 질,
그리고 TV에서 하던 세계명작 만화에 대한 추억이 있습니다."

"친숙한 이야기를 영어 원문으로 읽어 봐야겠다고 마음 먹고 샀던 원서들은
이제 애물단지가 되어 버렸습니다."

"재미있는 세계명작 하나 읽어 보려고 따져 보는 어려운 영문법,
모르는 단어 찾느라 이리저리 뒤져 봐야 하는 사전,
몇 장 넘겨 보기도 전에 지칩니다."

영어 독해력을 기르려면 술술 읽어가며 내용을 파악하는 것이
중요합니다. 현재 수능 시험에도 대세인 '직독직해' 스타일을 접목시
킨 〈**직독직해로 읽는 세계명작 시리즈**〉는 세계명작을 영어 원작으
로 쉽게 읽어갈 수 있도록 안내해 드릴 것입니다.

'직독직해' 스타일로 읽다 보면, 영문법을 들먹이며 따질 필요
가 없으니 쉽고, 끊어 읽다 보니 독해 속도도 **빨라집니다**. 이 습관
이 들여지면 어떤 글을 만나도 두렵지 않을 것입니다.

명작의 재미를 즐기며 영어 독해력을 키우는 두 마리의 토끼
를 잡으세요!

　〈직독직해로 읽는 세계명작 시리즈〉의 나의 소중한 파트너 오랜 친구 윤수, 쿨하게 번역 작업을 함께해 준 번역자 혜련 씨와 바쁜 일정 중에도 따뜻한 문자로 안부 묻던 일러스트레이터 은수 씨, 좋은 동역자 디자인 DX, 그리고 이 책이 출판될 수 있도록 늘 든든하게 지원해 주시는 랭귀지북스에 감사의 마음을 전합니다.

　마지막으로 내 삶의 이유가 되시는 하나님께 영광을 올려 드립니다.

더 콜링 김정희

목차

《크리스마스 캐럴》의 작가 찰스 존 허펌 디킨스

(Charles John Huffam Dickens, 1812년 2월 7일 – 1870년 6월 9일)는

빅토리아 시대에 활동한 영국 소설가입니다.

화가 시모어의 만화를 위해 쓰기 시작한

희곡 소설 〈픽위크 클럽〉을 분책으로 출판하여 일약 유명해졌습니다.

그는 특히 가난한 사람에 대한 깊은 동정을 보이고,

사회의 악습에 반격을 가하면서,

사회에 대한 실제의 일들의 묘사를 이야기 형식으로 완성했습니다.

후기 소설에는 초기의 넘치던 풍자는 약해졌지만,

구성의 치밀함과 사회 비평의 심화는 여전히 주목을 받았습니다.

그의 작품으로

자전적 요소가 짙은 〈데이비드 커퍼필드〉, 〈위대한 유산〉 등을 비롯,

〈올리버 트위스트〉, 〈크리스마스 캐럴〉, 〈두 도시의 이야기〉 등이 있습니다.

그가 1870년 사망하여 성공회 교회인
웨스트민스터 대성당의 시인들의 묘역에 안장되었는데,
그의 묘비에 쓰인 다음 문구를 보면,
당시 사람들이 얼마나 그를 사랑했는지 엿볼 수 있습니다.

He was a sympathiser to the poor, the suffering,
and the oppressed; and by his death,
one of England's greatest writers is lost to the world.

그는 가난하고 고통 받고 박해 받는 자들의 동정자였으며

그의 죽음으로 인해

세상은 영국의 가장 훌륭한 작가 중 하나를 잃었다.

《크리스마스 캐럴》(A Christmas Carol)은
영국의 소설가 찰스 디킨스가 쓴 중편 소설입니다.
1843년 발표되었으며, 그 후 해마다 발표된
5편의 《크리스마스 이야기》의 제1작으로
그의 대표작 중의 하나입니다.

자린고비 구두쇠인 주인공
스크루지(에브니저 스크루지 Ebenezer Scrooge)는
인정이라곤 손톱끝만치도 없는 수전노로,
크리스마스 전날 밤에 동업자의 유령을 만나
자기의 과거·현재·미래의 모습을 보게 되자
자신의 죄를 뉘우치고 사람다운 마음을 찾게 된다는 이야기입니다.
유령을 소설 속에 등장시키는 과감한 작가의 내용 구성은
《아라비안나이트》 등 다양한 이야기를 읽으면서 키운
상상력에 근거했다고 합니다.

스크루지가 어떻게 개과천선을 하게 되는지
원문의 의미를 잘 헤아리면서
읽어 보세요.

1

MARLEY'S GHOST I
말리의 유령 I

Marley was dead: / to begin with. There is no doubt /
말리는 죽었다:　　　　　거기에서 시작하겠다.　　의심의 여지가 없다

whatever about that. The register of his burial was signed
그 일에 대해서는 무엇이든.　　매장 기록부에 서명했다

/ by the clergyman, / the clerk, / the undertaker, / and the
　　　　목사와,　　　　　서기,　　　　장의사,

chief mourner. Scrooge signed it: / and Scrooge's name
그리고 상주가.　　스크루지도 거기에 서명했다:　　그리고 스크루지의 이름은 거래소

was good upon 'Change, / for anything he chose to put
에서도 확실했다,　　　　　　손에 넣고자 선택한 것은 무엇이든 갖는 것으로.

his hand to. Old Marley was as dead as a door-nail.
말리 영감은 대문의 대갈못처럼 죽었다.

Mind! I don't mean to say / that I know, / of my own
주의하시길! 말하려는 것이 아니다　　알고 있다고,　　내가 가진 지식을,

knowledge, / what there is particularly dead about
　　　　　대갈못에 특별히 죽음에 관한 뭔가 있다고.

a door-nail. I might have been inclined, / myself,
　　　　하고 싶었을 것이다,　　　　　나라면,

/ to regard / a coffin-nail / as the deadest piece of
　생각한다고　관에 박는 못을　철물점에서 가장 죽음에 유사한 물건이라고

ironmongery / in the trade. But the wisdom of our
　　　　　팔고 있는 물건 중.　하지만 우리 조상들의 지혜가 들어 있다

ancestors is / in the simile; / and my unhallowed hands
이　비유 속에;　　　그러니 내 부정한 손으로 그 지혜를 망치려는

shall not disturb it, / or the Country's done for.
것은 아니다,　　　　그랬다면 온 나라가 어떻게 되겠는가.

You will therefore permit me / to repeat, / emphatically, /
그러므로 여러분들은 허락해 줄 것이다　　반복하는 것을,　강조하여,

that Marley was as dead as a door-nail.
말리는 대갈못처럼 죽었다고.

Scrooge knew he was dead? Of course he did. How
스크루지는 그가 죽었다는 것을 알고 있었느냐고? 물론 알고 있었다.

could it be otherwise? Scrooge and he were partners
어떻게 모를 수 있겠는가?　　　　　스크루지와 말리는 동업자였다

/ for I don't know how many years. Scrooge was his
나로서는 몇 년 동안인지도 알 수 없을 만큼 오랫동안.　　　스크루지는 말리의 유일한 유언

sole executor, / his sole administrator, / his sole assign,
집행인이었고,　　　　유일한 유산 관리인이었으며,　　　　유일한 유산 위탁인이자,

/ his sole residuary legatee, / his sole friend, / and sole
유일한 재산 상속인이고,　　　　유일한 친구이면서,　　　유일한 문상객

mourner. And even Scrooge was not so dreadfully cut
이었다.　　　그런데 스크루지는 그다지 엄청나게 슬퍼하지도 않았으며

up / by the sad event, / but that he was an excellent
그 슬픈 사건에,　　　　훌륭한 사업 수완을 발휘하여

man of business / on the very day of the funeral, / and
장례식 당일에도,

solemnized it / with an undoubted bargain.
식을 치뤄냈다　　　정말 저렴하게.

Key Expression

as dead as a doornail : 완전히 죽은

예전에 성문에 박아두는 대못을 'doornail'이라고 불렀습니다. 적의 성문을 열 때는 수십 명의 병사들이 통나무를 들고 충격을 가했는데 이 때 성문이 죽은 듯이 꿈쩍도 안 하는 모습에서 'as dead as a doornail'이 '완전히 죽어버린'이라는 의미로 쓰이게 되었답니다.

ex) Old Marley was as dead as a door-nail.
말리 영감은 대갈못처럼 완전히 죽었다.

register 기록부 | clergyman 성직자, 목사 | clerk 서기, 기록계 | undertaker 장의사 | chief mourner
상주 | 'Change 거래소(=Exchange) | put to 대다 | door-nail (장식용, 보강용으로 문에 박은) 대갈못 | incline
마음이 기울다, 하고 싶은 생각이 들다 | coffin 관 | ironmongery 철물점 | trade 매매, 장사 | simile 직유 |
unhallowed 부정한, 신성하지 않은 | emphatically 단호하게, 강조하여 | sole 유일한 | executer 유언 집행자 |
administrator 유산 관리인 | assign 유산 위탁인 | residuary 잔여 재산의 | legatee 상속인 | mourner 문상객
| dreadfully 몹시, 엄청나게 | cut up 몹시 슬퍼하게 하다 | solemnize 엄숙하게 식을 치르다 | undoubted
의심할 바 없는, 진정한 | bargain 싼 값

13

The mention of Marley's funeral / brings me back to the
말리의 장례식에 관해 언급하니   그 시점으로 돌아가게 된다

point / I started from. There is no doubt / that Marley
처음 이야기를 시작했던. 의심의 여지가 없다   말리가 죽었다는 것은.

was dead. This must be distinctly understood, / or
이것은 분명히 알고 있어야 한다,

nothing wonderful can come of the story / I am going to
그러지 않으면 이야기에 놀라지 않을 수도 있다   내가 시작하려는.

relate. If we were not perfectly convinced / that Hamlet's
만약 우리가 만약 확실히 납득하지 않는다면   햄릿의 아버지가 죽었

Father died / before the play began, / there would be
다는 점을   연극이 시작되기 전에.   특별한 점이 없을지도 모른다

nothing more remarkable / in his taking a stroll / at
햄릿 아버지가 배회한다는 사실에

night, / in an easterly wind, / upon his own ramparts, /
밤중에,   동풍이 불어오는 가운데.   성벽 위를,

than there would be in any other middle-aged gentleman
다른 여느 중년 신사가

/ rashly turning out / after dark / in a breezy spot / — say
갑자기 나타나는 것보다   어두워진 후   바람 부는 곳에

Saint Paul's Churchyard / for instance — / literally / to
— 말하자면 세인트폴 성당 마당에   예를 들어 —   말 그대로

astonish his son's weak mind.
마음 약한 자신의 아들을 놀라게 하려고.

Scrooge never painted out / Old Marley's name. There it
스크루지는 지우지 않았다   고인인 말리의 이름을.   그 이름은 그대

stood, / years afterwards, / above the warehouse door: /
로 있었다.   몇 년이 지난 후에도,   상점 문 위에:

distinctly 명백히 | relate 이야기 하다 | remarkable 두드러진, 주목할 만한 | stroll 산책 | easterly 동쪽으로부터 | rampart 성벽 | rashly 성급하게, 경솔히 | turn out 참석하다, 모이다 | literally 정말로, 실제로 | astonish 놀라게 하다 | paint out 페인트칠로 지우다 | tight-fisted 인색한, 꽉 움켜진 | grindstone 맷돌(쉴새없이 일하는 모습을 비유하는 표현으로 쓰임) | wrench 비틀다 | grasp 움켜쥐다 | scrap 긁다 | clutch 꽉 쥐다 | covetous 턱없이 탐내는, 욕심 많은 | flint 부싯돌 | strike out (쳐서, 마찰하여) ~에 불(꽃)이 나게 하다 | self-contained 마음을 터놓지 않는 | solitary 고독한, 외로운 | nipped 꼬집다, 쥐어뜯다 | shrivelled 주름지다 | stiffened 경직시키다 | gait 걸음걸이 | shrewdly 약삭빠르게 | grating 신경을 건드리는 | frosty 얼어붙는 듯한 | rime 서리 | wiry 철사같이 질긴 | carry about 가지고 다니다, 휴대하다 | dog-days 삼복더위 | thaw 녹이다

Scrooge and Marley. The firm was known / as Scrooge
'스크루지와 말리'. 　　　　　　　　그 회사는 알려져 있었다

and Marley. Sometimes people new to the business /
'스크루지와 말리'로. 때때로 처음 거래하러 오는 사람들은

called Scrooge Scrooge, / and sometimes Marley, / but he
'스크루지 스크루지'라고 불렸고, 　　때로는 '말리'라고 불렀지만,

answered to both names. It was all the same to him.
스크루지는 둘 다 대답했다. 　　　그에게는 어차피 모든 것이 같았다.

Oh! But he was a tight-fisted hand at the grindstone,
아! 　하지만 스크루지는 맷돌을 꽉 쥔 손처럼 쉴새없이 일하는 구두쇠였다,

/ Scrooge! A squeezing, / wrenching, / grasping, /
스크루지! 쥐어짜고, 　　　　비틀고, 　　　움켜쥐고,

scraping, / clutching, / covetous, / old sinner! Hard and
긁어 모으고, 　한 번 쥐면 놓지 않는, 욕심이 많은, 　늙은 죄인! 　부싯돌처럼 단단

sharp as flint, / from which no steel had ever struck out
하고 날카로우며, 　어떤 쇠뭉치로 쳐도 불꽃이 시원하게 일지 않는;

generous fire; / secret, / and self-contained, / and solitary
비밀스럽고, 　마음을 터놓지 않고, 　　　껍질 속의 굴처럼

as an oyster. The cold within him / froze his old features,
외로운. 　　　내면의 냉기는 　　　　늙은 몸을 얼리고,

/ nipped his pointed nose, / shrivelled his cheek, /
뾰족한 코를 쥐어뜯으며, 　　　빰에 주름을 만들고,

stiffened his gait; / made his eyes red, / his thin lips blue;
걸음걸이마저 뻣뻣하게 했으며; 눈은 벌겋게 충혈되고, 　　　얇은 입술은 파래졌다;

/ and spoke out shrewdly / in his grating voice. A frosty
약삭빠른 말투에 배어나왔다 　건드리는 목소리로. 　　　얼어붙을 듯한 서

rime was / on his head, / and on his eyebrows, / and his
리가 내려 앉았다 머리에, 　　　눈썹에, 　　　　그리고 뻣뻣한

wiry chin. He carried his own low temperature always
턱수염에. 　그가 가는 곳이면 어디에나 찬바람이 불었다;

about with him; / he iced his office in the dog-days; / and
　　　　　　그는 삼복 더위에도 사무실을 얼렸고;

didn't thaw it one degree / at Christmas.
사무실 온도를 1도도 올리지 않았다 　크리스마스에도.

External heat and cold / had little influence / on Scrooge.
외부의 더위와 추위는   거의 영향을 미치지 않았다   스크루지에게.

No warmth could warm, / no wintry weather chill him.
어떤 온기도 따뜻하게 하지 못했고,   어떤 겨울 날씨도 그를 떨게 못하게 했다.

No wind that blew / was bitterer than he, / no falling
불어오는 어떤 바람도   그보다 더 매섭지 못했고,   내리는 어떤 눈도

snow was / more intent upon its purpose, / no pelting
        그 목적을 집요하게 이루지 못했으며,   퍼붓는 장대비도

rain / less open to entreaty. Foul weather didn't know /
        간절할 것 같지 않았다.   험악한 날씨마저도 알지 못했다

where to have him. The heaviest rain, / and snow, / and
어디에서 스크루지를 상대해야 할지. 폭우도,   눈도,

hail, / and sleet, / could boast of the advantage / over
우박도,   진눈깨비마저도,   그에 비하면 장점을 자랑할 수 있었다   그에게는

him / in only one respect. They often "came down"
단 한 가지 점에서.   그것들은 때때로 인심 좋게 "내리지만",

handsomely, / and Scrooge never did.
        스크루지는 절대 그런 법이 없었다.

Nobody ever stopped him in the street / to say, / with
아무도 길에서 그를 불러 세우지 않았다   말하기 위해,

gladsome looks, / "My dear Scrooge, / how are you?
반가운 표정으로,   "스크루지 씨,   안녕하세요?

When will you come to see me?" No beggars implored
언제 저를 보러 오시죠?"   거지들도 그에게 구걸하지 않았고

him / to bestow a trifle, / no children asked him / what it
        한 푼 달라고,   아이들도 묻지 않았으며   몇 시인지,

was o'clock, / no man or woman ever / once in all his life
몇 시인지,   남자이든 여자이든   평생 단 한 번도

/ inquired the way to such and such a place, / of Scrooge.
어디론가 가는 길을 물어보지 않았다,   스크루지에게.

---

intent 작정한 | pelting rain 퍼붓는 비 | open to ~하기 쉬운 | entreaty 간청, 애원 | foul (날씨가) 궂은,
험악한 | hail 우박 | sleet 진눈깨비 | in one respect 한 가지 점에서 | handsomely 인심 좋게 | gladsome
기쁜, 반가운 | implore 애원하다 | bestow ~을 주다 | trifle 푼돈 | tug 끌어 당기다 | court 안마당 | edge
along 서서히 나아가다

Even the blind men's dogs / appeared to know him; / and
심지어 맹도견들조차   그를 아는 것 같아서;

when they saw him coming on, / would tug their owners
스크루지가 오는 것을 보면,   자기 주인을 끌어 당겨서

/ into doorways and up courts; / and then would wag
  현관이나 안뜰로 들어갔고;   그리고 나서 꼬리를 흔들곤 했다

their tails / as though they said, / "No eye at all is better /
그들의 꼬리를   말하기라도 하는 듯이,   "아예 눈이 없는 것이 훨씬 나아

than an evil eye, / dark master!"
악마의 눈이 있는 것보다는,   앞 못 보는 주인님!"

But what did Scrooge care! It was the very thing / he
하지만 스크루지가 뭘 상관하겠는가!   이것이 바로 그것이다   그가

liked. To edge his way / along the crowded paths of life, /
좋아하는. 그의 길을 헤쳐나가기 위해   복잡한 인생길에서,

warning all human sympathy / to keep its distance, / was
사람들의 동정심을 경계하는 것은   거리를 두며,

what the knowing ones call "nuts" / to Scrooge.
소위 현명한 사람들이 말하는 "장땡"이었다   스크루지에게는.

Once upon a time / — of all the good days in the year,
어느 날 — 한 해의 가장 즐거운 날들 중 하루인,

/ on Christmas Eve — / old Scrooge sat busy / in his
크리스마스 이브였다 — 스크루지 영감은 바삐 일하며 앉아 있었다

counting-house. It was cold, / bleak, / biting weather: /
자신의 회계 사무실 안에서. 춥고, 살을 에는 듯한, 매서운 날씨였다:

foggy withal: / and he could hear the people / in the court
안개까지 껴 있었다: 그리고 그는 사람들 소리를 들을 수 있었다 밖의 골목에서,

outside, / go wheezing up and down, / beating their hands
숨을 오르락 내리락 쌕쌕거리며, 손으로 가슴을 치고,

upon their breasts, / and stamping their feet upon the
포장된 돌길에 발을 구르며 걸어가는

pavement stones / to warm them. The city clocks had only
몸을 녹이려고. 광장 시계는 이제 겨우 3시가 지났지만,

just gone three, / but it was quite dark already / — it had
벌써 꽤나 어두웠고

not been light all day — / and candles were flaring / in the
— 하루종일 밝지 않았다 — 촛불이 너울대고 있었다

windows of the neighboring offices, / like ruddy smears
이웃 사무실들의 창문에서, 붉은 얼룩처럼

/ upon the palpable brown air. The fog came pouring in /
짙은 갈색 공기에 스미는. 안개는 쏟아져 들어왔고

at every chink and keyhole, / and was so dense without, /
모든 틈과 열쇠 구멍으로, 무척 짙어서,

that although the court was of the narrowest, / the houses
가장 좁은 골목길이라도,

opposite were mere phantoms. To see the dingy cloud
반대편 집들이 단지 유령처럼 보였다. 우중충한 구름을 보면

/ come drooping down, / obscuring everything, / one
내려앉아, 모든 것을 감추는,

might have thought / that Nature lived hard by, / and was
누구나 생각했을지도 모른다 자연이 근처에 살면서 열심히,

brewing on a large scale.
대량의 구름을 만들어 내고 있다고.

The door of Scrooge's counting-house was open / that
스크루지의 회계 사무실 문은 열려 있었는데

he might keep his eye upon his clerk, / who in a dismal
자기의 서기를 감시하는 것일지도 모른다.   저 너머의 음침하고 작은

little cell beyond, / a sort of tank, / was copying letters.
방에서,   골방처럼 생긴,   서류를 옮겨 쓰고 있던.

Scrooge had a very small fire, / but the clerk's fire was
스크루지는 아주 작은 난로를 쬐고 있었지만,   서기의 난로는 훨씬 작아서

so very much smaller / that it looked like one coal. But
          석탄 한 덩어리처럼 보였다.

he couldn't replenish it, / for Scrooge kept the coal-box
하지만 서기는 석탄을 보충할 수 없었다.   스크루지가 석탄 상자를 가지고 있었기 때문에

/ in his own room; / and so surely / as the clerk came in
    자기 방에;   그러니 분명히   서기가 삽을 들고 들어가면,

with the shovel, / the master predicted / that it would be
          주인은 생각할 것이 틀림없었다

necessary for them to part. Wherefore the clerk put on
그만 헤어져야겠다고.   그 때문에 서기는 자신의 하얀 털실 목도리를

his white comforter, / and tried to warm himself at the
두르고,   촛불에라도 몸을 녹여 보려고 노력했다;

candle; / in which effort, / not being a man of a strong
    그런 노력에도,   풍부한 상상력을 가지지 못한 사람이라서,

imagination, / he failed.
          실패했다.

"A merry Christmas, / uncle! God save you!" / cried a
"메리 크리스마스,   삼촌!   하나님이 축복해 주시길!"

cheerful voice. It was the voice of Scrooge's nephew, /
명랑한 소리가 들려왔다. 스크루지 조카의 목소리였다,

who came upon him so quickly / that this was the first
아주 재빨리 다가와서   이 인사로 겨우 알아차렸다

intimation / he had of his approach.
          조카가 왔다는 사실을.

counting-house 회계 사무소 | bleak 살을 에는 듯한 | withal 이에 더하여, 게다가 | wheeze (숨쉬기가 힘이
들어서) 쌕쌕거리다 | ruddy 붉게 빛나는, 붉은 | smear 얼룩 | palpable 명백한, 짙은 | chink 틈 | dingy
우중충한 | droop down 늘어지다 | obscure 숨기다, 가리다 | brew 양조하다, 만들다 | dismal 우울한, 음침한 |
replenish 채우다, 보충하다 | wherefore 그 때문에 | comforter 털실 목도리 | intimation 암시, 넌지시 비침

"Bah!" / said Scrooge, / "Humbug!"
"흥!"　　　　스크루지가 말했다.　　　"헛소리하고 있군!"

He had so heated himself / with rapid walking / in the
그는 몸이 무척 상기되어　　　　빨리 걸어온 탓에

fog and frost, / this nephew of Scrooge's, / that he was all
안개와 서리 속에서,　　스크루지의 조카는,　　　　온몸이 달아올랐다;

in a glow; / his face was ruddy and handsome; / his eyes
　　　　　　　얼굴은 발그레하고 잘 생겼으며;　　　　눈은 빛났고,

sparkled, / and his breath smoked again.
　　　　　임김이 다시 뿜어져 나왔다.

"Christmas a humbug, / uncle!" / said Scrooge's nephew.
"크리스마스가 헛소리라니요,　　삼촌!"　　스크루지의 조카는 말했다.

"You don't mean that, / I am sure?"
"진심은 아니겠죠,　　　　　　맞죠?"

"I do," / said Scrooge. "Merry Christmas! What right have
"진심이야,"　　스크루지가 말했다.　"메리 크리스마스라니!　　네 놈이 도대체 무슨 권리

you to be merry? What reason have you to be merry?
로 즐거워 하는 거냐?　　즐거워 해야 하는 이유라도 있냐고?

You're poor enough."
가난한 주제에."

"Come, / then," / returned the nephew gaily. "What
"자,　　　그럼,"　　조카가 명랑하게 되물었다.

right have you to be dismal? What reason have you to be
"삼촌은 우울해야 할 권리라도 있으세요?　　시무룩해야 하는 이유라도 있냐고요?

morose? You're rich enough."
　　　　부자이시잖아요."

Scrooge having no better answer / ready on the spur / of
스크루지는 좋은 대답을 찾을 수 없어　　　즉시 준비된

the moment, / said, / "Bah!" again; / and followed it up /
그 순간,　　　　말한 뒤,　"흥!"하고 다시;　　연이어 말했다

with "Humbug."
"헛소리야"라고.

"Don't be cross, / uncle!" / said the nephew.
"화내지 마세요,　　　삼촌!"　　조카가 말했다.

humbug 사기, 협잡 | glow 달아오름, 훈훈함 | sparkle 빛나다 | dismal 울적한, 우울한 | morose 시무룩한 |
on the spur 전속력으로, 아주 급히

20　A Christmas Carol

"What else can I be," / returned the uncle, / "when I live in
"화 안 나게 됐냐," 삼촌이 대구했다, "멍청이들이 우글거리는

such a world of fools / as this? Merry Christmas! Out upon
세상에 살고 있는데 이렇게? 메리 크리스마스라니!

merry Christmas! What's Christmas time to you / but a
메리 크리스마스라고 말했어! 크리스마스가 네게 뭐란 말이냐

time for paying bills / without money; / a time for finding
내야 할 청구서만 잔뜩인 때잖아 돈도 없으면서;

yourself a year older, / but not an hour richer; / a time for
나이 한 살 더 먹는 걸 알게 될 뿐, 형편이 조금도 나아지지 않으면서;

balancing your books / and having every item in 'em /
장부 결산을 해야 하는데 장부 속의 모든 항목이

through a round dozen of months / presented dead against
일 년 열두 달 내내 적자인 것을 알게 될 뿐이지?

you? If I could work my will," / said Scrooge indignantly,
내가 할 수만 있다면," 스크루지는 분개하며 말했다,

/ "every idiot / who goes about / with 'Merry Christmas'
"머저리들은 모조리 돌아다니는 입에 '메리 크리스마스'를 달고,

on his lips, / should be boiled with his own pudding, / and
자기 푸딩과 함께 끓여서, 묻으면

buried / with a stake of holly through his heart. He should!"
좋으련만 가슴에 트리 장식용 나무 가지를 찔러서. 그래도 싸!"

"Uncle!" / pleaded the nephew.
"삼촌!" 조카가 항변했다.

"Nephew!" / returned the uncle sternly, / "keep Christmas
"조카야!" 삼촌이 단호하게 대답했다. "네 식대로 크리스마스를

in your own way, / and let me keep it in mine."
지내라, 그리고 나는 내 식대로 지내게 내버려 두란 말이야."

"Keep it!" / repeated Scrooge's nephew. "But you don't
"지내다니요!" 스크루지의 조카는 따라 했다. "하지만 크리스마스를

keep it."
지내지도 않잖아요."

"Let me leave it alone, / then," / said Scrooge. "Much good
"그렇게 하게 내버려 둬, 그럼," 스크루지는 말했다. "너나 좋은 일 많이

may it do you! Much good it has ever done you!"
생기거라! 지금까지 좋은 일이 많았나 보구나!"

"There are many things / from which I might have
많은 일들이 있어요   행복을 느낄 수 있었던,

derived good, / by which I have not profited, / I dare say,"
그 일로 돈을 벌지 못했을지라도,   감히 말하지만요,"

/ returned the nephew. "Christmas among the rest. But
조카는 대답했다.   "크리스마스도 그 중 하나예요.

I am sure / I have always thought of Christmas time, /
하지만 확신해요   항상 크리스마스에 대해 생각했어요,

when it has come round / — apart from the veneration /
크리스마스가 다가올 때면   — 경외심은 제쳐 두고라도

due to its sacred name and origin, / if anything belonging
성스러운 이름이나 유래 때문에 생기는,   크리스마스에 해당되는 건 무엇이든

to it / can be apart from that / — as a good time; / a kind,
제쳐 두고라도,   — 좋은 시간이라고;   친절을 베풀고,

/ forgiving, / charitable, / pleasant time; / the only time /
용서하며,   자비롭고,   즐거운 시간이라고;   그리고 유일한 시간이라고

I know of, / in the long calendar of the year, / when men
내가 아는,   1년이라는 긴 나날 속에서,   남자나 여자나

and women / seem by one consent / to open their shut-up
한 마음이 되어   닫혀 있던 가슴을 자유롭게 열고,

hearts freely, / and to think of people below them / as if
                자신보다 못한 사람들을 생각하는 때요

they really were fellow-passengers to the grave, / and not
진짜 무덤까지 함께 가는 길동무나 되는 것처럼,

another race of creatures / bound on other journeys. And
별종의 사람이 아니라   다른 여행길을 가는.

therefore, / uncle, / though it has never put a scrap of gold
그러니까,   삼촌,   크리스마스가 금이나 은 부스러기라도 넣어 준 적 없지만

or silver / in my pocket, / I believe / that it has done me
            내 주머니에,   난 믿어요   내게 행운을 주었고,

good, / and will do me good; / and I say, / God bless it!"
앞으로도 그럴 거라고;   그러니 말해요,   신이 축복하시길!"이라고.

---

work one's will 뜻을 이루다 | indignantly 분연히, 분개하여 | stake 말뚝, 막대기 | holly 트리 장식용 나무
plead 항변하다 | sternly 엄격하게, 준엄하게 | veneration 숭배, 존경심 | consent 동의, 묵인

The clerk in the Tank / involuntarily applauded.
골방에 있던 서기는   자신도 모르게 박수를 쳤다.

Becoming immediately sensible of the impropriety, /
즉시 적절하지 못한 행동임을 깨닫고,

he poked the fire, / and extinguished the last frail spark
서기는 불을 들쑤시다가,   마지막 남아 있던 약한 불씨를 영원히 꺼뜨리고 말았다.

forever.

"Let me hear / another sound from you," / said Scrooge,
"들려줘 보게   박수 소리를 한 번 더."   스크루지는 말했다,

/ "and you'll keep your Christmas / by losing your
"그러면 크리스마스를 보내게 될 거야   일자리를 잃어버린 채!

situation! You're quite a powerful speaker, / sir," / he
                        꽤나 감명적인 연설가로군,   조카님," 그는

added, / turning to his nephew. "I wonder / you don't go
덧붙였다,   조카 쪽으로 몸을 돌리며.   "궁금하군

into Parliament."
국회로 가지 않는 이유가."

"Don't be angry, / uncle. Come! Dine with us tomorrow."
"화내지 마세요,　삼촌.　오세요! 내일 저희와 같이 저녁 드세요."

Scrooge said / that he would see him / — yes, / indeed
스크루지는 말했다　보러 가겠다고　— 그렇다. 정말로 그렇게

he did. He went the whole length of the expression, / and
했다.　그는 온갖 소리를 늘어놓은 끝에,

said / that he would him / in that extremity / first.
말했다　보러 가겠다고　조카가 곤경에 빠지면　제일 먼저.

"But why?" / cried Scrooge's nephew. "Why?"
"하지만 왜요?"　조카가 외쳤다.　"왜 그러세요?"

"Why did you get married?" / said Scrooge.
"결혼은 왜 했니?"　스크루지가 말했다

"Because I fell in love."
"사랑하니까요."

"Because you fell in love!" / growled Scrooge, / as if that
"사랑하니까라고!"　스크루지는 투덜거렸다,

were the only one thing in the world / more ridiculous
마치 그 말이 세상에서 유일한 말이라는 듯이

than a merry Christmas. "Good afternoon!"
메리 크리스마스보다 더 어리석은.　"잘 가라!"

"Nay, / uncle, / but you never came to see me / before
"아니,　삼촌,　하지만 저를 보러 한 번도 안 오셨잖아요

that happened. Why give it as a reason / for not coming
결혼하기 전에도.　결혼을 핑계대시는 거예요　지금 오지 않는 것에 대해?"

now?"

"Good afternoon," / said Scrooge.
"잘 가라,"　스크루지는 말했다.

"I want nothing from you; / I ask nothing of you; / why
"삼촌한테 원하는 것은 아무것도 없어요;　아무것도 부탁하지 않아요;

cannot we be friends?"
친하게 지내면 안 되나요?"

"Good afternoon," / said Scrooge.
"잘 가라."　스크루지는 말했다.

involuntarily 실수로, 무심결에 | applaud 박수 갈채하다 | sensible 의식하고 있는 | impropriety 부적당,
어울리지 않음 | frail 약한 | in extremity 파산 직전에, 곤경에 빠져 | growl 투덜거리다 | nay 아니(=no)

"I am sorry, / with all my heart, / to find you so resolute.
"서운해요, 진심으로, 삼촌이 그렇게 고집을 피우시니.

We have never had any quarrel, / to which I have
우리는 싸운 적도 없었는데, 싸움에 관여한 적도 없고요.

been a party. But I have made the trial / in homage to
하지만 한 번 말해 본 거예요 크리스마스에 대한

Christmas, / and I'll keep my Christmas humor / to the
경외심으로, 전 제 크리스마스 기분을 지키겠어요

last. So A Merry Christmas, / uncle!"
끝까지. 그러니 메리 크리스마스, 삼촌!"

"Good afternoon!" / said Scrooge.
"잘 가라!" 스크루지는 말했다.

"And A Happy New Year!"
"그리고 새해 복 많이 받으세요!"

"Good afternoon!" / said Scrooge.
"잘 가라!" 스크루지가 말했다.

His nephew left the room / without an angry word,
조카는 방에서 나갔다 한 마디 성내는 말도 없이,

/ notwithstanding. He stopped at the outer door / to
그럼에도 불구하고. 조카는 현관에 멈춰서서

bestow the greetings of the season / on the clerk, / who,
크리스마스 인사를 건넸다 서기에게, 서기는,

/ cold as he was, / was warmer than Scrooge; / for he
몸은 추웠지만, 스크루지보다는 따뜻한 사람이었다;

returned them cordially.
진심으로 답 인사를 했으므로.

"There's another fellow," / muttered Scrooge; / who
"또 한 놈이 있군." 스크루지가 중얼거렸다; 서기가

overheard him: / "my clerk, / with fifteen shillings a
인사하는 것을 듣고서: "서기인 주제에, 일주일에 15실링 벌고,

week, / and a wife and family, / talking about a merry
처자식이 있으면서, 즐거운 크리스마스를 운운하는군.

Christmas. I'll retire to Bedlam."
내가 정신병원으로 들어가든지 해야지."

---

resolute 단호한 | homage 존경, 경의 | notwithstanding ~에도 불구하고 | bestow 주다, 수여하다 |
cordially 정성껏, 진심으로 | bedlam 정신병원

This lunatic, / in letting Scrooge's nephew out, / had
이 정신병자는,　　　조카를 보내고,

let two other people in. They were portly gentlemen, /
다른 두 사람을 맞이했다.　　　그들은 풍채가 좋은 신사이고,

pleasant to behold, / and now stood, / with their hats off,
호감 가는 사람들이었는데,　　지금 서 있었다,　　모자를 벗고,

/ in Scrooge's office. They had books and papers in their
스크루지의 사무실 안에.　　두 신사는 장부와 서류를 손에 들고,

hands, / and bowed to him.
스크루지에게 인사했다.

"Scrooge and Marley's, / I believe," / said one of the
"스크루지와 말리 상점이지요,　　맞습니까."　　신사들 중 한 사람이 말했다,

gentlemen, / referring to his list. "Have I the pleasure of
자신의 명부를 보면서.　　"뵐 수 있을까요

addressing / Mr. Scrooge, or Mr. Marley?"
스크루지 씨나 말리 씨를?"

"Mr. Marley has been dead / these seven years," /
"말리 씨는 죽었소　　　7년 전에,"

Scrooge replied. "He died seven years ago, / this very
스크루지가 대답했다.　　"7년 전에 죽었소,　　바로 오늘 밤."

night."

"We have no doubt / his liberality is well represented
"틀림없겠군요　　말리 씨의 관대한 마음씨를 잘 표현해 주실 거라

/ by his surviving partner," / said the gentleman, /
남은 동업자께서,"　　신사는 말했다,

presenting his credentials.
자신의 신분증을 내밀면서.

It certainly was; / for they had been two kindred spirits.
확실했다;　　두 사람은 비슷한 종류의 사람이라는 것이.

At the ominous word "liberality," / Scrooge frowned, /
"관대한 마음씨"라는 불길한 단어에,　　스크루지는 얼굴을 찌푸렸고,

and shook his head, / and handed the credentials back.
고개를 저으며,　　신분증을 돌려 주었다.

---

lunatic 정신병자 | portly 당당한, 우람한 | behold 보다, 주시하다 | liberality 마음이 후함,관대함 |
credentials (복수형) 증명서, 보증서, 자격 인증서 | kindred 동족, 동질 | ominous 불길한, 조짐이 나쁜

"At this festive season of the year, / Mr. Scrooge," / said
"일 년 중에서도 축제 기간인 이맘 때,   스크루지 씨,"

the gentleman, / taking up a pen, / "it is more than usually
신사는 말했다,   펜을 들며,   "어느 때보다 바람직한 일이죠

desirable / that we should make some slight provision /
조금이라도 기부를 하는 일은

for the Poor and destitute, / who suffer greatly / at the
가난하고 빈곤한 사람들을 위해,   굉장히 고통 받는

present time. Many thousands are in want of common
이런 때에.   수천 명의 이웃들은 생필품이 부족하고;

necessaries; / hundreds of thousands are in want of
              수십만 명의 이웃들은 쉴 곳마저 부족합니다

common comforts, / sir."
                  선생님."

"Are there no prisons?" / asked Scrooge.
"감옥은 없소?"   스크루지가 물었다.

"Plenty of prisons," / said the gentleman, / laying down
"감옥이야 많죠,"   신사가 말했다,

the pen again.
펜을 다시 내려 놓으면서.

"And the Union workhouses?" / demanded Scrooge. "Are
"그럼 부랑자 수용소는?"   스크루지가 캐물었다.

they still in operation?"
"아직 운영을 하고 있소?"

"They are. Still," / returned the gentleman, / "I wish / I
"그렇습니다.   아직 하죠," 신사가 대답했다.   "좋겠지만요

could say they were not."
그렇지 않다고 말씀드릴 수 있다면."

"The Treadmill and the Poor Law / are in full vigor, /
"징역 제도나 빈민 구제법은   제대로 되고 있군요,

then?" / said Scrooge.
그럼?"   스크루지가 말했다.

provision 대책, 양식 | destitute 빈민들 | common necessaries 생활 필수품 | common comfort 생활을
편하게 해 주는 물건 | workhouse 구빈원 | treadmill 발로 밟아 돌리는 바퀴(옛날 감옥에서 죄수에게 밟게 했다) |
in vigor (법률이) 유효하여

"Both very busy, / sir."
"둘 다 아주 잘 시행됩니다. 선생님."

"Oh! I was afraid, / from what you said at first, / that
"아! 걱정했소, 당신이 처음에 말한 것을 듣고,

something had occurred to stop them / in their useful
무슨 일이 생겨서 그 제도가 중단됐는지 하고 시행되는 중에."

course," / said Scrooge. "I'm very glad to hear it."
스크루지가 말했다. "그 말을 들으니 아주 기쁘군요."

"Under the impression / that they scarcely furnish /
"생각합니다 그 제도만으로는 줄 수 없다고

Christian cheer of mind or body / to the multitude," /
기독교의 도움을 물심양면으로 많은 사람들에게,"

returned the gentleman, / "a few of us are endeavoring /
신사가 대구했다. "저희들 몇 사람이 노력하고 있습니다

to raise a fund / to buy the Poor / some meat and drink,
기금을 조성하기 위해 빈민에게 사 줄 고기와 음료, 그리고 땔감을,

and means of warmth. We choose this time, / because it
이때를 택한 것은, 그런 때이니까요,

is a time, / of all others, / when Want is keenly felt, / and
모든 사람에게, 가난한 사람들은 더욱 빈곤을 느끼고,

Abundance rejoices. What shall I put you down for?"
부자들은 풍요로움을 즐기는. 성함은 뭐라고 적을까요?"

Key Expression

would rather : 차라리 ~하겠다

would rather는 '차라리 ~하겠다'라는 의미로 뒤에는 동사원형이 옵니다.
would rather A than B의 형태로 'B하느니 차라리 A하겠다'라는 의미로
쓰이기도 합니다.
had better + 동사원형(~하는 게 낫다)와 비교해서 기억해 두세요.

ex) If they would rather die, they had better do it.
만약 그들이 차라리 죽겠다고 한다면, 그런 사람은 죽는 것이 낫소.

"Nothing!" / Scrooge replied.
"아무것도!" 스크루지는 대답했다.

"You wish to be anonymous?"
"익명으로 하길 바라십니까?"

"I wish to be left alone," / said Scrooge. "Since you
"혼자 있기를 바라오," 스크루지가 말했다. "당신이 질문하니

ask me / what I wish, / gentlemen, / that is my answer.
하는 말인데 내가 뭘 바라는지, 신사 양반, 이것이 내 대답이오.

I don't make merry myself at Christmas / and I can't
난 크리스마스라고 즐겁지 않고

afford to make idle people merry. I help to support the
게으른 사람들을 즐겁게 해 줄 여유도 없소. 난 시설들을 지원하고 있고

establishments / I have mentioned / — they cost enough;
아까 말했던 — 비용이 충분히 들어요;

/ and those who are badly off / must go there."
그러니 살기 힘든 사람들은 거기로 보내시오."

"Many can't go there; / and many would rather die."
"그런 곳에 갈 수 없는 사람들도 많아요; 그리고 많은 사람들이 차라리 죽겠다고 합니다."

"If they would rather die," / said Scrooge, / "they had
"만약 그 사람들이 차라리 죽겠다고 한다면," 스크루지가 말했다, "그런 사람은 죽는

better do it, / and decrease the surplus population.
것이 낫소. 그러면 인구 과잉도 좀 줄어들 테고.

Besides / — excuse me — / I don't know that."
게다가 — 실례지만 — 그런 문제는 잘 모르오."

"But you might know it," / observed the gentleman.
"하지만 아실 것 같은데요," 신사는 말해 보았다.

"It's not my business," / Scrooge returned. "It's enough
"내가 상관할 바가 아니오," 스크루지는 대꾸했다. "충분하지

for a man / to understand his own business, / and not
자기 일이나 잘 알고,

to interfere with other people's. Mine occupies me
다른 사람들 일을 참견하지 않으면. 내 일만으로도 항상 정신 없소.

constantly. Good afternoon, / gentlemen!"
잘 가시오, 신사 양반!"

be under the impression that ~하다고 생각하고 있다 | furnish 공급하다, 제공하다 | multitude 대중 |
anonymous 익명의 | be off 살이 ~한

Seeing clearly / that it would be useless / to pursue their
확실히 알아차리고   소용없다는 것을   자신들의 의도를 전달하려

point, / the gentlemen withdrew. Scrooge resumed his
해 봐야,   신사들은 물러섰다.   스크루지는 자신의 일을 다시 시작했다

labors / with an improved opinion of himself, / and in a
자신의 생각에 더욱 확신을 가지며,

more facetious temper / than was usual with him.
더욱 즐거운 기분으로   평소보다.

Meanwhile / the fog and darkness thickened so, / that
한편   안개와 어두움은 더욱 짙어져서,

people ran about with flaring links, / proffering their
사람들은 일렁이는 횃불을 들고 바삐 뛰어다녔다,   길을 밝히는 일을 하면서

services to go / before horses in carriages, / and conduct
마차를 끄는 말 앞에서,

them on their way. The ancient tower of a church, /
사람들에게 길을 안내했다.   오래된 교회의 탑이,

whose gruff old bell was always peeping slily down at
항상 스크루지를 몰래 들여다 보며 매달려 있는 낡은 종이

Scrooge / out of a Gothic window in the wall, / became
벽으로 난 고딕풍 창문으로,   보이지 않게

invisible, / and struck the hours and quarters / in the
되었고,   한 시간마다 그리고 15분마다 울렸다   구름 속에서,

clouds, / with tremulous vibrations afterwards / as if
길게 떨리는 울림과 함께   마치 이가

its teeth were chattering / in its frozen head up there.
추위로 딱딱 소리를 내며 떨리듯이   얼어붙은 머리에서.

The cold became intense. In the main street, / at the
추위는 더욱 심해졌다.   큰 길 가에,

corner of the court, / some laborers were repairing the
골목 한 귀퉁이에서는,   일꾼들이 가스관을 고치고 있었고,

gas-pipes, / and had lighted a great fire in a brazier,
통에 큰 불을 펴 놓은 채,

---

facetious 농담의, 익살맞은 | link 횃불 | proffer 내놓다, 제공하다 | gruff 퉁명스러운 | tremulous 떨리는
| brazier 화로 | rapture 환희, 황홀경 | water-plug 소화전 | solitude 고독, 쓸쓸함 | sullenly 시무룩하게,
뚱하게 | congealed 얼다, 응결하다 | misanthropic 인간혐오의, 염세적인 | sprig 잔가지 | berry 과실, 열매 |
crackle 탁탁 소리내다 | poulterer 새 장수, 가금상 | pageant 구경거리

/ round which a party of ragged men and boys / were
그 주위에는 누더기를 입은 어른들과 아이들이

gathered: / warming their hands / and winking their eyes
모여 있었다:　　손을 녹이고　　　　　　　눈을 깜빡이면서

/ before the blaze / in rapture. The water-plug being left
불길 앞에서　　　　황홀경에 빠져.　　소화전은 홀로 내팽개쳐져서,

in solitude, / its overflowings sullenly congealed, / and
　　　　　흘러 나온 물이 흉한 모습으로 얼어서,

turned to misanthropic ice. The brightness of the shops /
기괴한 모양의 얼음이 되었다.　　　가게에서 나오는 밝은 불빛은

where holly sprigs and berries crackled / in the lamp heat
호랑가시나무 가지와 열매가 탁탁 소리를 내던　　　창문의 램프 불빛 속에서,

of the windows, / made pale faces ruddy / as they passed.
　　　창백한 얼굴을 붉게 물들였다　　　사람들이 지나갈 때.

Poulterers' and grocers' trades / became a splendid joke: /
푸줏간과 식료품점은　　　　　　　유쾌한 농담판이 되었다:

a glorious pageant, / with which it was next to impossible
신나는 구경거리인,　　　거의 믿기 힘들도록

to believe / that such dull principles / as bargain and sale /
　　　지루한 원칙들이　　　　　흥정이니 매매같은

had anything to do.
관련되어 있는 곳이라고.

Key Expression

next to : 거의

next to는 특히 부정어 앞에서 '거의, ~에 버금가는'(=almost, nearly)라는 의미로 쓰입니다.
이 외에도 위치 상 '~바로 옆에', 순서 면에서 '~ 다음의' 등의 뜻도 있습니다.

ex) A glorious pageant, with which it was next to impossible to believe that such dull principles as bargain and sale had anything to do.
홍정이나 매매같은 지루한 원칙들과 관련이 있다고는 거의 믿을 수 없는 신나는 구경거리였다.

The Lord Mayor, / in the stronghold of the mighty
시장은, 거대한 요새같은 관저 안에서,

Mansion House, / gave orders / to his fifty cooks
지시를 내렸다 50명의 요리사와 집사들에게

and butlers / to keep Christmas / as a Lord Mayor's
크리스마스를 준비하라고 시장 관저에 걸맞게;

household should; / and even the little tailor, / whom he
또한 변변찮은 재봉사마저,

had fined five shillings / on the previous Monday / for
5실링의 벌금을 물었던 지난 월요일에

being drunk and bloodthirsty / in the streets, / stirred up
술에 취해 폭력을 휘두른 죄로 길에서,

tomorrow's pudding / in his garret, / while his lean wife
이튿날 먹을 푸딩을 젓고 있었다 자신의 다락방에서, 여윈 아내와 아이가

and the baby / sallied out to buy the beef.
신이 나서 쇠고기를 사러 나간 사이에.

Foggier yet, / and colder. Piercing, / searching, / biting
안개는 더 짙어졌고, 더욱 추워졌다. 살을 에이고, 몸을 휘젓는, 혹독한 추위

cold. If the good *Saint Dunstan had but nipped the
였다. 만약 자비로운 성 던스턴이 악마의 코를 쥐어 뜯었더라도

Evil Spirit's nose / with a touch of such weather as that,
이런 날씨를 이용해서,

/ instead of using his familiar weapons, / then indeed he
자신에게 익숙한 무기를 쓰는 대신,

would have roared to lusty purpose. The owner of one
정말로 호탕하게 웃을 수 있으리라. 빈약한 코의 어린 어린 아이가,

scant young nose, / gnawed and mumbled by the hungry
추위와 굶주림에 뜯기고 씹혀버린

cold / as bones are gnawed by dogs, / stooped down /
개들이 물어뜯은 뼈처럼, 허리를 굽혀

at Scrooge's keyhole / to regale him / with a Christmas
스크루지 사무실의 열쇠 구멍에 대고 그를 기쁘게 해 주려고 크리스마스 캐럴을 불렀다:

carol: / but at the first sound of / "God bless you, / merry
하지만 첫 소절이 "하나님이 축복하시길,

gentleman! May nothing you dismay!"
즐거운 신사분! 아무것도 당신을 슬프게 하지 못하리라!"였다.

Scrooge seized the ruler / with such energy of action, /
스크루지는 자를 쥐었고   힘차게 덥썩,

that the singer fled in terror, / leaving the keyhole / to the
그러자 아이는 겁에 질려 달아났다.   열쇠 구멍을 남겨둔 채

fog and even more congenial frost.
안개와 한층 더 잘 어울리는 서리 속에.

At length / the hour of shutting up the counting-house /
마침내   회계사무소 문을 닫을 시간이

arrived. With an ill-will Scrooge dismounted from his
다가왔다.   성미 고약한 스크루지가 그의 의자에서 내려옴으로써,

stool, / and tacitly admitted the fact / to the expectant
그 사실을 무언으로 인정하자   기대하고 있는 서기에게

clerk / in the Tank, / who instantly snuffed his candle
골방에서,   서기는 바로 촛불을 끄고,

out, / and put on his hat.
모자를 썼다.

Key Expression

may를 사용한 기원문 만들기

기원이나 소망을 나타낼 때 조동사 may를 사용합니다.
may를 사용한 기원문의 형태는 다음과 같습니다. 동사원형을 사용하고 ?(물음표)
로 끝나지 않는다는 점에서 may 의문문과 구별됩니다.

▶ May + 주어 + 동사원형 : 부디 ~ 이기를
▶ May + 주어 + never + 동사원형 : 부디 ~ 이 아니기를

ex) May nothing you dismay!
    아무것도 당신을 슬프게 하지 않길!

---

*성 더스턴. 대장장이와 보석 세공인의 수호성인. 잉글랜드 수도원의 재건자이자 유명한 음악가이며 숙련된
청공예이며 불에 달군 젓가락으로 악마를 내쫓았다고 전해진다.

stronghold 요새, 성채 | bloodthirsty 폭력적인, 살기를 띤 | garret 다락방 | lean 여윈, 마른 | sally 기운차게
나가다 | lusty 원기 있는, 활발한 | scant 작은, 빈약한 | gnaw 갉아 먹다 | mumble 우물쭈물 씹다 | stoop
허리를 굽히다 | regale 기쁘게 하다 | congenial 잘 어울리는 | at length 결국은, 마침내 | tacitly 무언으로 |
snuff 촛불을 끄다

"You'll want all day to-morrow, / I suppose?" / said
"내일 하루종일 쉬고 싶지,   그렇겠지?"

Scrooge.
스크루지가 말했다.

"If quite convenient, / sir."
"괜찮다면요,   사장님."

"It's not convenient," / said Scrooge, / "and it's not fair. If
"괜찮지 않아,"   스크루지가 말했다,   "그리고 공평하지도 않아.

I was to stop half-a-crown for it, / you'd think yourself ill-
만약 쉰 대가로 반 크라운을 뺀다면,   억울하다고 생각하겠지,

used, / I'll be bound?"
그렇지?"

The clerk smiled faintly.
서기는 희미하게 웃었다.

"And yet," / said Scrooge, / "you don't think me ill-used, /
"그러나,"   스크루지는 말했다,   "내가 억울하다고는 생각하지 않겠지,

when I pay a day's wages / for no work."
하루치 급여를 줘야 하는데   일을 하지 않는데도."

The clerk observed / that it was only once a year.
서기는 말해 보았다   일 년에 오직 한 번뿐이지 않느냐고.

"A poor excuse / for picking a man's pocket / every twenty-
"말도 안 되는 변명이야   남의 주머니를 채가려는   매년 12월 25일에!"

fifth of December!" / said Scrooge, / buttoning his great-
스크루지는 말했다,   두꺼운 코트의 단추를 턱까지 채우며.

coat to the chin. "But I suppose you must have the whole
"자네가 내일 하루종일 쉬어야겠다는 것이군.

day. Be here all the earlier next morning."
그 다음 날 아침에는 더 일찍 나오게."

The clerk promised / that he would; / and Scrooge walked
서기는 약속했다   그러겠다고;   그리고 스크루지는 걸어나갔다

out / with a growl. The office was closed / in a twinkling,
투덜거리며.   사무실은 닫혔고   눈 깜짝하는 사이에

/ and the clerk, / with the long ends of his white comforter
서기는,   하얀 목도리의 끝자락을

/ dangling below his waist / (for he boasted no great-coat),
허리 아래로 늘어뜨리고   (두꺼운 코트가 없다는 것을 자랑이라도 하듯이),

/ went down a slide on Cornhill, / at the end of a lane of
콘힐 언덕에서 미끄럼을 탔다,   줄 서 있는 사내 아이들 꽁무니에 서서,

boys, / twenty times, / in honor of its being Christmas Eve,
스무 번 쯤,   크리스마스 이브를 축하하며,

/ and then ran home to Camden Town / as hard as he could
그리고 나서 캠든 타운에 있는 집으로 달려갔다   할 수 있는 한 서둘러서,

pelt, / to play at blindman's-buff.
술래잡기 놀이를 하기 위해.

ill-use 혹사하다 | I'll be bound 꼭이다, 내가 보증한다 | great-coat 천이 두꺼운 외투 | twinkling 눈 깜박할
사이 | dangling 아래로 드리워지다 | pelt 서두르다 | blindman's-buff 술래잡기 놀이

A. 다음 문장을 해석해 보세요.

(1) To edge his way along the crowded paths of life, / warning all human sympathy to keep its distance, / was what the knowing ones call "nuts" / to Scrooge.

→

(2) To see the dingy cloud come / drooping down, / obscuring everything, / one might have thought / that Nature lived hard by, / and was brewing on a large scale.

→

(3) If I could work my will," / said Scrooge indignantly, / "every idiot who goes about / with 'Merry Christmas' on his lips, / should be boiled with his own pudding, / and buried / with a stake of holly through his heart.

→

(4) We choose this time, / because it is a time, / of all others, / when Want is keenly felt, and Abundance rejoices.

→

B. 다음 주어진 문장이 되도록 빈칸에 써서 넣으세요.

(1) 말리 영감은 대갈못처럼 완전히 죽었다.

→

(2) 즐거워 할 권리라도 있나?

→

(3) 네 식대로 크리스마스를 지내라, 그리고 나는 내 식대로 지내게 내버려 두란 말이야.

→

A. (1) 복잡한 인생길을 헤쳐 나가기 위해, 사람들의 동정심 따위는 가까이 하지 못하도록 하는 것이 스크루지에게는 소위 현명한 사람들이 말하는 '장땡이'었다. (2) 우중충한 구름이 모든 것을 감추며 내려앉은 것을 보면, 자연이 근처에 살면서 열심히 대규모로 구름을 만들어 낸다고 누구나 생각했을지도 모른다. (3) 스크루지는 분개하며 말했다. '내가 할 수만 있다면, 입에 '메리 크리스마스'를 달고 돌아다니는 머저리

(4) 만약 그들이 차라리 죽겠다고 한다면, 그렇게 하는 게 낫지.

→

C. 다음 주어진 문구가 알맞은 문장이 되도록 순서를 맞춰 보세요.

(1) 그가 가는 곳이면 어디에나 찬바람이 불었다.
(him / own / carried / He / temperature / low / about / with / his / always)
→

(2) 그 일에 대해서는 무엇이든 의심의 여지가 없다.
(no / whatever / There / that / is / doubt / about)
→

(3) 어떻게 그렇지 않을 수 있겠는가?
(otherwise / could / How / be / it)
→

(4) 아무것도 당신을 슬프게 하지 않길!
(nothing / May / dismay / you)
→

D. 다음 단어에 대한 맞는 설명과 연결해 보세요.

(1) wrench   ▶   ◀ ① healthy and full of strength
(2) bestow   ▶   ◀ ② twist it and injure
(3) intimation   ▶   ◀ ③ give or present
(4) lusty   ▶   ◀ ④ indirect suggestion or sign

2

MARLEY'S GHOST II
말리의 유령 II

Scrooge took his melancholy dinner / in his usual
스크루지는 음침한 저녁을 먹었다

melancholy tavern; / and having read all the newspapers,
늘 가는 음침한 선술집에서; 그리고 신문을 죄다 읽으며,

/ and beguiled the rest of the evening / with his banker's-
나머지 저녁 시간을 때우고 은행 장부를 뒤적이며,

book, / went home to bed. He lived in chambers / which
잠을 자러 집으로 갔다. 스크루지는 집에 살고 있었다

had once belonged to his deceased partner. They were a
한때는 죽은 동업자의 소유였던.

gloomy suite of rooms, / in a lowering pile of building
그 집에는 우중충한 방들이 있었고, 공터에 쌓여있는 허접한 골재 더미 가운데,

up a yard, / where it had so little business to be, / that
거의 집이 있을 만한 곳이 아니어서,

one could scarcely help fancying / it must have run there
생각할 수밖에 없었다 그곳에 자리잡은 것이 틀림없다고

/ when it was a young house, / playing at hide-and-seek
갓 지어졌을 때, 다른 집들과 숨바꼭질을 하다가,

with other houses, / and forgotten the way out again. It
다시 나가는 길을 잊어버려.

was old enough now, / and dreary enough, / for nobody
지금은 너무 낡고, 너무 음침해서,

lived in it but Scrooge, / the other rooms being all let out
스크루지 말고는 아무도 살지 않았다, 다른 방들은 사무실로 세를 주고 있었다.

as offices. The yard was so dark / that even Scrooge, /
공터는 너무 어두워서 스크루지조차도,

who knew its every stone, / was fain to grope with his
돌멩이 하나까지 알고 있는, 손으로 더듬어서 길을 찾아야만 했다.

hands.

tavern 선술집 | beguile [무료함 따위를] 달래다 | chamber 방, 침실 | fancy 상상하다 | dreary 황량한 | fain 어쩔 수 없이 ~하는 | grope 손으로 더듬어 찾다 | meditation 명상, 묵상 | alderman 시의회 의원 | livery 조합원

The fog and frost so hung / about the black old gateway
안개와 서리가 짙게 드리워져 낡고 시커먼 대문 주변에는,

of the house, / that it seemed as if the Genius of the
날씨를 주관하는 신이

Weather / sat in mournful meditation on the threshold.
슬픈 명상에 잠겨 문간에 앉아 있는 듯 했다.

Now, / it is a fact, / that there was nothing at all particular
자, 사실, 전혀 특별할 것은 없었다

/ about the knocker on the door, / except that it was very
현관 문고리에는, 아주 크다는 것 외에.

large. It is also a fact, / that Scrooge had seen it, / night
또한 사실이다. 스크루지가 그 문고리를 봐 왔다고.

and morning, / during his whole residence in that place;
아침 저녁으로, 그 집에 주거하는 동안 계속;

/ also that Scrooge had as little / of what is called fancy
또한 스크루지에게 거의 없다는 것도 상상력이라 부르는 것이

about him / as any man in the city of London, / even
런던에 있는 여느 사람들처럼,

including / — which is a bold word — / the corporation,
포함해도 — 감히 말하자면 — 시청 직원이나,

/ aldermen, / and livery. Let it also be borne in mind /
시의원, 그리고 조합원을. 또한 염두에 둬야 한다

that Scrooge had not bestowed one thought / on Marley,
스크루지는 한 번도 생각해 본 적이 없으며 말리에 대해,

/ since his last mention / of his seven years' dead partner
마지막으로 언급한 이후로 7년 전 오후에 죽은 동업자에 대해.

that afternoon. And then let any man explain to me, / if
그러나 누구든 내게 설명해 주시라,

he can, / how it happened / that Scrooge, / having his key
할 수 있다면, 어떻게 일어났는지 스크루지가,

in the lock of the door, / saw in the knocker, / without its
현관의 자물쇠에 열쇠를 꽂았을 때, 문고리에서 보는 일이,

undergoing any intermediate process of change / — not a
아무 변화도 없이 — 문고리가

knocker, / but Marley's face.
아니고, 말리의 얼굴을.

Marley's face. It was not in impenetrable shadow / as the
말리의 얼굴.　　　그것은 분간할 수 없는 어둠에 묻혀 있는 것이 아니라,

other objects in the yard were, / but had a dismal light
마당에 있는 다른 물건들처럼,　　　음침한 빛을 뿜고 있었다,

about it, / like a bad lobster in a dark cellar. It was not
어두운 지하실에 있는 썩은 바닷가재처럼.　　　화가 났거나 무서운

angry or ferocious, / but looked at Scrooge / as Marley
얼굴이 아니었지만,　　　스크루지를 보고 있었다　　　말리가 살아 있을 때

used to look: / with ghostly spectacles / turned up on its
보던 것처럼:　　유령같은 안경을 걸치고

ghostly forehead. The hair was curiously stirred, / as if
유령같은 이마 위에.　　머리가 기괴하게 나부꼈다.　　　숨결이나

by breath or hot air; / and, / though the eyes were wide
뜨거운 바람에 날린 것처럼;　　그리고,　눈을 크게 뜨고 있었지만,

open, / they were perfectly motionless. That, / and its
전혀 움직이지 않고 있었다.　　　　그것은,　　그리고 그

livid colour, / made it horrible; / but its horror seemed to
창백한 색은,　　소름끼치게 만들었지만;　　그 공포는 마치

be / in spite of the face / and beyond its control, / rather
자신의 얼굴임도 불구하고　　통제 불가능한 듯 보였다,

than a part of its own expression.
얼굴 표정이 아니라.

As Scrooge looked fixedly at this phenomenon, / it was a
스크루지가 이 형상을 뚫어지게 쳐다보자,

knocker again.
다시 문고리로 변했다.

To say / that he was not startled, / or that his blood was
말한다면　　스크루지가 놀라지 않았거나,

not conscious of a terrible sensation / to which it had
그의 피가 섬뜩한 느낌을 받지 않았다고

been a stranger from infancy, / would be untrue. But he
태어나서 한 번도 겪어 보지 않은 일에,　　　거짓말일 것이다.

put his hand upon the key / he had relinquished, / turned
하지만 그는 열쇠를 다시 손에 쥐고　　　떨어뜨렸던,

it sturdily, / walked in, / and lighted his candle.
힘껏 돌려,　　걸어 들어가서,　　초에 불을 붙였다.

impenetrable 꿰뚫을 수 없는 | ferocious 흉포한, 사나운 | spectacles 안경 | livid 흙빛의, 창백한 | fixedly
꼼짝 않고 | relinquish [쥐고 있던 것을] 늦추다 | sturdily 기운차게

He did pause, / with a moment's irresolution, / before
그는 멈춰서서,   잠시 동안 망설이며,

he shut the door; / and he did look cautiously behind it
문을 닫기 전에;   문 뒤를 주의 깊게 들여다 보았다

/ first, / as if he half expected / to be terrified with the
먼저,   조금은 각오했다는 듯이   말리의 길게 땋은 머리를 보고 놀라게

sight of Marley's pigtail / sticking out into the hall. But
될 것을   현관 안으로 쑥 들어오는.

there was nothing / on the back of the door, / except the
하지만 아무것도 없었고   문 뒤에는,

screws and nuts / that held the knocker on, / so he said /
나사와 너트 외에는   문고리를 고정하는,   그는 말하고는

"Pooh, pooh!" / and closed it with a bang.
"흥, 쳇!"이라고   쾅 하고 문을 닫았다.

Key Expression

충돌을 표현하는 단어들

bang은 부딪힐 때 나는 '쾅, 쿵, 탁' 등의 소리를 표현하며 동사 혹은 명사로 쓰입니다. 또한 '탕'하는 총소리를 표현하는 감탄사로도 쓰입니다.
bang과 같이 충돌을 표현하는 말로는 thump, bump, slam 등이 있습니다. 또한 bang보다 더 큰 소리로 천둥이나 대포 소리를 표현하는 말에는 boom이 있습니다.

ex) He closed it with a bang.
그는 쾅 하고 문을 닫았다.
The cellar-door flew open with a booming sound.
지하실 문이 꽝 하는 소리와 함께 확 열렸다.

The sound resounded through the house / like thunder.
그 소리는 집 안에 울려 퍼졌다 / 천둥처럼.

Every room above, / and every cask / in the wine-
위층에 있는 모든 방과, / 모든 술통이

merchant's cellars below, / appeared to have a separate
아래층 와인 상인의 지하 창고에 있는, / 제각각 그 소리를 메아리로 보내는 듯 했다.

peal of echoes of its own. Scrooge was not a man / to
스크루지는 그런 사람이 아니었다

be frightened by echoes. He fastened the door, / and
메아리에 놀라는. / 그는 문을 잠그고,

walked across the hall, / and up the stairs; / slowly too: /
복도를 가로질러 걸어서, / 위층으로 올라갔다; / 역시 느릿느릿:

trimming his candle / as he went.
초의 심지를 다듬으며 / 가면서.

You may talk vaguely / about driving a coach-and-six /
모호하게 말할 수도 있겠지만 / 육두마차를 끌고

up a good old flight of stairs, / or through a bad young
오래 되었지만 튼튼한 계단을 오르는 것이라거나, / 국회에서 갓 통과된 악법을 뚫고 지나가는

Act of Parliament; / but I mean to say / you might have
것이라고; / 난 말하고자 한다

got a hearse up that staircase, / and taken it broadwise,
영구차가 그 계단을 올라갈 수 있을 정도라고, / 마차를 옆으로 돌려서,

/ with the splinter-bar towards the wall / and the door
차체는 벽 쪽을 향하게 하고

towards the balustrades: / and done it easy. There was
문은 난간을 향하게 한 채: / 그것도 쉽게.

plenty of width for that, / and room to spare; / which is
그 정도로 계단 폭이 충분히 넓어서, / 남는 공간이 있다;

perhaps the reason / why Scrooge thought / he saw a
그것이 아마도 이유일 것이다 / 스크루지가 생각했던

locomotive hearse going on / before him / in the gloom.
영구차가 지나가는 것을 봤다고 / 자기 앞으로 / 어둠 속에서.

---

irresolution 결단력 없음, 우유부단 | pigtail 땋아 늘어뜨린 머리 | cask 통 | peal 굉음 | coach-and-six 말 여섯 필이 끄는 마차 | flight 층계참까지의 일련의 계단 | hearse 영구마차 | broadwise 옆으로 | splinter-bar (마차 따위의) 용수철을 받치는 가로장 | balustrade 난간 | locomotive 기관차, 이동하는, 움직이는 | gloom 어두컴컴한 곳

Half-a-dozen gas-lamps out of the street / wouldn't have
거리에서 대여섯 개의 가스등을 가져온다 해도   계단 입구조차 충분히

lighted the entry too well, / so you may suppose / that it
밝힐 수 없을 테니,   짐작할 수 있을 것이다

was pretty dark / with Scrooge's dip.
상당히 어두웠다는 것을   스크루지의 양초 하나만으로는.

Up Scrooge went, / not caring a button for that. Darkness
스크루지는 계단을 올라갔다.   그런 어둠에는 전혀 신경 쓰지 않고.   어둡게 하면 돈

is cheap, / and Scrooge liked it. But before he shut his
이 적게 드니.   스크루지는 그것이 좋았다.   하지만 육중한 방문을 닫기 전에,

heavy door, / he walked through his rooms / to see that
그는 방마다 돌아다녔다   모든 것이 괜찮은지

all was right. He had just enough recollection of the face
확인했다.   말리의 얼굴이 계속 떠올라서

/ to desire to do that.
그렇게 확인하고 싶어졌다.

Sitting-room, / bedroom, / lumber-room. All as they
거실,   침실,   창고.   모든 것이 그대로였다.

should be. Nobody under the table, / nobody under the
탁자 밑에도 아무도 없었고,   소파 밑에도 아무도 없었다;

sofa; / a small fire in the grate; / spoon and basin ready;
벽난로 안의 희미한 불꽃;   준비해 놓은 숟가락과 물그릇;

/ and the little saucepan of gruel / (Scrooge had a cold
묽은 죽이 들어 있는 작은 냄비도 그대로였다   (스크루지는 감기에 걸려 있었다)

in his head) / upon the hob. Nobody under the bed; /
화덕 위에 놓은.   침대 밑에도 아무도 없었다;

nobody in the closet; / nobody in his dressing-gown, /
옷장 안에도 아무도 없었고;   그의 실내복 안에도 아무도 없었다.

which was hanging up / in a suspicious attitude / against
걸려 있던   수상한 모습으로

the wall. Lumber-room as usual. Old fire-guard, / old
벽에.   창고도 여전했다.   낡은 난로 철망,

shoes, / two fish-baskets, / washing-stand on three legs, /
낡은 신발,   두 개의 생선 바구니,   삼발이 세면대,

and a poker.
그리소 부지깽이도 그대로였다.

Quite satisfied, / he closed his door, / and locked himself
꽤 만족스러워서,   그는 방문을 닫았고,   안에서 문을 잠궜다;

in; / double-locked himself in, / which was not his
이중으로 잠궜는데,   평소에 하는 행동은 아니었다.

custom. Thus secured against surprise, / he took off his
이렇게 갑작스러운 일에 대해 대비하고 나서,   넥타이를 풀고;

cravat; / put on his dressing-gown and slippers, / and his
실내복을 입고 실내화를 신고,   나이트캡을

nightcap; / and sat down before the fire / to take his gruel.
쓰고서;   난로 앞에 앉았다   귀리죽을 먹으려고.

It was a very low fire indeed; / nothing on such a bitter
아주 약한 불이었다;   그렇게 추운 밤에는 있으나마나였다.

night. He was obliged to sit close to it, / and brood over it,
그는 불 가까이 앉아,   몸을 숙여야만 했다,

/ before he could extract / the least sensation of warmth /
그제서야 쬘 수 있었다   따뜻한 기운을 조금이라도

from such a handful of fuel.
한 줌밖에 안 되는.

Key Expression

be obliged to : 하는 수 없이 ~하다, 부득이 ~하다
oblige는 주로 수동태로 쓰이기 때문에 be obliged to의 형태로 '하는 수 없이
~하다'라는 의미로 강요에 의한 의무를 표현합니다.
이 밖에도 obliged는 '감사한, 고마운'이라는 뜻으로, be obliged for의 형태로
쓰이면 감사를 표현하거나 정중한 부탁을 할 때 격식을 갖춘 표현이 됩니다.

ex) He was obliged to sit close to it, and brood over it.
   그는 불 가까이 앉아 몸을 숙여야만 했다.

dip 실 심지를 넣은 양초 | button 쓸모 없는 것, 소량 | grate 벽난로 | basin 물그릇 | gruel (특히 과거 가난한
사람들이 먹던) 귀리죽 | hob 벽난로 안쪽의 시렁 | cravat 넥타이 | be obliged to 어쩔 수 없이 ~하다 | brood
over 내리 덮다

The fireplace was an old one, / built by some Dutch
벽난로는 오래된 것이었다,   오래 전에 네덜란드 상인에 의해

merchant long ago, / and paved all round with quaint
만들어졌으며,   색다른 네덜란드 타일로 둘레가 장식된 것이었다.

Dutch tiles, / designed to illustrate the Scriptures. There
              성서 이야기가 그려지도록 설계하여.

were Cains and Abels, / Pharaoh's daughters; / Queens
카인과 아벨,   파라오의 딸들이 있었고;   시바의 여왕들,

of Sheba, / Angelic messengers / descending through
            천사 메신저들   하늘에서 내려오는

the air / on clouds like feather-beds, / Abrahams, /
        깃털 베개같은 구름을 타고,   아브라함,

Belshazzars, / Apostles putting off to sea in butter-boats,
벨사자르,   종지같은 배를 타고 바다로 떠나는 사도 등,

/ hundreds of figures / to attract his thoughts; / and yet
  수백 명의 인물들이 그려져 있었다 그의 생각을 사로잡은;

that face of Marley, / seven years dead, / came like the
그런데 말리의 얼굴이,   7년 전에 죽은,

ancient Prophet's rod, / and swallowed up the whole.
고대 예언자의 지팡이처럼 나타나서,   모든 것을 집어 삼켰다.

If each smooth tile had been a blank / at first, / with
만약 매끄러운 타일에 아무것도 그려져 있지 않아서   처음부터,

power to shape some picture / on its surface / from the
어떤 그림을 그려낼 수 있었다면   타일 표면에

disjointed fragments of his thoughts, / there would have
스크루지의 혼란스러운 생각의 단편들로부터 비롯된,

been a copy of old Marley's head / on every one.
늙은 말리의 얼굴이 그려졌을 것이다   타일 하나하나마다.

"Humbug!" / said Scrooge; / and walked across the
"헛것이야!"   스크루지는 말하며;   방 안에서 왔다갔다 했다.

room.

---

quaint 색다르고 재미있는, 별난 | Scriptures 성서 | Apostles 사도들 | butter-boat 배 모양의 소스 그릇

After several turns, / he sat down again. As he threw
몇 바퀴를 돌고 나서,   그는 다시 앉았다.

his head back in the chair, / his glance happened to rest
머리를 의자에 기대자,   눈길이 종에 머물렀다,

upon a bell, / a disused bell, / that hung in the room, /
                사용하지 않는 종이었다.   방 안에 걸려 있는,

and communicated / for some purpose / now forgotten
연락을 취하는데 썼던   어떤 목적으로   지금은 기억나지 않는

/ with a chamber / in the highest story of the building.
        방과   건물 꼭대기 층에 있는.

It was with great astonishment, / and with a strange, /
소스라치도록 놀랍고,   기괴하며,

inexplicable dread, / that as he looked, / he saw this bell
설명할 수 없을 정도로 두려웠다,   바라보았는 순간,   종이 흔들리기 시작하는 것

begin to swing. It swung so softly in the outset / that it
을 보자.   처음에는 아주 부드럽게 흔들려서

scarcely made a sound; / but soon it rang out loudly, /
거의 소리가 나지 않았지만;   곧 시끄럽게 울리더니,

and so did every bell in the house.
집 안의 모든 종도 따라 울렸다.

Key Expression♟

so + 동사 + 주어 : ~도 역시 그렇게 하다
so가 문장 앞에 나와 앞의 행동에 대한 동의나 확인, 반복을 표현할 때 뒤따르는
주어 + 동사의 순서가 도치됩니다.

ex) Soon it rang out loudly, and so did every bell in the house.
곧 그것이 시끄럽게 울리자, 집 안의 모든 종도 따라 울렸다.

inexplicable 설명할 수 없는, 불가사의한 | dread 공포 | outset 착수, 시작, 발단 | clanking (무거운 쇠사슬
등이) 절거덕 소리를 내는 | cask 통 | booming 쾅 울리는

This might have lasted / half a minute, / or a minute,
종소리는 울린 듯 했다   30초 아니면,   일 분 정도,

/ but it seemed an hour. The bells ceased / as they had
한 시간처럼 느껴졌다.   종소리는 멈췄다   시작했을 때처럼.

begun, / together. They were succeeded by a clanking
다같이.   종소리에 이어 절거덕거리는 소리가 들렸다.

noise, / deep down below; / as if some person were
저 멀리 아래쪽에서;   마치 누군가 끌고 다니는 것처럼

dragging / a heavy chain / over the casks / in the wine-
무거운 쇠사슬을   술통을 묶어 놓은

merchant's cellar. Scrooge then remembered / to have
와인 상인의 지하 창고에서.   스크루지는 그때 기억해 냈다   들은 적 있는

heard / that ghosts in haunted houses / were described /
이야기를   유령의 집 유령들은   묘사된

as dragging chains.
쇠사슬을 끌고 다닌다고.

The cellar-door flew open / with a booming sound, /
지하 창고 문이 확 열리더니   꽝 하는 소리와 함께,

and then he heard the noise much louder, / on the floors
그 소리는 더 크게 들렸다,   아래층 위에서;

below; / then coming up the stairs; / then coming straight
그 다음 계단에서 소리가 나더니;   곧장 스크루지의 방으로 향했다.

towards his door.

"It's humbug still!" / said Scrooge. "I won't believe it."
"더욱 말도 안 돼!"   스크루지는 말했다.   "믿지 않을 거야."

His color changed though, / when, / without a pause, / it
하지만 그의 낯빛이 바뀌었다,   그때,   쉬지도 않고,

came on through the heavy door, / and passed into the
그 소리가 육중한 방문을 통과하여,   방으로 들어와서

room / before his eyes. Upon its coming in, / the dying
그의 눈 앞으로 다가오자.   그것이 들어올 때,   꺼져가던 불빛이

flame leaped up, / as though it cried, / "I know him; /
확 피어 올랐다가,   외치기라도 하는 듯이,   "이게 뭔지 알아요;

Marley's Ghost!" / and fell again.
말리의 유령이에요!"라고   다시 수그러들었다.

The same face: / the very same. Marley / in his pigtail,
같은 얼굴이었다: 바로 그 얼굴이었다.   말리였다   꽁지 머리에.

/ usual waistcoat, / tights and boots; / the tassels on the
늘 입던 조끼와,   긴 양말과 부츠를 신은;   뻣뻣한 부츠에 달린 장식 술과,

latter bristling, / like his pigtail, / and his coat-skirts,
그의 꽁지 머리같은,   코트 자락과,

/ and the hair upon his head. The chain he drew / was
머리카락까지 똑같았다.   그가 끌고 다니는 쇠사슬은

clasped about his middle. It was long, / and wound
허리에 휘감겨 있었다.   쇠사슬은 길고,   그를 감고 있었다

about him / like a tail; / and it was made / (for Scrooge
꼬리처럼;   만든 것이었다

observed it closely) / of cash-boxes, / keys, / padlocks, /
스크루지는 자세히 관찰했다)   현금 상자와,   열쇠,   자물쇠,

ledgers, / deeds, / and heavy purses wrought in steel.
장부,   증서,   그리고 무거운 지갑으로   쇠로 만든.

His body was transparent; / so that Scrooge, / observing
말리의 몸은 투명해서;   스크루지가,   그를 바라볼 때,

him, / and looking through his waistcoat, / could see the
조끼를 통과하여,   단추 두 개까지 보였다

two buttons / on his coat behind.
코트 뒤쪽에 달린.

Key Expression ❗

be made of : ~으로 만들어지다

동사 make가 수동태형식으로 쓰일 때 뒤에 전치사 of 혹은 from을 사용하여 재료를 나타냅니다.

▶ be made of : 물리적 변화
▶ be made from : 화학적 변화

ex) It was made of cash-boxes, keys, padlocks, ledgers, deeds, and heavy purses wrought in steel.
그것은 현금 상자와, 열쇠, 자물쇠, 장부, 증서, 그리고 쇠로 만든 무거운 지갑으로 만들어졌다.

* have no bowels : '창자가 없다'라는 말은 '동정심이 없다'라는 뜻으로 성경에서 유래한 표현이다.

waistcoat 조끼 | tassel 장식술 | bristling 거센 털 | clasp 휘감기다 | wrought 가공한 | bowel 창자, 동정심 | incredulous 믿기지 않는 | caustic 빈정대는

Scrooge had often heard / it said / that Marley *had no
스크루지는 종종 듣곤 했지만   말하는 것을 말리가 창자 빠진 인간이라고.

bowels, / but he had never believed it / until now.
        믿은 적은 없었다   지금까지.

No, / nor did he believe it even now. Though he looked
아니,   그는 지금도 믿을 수 없었다.   유령을 쳐다 보고 있었지만

the phantom / through and through, / and saw it standing
              계속해서,   또 자신 앞에 서 있는 모습까지

before him; / though he felt / the chilling influence / of
봤지만;   느끼고 있었지만   오싹한 냉기를   차갑게

its death-cold eyes; / and marked / the very texture of
얼어붙은 눈동자에서 나오는; 또한 알아보았지만 접혀 있는 손수건의 질감까지

the folded kerchief / bound about its head and chin, /
                    유령의 머리와 턱을 감싸고 있는.

which wrapper he had not observed before; / he was still
전에는 본 적이 없었던;   스크루지는 여전히

incredulous, / and fought against his senses.
믿기지 않았고,   자신의 감각이 잘못되었나 의심했다.

"How now!" / said Scrooge, / caustic and cold as ever.
"지금 무슨 일이지!" 스크루지가 말했다.   여느 때처럼 차갑고 빈정대는 말투로.

"What do you want with me?"
"내게 뭘 바라는 건가?"

"Much!"/ — Marley's voice, / no doubt about it.
"많지!"   — 말리의 목소리였고,   의심의 여지가 없었다.

"Who are you?"
"누군가?"

"Ask me / who I was."
"물어보게   내가 누구였느냐고."

"Who were you then?" / said Scrooge, / raising his voice.
"그럼 누구였나?"   스크루지가 말했다,   목소리를 높이면서.

"You're particular, / for a shade." He was going to say
"유별나군,   유령치고는."   그는 말할 뻔 했다

"to a shade," / but substituted this, / as more appropriate.
"그 유령 주제에"라고,   하지만 바꿔 말했다,   좀 더 적절한 표현으로.

"In life / I was your partner, / Jacob Marley."
"살아있을 때 자네 동업자였던,   제이콥 말리라네."

"Can you / — can you sit down?" / asked Scrooge, /
"자네 — 앉을 수 있나?" 스크루지가 물었다,

looking doubtfully at him.
의심하는 표정으로 그를 바라보면서.

"I can."
"그럼."

"Do it, / then."
"앉아보게, 그럼."

Scrooge asked the question, / because he didn't know /
스크루지는 그렇게 물었다, 왜냐하면 알지 못했고

whether a ghost so transparent / might find himself in a
그렇게 투명한 유령이 의자에 앉을 수 있을지를;

condition to take a chair; / and felt / that in the event of
느꼈기 때문에 혹시 앉을 수 없는 경우에,

its being impossible, / it might involve the necessity / of
유령에게 필요할 수도 있다고

an embarrassing explanation. But the ghost sat down /
당황해 하며 설명해야 할. 하지만 유령은 앉았다

on the opposite side of the fireplace, / as if he were quite
벽난로의 맞은편에, 마치 꽤 익숙한 일이라는 듯.

used to it.

"You don't believe in me," / observed the Ghost.
"자네는 나를 믿지 않는군," 유령이 말했다.

"I don't," / said Scrooge.
"믿지 않네," 스크루지가 말했다.

"What evidence would you have / of my reality / beyond
"어떤 증거가 필요한가 내 존재를 증명하기 위한

that of your senses?"
자네의 감각보다 더한?"

"I don't know," / said Scrooge.
"모르겠네," 스크루지가 말했다.

"Why do you doubt your senses?"
"왜 자신의 감각을 의심하나?"

blot 얼룩 | gravy 육즙 | by any means 어떻게 해서라도 | waggish 익살스러운 | spectre 유령, 귀신 |
marrow 골수 | deuce 액운, 재앙 | infernal 지옥의 | agitate 뒤흔들다, 동요하게 하다

"Because," / said Scrooge, / "a little thing affects them. A
"왜냐하면," 스크루지는 말했다, "아주 사소한 일이 감각에 영향을 주니까.

slight disorder of the stomach / makes them cheats. You may
뱃속이 조금만 불편해도 감각을 속일 수 있네.

be an undigested bit of beef, / a blot of mustard, / a crumb of
자네는 소화가 덜 된 쇠고기 조각일 수도 있고, 겨자 얼룩이나, 치즈 부스러기,

cheese, / a fragment of an underdone potato. There's more of
덜 익은 감자 조각일 수도 있지. 육즙 냄새가 난다고

gravy / than of grave / about you, / whatever you are!"
무덤 냄새라기 보다 자네에게는, 자네가 무엇이든 간에!"

Scrooge was not much in the habit of cracking jokes, / nor
스크루지는 농담을 잘하는 편도 아니고, 농담할

did he feel, / in his heart, / by any means waggish then.
기분도 아니었다. 마음속에서는, 어떤 식으로든지 우스꽝스럽게.

The truth is, / that he tried to be smart, / as a means of
사실은, 정신을 차리려고 노력하고 있었다,

distracting his own attention, / and keeping down his terror;
자기 자신의 주의를 흩뜨려뜨리고, 공포심을 억누르려고;

/ for the spectre's voice disturbed / the very marrow in his
왜냐하면 유령의 목소리는 무서웠기 때문이다 뼈 속 골수까지 오싹하게 만들 만큼.

bones.

To sit, / staring at those fixed glazed eyes, / in silence / for
앉으려니, 자기에게 고정된 흐릿한 눈을 바라보며, 침묵 속에서

a moment, / would play, / Scrooge felt, / the very deuce
잠시라도, 생길 것 같았다, 스크루지가 느끼기에. 끔찍한 일이 벌어질 것 같았다.

with him. There was something very awful, / too, / in the
아주 끔찍했다, 또한,

spectre's being provided / with an infernal atmosphere of its
유령이 내뿜는 공기에는 지옥같은 분위기를 자아내며.

own. Scrooge could not feel it himself, / but this was clearly
스크루지 자신은 느끼지 못했지만, 분명히 끔찍했다;

the case; / for though the Ghost sat perfectly motionless, / its
유령은 꿈쩍하지 않고 있었지만, 그의

hair, / and skirts, / and tassels, / were still agitated / as by the
머리, 옷자락, 그리고 장식술은, 여전히 흔들리고 있었다 오븐에서 나오

hot vapour from an oven.
는 뜨거운 증기에라도 날리듯.

"You see this toothpick?" / said Scrooge, / returning
"이 이쑤시개 보이나?" 스크루지는 말했다,

quickly to the charge, / for the reason just assigned; / and
재빨리 원래의 임무로 돌아가며, 방금 설명했던 이유로 인해;

wishing, / though it were only for a second, / to divert
그리고 바랐다, 잠깐이라도,

the vision's stony gaze from himself.
유령의 고정된 시선을 피할 수 있기를.

"I do," / replied the Ghost.
"보이네." 유령이 대답했다.

"You are not looking at it," / said Scrooge.
"보고 있지도 않잖아." 스크루지가 말했다.

"But I see it," / said the Ghost, / "notwithstanding."
"하지만 보이네." 유령이 말했다. "보고 있지 않아도."

"Well!" / returned Scrooge, / "I have but to swallow this,
"그렇군!" 스크루지는 말했다, "난 이거나 삼켜야겠어,

/ and be for the rest of my days persecuted / by a legion
그리고 내 남은 인생 동안 박해 받는 수밖에 도깨비 군단에게,

of goblins, / all of my own creation. Humbug, / I tell you!
모두 내가 만들어낸 상상일 뿐이야. 엉터리야, 정말이지!

humbug!"
헛소리라고!"

At this / the spirit raised a frightful cry, / and shook its
그러자 유령은 섬뜩하게 고함을 지르며, 쇠사슬을 흔들어댔고

chain / with such a dismal and appalling noise, / that
그야말로 음침하고 소름 끼치는 소리를 내며,

Scrooge held on tight to his chair, / to save himself from
스크루지는 의자를 꼭 붙들었다, 기절하지 않으려고.

falling in a swoon. But how much greater was his horror,
하지만 그 공포가 얼마나 대단했을까,

/ when the phantom taking off the bandage / round its
유령이 붕대를 풀어서 머리를 감싸고 있는,

head, / as if it were too warm to wear indoors, / its lower
마치 집 안에서 하고 있기 너무 덥다는 듯이,

jaw dropped down upon its breast!
유령의 아래턱이 가슴으로 툭 떨어졌을 때!

Scrooge fell upon his knees, / and clasped his hands
스크루지는 털썩 무릎을 꿇고,   얼굴 앞에서 두 손을 모았다.

before his face.

"Mercy!" / he said. "Dreadful apparition, / why do you
"자비를 베푸소서!" 그는 말했다.   "무서운 유령이시어,

trouble me?"
왜 저를 괴롭히십니까?"

"Man of the worldly mind!" / replied the Ghost, / "do
"속물스러운 인간이여!"   유령이 대답했다,

you believe in me or not?"
"나를 믿느냐 믿지 않느냐?"

"I do," / said Scrooge. "I must. But why do spirits walk
"믿습니다."   스크루지는 말했다.   "믿어야겠죠. 하지만 왜 유령들이 세상을 돌아다니고,

the earth, / and why do they come to me?"
왜 내게 오셨습니까?"

"It is required of every man," / the Ghost returned, /
"모든 인간이 그래야만 한다,"   유령이 대답했다,

"that the spirit within him / should walk abroad / among
"인간 안에 들어 있는 영혼은   다녀야 하고

his fellowmen, / and travel far and wide; / and if that
사람들 사이를,   멀리 그리고 널리 여행해야 한다;

spirit goes not forth in life, / it is condemned to do so /
만약 영혼이 살아 생전 다니지 않았다면,   여행을 해야만 하는 운명이다

after death. It is doomed / to wander through the world
죽은 후에라도. 숙명이라니   세상을 돌아다니며

/ — oh, woe is me! — / and witness / what it cannot
— 아, 슬프도다! —   지켜봐야 하는 것이   함께 할 수 없는 것을,

share, / but might have shared / on earth, / and turned to
하지만 함께했을텐데   이승에 있다면,   그리고 행복해졌을텐데!"

happiness!"

---

charge 임무 | have but to do ~하기만 하면 된다 | persecuted 박해하다, 괴롭히다 | legion 군단 | goblin
마귀, 도깨비 | swoon 기절, 졸도 | apparition 유령, 망령 | worldly 세속적인 | condemn 선고하다, 운명 짓다

Again / the spectre raised a cry, / and shook its chain /
다시 한 번 유령은 소리를 지르고, 쇠사슬을 흔들어대며

and wrung its shadowy hands.
그림자같은 손을 비틀었다.

"You are fettered," / said Scrooge, / trembling. "Tell me
"족쇄를 차고 있군요," 스크루지가 말했다, 떨면서.

why?"
"왜 그렇습니까?"

"I wear the chain / I forged in life," / replied the Ghost.
"쇠사슬을 차고 있지 살아 생전 만든," 유령이 대답했다.

"I made it / link by link, / and *yard by yard; I girded
"내가 만들었지 한 고리씩, 1야드씩 늘려갔어; 그걸 둘렀네

it on / of my own free will, / and of my own free will / I
  내 자유의지로, 그리고 내 자유의지로

wore it. Is its pattern strange to you?"
찬 거지. 모양이 낯선가?"

Scrooge trembled more and more.
스크루지는 점점 더 심하게 떨었다.

"Or would you know," / pursued the Ghost, / "the weight
"아니면 알고 싶은가," 유령은 계속했다.

and length of the strong coil / you bear yourself? It was
"쇠사슬의 무게와 길이를 자네가 지고 있는?

full as heavy and as long as this, / seven Christmas Eves
자네 쇠사슬은 이것만큼 무겁고 길었어. 7년 전 크리스마스 이브에.

ago. You have labored on it, / since. It is a ponderous
  자넨 계속 늘려왔지, 그때 이후로.

chain!"
아주 무거운 쇠사슬이 되었네!"

Scrooge glanced about him / on the floor, / in the
스크루지는 자신을 살펴 보았지만 바닥을,

expectation of finding / himself surrounded / by some
발견할까 봐 자신이 감겨 있는 모습을

fifty or sixty **fathoms of iron cable: / but he could see
5,60패덤의 쇠사슬에 둘러싸인: 아무것도 볼 수 없었다.

nothing.

"Jacob," / he said, / imploringly. "Old Jacob Marley, / tell
"제이콥," 그는 말했다, 애원하듯. "옛 친구 제이콥 말리,

me more. Speak comfort to me, / Jacob!"
더 말해 주게. 내게 위안을 좀 주게나, 제이콥!"

"I have none to give," / the Ghost replied. "It comes from
"난 해 줄 말이 없네," 유령이 대답했다. "그것은 다른 세상의 일

other regions, / Ebenezer Scrooge, / and is conveyed by
이네, 에브니저 스크루지, 다른 부류의 성직자들이 전해

other ministers, / to other kinds of men. Nor can I tell
주는 것이지, 자네와 다른 종류의 사람들에게. 또 말해 줄 수도 없네,

you / what I would. A very little more is / all permitted
내가 뭘 줄 것인지. 아주 작은 것만 내게 허락되어 있지.

to me. I cannot rest, / I cannot stay, / I cannot linger
난 쉴 수도 없고, 머물 수도 없고, 어딘가에서 꾸물거릴 수도 없네.

anywhere. My spirit never walked / beyond our counting
내 영혼은 결코 걸어간 적이 없었네 우리의 회계사무실 밖으로

–house / —— mark me! — / in life / my spirit never roved
— 나를 보게! — 살아있을 때 내 영혼은 결코 배회한 적 없었고

/ beyond the narrow limits of our money-changing hole; /
우리의 좁은 환전 창구 구멍 밖으로;

and weary journeys lie / before me!"
그래서 이제 힘든 여행길이 있는 것이지 내 앞에는! "

Key Expression 🔑

명사 by 명사 : ~씩

전치사 by는 '명사 by 명사'의 형태로 사용되어 어떤 일이 일어나는 속도를 표현할 수 있습니다.

▶ day by day : 나날이, 날마다
▶ bit by bit : 조금씩
▶ two by two : 둘씩
▶ hour by hour : 시시각각

ex) I made it link by link, and yard by yard.
　　내가 그것을 한 고리 한 고리 만들어 한 야드씩 늘려갔어.

---

*1야드는 91.44센티미터
**1패덤은 약 1.83미터. 주로 바다의 깊이를 잴 때 쓰이는 단위

wring 비틀다 | fetter 족쇄를 채우다 | forge (노력하여) 만들어 내다 | gird on 둘러싸다, 에워싸다 | ponderous
육중한 | imploringly 애원하여 | linger 꾸물거리다 | rove 배회하다, 헤매다 | weary 지친, 힘든

It was a habit with Scrooge, / whenever he became
스크루지의 버릇이었다,　　　　　무슨 일을 생각할 때마다,

thoughtful, / to put his hands in his breeches pockets.
바지 주머니에 손을 찔러 넣는 것은.

Pondering on what the Ghost had said, / he did so now, /
유령이 한 말을 곰곰이 생각하면서,　　　이제 그렇게 손을 넣었다,

but without lifting up his eyes, / or getting off his knees.
눈을 내리깐 채,　　　무릎을 꿇고.

"You must have been very slow about it, / Jacob,"
"자네는 아주 느긋하게 있었나 보군,　　　제이콥,"

Scrooge observed, / in a business-like manner, / though
스크루지가 말했다,　　　장사꾼같은 태도로,

with humility and deference.
겸손하고 공손했지만.

"Slow!" / the Ghost repeated.
"느긋하게라니!" 유령은 되풀이 해 말했다.

"Seven years dead," / mused Scrooge. "And travelling all
"죽은 지 7년 동안, "　　　스크루지는 생각에 잠겼다.　"내내 여행을 다녔으니 말이

the time!"
지!"

"The whole time," / said the Ghost. "No rest, / no peace.
"내내,"　　　유령은 말했다.　　　"휴식도 없고,　평화도 없었네.

Incessant torture of remorse."
후회로 인해 끊임없이 고통스러웠지."

"You travel fast?" / said Scrooge.
"빨리 다니나?"　　　스크루지가 말했다.

"On the wings of the wind," / replied the Ghost.
"바람의 날개를 타고 다니지."　　　유령이 대답했다.

"You might have got over a great quantity of ground / in
"아주 많은 곳을 다녔겠는데

seven years," / said Scrooge.
7년 동안,"　　　스크루지가 말했다.

---

breeches 바지 | humility 겸손, 비하 | difference 존경 | muse 명상에 잠기다, 골똘히 생각하다 | incessant
그칠 새 없는, 부단한 | remorse 후회, 양심의 가책 | hideously 소름끼치게 | ward 파수꾼 | indict 기소하다,
고발하다 | susceptible 허용하는, 가능한 | falter 움찔하다, 망설이다

The Ghost, / on hearing this, / set up another cry, / and
유령은, 이 말을 듣자, 또 다시 울부짖으며,

clanked its chain / so hideously / in the dead silence of
쇠사슬을 덜그럭거렸다 소름끼치도록 죽은 듯한 조용한 밤에,

the night, / that the Ward would have been justified / in
야경꾼이 기소해도 정당할 정도였다

indicting it / for a nuisance.
소란죄로.

"Oh! Captive, / bound, / and double-ironed," / cried the
"아! 속박되고, 얽매이고, 쇠사슬에 이중으로 휘감겼으니,"

phantom, / "not to know, / that ages of incessant labour
유령이 소리쳤다, "몰랐다니, 끊임없이 일하는 시간 동안

/ by immortal creatures, / for this earth must pass into
불멸의 존재들이, 이승의 삶은 영원의 세계로 가야 한다는 것을

eternity / before the good of which it is susceptible / is
세상이 허용하는 즐거움을

all developed. Not to know / that any Christian spirit
채 펼치지도 못하고, 몰랐다니 선한 일을 하는 어느 기독교 영혼이라도

working kindly / in its little sphere, / whatever it may
이 작은 세상에서, 그것이 무엇이든,

be, / will find its mortal life too short / for its vast means
유한한 이 삶은 너무 짧다는 것을 그 방대한 유용성을 발휘하기

of usefulness. Not to know / that no space of regret can
에는. 몰랐다니 아무리 후회해도 다시 고칠 수 없다는 것을

make amends / for one life's opportunity misused! Yet
잘못 사용한 단 한 번의 인생이란 기회를! 그러나

such was I! Oh! Such was I!"
난 그랬었다! 아! 난 그랬었어!"

"But you were always a good man of business, / Jacob,"
"하지만 자네는 항상 훌륭한 사업가였지 않나, 제이콥,"

faltered Scrooge, / who now began to apply this to
스크루지는 머뭇거리렸다, 이제 이 말을 자기 자신에게 사용하고 있었다.

himself.

"Business!" / cried the Ghost, / wringing its hands
"사업이라니!" 유령이 소리쳤다, 다시 손을 움켜 잡으며.

again. "Mankind was my business. The common welfare
"인류를 위한 내 사업이었어야 했어. 모든 이의 행복을 위한 사업이었어

was my business; / charity, / mercy, / forbearance,
야 해; 자선, 자비, 관용,

/ and benevolence, / were, all, / my business. The
그리고 선행, 그 모든 것이, 내 사업이었어야 했어.

dealings of my trade / were but a drop of water / in the
내가 했던 거래는 물 한 방울에 지나지 않았어

comprehensive ocean / of my business!"
광대한 바다 속의 내가 했어야 하는 사업이라는!"

It held up its chain at arm's length, / as if that were the
유령은 쇠사슬을 번쩍 들어 올리고는, 그것이 이 모든 헛된 슬픔의

cause of all its unavailing grief, / and flung it heavily /
원인이라도 된다는 듯이, 거칠게 내던졌다

upon the ground again.
다시 바닥 위로.

"At this time of the rolling year," / the spectre said, / "I
"흘러가는 일 년 중에 이맘 때가," 유령이 말했다,

suffer most. Why did I walk / through crowds of fellow-
"가장 괴롭다네. 나는 왜 걸어갔던가 이웃 사람들 사이를

beings / with my eyes turned down, / and never raise
눈을 내리깐 채, 눈을 들어 바라보지 않았던가

them / to that blessed Star / which led the Wise Men / to
거룩한 별을 동방 박사들을 이끌었던

a poor abode! Were there no poor homes / to which its
가난한 이들의 거처로! 가난한 집들이 없었단 말인가

light would have conducted me!"
날 인도할 별빛이!"

Scrooge was very much dismayed / to hear the spectre
스크루지는 공포에 질려 유령이 계속 말하는 것을 듣고

going on / at this rate, / and began to quake exceedingly.
이런 식으로, 몹시 떨기 시작했다.

"Hear me!" / cried the Ghost. "My time is nearly gone."
"내 말을 들게나!" 유령이 소리쳤다. "내 시간은 거의 끝났네."

"I will," / said Scrooge. "But don't be hard upon me!
"듣겠네."   스크루지는 말했다.   "하지만 너무 가혹하게 하지는 말게나!

Don't be flowery, / Jacob! Pray!"
과장하지 말게,   제이콥! 부탁하네!"

"How it is / that I appear before you / in a shape / that you
"어떻게   내가 자네 앞에 나타났는지   모습으로   자네가 볼 수

can see, / I may not tell. I have sat invisible beside you /
있는,   말하지 않겠네.   자네 옆에 보이지 않는 모습으로 앉아 있었다네

many and many a day."
여러 번, 하루에도 여러 번.

It was not an agreeable idea. Scrooge shivered, / and
그것은 기분 좋은 말은 아니었다.   스크루지는 몸서리치며,

wiped the perspiration from his brow.
이마에 맺힌 땀을 닦았다.

Key Expression ♥

whatever it may be : 그것이 무엇이든 간에
whatever it may be는 '그것이 무엇이든 간에'라는 의미로 기억하세요.
이때 whatever는 양보의 의미를 가진 복합관계대명사입니다.

ex) Not to know that any Christian spirit working kindly in its little sphere, what
    ever it may be, will find its mortal life too short for its vast means of
    usefulness.
    이 작은 지구에서 무엇이든 간에 자비로운 일을 하는 기독교의 영혼도 인간의
    유한한 삶이 너무 짧다는 것을 몰랐다니.

wring 꽉 움켜 잡다 | forbearance 용서, 관용 | benevolence 자비심, 선행 | comprehensive 광범위한
| unavailing 무익한, 헛된 | abode 거처 | dismay 공포 따위로 당황하다 | at this rate 이런 식으로 |
exceedingly 대단히, 몹시 | flowery 미사 여구를 쓴 | agreeable 기분 좋은

"That is no light part of my penance," / pursued the
"그것은 내 속죄의 하나이지만 쉬운 일이 아니지,"   유령은 계속했다.

Ghost. "I am here to-night to warn you, / that you have
"난 오늘 밤 자네에게 경고하기 위해 온 거네,

yet a chance and hope / of escaping my fate. A chance
자네에겐 아직 기회와 희망이 있다고   나같은 운명을 피해 갈 수 있는.

and hope of my procuring, / Ebenezer."
내가 주는 한 번의 기회와 희망이네,   에브니저."

"You were always a good friend to me," / said Scrooge.
"자네는 언제나 나의 좋은 친구였지,"   스크루지는 말했다.

"Thank'ee!"
"고맙네!"

"You will be haunted," / resumed the Ghost, / "by Three
"나타날 것이네,"   유령은 계속해서 말했다,

Spirits."
"세 유령이."

Scrooge's countenance fell / almost as low as the Ghost's
스크루지의 안색이 창백해졌다   유령만큼이나.

had done.

"Is that the chance and hope / you mentioned, / Jacob?"
"그것이 기회이고 희망인가   자네가 언급했던,   제이콥?"

he demanded, / in a faltering voice.
그는 질문했다,   더듬거리는 목소리로.

"It is."
"그렇네."

"I — I think / I'd rather not," / said Scrooge.
"내 — 내 생각에는   안 만났으면 좋겠네,"   스크루지는 말했다.

"Without their visits," / said the Ghost, / "you cannot
"유령들이 방문하지 않으면,"   유령이 말했다,   "자네는 피할 희망이 없네

hope to shun / the path I tread. Expect the first /
            내가 걸었던 길을.   첫 번째 유령을 기다리게

tomorrow, / when the bell tolls One."
내일,   시계가 1시를 울릴 때."

penance 회개, 참회 | procure ~을 설득하여 시키다 | countenance 안색 | shun 피하다, 비키다 | tread 밟다,
걷다 | toll 치다, 울리다 | look to 돌보다, 주의하다, 기대하다

64   A Christmas Carol

"Couldn't I take 'em all at once, / and have it over, /
"세 유령을 한꺼번에 보고,   끝낼 수는 없을까,

Jacob?" / hinted Scrooge.
제이콥?"   스크루지가 넌지시 물었다.

"Expect the second / on the next night / at the same hour.
"두 번째 유령을 기다리게   그 다음 날 밤   같은 시간에.

The third upon the next night / when the last stroke of
세 번째 유령은 그 다음 날 밤 올 것이네   열두 번째 시계 소리가

Twelve / has ceased to vibrate. Look to see me no more; /
         떨림을 멈출 때.   더 이상 내게 기대하지 말고;

and look that, / for your own sake, / you remember / what
돌아보게,   자신을 위해,   기억하게

has passed between us!"
우리 사이에 있었던 일을!"

When it had said these words, / the spectre took its
유령은 이 말을 하고는,   탁자에서 붕대를 집어,

wrapper from the table, / and bound it round its head,
머리에 다시 둘러 감았다,

/ as before. Scrooge knew this, / by the smart sound its
전처럼.   스크루지는 알 수 있었다,   유령의 치아가 내는 날카로운 소리를

teeth made, / when the jaws were brought together / by
통해서,   턱이 서로 맞춰졌다는 것을

the bandage. He ventured to raise his eyes again, / and
붕대를 이용해.   겨우 다시 눈을 들어 살펴보니,

found his supernatural visitor / confronting him / in an
초자연적인 방문자를 볼 수 있었다   자신을 마주하고 서 있는

erect attitude, / with its chain wound over and about its
꼿꼿한 자세로,   쇠사슬을 팔에 두른 채.

arm.

The apparition walked backward from him; / and at
유령은 뒷걸음질치며 그에게서 물러났다;

every step it took, / the window raised itself a little, / so
한 걸음씩 물러날 때마다, 창문이 저절로 조금씩 올라가더니,

that when the spectre reached it, / it was wide open.
유령이 창문에 다다랐을 때는, 활짝 열려 있었다.

It beckoned Scrooge to approach, / which he did. When
유령을 스크루지에게 다가오라고 손짓했고, 그는 다가갔다.

they were within two paces of each other, / Marley's
유령과의 사이에 두 발자국 정도 남았을 때,

Ghost held up its hand, / warning him to come no nearer.
말리는 손을 들었다, 더 이상 다가오지 말라고 경고하며.

Scrooge stopped.
스크루지는 멈췄다.

Not so much in obedience, / as in surprise and fear:
복종하기 위해서라기보다는, 놀라움과 공포 때문이었다:

/ for on the raising of the hand, / he became sensible
말리가 손을 들었을 때, 스크루지는 이상한 소리가 나는

of confused noises / in the air; / incoherent sounds
것을 알아챘다 허공 속에서; 알아들을 수 없는

/ of lamentation and regret; / wailings inexpressibly
비탄과 후회에 잠긴;

sorrowful and self-accusatory. The spectre, / after
표현할 수 없이 슬프고 자책하는 울부짖음을. 유령은,

listening for a moment, / joined in the mournful dirge; /
잠시 동안 귀를 기울이더니, 그 슬픔의 장송가를 따라 부르며;

and floated out upon the bleak, dark night.
음침하고, 어두운 밤 속으로 날아갔다.

Scrooge followed to the window: / desperate in his
스크루지는 창문쪽으로 따라 갔다: 호기심을 참지 못하고.

curiosity. He looked out.
그는 내다 보았다.

---

confront 직면하다, 마주 보다 | erect 직립한, 곧추 서 있는 | apparition 유령, 망령 | beckon 신호하다, 부르다 |
incoherent (소리가) 잘 알아들을 수 없는 | lamentation 비탄, 애도 | wail 울부짖다 | inexpressibly 표현할 수
없이 | self-accusatory 자책하는 | dirge 장송가 | bleak 음침한

The air was filled with phantoms, / wandering hither
하늘에는 유령들로 가득 차 있었다.   이리저리 떠돌아 다니는

and thither / in restless haste, / and moaning / as they
             불안하게,   신음 소리를 내며   지날 때마다.

went. Every one of them wore chains / like Marley's
       모두 쇠사슬을 감고 있었다   말리의 유령처럼;

Ghost; / some few / (they might be guilty governments)
몇몇은   (아마 죄를 지은 공무원들일 것이다)

/ were linked together; / none were free. Many had been
  같이 묶여 있었다;   아무도 자유롭지 못했다.   많은 유령들은 스크루지와

personally known to Scrooge / in their lives. He had
개인적으로 알고 지냈었다   살아있을 때.

been quite familiar / with one old ghost, / in a white
스크루지는 꽤 친분이 있었다   한 늙은 유령과,   하얀 코트를 입고 있는,

waistcoat, / with a monstrous iron safe / attached to its
             괴물같은 쇠 금고를   발목에 차고 있는,

ankle, / who cried piteously / at being unable to assist /
애처롭게 울부짖고 있었다   도와줄 수 없어서

a wretched woman with an infant, / whom it saw below,
아기와 함께 있는 불쌍한 여인을,   내려다보며,

/ upon a door-step. The misery with them all was, /
  현관에 앉아 있는.   그 모든 유령들의 불행은,

clearly, / that they sought to interfere, / for good, / in
분명히,   끼어들고 싶지만,   선의로,

human matters, / and had lost the power / for ever.
인간 세상의 문제에,   그럴 힘이 없다는데 있었다   영원히.

Whether these creatures faded into mist, / or mist
이 유령들이 안개 속으로 사라졌는지,   아니면 안개가

enshrouded them, / he could not tell. But they and their
그들을 덮어 가렸는지,   그는 알 수 없었다.   하지만 유령들과 그들의 목소리는

spirit voices / faded together; / and the night became / as
             함께 사라졌다;   그리고 밤이 돌아왔다

it had been / when he walked home.
예전 모습으로   자신이 집에 왔던 때의.

---

hither and thither 여기저기로 | moan 신음하다 | piteously 애처롭게 | enshroud ~을 덮어 가리다 | repose
휴식하다

68 A Christmas Carol

Scrooge closed the window, / and examined the door / by
스크루지는 창문을 닫고,   문을 살펴보았다

which the Ghost had entered. It was double-locked, / as
유령이 들어왔던.   문은 이중으로 잠겨 있었고,

he had locked it / with his own hands, / and the bolts were
그가 잠궜던 것처럼   자기 손으로,   나사는 풀리지 않은 채였다.

undisturbed. He tried to say "Humbug!" / but stopped at
                  그는 "헛소리!"라고 말하려다가   첫 음절에서 멈췄다.

the first syllable. And being, / from the emotion he had
              그리고,   그가 겪은 감정 때문인지,

undergone, / or the fatigues of the day, / or his glimpse
              아니면 그날의 피로 때문인지,   혹은 보이지 않는 세상을

of the Invisible World, / or the dull conversation of the
들여다 본 탓인지,   또는 유령과의 지루한 대화 때문이었는지,

Ghost, / or the lateness of the hour, / much in need of
          아니면 늦은 시간이라서,   휴식이 필요해졌던 것인지;

repose; / went straight to bed, / without undressing, / and
              곧바로 잠자리에 들어,   옷도 벗지 않고,

fell asleep upon the instant.
즉시 곯아 떨어졌다.

Key Expression ♀

복장을 나타내는 전치사 in

옷을 입은 모습을 표현할 때는 전치사 in를 사용합니다.
반면 옷이 아닌 액세서리를 표현할 때에는 with를 사용하는 것에 주의하세요.

ex) He had been quite familiar with one old ghost, in a white waistcoat, with a
monstrous iron safe attached to its ankle.
그는 하얀 코트를 입고 괴물같은 쇠 금고를 발목에 찬 노인 유령은 꽤 익숙했다.

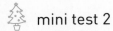 mini test 2

A. 다음 문장을 해석해 보세요.

(1) The yard was so dark / that even Scrooge, / who knew its every stone, / was fain to grope with his hands.
→

(2) Its horror seemed to be / in spite of the face and beyond its control, / rather than a part of its own expression.
→

(3) Upon its coming in, / the dying flame leaped up, / as though it cried, / "I know him; / Marley's Ghost!" / and fell again.
→

(4) It is doomed / to wander through the world / and witness / what it cannot share!
→

B. 다음 주어진 문구가 알맞은 문장이 되도록 순서를 맞춰 보세요.

(1) 모든 것이 있어야 하는 그대로였다.
(as / should / be / they / All)
→

(2) 왜 난 <u>눈을 내리깐 채 이웃들 사이를 뚫고</u> 걸어 갔던 것인가.
(with / crowds / of / through / my eyes / fellow beings / down / turned)
Why did I walk _____
_____ .

(3) 너무 가혹하게는 하지 말게나!
(upon / Don't / me / hard / be)
→

 !

A. (1) 공터는 너무 어두워서 돌멩이 하나까지 알고 있는 스크루지조차도, 손으로 더듬어서 길을 찾아야만 했다. (2) 그 얼굴에도 불구하고, 공포는 얼굴이 표현하는 무엇이라기보다, 그 이상의 뭔가에 있는 듯 했다. (3) 그것이 들어오자, 꺼져가던 불빛은 '이게 뭔지 알아요; 말리의 유령이에요'라고 외치는 듯, 확 피어 올

A Christmas Carol

(4) 복종하는 의미라기 보다 는, 놀라움과 공포 때문이었다.
[as / Not / fear / so / in / in / much / and / surprise / obedience,]
→

C. 다음 주어진 문장이 본문의 내용과 맞으면 T, 틀리면 F에 동그라미 하세요.

(1) When Scrooge had his key in the lock of the door, he saw
    Marley's face.
    [T / F]

(2) Scrooge wasn't very surprised when he saw his old friend.
    [T / F]

(3) When Scrooge went up to his room, he saw a mess in it.
    [T / F]

(4) After the journey with Marley, Scrooge had to stay up all
    night.
    [T / F]

D. 의미가 비슷한 것끼리 서로 연결해 보세요.

(1) grope   ▶   ◀ ① beginning
(2) outset   ▶   ◀ ② hang
(3) agitate   ▶   ◀ ③ ponder
(4) muse   ▶   ◀ ④ search

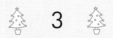

3

THE FIRST OF THE THREE SPIRITS I
첫 번째 유령 I

When Scrooge awoke, / it was so dark, / that looking out
스크루지는 잠에서 깨어났을 때,　　너무 어두워서,　　침대 밖을 살펴보니,

of bed, / he could scarcely distinguish / the transparent
거의 구별할 수 없었다

window / from the opaque walls / of his chamber. He
투명한 창문과　불투명한 벽을　　　그의 방의.

was endeavoring to pierce the darkness / with his ferret
그는 어둠을 뚫고 보려고 노력했다　　　　　탐색하는 눈빛으로,

eyes, / when the chimes of a neighboring church / struck
근처의 교회 종소리가　　　　　15분마다

the four quarters. So he listened for the hour.
종이 네 번 울렸다.　　그는 시간을 알아보려고 귀를 기울였다.

To his great astonishment / the heavy bell went on / from
놀랍게도　　　　그 둔탁한 종은 계속 울렸다　　여섯 번

six to seven, / and from seven to eight, / and regularly up
을 넘겨 일곱 번,　일곱 번에서 여덟 번,　　그리고 규칙적으로 열두 번

to twelve; / then stopped. Twelve! It was past two / when
까지 치더니;　멈췄다.　12시였다!　2시가 넘은 시각이었다　그가 잠자

he went to bed. The clock was wrong. An icicle must
리에 들었을 때는.　시계가 고장난 것이었다.　고드름이 작동에 문제를

have got into the works. Twelve!
일으켰음이 틀림없다.　　12시라니!

He touched the spring of his repeater, / to correct this
그는 시계 스프링을 만졌다,

most preposterous clock. Its rapid little pulse beat twelve:
이 뒤죽박죽인 시간을 제대로 알려고.　그 시계의 작은 진동이 빠르게 열두 번을 치더니:

/ and stopped.
멈췄다.

"Why, / it isn't possible," / said Scrooge, / "that I can
"아니,　이건 불가능해."　스크루지가 말했다,

have slept through a whole day / and far into another
"내가 하루종일 낮잠을 자고　　　또 다시 밤이 되었단 말인가.

night. It isn't possible / that anything has happened to the
말도 안 되는데   태양에게 무슨 일이 생긴다는 건,

sun, / and this is twelve at noon!"
그런데 낮 12시라니!"

The idea being an alarming one, / he scrambled out of
예고했던 1시가 된다는 생각에,   그는 침대에서 뛰어 나와,

bed, / and groped his way to the window. He was obliged
더듬거리며 창문으로 다가갔다.

to rub the frost off / with the sleeve of his dressing-gown
성애를 닦아야만 했지만   잠옷 소매 자락으로

/ before he could see anything; / and could see very little
뭔가를 보기 위해서는: 거의 아무것도 보이지 않았다.

then. All he could make out was, / that it was still very
그가 알아낼 수 있었던 것은,

foggy and extremely cold, / and that there was no noise
아직 안개가 짙고 무척 춥다는 것과,   사람들의 소리가 들리지 않는다는 것이었다

of people / running to and fro, / and making a great stir,
이리저리 뛰어다니거나,   시끌벅적한 소동을 빚는,

/ as there unquestionably would have been / if night had
당연히 있어야 할

beaten off bright day, / and taken possession of the world.
낮이 밤을 이기고,   세상을 차지해 버렸다면.

Key Expression 🔑

to one's + 감정 추상명사 : ~하게도

감정을 나타내는 형용사 앞에 to one's를 붙이면 '(~가) ~하게도'라는 뜻으로 부사의 의미를 띠게 됩니다.

▶ to one's astonishment : 놀랍게도 (=astonishingly)

▶ to one's surprise : 놀랍게도 (=surprisingly)

▶ to one's sorrow : 슬프게도 (=sorrowfully)

▶ to one's delight : 즐겁게도 (=delightfully)

▶ to one's satisfaction : 만족스럽게도 (=satisfactorily)

ex) To his great astonishment the heavy bell went on from six to seven, and from seven to eight, and regularly up to twelve.

놀랍게도 그 둔탁한 종소리는 여섯 번에서 일곱 번, 다시 일곱 번에서 여덟 번으로, 그리고 열두 번이 될 때까지 규칙적으로 늘어났다.

opaque 불투명한 | ferret 탐색자 | chime 종, 종소리 | icicle 고드름 | repeater (1시간 혹은 15분 단위로)
반복해서 치는 시계(=repeating watch) | preposterous 불합리한, 뒤죽박죽의 | scramble 급히 이동시키다

This was a great relief, / because "three days after sight
이것은 아주 다행스러운 일이었다.   왜냐하면 "이 어음을 받고 사흘 후에

of this First of Exchange / pay to Mr. Ebenezer Scrooge
                          에브니저 스크루지나 그의 대리인에게 지불하시오,"

or his order," / and so forth, / would have become a mere
와 같은 것은,   미국의 국채처럼 쓸모없는 것이 되었을지

*United States' security / if there were no days to count
모르니까   만약 셀 날짜가 없었다면.

by.

Scrooge went to bed again, / and thought, / and thought,
스크루지는 다시 침대로 돌아가서,   생각하고,   생각하고,

/ and thought it over and over and over, / and could make
그 일을 계속해서 생각했지만,   아무 결론도 내릴 수 없었

nothing of it. The more he thought, / the more perplexed
다.   생각하면 생각할수록,   그는 더욱 혼란스러워졌고;

he was; / and the more he endeavored / not to think, / the
노력하면 노력할수록   생각하지 않으려고,

more he thought.
더 생각하게 되었다.

Key Expression

the + 비교급 ~, the 비교급 … : ~하면 할수록 더욱 …하다
비교급을 사용한 특수 구문의 하나입니다.
원칙적으로 다음과 같은 형태로 사용하지만, 'The more, the better.(많을수록 좋다)'처럼 간결하게 표현하는 경우도 있습니다.

▶ the + 비교급 + 주어 + 동사, the + 비교급 + 주어 + 동사
▶ the + 비교급 + 명사, the + 비교급 + 명사

ex) The more he thought, the more perplexed he was; and the more he endeav
ored not to think, the more he thought.
생각하면 생각할수록 그는 더욱 혼란스러워졌고; 생각하지 않으려고 노력하면
노력할수록 더욱 생각났다.

Marley's Ghost bothered him exceedingly. Every time
말리의 유령은 그를 엄청나게 괴롭혔다.

he resolved within himself, / after mature inquiry, /
그가 속으로 결론을 내릴 때마다, 신중한 질문들 끝에,

that it was all a dream, / his mind flew back again, /
모든 것이 꿈이었다고, 그의 마음은 되돌아갔고,

like a strong spring released, / to its first position, / and
강력한 스프링이 풀린 것처럼, 처음 자리로,

presented the same problem / to be worked all through, /
같은 질문을 하곤 했다 계속해서 풀려고 했던,

"Was it a dream or not?"
"그건 꿈이었나 아니었나?"

Scrooge lay in this state / until the chime had gone three
스크루지는 이런 상태로 누워 있었다 15분 시계 소리가 세 번 더 울릴 때까지,

quarters more, / when he remembered, / on a sudden, /
그때 기억났다, 갑자기,

that the Ghost had warned him of a visitation / when the
유령이 방문할 것이라고 경고했던 것이 시계 소리가

bell tolled one. He resolved to lie awake / until the hour
1시를 알리자. 그는 깨어 있겠다고 결심했다

was passed; / and, / considering / that he could no more
그 시간이 될 때까지; 그리고, 생각하면 더 이상 잠드는 것이 힘들다면

go to sleep / than go to Heaven, / this was perhaps the
천국에 가는 것보다 더, 이것은 가장 현명한 결정이었다

wisest resolution / in his power.
그가 할 수 있는 한.

---

*1930년대 미국의 대공황으로 채권의 가치가 떨어졌던 것을 비유한 표현

First of Exchange 제1어음(최초로 발행된 어음을 제1어음, 이를 담보로 발행된 어음을 제2어음이라고 함) |
perplexed 당황한, 난처한 | resolve 결심하다, 결의하다

The quarter was so long, / that he was more than
15분이 너무 길어서, 그는 여러 번 생각했다

once convinced / he must have sunk into a doze
자신이 깜박 졸아서,

unconsciously, / and missed the clock. At length / it
시계 소리를 놓쳤음에 틀림없다고. 마침내,

broke upon his listening ear.
귀 기울이던 귀에 종소리가 들렸다.

"Ding, dong!"
"딩, 동!"

"A quarter past," / said Scrooge, / counting.
"15분 지났다," 스크루지는 말했다, 세면서.

"Ding, dong!"
"딩, 동!"

"Half-past!" / said Scrooge.
"30분이야!" 스크루지는 말했다.

"Ding, dong!"
"딩, 동!"

"A quarter to it," / said Scrooge.
"15분 남았어," 스크루지는 말했다.

"Ding, dong!"
"딩, 동!"

"The hour itself," / said Scrooge, / triumphantly, / "and
"1시가 되었군." 스크루지는 말했다, 의기양양해서,

nothing else!"
"아무 일도 생기지 않는데!"

He spoke before the hour bell sounded, / which it now
그는 시간을 알리는 종이 울리기 전에 말했는데, 그때 종소리가 울렸다

did / with a deep, / dull, / hollow, / melancholy One.
깊고, 둔탁하며, 공허하고, 우울한 한 번의 종소리가.

Light flashed up in the room / upon the instant, / and the
밝은 불빛이 방 안에 비치더니 갑자기,

curtains of his bed were drawn.
침대 커튼이 젖혀졌다.

The curtains of his bed were drawn aside, / I tell you, /
침대 커튼이 옆으로 젖혀졌다,   말하자면,

by a hand. Not the curtains at his feet, / nor the curtains
어떤 손에 의해.   발치에 있는 커튼도 아니고,   등에 있는 커튼도 아니며,

at his back, / but those to which his face was addressed.
바로 얼굴 앞에 있는 커튼이었다.

The curtains of his bed / were drawn aside; / and
침대의 커튼이   옆으로 젖혀졌다;   그러자 스크루지는,

Scrooge, / starting up into a half-recumbent attitude, /
몸을 반쯤 일으키다가,

found himself face to face / with the unearthly visitor
얼굴이 마주쳤다   이 세상에 존재할 것 같지 않은 방문객과

/ who drew them: / as close to it / as I am now to you, /
커튼을 젖힌: 가깝게   나와 여러분과의 거리만큼,

and I am standing / in the spirit / at your elbow.
그리고 나는 서 있다   정신적으로   여러분의 팔꿈치 거리에.

It was a strange figure / — like a child: / yet not so like
이상하게 생긴 얼굴이었다   — 어린 아이같은: 그러나 그렇게 어린 아이같

a child / as like an old man, / viewed through some
지는 않고   노인같기도 했다   어떤 초자연적인 매개체를 통해 보여서,

supernatural medium, / which gave him the appearance /
모습으로 보였다

of having receded from the view, / and being diminished
시야에서 희미해지는 듯한,

to a child's proportions. Its hair, / which hung about its
그리고 어린 아이처럼 작아 보였다.   그 유령의 머리는,

neck and down its back, / was white as if with age; / and
목과 등까지 내려 와 있던,   나이가 들어 하얗게 센 것 같았지만;

yet the face had not a wrinkle in it, / and the tenderest
얼굴에는 주름 하나 없었으며,

recumbent 드러누운 | medium 매개물 | recede 옅어지다, 희미해지다 | diminish 작게 하다, 축소하다 |
proportion 비율

bloom was on the skin. The arms were very long and
피부에는 희미한 홍조가 있었다.   팔은 굉장히 길고 근육질이었으며;

muscular; / the hands the same, / as if its hold were of
                손도 같았다.   마치 악력이 매우 셀 것 같이.

uncommon strength. Its legs and feet, / most delicately
                다리와 발은,   가장 섬세하게 생긴

formed, / were, / like those upper members, / bare. It
        모습이었다. 다른 부분과 마찬가지로,   맨살의.

wore a tunic of the purest white; / and round its waist
유령은 새하얀 튜닉을 입고;   허리에는 두르고 있었는데

was bound / a lustrous belt, / the sheen of which was
        번쩍이는 허리띠를,   허리띠의 광채가 아름다웠다.

beautiful. It held a branch of fresh green holly / in its
        싱싱한 초록색의 호랑가시나무 가지를 들고 있었고   손에는;

hand; / and, / in singular contradiction / of that wintry
        그리고,   기묘하게 어울리지 않는 모습으로   겨울을 상징하는 그 가지와,

emblem, / had its dress trimmed / with summer flowers.
        옷은 장식되어 있었다   여름 꽃들로.

But the strangest thing about it was, / that from the
하지만 가장 이상한 점은,   머리에 있는 관으로부터

crown of its head / there sprung a bright clear jet of light,
        밝고 눈부신 불빛이 쏟아지고 있는 것이었다.

/ by which all this was visible; / and which was doubtless
그 빛으로 인해 이 모든 것이 보였다;   또한 분명한 것은 사용한다는 점이었다,

the occasion of its using, / in its duller moments, / a great
                유령이 덜 바쁠 때에는,

extinguisher / for a cap, / which it now held under its
불 끄는 도구로   모자를,   지금의 팔 밑에 끼고 있는.

arm.

---

bloom 뺨의 홍조 | tunic 튜닉(허리 아래까지 내려오는 여성용 옷옷) | lustrous 번쩍이는 | sheen 번쩍임, 광채 |
singular 기묘한, 기이한 | contradiction 반대, 모순 | emblem 상징, 표상 | trim ~을 장식하다

Even this, / though, / when Scrooge looked at it / with
이것조차, 그러나, 스크루지가 바라보았을 때

increasing steadiness, / was not its strangest quality. For
안정을 되찾으며, 가장 이상한 점은 아니었다.

as its belt sparkled and glittered / now in one part and
유령의 허리띠가 불꽃을 내며 번쩍 빛났다가 이쪽 저쪽에서,

now in another, / and what was light / one instant, / at
밝아졌다가 한 순간,

another time was dark, / so the figure itself fluctuated /
다음 순간 어두워지면서, 유령의 모습이 변했다

in its distinctness: / being now a thing with one arm, /
전혀 다르게: 팔이 하나였다가,

now with one leg, / now with twenty legs, / now a pair
다리가 하나가 되더니, 다리가 스무 개였다가,

of legs without a head, / now a head without a body: / of
머리 없이 다리가 두 개가 되기도 하고, 몸통 없이 머리만 있기도 했다:

which dissolving parts, / no outline would be visible / in
없어진 부분은, 윤곽도 보이지 않았다

the dense gloom / wherein they melted away. And in the
짙은 어둠 속에 녹아들어 버린 것처럼. 이런 놀라운 현상이

very wonder of this, / it would be itself again; / distinct
벌어지는 가운데, 유령은 다시 원래 모습으로 돌아왔다;

and clear as ever.
전처럼 분명하고 선명한 모습으로.

"Are you the Spirit, / sir, / whose coming was foretold to
"당신이 그 유령인가요, 유령님, 제게 찾아오신다던?"

me?" / asked Scrooge.
스크루지가 물었다.

"I am!"
"그렇다!"

The voice was soft and gentle. Singularly low, / as
목소리는 부드럽고 온화했다. 기묘하게 나지막하여,

if instead of being so close beside him, / it were at a
그의 옆 가까이에서 들려온다기 보다,

distance.
멀리서 들려오는 것 같았다.

"Who, / and what are you?" / Scrooge demanded.
"누구, 아니 무슨 유령인가요?" 스크루지가 물었다.

"I am the Ghost of Christmas Past."
"나는 과거의 크리스마스 유령이다."

"Long Past?" / inquired Scrooge: / observant of its
"먼 과거인가요?" 스크루지가 물었다:

dwarfish stature.
유령의 난쟁이같은 모습을 관찰하면서.

"No. Your past."
"아니다. 네 과거다."

Perhaps, / Scrooge could not have told anybody why, /
아마도, 스크루지는 이유를 설명할 수 없었겠지만,

if anybody could have asked him; / but he had a special
만약 누군가 물어본다면; 특히 보고 싶어져서

desire to see / the Spirit in his cap; / and begged him to
유령이 모자 쓴 모습을; 모자를 써 달라고 간청했다.

be covered.

"What!" / exclaimed the Ghost, / "would you so soon
"뭐라고!" 유령이 소리쳤다, "그렇게 빨리 끄고 싶단 말이구나,

put out, / with worldly hands, / the light / I give? Is it not
네 세속적인 손으로, 그 빛을 내가 주는? 충분하지 않단

enough / that you are one of those / whose passions made
말이냐 네가 그들 중 하나이거늘 욕망으로 이 모자를 만들어,

this cap, / and force me / through whole trains of years /
내게 강요한 수많은 세월 동안

to wear it low / upon my brow!"
모자를 쓰도록 아주 깊이!"

---

fluctuate 계속 변화하다 | distinctness 확연함 | gloom 어스름, 어둑어둑함 | singularly 아주, 몹시, 특이하게 |
dwarfish 난쟁이 같은, 왜소한 | stature 신장, 키

Scrooge reverently disclaimed / all intention to offend
스크루지는 공손하게 부인했다   기분을 상하게 하려는 의도는 아니며

/ or any knowledge / of having wilfully "bonneted" the
아는 바도 전혀 없었다고   유령에게 고의로 "모자를 씌웠다"는 것에 대해

Spirit / at any period of his life. He then / made bold to
평생 한 순간도.   그리고 나서   용기를 내어 물었다

inquire / what business brought him there.
            무슨 일로 왔는지.

"Your welfare!" / said the Ghost.
"네 행복을 위해서이다!"   유령이 말했다 .

Scrooge expressed himself much obliged, / but could not
스크루지는 고맙다고 말하기는 했지만,   하지 않을 수 없었다

help thinking / that a night of unbroken rest / would have
           방해 받지 않고 하룻밤 휴식을 취하는 것이

been more conducive to that end. The Spirit must have
훨씬 도움이 되었을 것이라고.   유령은 그의 생각을 읽은 것이 틀림

heard him thinking, / for it said immediately:
없었다,   바로 말한 것으로 봐서:

Key Expression ♪

cannot help −ing : ~하지 않을 수 없다
조동사 can을 이용한 숙어 표현으로 '~하지 않을 수 없다', 즉 '할 수 밖에 없다,
어쩔 수 없이 해야 한다'라는 뜻입니다. 같은 의미의 숙어들을 함께 기억하세요.

▶ cannot help −ing
   = cannot but + 동사원형
   = have no choice but to + 동사원형
   = be forced to + 동사원형

ex) Scrooge expressed himself much obliged, but could not help thinking that a
    night of unbroken rest would have been more conducive to that end.
    스크루지는 고맙다고 말하기는 했지만, 하룻밤의 휴식을 방해 받지 않았다면
    훨씬 도움이 되었을 것이라고 생각하지 않을 수 없었다.

"Your reclamation, / then. Take heed!"
"너를 교화시키려고 왔다,   그러니.   조심해라!"

It put out its strong hand / as it spoke, / and clasped him
유령은 강인한 손을 뻗어   말하면서,

gently by the arm.
스크루지의 팔을 가볍게 움켜잡았다.

"Rise! And walk with me!"
"일어나라! 그리고 나와 같이 가자!"

It would have been in vain / for Scrooge to plead /
소용없을 것 같았다   스크루지가 간청한다 해도

that the weather and the hour were not adapted / to
날씨와 시간이 적합하지 않다고

pedestrian purposes; / that bed was warm, / and the
돌아다니기에는;   침대는 따뜻하지만,

thermometer a long way below freezing; / that he was
기온은 영하를 훨씬 밑도는 데다가;

clad but lightly / in his slippers, / dressing-gown, / and
자신은 가벼운 차림이라고   슬리퍼에,   잠옷을 걸치고,

nightcap; / and that he had a cold upon him / at that time.
나이트캡을 쓴;   또한 감기에 걸릴 거라고   그런 시간에 나가면.

The grasp, / though gentle as a woman's hand, / was not
움켜잡은 손은,   여자의 손이 움켜쥔 것처럼 부드러웠지만,

to be resisted. He rose: / but finding / that the Spirit made
저항할 수 없었다.   그는 일어났지만: 알아차리자   유령이 창문 쪽으로 가는 것을,

towards the window, / clasped his robe / in supplication.
       유령의 옷자락을 쥐었다   애원하면서.

"I am a mortal," / Scrooge remonstrated, / "and liable to
"나는 인간입니다,"   스크루지는 항의했다,   "떨어지고 말 거예요."

fall."

---

reverently 공경하여 | disclaim 부인하다 | bonnet 모자를 씌우다 | conducive 도움이 되는, 촉구하는
| reclamation 교화 | heed 조심 | pedestrian 도보의 | clad 차려 입은 | supplication 간청, 애원 |
remonstrate 항의하다 | liable ~할 것 같은(likely)

"Bear but a touch of my hand there," / said the Spirit, /
"내 손이 닿기만 한다면," 유령은 말했다,

laying it upon his heart, / "and you shall be upheld / in
스크루지의 가슴에 손을 얹으며 "넌 떠오를 수도 있다

more than this!"
이보다 더 높은 곳도!"

As the words were spoken, / they passed through the
말이 끝나자, 그들은 벽을 통과하여,

wall, / and stood upon an open country road, / with fields
탁 트인 시골길에 서 있었다. 양쪽에 들판이 펼쳐진.

on either hand. The city had entirely vanished. Not a
양쪽에 들판이 펼쳐진. 도시는 완전히 사라져 버렸다.

vestige of it was to be seen. The darkness and the mist
흔적조차 보이지 않았다. 어둠과 안개도 사라져서

had vanished / with it, / for it was a clear, / cold, / winter
도시와 함께, 맑고, 추운, 겨울날이

day, / with snow upon the ground.
었다, 땅에는 눈이 쌓인.

"Good Heaven!" / said Scrooge, / clasping his hands
"이럴 수가!" 스크루지가 말했다, 두 손을 맞잡고,

together, / as he looked about him. "I was bred in this
주변을 돌아보며. "저는 이곳에서 자랐습니다.

place. I was a boy here!"
여기에서 어린 시절을 보냈어요!"

---

uphold 들어올리다 | vestige 흔적, 자국 | Good Heaven 저런 | breed 가르치다, 양육하다 | instantaneous
즉시의, 순간적인 | odour 냄새, 향기 | fervor 열렬, 열성

The Spirit gazed upon him mildly. Its gentle touch, /
유령은 그를 부드럽게 응시했다.　유령의 부드러운 손길은,

though it had been light and instantaneous, / appeared
비록 가볍고 순간적이었지만,

still present / to the old man's sense of feeling. He was
아직도 남아 있었다　늙은이의 감각 속에.

conscious of a thousand odours / floating in the air, /
수천 가지 향기가 느껴지고　공기 중에 떠 다니는,

each one connected with / a thousand thoughts, / and
각 향기는 연결되어 있었다　수천 가지의 생각과,

hopes, / and joys, / and cares / long, long, forgotten!
희망,　기쁨,　그리고 걱정들과　아주 오래 전에 잊어버린!

"Your lip is trembling," / said the Ghost. "And what is
"네 입술이 떨리는구나,"　유령이 말했다.

that upon your cheek?"
"네 뺨에 난 것은 무엇인가?"

Scrooge muttered, / with an unusual catching in his
스크루지는 더듬더듬 말하며,　평소와는 다른 목이 멘 목소리로,

voice, / that it was a pimple; / and begged the Ghost / to
여드름이라고;　유령에게 간청했다

lead him / where he would.
데려가 달라고　그가 자란 곳으로.

"You recollect the way?" / inquired the Spirit.
"길을 기억하느냐?"　유령이 물었다.

"Remember it!" / cried Scrooge with fervor; / "I could
"당연히 기억합니다!"　스크루지는 열띤 목소리로 소리쳤다;

walk it blindfold."
"눈 감고도 갈 수 있어요."

"Strange to have forgotten it / for so many years!" /
"잊어버려서 낯설텐데　그렇게 오랫동안!"

observed the Ghost. "Let us go on."
유령은 떠 보았다.　"가도록 하자."

They walked along the road, / Scrooge recognising /
그들은 길을 따라 걸었고, 스크루지는 알아보았다

every gate, / and post, / and tree; / until a little market-
대문 하나, 말뚝 하나, 나무 한 그루까지도; 마침내 작은 시장이 보였고

town / appeared in the distance, / with its bridge, / its
저 멀리에, 다리와,

church, / and winding river. Some shaggy ponies now
교회와, 굽이쳐 도는 강물도 보였다. 털이 덥수룩한 조랑말 몇 마리가 보였다

were seen / trotting towards them / with boys upon their
그들을 향해 달려오는 등에 남자 아이들을 태우고,

backs, / who called to other boys / in country gigs and
아이들은 다른 아이들을 불렀다 달구지와 짐마차에 타고 있는

carts, / driven by farmers. All these boys were in great
농부가 끄는. 아이들은 모두 신이 나서,

spirits, / and shouted to each other, / until the broad
서로 소리쳐 불렀다,

fields were so full of merry music, / that the crisp air
그러자 넓은 벌판이 즐거운 음악 소리로 가득 차서, 청명한 공기마저 웃는 듯 했다

laughed / to hear it!
그 소리를 듣고!

"These are but shadows of the things / that have been," /
"이것들은 모두 환영일 뿐이다 과거에 있었던 일의."

said the Ghost. "They have no consciousness of us."
유령은 말했다. "저들은 우리를 의식하지 못한다."

The jocund travellers came on; / and as they came, /
그 즐거운 여행자들이 다가왔고; 그들이 다가올 때,

Scrooge knew and named them every one. Why was he
스크루지는 한 명 한 명 이름까지 알고 있었다.

rejoiced beyond all bounds / to see them! Why did his
그는 왜 한없이 기뻐했을까 그들을 보고! 왜 그의 차가운 눈이

cold eye glisten, / and his heart leap up / as they went
반짝거렸고, 심장이 뛰었을까 그들이 지나갈 때!

past! Why was he filled with gladness / when he heard /
그는 왜 기쁨에 가득 찼을까 들었을 때

them give each other Merry Christmas, / as they parted
소년들이 서로 크리스마스 인사를 주고 받는 것을,

at cross-roads and bye-ways, / for their several homes!
교차로와 갈림길에서 헤어지면서, 각자의 집으로 가기 위해!

Key Expression 🎵

접속사 until의 해석

접속사 until은 '~때까지'라는 뜻을 지니고 있어요.
하지만 영어 문장을 해석하다 보면 until절을 먼저 해석하기 보다 주절의 행동
이 일어난 후 until절의 행동이 일어난 것으로 순차적인 과정으로 해석하는 게
자연스러울 때가 많답니다.
이때 until은 '그러자', 혹은 '마침내' 등으로 이해하면 됩니다.

ex) They walked along the road, Scrooge recognising every gate, and post, and
tree; until a little market town appeared in the distance.
그들은 길을 따라 걸었고, 스크루지는 대문 하나, 말뚝 하나, 나무 한 그루까지
도 알아보았다; 그리고 마침내 저 멀리에 작은 시장이 나타났다.
All these boys were in great spirits, and shouted to each other, until the
broad fields were so full of merry music, that the crisp air laughed to hear it!
이 소년들은 모두 신이 나서, 서로 소리쳐 불렀고, 그러자 넓은 벌판이 즐거운
음악 소리로 가득 차서, 청명한 공기마저 그 소리를 듣고 웃는 듯 했다.

What was merry Christmas to Scrooge? Out upon merry
즐거운 크리스마스는 스크루지에게 무엇이었던가?   즐거운 크리스마스라니!

Christmas! What good had it ever done to him?
크리스마스가 그에게 무슨 이득이 되었단 말인가?

"The school is not quite deserted," / said the Ghost. "A
"학교가 텅 빈 것은 아니구나."   유령이 말했다.

solitary child, / neglected by his friends, / is left there
"외로운 아이가,   친구들에게 무시당한,   저기에 아직 남아 있다."

still."

Scrooge said / he knew it. And he sobbed.
스크루지가 말했다   알고 있다고.   그리고 그는 흐느껴 울었다.

They left the high-road, / by a well-remembered lane, /
그들은 큰 길을 벗어나,   스크루지가 잘 기억하고 있는 골목길로 가서,

and soon approached a mansion of dull red brick, / with
이내 우중충한 붉은 벽돌 저택으로 다가갔다,

a little weathercock-surmounted cupola, / on the roof, /
작은 수탉 모양의 풍향계가 달려 있고,   지붕 위에는,

and a bell hanging in it. It was a large house, / but one
그 안에 종이 매달려 있었다.   대저택이었으나,

of broken fortunes; / for the spacious offices were little
쇠락한 집이었다;   넓은 방들은 거의 사용되지 않는 듯 했고,

used, / their walls were damp and mossy, / their windows
벽은 축축하고 이끼가 가득했으며,   창문은 깨져 있고,

broken, / and their gates decayed. Fowls clucked and
대문은 썩어 있었다.   닭들이 꼬꼬댁거리며 활개쳤고

strutted / in the stables; / and the coach-houses and sheds
우리에서;   차고와 헛간에는 풀이 가득했다.

were over-run with grass. Nor was it more retentive of its
옛 영화는 남아 있지 않았다,

ancient state, / within; / for entering the dreary hall, / and
집 안에는;   황량한 복도에 들어서서,

---

weathercock 수탉 모양의 풍향계 | surmounted ~위에 놓다, 얹다 | cupola 둥근 지붕 | fowl 닭 | cluck
꼬꼬하고 울다 | strut 걷다, 활보하다 | stable 마구간 | retentive 유지하는, 보존하는 | dreary 황량한 | savor
기색, 경향 | deal 전나무 | form 긴 의자

glancing through the open doors of many rooms, / they
열려 있는 문으로 방들을 들여다보니,

found them / poorly furnished, / cold, / and vast. There
보였다   가구가 갖춰져 있지 않고,   으스스하며,   휑한 모습이.

was an earthy savor in the air, / a chilly bareness in the
공기에서는 흙내가 났고,   방 안에는 싸늘하고 휑함이 감돌아서,

place, / which associated itself / somehow with too much
떠올랐다   촛불만 너무 많이 켜 놓은 식탁이,

getting up by candle-light, / and not too much to eat.
                              먹을 것이 별로 없이.

They went, / the Ghost and Scrooge, / across the hall, / to
지나갔다,   유령과 스크루지는,   현관을 가로 질러,

a door / at the back of the house. It opened before them, /
문으로   집 뒤 편에 있는.   그 문이 열리자,

and disclosed / a long, / bare, / melancholy room, / made
드러났다   길고,   황량하며,   음침한 방이,   더욱 황량

barer still / by lines of plain deal forms and desks. At one
해 보였다   평범한 전나무 의자와 책상들 줄지어 있어.   이 의자 중

of these / a lonely boy was reading / near a feeble fire; /
하나에   외로운 소년이 책을 읽고 있었고   희미한 난로 옆에서;

and Scrooge sat down upon a form, / and wept to / see
스크루지는 의자 하나에 걸터 앉아서,   흐느껴 울었다

his poor forgotten self / as he used to be.
잊어버렸던 가엾은 자신을 보고   과거에 모습이던.

Key Expression

do good : (~에게) 도움이 되다

do good은 '(~에게) 도움이 되다, 이롭다'라는 의미를 가진 표현입니다. 뒤에 전치사 to를 붙여 도움이 되는 대상을 표현하지요.
반대로 '해가 되다, 해롭다'라는 의미를 표현하려면 good 대신에 harm을 사용합니다.

ex) What good had it ever done to him?
    그것이 그에게 무슨 도움이 되었단 말인가?

Not a latent echo in the house, / not a squeak and scuffle
집 안에 숨어 있던 메아리도,　　　　　　　　쥐들이 찍찍거리며 싸우는 소리도

from the mice / behind the panelling, / not a drip from
　　　　　　벽 뒤에서,　　　　　　　　반쯤 녹은 배수관에서 똑똑

the half-thawed water-spout / in the dull yard behind, /
떨어지는 물방울 소리도,　　　　　　칙칙한 뜰 뒤편에 있는,

not a sigh among the leafless boughs / of one despondent
헐벗은 나뭇가지 사이에서 나는 한숨 소리도　　늘어진 포플라 나무의,

poplar, / not the idle swinging / of an empty store-house
　　　　덜컹거리며 흔들리는 소리도　　빈 창고 문에서 나는,

door, / no, / not a clicking in the fire, / but fell upon the
　　　아니,　　불이 탁탁거리는 소리도,　　스크루지의 가슴을 치지 않는

heart of Scrooge / with a softening influence, / and gave
것이 없었다　　　　　마음을 여리게 하고,

a freer passage to his tears.
하염없이 눈물 흘리게 하며.

latent 잠복해 있는 | squeak 찍찍우는 소리 | scuffle 맞붙잡고 싸우다 | panelling 판벽널 | thaw 녹다 |
bough 가지 | despondent 낙담한 | intent 집중되어 있는 | garment 옷 | bridle 고삐 | ecstasy 황홀경, 도취,
흥분 | yonder 저쪽의 | groom 마부 | serve a person right 고소하다, 꼴 좋다

The Spirit touched him on the arm, / and pointed to his
유령은 스크루지의 팔을 치더니,   꼬마 스크루지를 가리켰다,

younger self, / intent upon his reading. Suddenly a man,
독서에 열중하고 있는.   갑자기 한 남자가,

/ in foreign garments: / wonderfully real and distinct to
이국적인 옷을 입고: 놀랍게도 생생하고 분명한 모습으로:

look at: / stood outside the window, / with an axe stuck
창문 밖에 서 있었던,   허리춤에 도끼를 찬 채,

in his belt, / and leading by the bridle / an ass laden with
고삐를 잡고서   장작을 실은 당나귀의.

wood.

"Why, / it's Ali Baba!" / Scrooge exclaimed in ecstasy.
"아니,   알리 바바예요!"   스크루지는 흥분에 차서 소리쳤다.

"It's dear old honest Ali Baba! Yes, / yes, / I know! One
"저 사람은 정직한 알리 바바 영감님!   그래,   그래,   알겠어요!

Christmas time, / when yonder solitary child was left
어느 크리스마스에,   저 외로운 아이가 여기에 혼자 남았을 때,

here all alone, / he did come, / for the first time, / just
혼자 남았을 때,   알리 바바가 왔어요,   처음으로,   바로 저

like that. Poor boy! And Valentine," / said Scrooge, /
모습으로.   불쌍한 아이야!   그리고 발렌틴,"   스크루지가 말했다,

"and his wild brother, / Orson; / there they go! And
"그리고 야생에서 자란 동생,   오르송: 저기 오는군요!"

what's his name, / who was put down in his drawers, /
그리고 이름이 뭐더라,   속옷 차림으로 두워 있는 사람이요,

asleep, / at the Gate of Damascus; / don't you see him!
잠든 채로,   다마스커스 성문 앞에: 보이지 않나요!

And the Sultan's Groom / turned upside down by the
그리고 술탄의 마부가 있어요   지니가 거꾸로 처박았던:

Genii; / there he is upon his head! Serve him right. I'm
머리가 처박힌 채 있네요!   꼴 좋다.

glad of it. What business had he to be married to the
속이 시원하군.   공주하고 결혼할 생각을 하다니!"

Princess!"

earnestness 열정 | creek 시내, 샛강

A Christmas Carol

To hear Scrooge expending / all the earnestness of his
스크루지가 말하는 것을 듣게 된다면   온 열정을 다해

nature / on such subjects, / in a most extraordinary
그런 주제들에 대해,   아주 희한한 목소리로

voice / between laughing and crying; / and to see
웃는 것도 우는 것도 아닌;

his heightened and excited face; / would have been a
또 상기되고 흥분된 얼굴을 보게 된다면;   엄청 놀랄 것이다

surprise / to his business friends / in the city, / indeed.
거래처 동료들은   도시에 있는,   정말로.

"There's the Parrot!" / cried Scrooge. "Green body and
"앵무새가 있어요!"   스크루지는 소리쳤다.   "초록색 몸뚱이에 노란 꼬리,

yellow tail, / with a thing like a lettuce / growing out of
상추같이 생긴 것이

the top of his head; / there he is! Poor Robin Crusoe, /
머리 위에 솟아 나와 있어요;   앵무새가 있어요! 불쌍한 로빈슨 크루소,

he called him, / when he came home again / after sailing
앵무새가 불렀죠.   로빈슨 크루소가 다시 집에 돌아왔을 때   섬을 일주하고 나서.

round the island. 'Poor Robin Crusoe, / where have
'불쌍한 로빈슨 크루소,   어디에 있다가 오는 거야,

you been, / Robin Crusoe?' The man thought / he was
로빈슨 크루소?'   그는 생각했죠

dreaming, / but he wasn't. It was the Parrot, / you know.
꿈꾸고 있다고,   하지만 아니었어요.   그건 앵무새였어요,   알다시피.

There goes *Friday, / running for his life / to the little
프라이데이가 가요,   죽어라 달려가네요   작은 개울로!

creek! Halloa! Hoop! Halloo!"
어이!   이봐!   이보라고!"

Then, / with a rapidity of transition / very foreign to his
그러더니,   갑자기 바뀌어서   평소 그의 성격과는 아주

usual character, / he said, / in pity for his former self, /
다르게,   말하고는,   자신의 어린 시절에 대한 연민에 빠져,

"Poor boy!" / and cried again.
"가여운 아이야!"라고   다시 울었다.

---

*Friday 프라이데이 : 〈로빈슨 크루소〉에 나오는 로빈슨의 무인도 시절 동료였던 야만인의 이름. 다른 야만
인 부족 무리에서 탈출한 그를 구해 주고 '프라이데이'라는 이름을 지은 후 교육시켰다.

"I wish," / Scrooge muttered, / putting his hand in his
"했다면 좋을텐데," 스크루지는 중얼거렸다.   손을 주머니에 찌르고,

pocket, / and looking about him, / after drying his eyes
주위를 돌아보며,   소매 자락으로 눈물을 닦아낸 후:

with his cuff: / "but it's too late now."
"하지만 이젠 너무 늦었어요."

"What is the matter?" / asked the Spirit.
"뭐가 문제인가?"   유령은 물었다.

"Nothing," / said Scrooge. "Nothing. There was a boy
"아닙니다."   스크루지는 말했다.   "아무것도 아니에요. 소년이 있었어요

/ singing a Christmas Carol / at my door last night. I
크리스마스 캐럴을 부르던   어젯밤 우리 집 대문에서.

should like to have given him something: / that's all."
뭔가를 줬더라면 좋았을텐데: 그 뿐이에요."

The Ghost smiled thoughtfully, / and waved its hand: /
유령은 사려 깊게 미소짓더니,   손을 흔들었다:

saying as it did so, / "Let us see another Christmas!"
말하면서,   "다른 크리스마스를 보자!"

plaster 회반죽, 벽토 | lath 욋가지 | dart 돌진하다

Scrooge's former self grew larger / at the words, / and
꼬마 스크루지는 성장한 모습이 되었고   그 말이 끝나자,

the room became a little darker and more dirty. The
방은 더욱 어둡고 더럽게 변했다.

panels shrunk, / the windows cracked; / ·fragments of
벽의 판자는 우그러들었고, 창문에는 금이 갔다:

plaster fell out of the ceiling, / and the naked laths were
회칠 조각들이 천정에서 떨어져서,   대신 윗가지가 드러나 보였다:

shown instead; / but how all this was brought about, /
하지만 이 모든 일이 어떻게 일어났는지,

Scrooge knew no more than you do. He only knew / that
스크루지는 여러분과 마찬가지로 알지 못했다.   그는 다만 알 뿐이었다

it was quite correct; / that everything had happened so; /
그 모습이 꽤 정확하다는 것만;   모든 것이 실제 일어났던 일이다;

that there he was, / alone again, / when all the other boys
그곳에 그가 있었다,   다시 혼자가 되어,   다른 모든 아이들이 집에 돌아갈 때면

had gone home / for the jolly holidays.
즐거운 크리스마스를 보내러.

He was not reading now, / but walking up and down
그는 이번에는 책을 읽지 않고,   절망스럽게 이리저리 걸어 다니고 있었다.

despairingly. Scrooge looked at the Ghost, / and with
스크루지는 유령을 쳐다보았고,

a mournful shaking of his head, / glanced anxiously
슬프게 고개를 내저으며,   걱정스럽게 문 쪽을 힐끔 보았다.

towards the door.

It opened; / and a little girl, / much younger than the boy,
문이 열리고;   작은 소녀가,   소년보다 훨씬 어린,

/ came darting in, / and putting her arms about his neck,
곧바로 들어와서,   그의 목에 팔을 두르고,

/ and often kissing him, / addressed him as her "Dear,
연신 입을 맞추며,   그를 "오빠, 오빠."라고 불렀다.

dear brother."

"I have come to bring you home, / dear brother!" / said
"오빠를 집에 데려가려고 왔어,   오빠!"

the child, / clapping her tiny hands, / and bending down
아이는 말했다,   작은 손으로 손뼉을 치고,   허리를 굽히고 웃으며,

to laugh. "To bring you home, home, home!"
                    "오빠를 집에 데려가려고 왔어, 집, 집이라고!"

"Home, / little Fan?" / returned the boy.
"집이라고,   팬?"   소년은 되물었다.

"Yes!" / said the child, / brimful of glee. "Home, / for
"그래!"   아이는 말했다,   기쁨에 가득 차서.   "집에 가는 거야,

good and all. Home, / forever and ever. Father is so much
영원히.   집,   아주 가는 거라고.   아빠는 훨씬 상냥해지셨어

kinder / than he used to be, / that home's like Heaven!
전보다,   그래서 집이 천국같아!

He spoke so gently to me / one dear night / when I was
아빠가 아주 다정하게 말씀하셨어   요전 날 밤에   내가 자러 가려는데,

going to bed, / that I was not afraid to ask him / once
                    그래서 겁내지 않고 물어봤어   다시 한 번

more / if you might come home; / and he said / yes, / you
다시   오빠가 집에 와도 되느냐고;   그랬더니 말씀하셨어 그래,

should; / and sent me / in a coach / to bring you. And
데려와야지;   그리고 날 보냈었어   마차에 태워   오빠를 데리러.

you're to be a man!" / said the child, / opening her eyes, /
오빠는 곧 어른이 될 거잖아!"   아이는 말했다,   눈을 크게 뜨며,

"and are never to come back here; / but first, / we're to be
"이제 다시는 여기에 돌아오지 않을 거야;   하지만 먼저,   우리는 함께 있을

together / all the Christmas long, / and have the merriest
거고   크리스마스 휴가 내내 ,

time in all the world."
세상에서 가장 즐거운 시간을 보낼 거야."

"You are quite a woman, / little Fan!" / exclaimed the
"너도 아가씨가 다 됐는걸,   팬!"   소년이 외쳤다.

boy.

---

brimful 넘칠듯한 | glee 큰 기쁨, 환희 | for good and all 영원히

She clapped her hands and laughed, / and tried to
팬은 손뼉을 치고 웃으며,   오빠의 머리를 만지려고 했지만;

touch his head; / but being too little, / laughed again,
너무 작아서 닿지 않자,   다시 웃으면서,

/ and stood on tiptoe to embrace him. Then she began
까치발로 서서 오빠를 껴안았다.   그리고 나서 오빠를 끌어당기기

to drag him, / in her childish eagerness, / towards the
시작했고,   어린 아이처럼 졸라대며,   문 쪽으로;

door; / and he, / nothing loth to go, / accompanied her.
그리고 그는,   싫어하는 기색 없이,   동생을 따라 갔다.

A terrible voice in the hall cried, / "Bring down Master
무시무시한 소리가 현관에서 울렸다,   "스크루지 군의 짐을 갖고 내려오게,

Scrooge's box, / there!" / and in the hall / appeared the
           저기로!"   그리고 복도에

schoolmaster himself, / who glared on Master Scrooge
교장 선생님이 나타나더니,   스크루지를 바라보며

/ with a ferocious condescension, / and threw him into
  무섭고 생색내는 태도로,   겁에 질리게 했다

a dreadful state of mind / by shaking hands with him.
                        악수를 하며,

He then conveyed him and his sister / into the veriest
그리고는 스크루지와 여동생을 데려갔다   아주 낡은 우물같은 안쪽으로

old well / of a shivering best-parlor / that ever was
           오싹한 응접실의   지금까지 본 적이 없는,

seen, / where the maps upon the wall, / and the celestial
       그 방에는 벽에 지도가 걸려 있고,   천체의와 지구본이

and terrestrial globes / in the windows, / were waxy
                        창가에 놓인,   납처럼 창백한 빛이었다.

with cold. Here he produced / a decanter of curiously
          여기에서 교장은 꺼내 오더니   이상할 정도로 순한 포도주 한 병과,

light wine, / and a block of curiously heavy cake, /
           이상할 정도로 딱딱한 케이크 한 조각을,

and administered instalments of those dainties / to the
이 진수성찬을 차렸다

young people: / at the same time, / sending out a meagre
어린 친구들에게: 그와 동시에,   깡마른 하인을 보내

servant / to offer a glass of "something" / to the postboy,
        "마실 것" 한 잔을 권하게 했다   배달부에게,

/ who answered / that he thanked the gentleman, / but
  하지만 배달부는 대답했다   신사분께 고맙지만,

---

ferocious 흉포한, 사나운 | condescension 공손, 저자세 | parlor 응접실 | celestial 천체의 | terrestrial
globe 지구의 | waxy 밀납같은, 창백한 | instalment 전시, 전람(=installation) | dainties (복수형) 맛있는 것,
진수성찬 | meagre 빈약한, 변변찮은 | tap 술 | chaise 역마차 | bid (인사를) 드리다 | sweep 굽은 길 | hoar-
frost (흰)서리 | wither 시들다 | gainsay 반박하다 | forbid 금지하다

if it was the same tap / as he had tasted before, / he had
만약 같은 술이라면   전에 맛보았던 것과,

rather not. Master Scrooge's trunk being / by this time
사양하겠다고.   스크루지의 가방을   이때

/ tied on to the top of the chaise, / the children bade the
마차 지붕 위에 얹어 끈으로 묶었고,

schoolmaster good-bye right willingly; / and getting
두 아이는 흔쾌히 교장에게 작별 인사를 하고;   마차에 올라,

into it, / drove gaily down the garden-sweep: / the quick
즐겁게 정원길을 달려 내려갔다:

wheels dashing / the hoar-frost and snow / from off the
바퀴는 빠르게 돌진했다   서리와 눈을 뚫고

dark leaves of the evergreens / like spray.
상록수의 짙은 색 잎에서 떨어진   물보라처럼.

"Always a delicate creature, / whom a breath might have
"언제나 가냘픈 아이였지,   숨결에라도 시들 것 같은."

withered," / said the Ghost. "But she had a large heart!"
            유령이 말했다.   "하지만 넓은 마음을 가졌었어!"

"So she had," / cried Scrooge. "You're right. I will not
"그랬지요,"   스크루지가 소리쳤다.   "맞습니다.   반박하지 않겠어요,

gainsay it, / Spirit. God forbid!"
             유령님.   신도 금하실 것입니다!"

"She died a woman," / said the Ghost, / "and had, / as I
"그 아이는 어른이 되어 죽었지."   유령은 말했다.   "그리고 있었는데,   내 생각

think, / children."
에는,   아이들이."

"One child," / Scrooge returned.
"하나 있었지요,"   스크루지가 대답했다.

"True," / said the Ghost. "Your nephew!"
"그렇지,"   유령이 말했다.   "네 조카로군!"

Scrooge seemed uneasy in his mind; / and answered
스크루지는 마음이 불편해 보이며;   짧게 대답했다,

briefly, / "Yes."
        "그렇습니다"라고.

🎄 mini test 3

A. 다음 문장을 해석해 보세요.

(1) To his great astonishment / the heavy bell went on / from six to seven, / and from seven to eight, / and regularly up to twelve.
→

(2) "It isn't possible," / said Scrooge, / "that I can have slept through a whole day / and far into another night.
→

(3) Every time he resolved within himself, / after mature inquiry, / that it was all a dream, / his mind flew back again, / like a strong spring released, / to its first position.
→

(4) He answered he thanked the gentleman, but if it was the same tap as he had tasted before, he had rather not.
→

B. 다음 주어진 문장이 되도록 빈칸에 써 넣으세요.

(1) 생각하면 생각할수록, 그는 더욱 혼란스러워졌다.

→

(2) 그는 하룻밤의 휴식을 방해 받지 않았다면 훨씬 도움이 되었을 것이라고 <u>생각하지 않을 수 없었다</u>.

[   ] that a night of unbroken rest would have been more conducive to that end.

(3) 유령은 그의 생각을 들었음이 틀림없었다.

→

(4) 너는 어른이 되어 이곳에 다시는 돌아오지 않겠지.

→

A. (1) 놀랍게도 그 둔탁한 종소리는 여섯 번에 서 일곱 번, 다시 일곱 번에서 여덟 번으로, 그리고 열두 번이 될 때까지 규칙적으로 늘어났다. (2) 스크루지는 "내가 하루종일 낮잠을 자고 또 다른 밤이라니 이건 불가능해."라고 말했다. (3) 신중한 질문들 끝에, 그가 속으로 모든 것이 꿈이었다고 결론 내릴 때마다, 그의 마음은 강력한 스프링이 풀

A Christmas Carol

C. 다음 주어진 문구가 알맞은 문장이 되도록 순서를 맞춰 보세요.

(1) 그는 그리고 나서 용기를 내어 무슨 일로 왔는지 묻기까지 했다.
   (there / business / him / brought / what)
   He then made bold to inquire _____
   _____ .

(2) 페터는 잠시 동안 겁에 질렸어.
   (done / What / ever / had / him / to / it / good)
   →

(3) 움켜잡은 손은, 비록 여자의 손이 움켜쥔 것처럼 부드러웠지만, 저항할 수 없었다.
   (gentle / a / though / hand / woman's / as)
   The grasp, _____ ,
   was not to be resisted.

(4) 내 식대로 지내게 내버려 둬.
   (mine / keep / Let / me / it / in)
   →

D. 다음 단어에 대한 맞는 설명과 연결해 보세요.

(1) perplexed　　　▶　　　◀ ① confused and slightly worried

(2) fluctuate　　　▶　　　◀ ② a prayer to God

(3) supplication　　▶　　　◀ ③ hidden and not obvious

(4) latent　　　　▶　　　◀ ④ change a lot in an irregular way

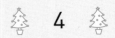

THE FIRST OF THE THREE SPIRITS II
첫 번째 유령 II

Although they had but that moment / left the school
얼마 지나지 않았지만   학교를 떠난 지,

behind them, / they were now in the busy thoroughfares
이제 복잡한 시내 대로에 있었다.

of a city, / where shadowy passengers passed and
행인들의 환영이 지나다니고;

repassed; / where shadowy carts and coaches battled for
짐마차와 승합마차의 환영이 앞다투어 지나가며,

the way, / and all the strife and tumult of a real city were.
진짜 도시의 모든 분투와 법석이 있는 곳이었다.

It was made plain enough, / by the dressing of the shops,
충분히 명백하게 알 수 있었다.   가게들이 단장한 모습으로 보아,

/ that here too it was Christmas time again; / but it was
여기도 역시 크리스마스 무렵이라는 것을;   하지만 저녁이었고,

evening, / and the streets were lighted up.
거리에는 불이 켜져 있었다.

Key Expression

leave ~ behind : 두고 떠나다

leave는 '떠나다, 남겨두다'의 뜻을 가진 동사입니다. leave가 behind와 결합하면 '~을 잊고 가다, 두고 떠나다, 뒤에 남기다'라는 뜻을 나타냅니다.
때에 따라 '(가족·재산·명성·기록·피해 등을) 남기고 죽다'라는 의미로 쓰이기도 합니다.
또한 leave ~ behind가 수동태로 쓰이면 '~을 훨씬 앞서다'라는 뜻을 표현하기도 합니다.

ex) Although they had but that moment left the school behind them, they were
now in the busy thoroughfares of a city.
학교를 두고 떠난 지 얼마 지나지 않았지만, 그들은 이제 도시의 복잡한 큰 길에
있었다.

The Ghost stopped / at a certain warehouse door, / and
유령은 문 앞에서 멈춰 서더니   어떤 상점의 문 앞에서,

asked Scrooge / if he knew it.
스크루지에게 물었다   이곳을 아느냐고.

"Know it!" / said Scrooge. "Was I apprenticed here!"
"알죠!"   스크루지는 말했다.   "여기에서 견습 생활을 했어요!"

They went in. At sight of an old gentleman in a Welsh
그들은 안으로 들어갔다. 웨일스식의 가발을 쓴 노신사를 보고,

wig, / sitting behind such a high desk, / that if he had
아주 높은 책상 뒤에 앉아 있는데,

been two inches taller / he must have knocked his head
만약 2인치만 더 컸더라도   천정에 머리를 부딪치고 말았을 것처럼 보이는,

against the ceiling, / Scrooge cried in great excitement:
스크루지는 몹시 흥분해서 소리쳤다.

"Why, / it's old Fezziwig! Bless his heart; / it's Fezziwig
"아니,   페치위그 어르신이에요!   그분에게 축복이 내리길;   페치위그 어르신이

alive again!"
다시 살아났어요!"

Old Fezziwig laid down his pen, / and looked up at
페치위그 영감은 펜을 내려 놓고,   시계를 올려다 보았다.

the clock, / which pointed to the hour of seven. He
시계는 7시를 가리키고 있었다.

rubbed his hands; / adjusted his capacious waistcoat; /
그는 손을 비비고;   헐렁한 외투를 고쳐 입고는;

laughed all over himself, / from his shoes to his organ of
온몸으로 웃어대며,   머리끝부터 발끝까지 기쁨에 차서;

benevolence; / and called out / in a comfortable, / oily, /
소리쳤다   편안하고,   구성지고,

rich, / fat, / jovial voice:
성량 풍부하고, 윤택하고, 즐거운 목소리로:

"Yo ho, / there! Ebenezer! Dick!"
"어이,   거기!   에브니저!   딕!"

---

thoroughfare 도로 | strife 분투, 분쟁 | tumult 소동, 소란 | capacious 널직한 | benevolence 자비심, 선의
| jovial 유쾌한, 명랑한

Scrooge's former self, / now grown a young man, / came
과거의 스크루지가, 이제 젊은 청년으로 자란,

briskly in, / accompanied by his fellow-'prentice.
기운차게 들어왔다, 동료 견습생과 함께.

"Dick Wilkins, / to be sure!" / said Scrooge to the Ghost.
"딕 윌킨스예요, 확실해요!" 스크루지는 유령에게 말했다.

"Bless me, / yes. There he is. He was very much attached
"세상에, 그래요. 딕이 저기 있군요. 나랑 항상 같이 다녔지요,

to me, / was Dick. Poor Dick! Dear, dear!"
딕이에요. 불쌍한 딕! 저런, 저런!"

"Yo ho, / my boys!" / said Fezziwig. "No more work
"어이, 자네들!" 페치위그가 말했다. "오늘 밤은 그만하게.

to-night. Christmas Eve, / Dick. Christmas, / Ebenezer!
크리스마스 이브이지 않나, 딕. 크리스마스야, 에브니저!

Let's have the shutters up," / cried old Fezziwig, / with
문을 닫자고," 페치위그 영감은 소리쳤다,

a sharp clap of his hands, / "before a man can say Jack
활기차게 손뼉을 치면서, "순식간에 끝내자고!"

Robinson!"

Key Expression ❢

before you can say Jack Robinson : 눈 깜짝할 사이에

before you can say Jack Robinson는 '눈 깜짝할 사이에'라는 의미로
재빨리, 순간적으로 일어나는 일을 표현할 때 쓰는 관용어구입니다.
이때 you 대신 one, a man과 같은 일반적인 사람을 나타내는 주어를 사용
할 수 있습니다.
이 표현에는 재미있는 유래가 있습니다.
16세기 영국에 Jack Robinson이라는 사람이 있었는데, 말이 매우 빠르고 남
에 일에 참견하기 좋아하는 인물했습니다. 어느 날 회의에 잭 로빈슨이 나타나지
않자 사회자가 그가 나타나 참견하기 전에 재빨리 문제를 처리하자는 말을 했고,
이때부터 before you(one) can say Jack Robinson은 '눈 깜짝할 사이
에, 순식간에'라는 뜻를 가지게 되었습니다.

ex) Let's have the shutters up before a man can say Jack Robinson!
재빨리 덧문을 닫읍시다!

briskly 기세 좋게 | panting 헐떡거리는 | agility 민첩, 경쾌 | snug 아늑한, 편안한

You wouldn't believe / how those two fellows went at it!
믿지 못할 것이다　　　　　　　이 두 청년들이 얼마나 순식간에 일을 해치웠는지!

They charged into the street / with the shutters / — one,
그들은 문 밖으로 달려 나가　　　　　덧문을 들고　　　　　— 하나, 둘,

two, three — / had 'em up in their places / — four, five,
셋 세는 동안 —　　　제자리에 고정하고　　　　　— 넷, 다섯, 여섯 세

six — / barred 'em and pinned 'em / — seven, eight,
는 동안 —　　덧문을 끼우고 빗장을 질렀으며　　　— 일곱, 여덟, 아홉 만에 —

nine — / and came back / before you could have got to
　　　다시 들어왔다　　　　열둘을 채 세기도 전에.

twelve, / panting like race-horses.
　　　경주마처럼 헐떡거리며.

"Hilli-ho!" / cried old Fezziwig, / skipping down from
"이야호!"　　　　페치위그 영감은 소리쳤다.　　　높은 책상에서 뛰어내리며,

the high desk, / with wonderful agility. "Clear away, /
　　높은 책상에서　　　놀라울 정도로 민첩하게.　　　　"말끔히 치우고,

my lads, / and let's have lots of room here! Hilli-ho, /
젊은이들,　　　여기에 넓은 공간을 만들자고!　　　　이야호,

Dick! Chirrup, / Ebenezer!"
딕!　　기운 내,　　에브니저!"

Clear away! There was nothing / they wouldn't have
모두 치웠다!　　아무것도 없었다　　　　치우지 않은 것도,

cleared away, / or couldn't have cleared away, / with old
　　　　치우지 못할 것도,

Fezziwig looking on. It was done in a minute. Every
페치위그 영감이 보고 있으니.　　　모든 것이 순식간에 끝났다.

movable was packed off, / as if it were dismissed from
옮길 수 있는 것은 모두 싸서 치우고,　　　사용하지 않을 것처럼

public life / for evermore; / the floor was swept and
　　　　　앞으로 더 이상은;　　마루 바닥을 쓸고 닦았고,

watered, / the lamps were trimmed / fuel was heaped /
　　전등도 손질했으며,　　　　　　　　장작을 쌓아두었다

upon the fire; / and the warehouse was / as snug, / and
난로 위에;　　　그래서 상점은　　　　　아늑하고,

warm, / and dry, / and bright a ball-room, / as you would
따뜻하며,　　녹눅하지 않고,　　무도장처럼 환했다,　　　여러분도 가 보고 싶어

desire to see / upon a winter's night.
할 만큼　　　겨울 밤에.

105

In came a fiddler with a music-book, / and went up to
바이올린 연주가가 악보를 들고 들어와서,   높은 책상으로 올라가더니,

the lofty desk, / and made an orchestra of it, / and tuned
책상을 오케스트라 삼아,   쉰 가지의 배 아픈

like fifty stomach-aches. In came Mrs. Fezziwig, / one
소리를 내며 악기를 조율했다.   페치위그 부인이 들어왔다,

vast substantial smile. In came the three Miss Fezziwigs,
크게 환한 미소를 지으며.   페치위그 씨의 세 딸이 들어왔다,

/ beaming and lovable. In came the six young followers
빛이 나며 사랑스러운.   세 딸을 추종하는 여섯 명의 청년들이 들어왔다

/ whose hearts they broke. In came all the young men
애를 태우며.   모든 젊은 남자와 여자들이 들어왔다

and women / employed in the business. In came the
페치위그 씨가 고용하고 있는.   하녀가 들어왔다,

housemaid, / with her cousin, / the baker. In came
사촌과 함께,   제빵사인.   요리사가 들어왔다,

the cook, / with her brother's particular friend, / the
하녀 오빠의 특별한 친구와 함께,   우유 배달부

milkman. In came the boy from over the way, / who was
와 함께.   길 건너에서 소년이 들어왔는데,

suspected of not having board enough / from his master;
밥도 제대로 얻어 먹지 못하는 것 같은   주인에게;

/ trying to hide himself / behind the girl from next door
숨으려고 애를 쓰면서   옆집 소녀 뒤에

/ but one, / who was proved to have had her ears pulled
그 소녀는,   귀를 뜯기곤 한다고 알려진

/ by her mistress. In they all came, / one after another;
여주인에게.   그들 모두 들어왔다,   한 명씩;

/ some shyly, / some boldly, / some gracefully, / some
어떤 이는 수줍어하며, 어떤 이는 당당하게,   어떤 이는 우아하게,

awkwardly, / some pushing, / some pulling; / in they
어떤 이는 어색하게,   어떤 이는 밀면서,   어떤 이는 끌면서;   모두 들어왔다,

all came, / anyhow and everyhow. Away they all went,
각양각색으로.   모두 나가서,

/ twenty couple at once; / hands half round / and back
바로 스무 커플이 되어; 손을 반바퀴 돌렸다가

again the other way; / down the middle and up again;
다시 반대쪽으로 돌렸다; 가운데로 모였다가 다시 퍼져 나갔다가;

/ round and round / in various stages of affectionate
빙글빙글 돌고 여러 가지 모습으로 군무 형상을 만들었다;

grouping; / old top couple / always turning up / in the
먼저 선두에 섰던 커플이 항상 돌곤 해서

wrong place; / new top couple starting off again, / as
틀린 곳에서; 새로 선두에 선 커플이 다시 시작했다,

soon as they got there; / all top couples at last, / and not
선두 자리에 서자마자; 결국 모든 커플이 선두에 서게 되고, 뒤따라서 도와

a bottom one to help them! When this result was brought
야 하는 커플이 하나도 없게 되어 버렸다! 이런 식의 결과가 나오게 되자,

about, / old Fezziwig, / clapping his hands / to stop
페치위그 영감은, 박수를 치며 군무를 중단시킨

the dance, / cried out, / "Well done!" / and the fiddler
다음, 외쳤고, "잘들 했어요!"

plunged his hot face / into a pot of porter, / especially
연주가는 뜨거워진 얼굴을 담갔다 흑맥주 통에,

provided for that purpose. But scorning rest, / upon his
얼굴을 담그라고 특별히 준비된. 하지만 쉬는 것을 수치스럽게 여겨,

reappearance, / he instantly began again, / though there
다시 무대에 나타나, 즉시 연주를 시작했다, 춤추는 사람이 아직

were no dancers yet, / as if the other fiddler had been
없음에도 불구하고, 마치 그 전의 연주가가 집으로 실려가서,

carried home, / exhausted, / on a shutter, / and he were
기진맥진해서, 덧문 위에, 자기가 새로운 악사라도

a bran-new man / resolved to beat him out of sight, / or
된다는 듯이 그 전 연주가를 쫓아 버리기로 했거나,

perish.
죽기라도 하겠다고 결심한 듯이.

---

lofty 우뚝 솟은, 높은 | substantial 상당한 | board 식사 | affectionate 애정 어린 | plunge 처넣다, 담그다 |
porter 흑맥주 | scoring ~을 치사하게 생각하다 | perish 죽다, 무너지다

There were more dances, / and there were forfeits, /
춤을 좀 더 추고, 벌금 게임을 한 다음,

and more dances, / and there was cake, / and there was
다시 춤을 좀 더 추었다, 그리고 나서 케이크가 나왔고, 니거스주와,

negus, / and there was a great piece of Cold Roast, / and
커다란 구운 고기 덩어리,

there was a great piece of Cold Boiled, / and there were
삶은 커다란 고기 덩어리, 그리고 민스 파이와,

mince-pies, / and plenty of beer. But the great effect of
엄청나게 많은 맥주가 나왔다. 하지만 그날 저녁 가장 큰 구경거리는

the evening / came after the Roast and Boiled, / when
구운 고기와 삶은 고기 다음에 나왔다,

the fiddler / (an artful dog, / mind! The sort of man / who
연주가가 (솜씨 좋은 사람이다, 주목하시라! 그런 사람이었다

knew his business better than / you or I could have told
자신이 해야 할 일을 잘 아는 여러분이나 내가 말하지 않아도!)

it him!) / struck up / "Sir Roger de Coverley." / Then old
연주했을 때였다 "로저 드 코벌레이 경"을. 그러자 페치위그

Fezziwig stood out / to dance with Mrs. Fezziwig. Top
영감님이 일어섰다 부인과 함께 춤을 추려고. 선두가

couple, / too; / with a good stiff piece of work cut out for
되었다, 역시; 매우 고생하면서;

them; / three or four and twenty pair of partners; / people
스물 서너 쌍 때문에;

who were not to be trifled with; / people who would
우습게 봐서는 안 될 사람들; 춤을 추려는 사람들이었다,

dance, / and had no notion of walking.
걸을 생각이 없이.

But if they had been twice as many / — ah, four times
하지만 두 배는 많은 사람이 있다 해도 — 아, 네 배나 많이 —

— / old Fezziwig would have been a match for them, /
페치위그 영감은 상대할 수 있었을 것이었다.

and so would Mrs. Fezziwig. As to her, / she was worthy
그리고 페치위그 부인도 마찬가지였다. 부인으로 말하자면, 페치위그 씨의 반려자가 될

to be his partner / in every sense of the term.
가치가 있는 사람이었다 모든 면에서.

forfeit 벌금 놀이 | negus 니거스 주(포도주, 더운 물, 설탕, 향료, 레몬 따위를 섞은 음료) | strike up 연주하다 |
have one's work cut out 애먹다, 매우 고생하다 | trifle 소홀히 하다 | notion 의향, 의지

If that's not high praise, / tell me higher, / and I'll use
만약 이 말이 칭송이 되지 않는다면,   더 멋진 방법을 말해 달라,   내가 써 먹을 테니.

it. A positive light appeared to issue / from Fezziwig's
자신만만한 빛이 쏟아져 나왔다   페치위그의 종아리에서.

calves. They shone in every part of the dance / like
부부의 춤은 매 순간 빛났다

moons. You couldn't have predicted, / at any given time,
달처럼.   예상할 수 없었을 것이다.   어느 순간에도,

/ what would have become of them next. And when old
그들이 다음 순간 무슨 춤을 출지.

Fezziwig and Mrs. Fezziwig / had gone all through the
페치위그 영감과 페치위그 부인이   춤을 다 추고 나서;

dance; / advance and retire, / both hands to your partner,
앞으로 갔다 물러섰다.   파트너와 두 손을 맞잡고,

/ bow and curtsey, / corkscrew, / thread-the-needle,
남녀가 인사를 하고,   나선형으로 움직이다가,

and back again to your place; / Fezziwig "cut"— cut so
손을 맞잡고 커플들을 빠져나가게 하거나,   페치위그는 "공중에서 발 부딪치기"도 했다

deftly, / that he appeared to wink with his legs, / and
— 매우 능숙해서, 다리로 윙크를 하는 듯 보일 정도였다,

came upon his feet again / without a stagger.
그리고 나서 다시 내려왔다   비틀거리지도 않고.

When the clock struck eleven, / this domestic ball broke
시계가 11시를 치자, 이 실내 무도회는 끝났다.

up. Mr. and Mrs. Fezziwig took their stations, / one on
페치위그 부부는 자리를 잡고,

either side of the door, / and shaking hands with every
현관문 양편에, 모든 사람과 한 사람씩 악수를 나누며

person individually / as he or she went out, / wished him
돌아가는,

or her a Merry Christmas. When everybody had retired /
메리 크리스마스라고 인사하면서. 모든 사람이 돌아가자

but the two 'prentices, / they did the same to them; / and
두 견습생을 제외하고, 페치위그 부부는 그들에게도 똑같이 인사했다;

thus the cheerful voices died away, / and the lads were
그리고 즐거운 목소리들이 멀어지자, 청년들은 자신들의 침대로 갔다;

left to their beds; / which were under a counter in the
가게 뒤 편의 계산대 아래에 있는.

back-shop.

During the whole of this time, / Scrooge had acted / like a
이 모든 시간 동안, 스크루지는 행동했다

man out of his wits. His heart and soul were in the scene,
정신 나간 사람처럼. 그의 가슴과 영혼은 그 파티 장면과,

/ and with his former self. He corroborated everything,
자신의 옛 모습과 같이 있었다. 그는 모든 것을 확인했고,

/ remembered everything, / enjoyed everything, / and
모든 것을 기억해 냈으며, 모든 것을 즐겼고,

underwent the strangest agitation. It was not until now, /
매우 낯선 흥분을 경험했다. 지금까지 기억하지 못하다가

when the bright faces of his former self and Dick / were
밝은 얼굴인 과거의 그와 딕이

turned from them, / that he remembered the Ghost, / and
그들로부터 얼굴을 돌렸을 때, 그는 유령을 기억해 냈고,

became conscious / that it was looking full upon him, /
의식하게 되었다 유령이 자신을 주시하고 있다는 것을,

while the light upon its head burnt very clear.
머리에 있는 빛이 아주 환하게 타오르면서.

calf 장딴지, 종아리 | cut 발과 발을 부딪치다 | deftly 교묘하게, 능숙하게 | corroborate 확증하다, 입증하다 |
agitation 동요, 흥분

"A small matter," / said the Ghost, / "to make these silly
"사소한 일이군," 유령은 말했다. "이런 어리석은 사람들을

folks / so full of gratitude."
감격하게 만드는 것은."

"Small!" / echoed Scrooge.
"사소하다고요!" 스크루지가 되풀이 말했다.

The Spirit signed to him / to listen to the two
유령은 그에게 신호했고 두 견습생이 하는 말을 들으라고,

apprentices, / who were pouring out their hearts / in
진심을 쏟아내고 있는

praise of Fezziwig: / and when he had done so, / said,
페치위그를 칭송하며: 그리고 스크루지가 그들의 말을 들었을 때, 유령이 말했다.

"Why! Is it not? He has spent / but a few pounds of your
"자! 그렇지 않은가? 페치위그는 썼을 뿐이다 단지 너희 인간 세상의 돈 몇 파운드:

mortal money: / three or four perhaps. Is that so much /
아마도 3~4파운드 정도. 그것이 그렇게 대단한가

that he deserves this praise?"
이런 칭송을 받을 만큼?"

"It isn't that," / said Scrooge, / heated by the remark,
"그런 것이 아닙니다." 스크루지는 대답했다. 유령의 말에 흥분해서,

/ and speaking unconsciously / like his former, / not
무의식 중에 말하며 과거의 그처럼.

his latter, self. "It isn't that, / Spirit. He has the power
현재의 자신이 아니라. "그런 것이 아니에요, 유령님. 페치위그 씨는 힘을 갖고 있어요

/ to render us happy or unhappy; / to make our service
우리를 기쁘게 하거나 불행하게 할 수도 있는; 우리의 일을 가볍게도 부담스럽게도

light or burdensome; / a pleasure or a toil. Say / that his
만들 수 있는; 즐겁거나 고생스럽게 할 수 있는. 말하자면

power lies in words and looks; / in things so slight and
영감님의 힘은 말이나 표정에서; 또 아주 보잘것없고 하찮은 일에 들어

insignificant / that it is impossible to add and count 'em
있어서 셈하거나 헤아릴 수 없다고 해서:

up: / what then? The happiness he gives, / is quite as
그러면 어떻습니까? 영감님이 주시는 행복감이, 이렇게나 대단한데요

great / as if it cost a fortune."
대단한 재산을 쓴 것처럼."

He felt the Spirit's glance, / and stopped.
그는 유령이 힐끔 보는 것을 느꼈고,　　　말을 멈췄다.

"What is the matter?" / asked the Ghost.
"무엇이 문제인가?"　　　　유령은 물었다.

"Nothing particular," / said Scrooge.
"별 거 아닙니다."　　　스크루지는 말했다.

"Something, / I think?" / the Ghost insisted.
"뭔가 있는 것 같은데, / 내 생각에는?"　유령이 캐물었다.

"No," / said Scrooge, "No. I should like to be able to say
"아닙니다." 스크루지가 말했다. "아니요. 그저 한두 마디 건넬 수 있었으면 했어요

a word or two / to my clerk / just now. That's all."
내 직원에게　지금.　그게 다입니다."

His former self turned down the lamps / as he gave
청년 시절의 스크루지는 등잔을 껐다

utterance to the wish; / and Scrooge and the Ghost again
스크루지가 소원을 중얼거릴 때; 스크루지와 유령은 다시 섰다

stood / side by side / in the open air.
나란히　공중에서.

"My time grows short," / observed the Spirit. "Quick!"
"내 시간이 줄어들고 있다."　유령은 말했다.　"서두르자!"

Key Expression

the former vs the latter
the former와 the latter는 앞에서 말했던 것을 다시 받을 때 쓰는 '전자와 후자', 혹은 '전반부와 후반부'의 의미로 짝을 이루어 쓰는 표현입니다. 하지만 이 글에서는 과거의 스크루지(the former)와 현재의 스크루지(the latter)의 뜻을 표현합니다.

ex) "It isn't that," said Scrooge, heated by the remark, and speaking unconsciously like his former, not his latter, self.
"그런 것이 아닙니다." 스크루지는 유령이 말에 흥분해서, 무의식 중에 현재의 그 자신이 아닌 과거의 그처럼 말했다.

render 행하다 | toil 노고, 수고

This was not addressed / to Scrooge, / or to any one
이 말은 한 것이 아니었지만   스크루지나,   다른 사람에게

/ whom he could see, / but it produced an immediate
그가 볼 수 있는,   즉각적인 효과를 나타냈다.

effect. For again Scrooge saw himself. He was older
스크루지는 다시 자신을 보고 있었다.   그는 이제 좀 더 나이가 들었다;

now; / a man in the prime of life. His face had not the
인생의 황금기에 있는 남자였다.   그의 얼굴에는 눈에 거슬리고 경직된

harsh and rigid lines / of later years; / but it had begun to
주름들이 아직은 없었지만   나중에 나타날;   나타나고 있었다

wear / the signs of care and avarice. There was an eager,
근심과 탐욕의 징조가.   열망,

/ greedy, / restless motion / in the eye, / which showed
탐욕,   초조한 기색이 있었고   그의 눈에,   욕망을 보여 준

the passion / that had taken root, / and where the shadow
뿌리를 내린,   그 눈동자에는 나무의 그늘이 자라면서

of the growing tree / would fall.
드리워지고 있었다.

He was not alone, / but sat by the side of a fair young girl
그는 혼자가 아니었고,   아름다운 젊은 아가씨의 옆에 앉아 있었다

/ in a mourning-dress: / in whose eyes / there were tears,
상복을 입은: 그녀의 눈에는   눈물이 고여 있었다,

/ which sparkled in the light / that shone out of the Ghost
그 눈물이 빛에 비쳐 반짝거리는   과거 크리스마스 유령이 내뿜는.

of Christmas Past.

"It matters little," / she said, / softly. "To you, / very
"중요하지 않죠,"   그녀가 말했다, 부드럽게.   "당신에게는,   아무것도 아니죠.

little. Another idol has displaced me; / and if it can cheer
다른 우상이 나를 대신했으니까요;   그 우상이 당신을 기쁘게 하고

and comfort you / in time / to come, / as I would have
위로해 주며   때맞춰   온다면,   내가 노력했을 것처럼,

tried to do, / I have no just cause to grieve."
난 슬퍼할 이유가 없어요."

"What Idol has displaced you?" / he rejoined.
"어떤 우상이 당신을 대신했다는 것이지?"   그는 다시 물었다.

"A golden one."
"황금이라는 우상이죠."

"This is the even-handed dealing of the world!" / he said.
"이것이 바로 세상의 공평한 취급이라는 것인가!"   그는 말했다.

"There is nothing / on which it is so hard as poverty; /
"아무것도 없고   가난처럼 힘든 것은;

and there is nothing / it professes to condemn with such
아무것도 없지   그렇게 가혹하게 비난받는 것도

severity / as the pursuit of wealth!"
부를 추구하는 것만큼!"

"You fear the world too much," / she answered, / gently.
"당신은 세상을 너무 두려워하는군요."   그녀는 대답했다.   부드럽게.

"All your other hopes / have merged into the hope / of
"다른 희망들은   그 희망 안에 합쳐졌어요

being beyond the chance of its sordid reproach. I have
더러운 비난을 받지 않으려는.

seen your nobler aspirations / fall off one by one, / until
난 당신의 더 숭고한 열망을 지켜봤죠   하나씩 하나씩 떨어져 나갔던,

the master-passion, / Gain, / engrosses you. Have I not?"
마침내 그 가장 큰 욕망,   돈 버는 일에, 당신이 몰두하게 되 버렸죠. 아닌가요?"

"What then?" / he retorted. "Even if I have grown so
"그래서 어쨌다는 것이지?" 그가 비꼬았다.   "내가 훨씬 더 현명해졌다고 한들,

much wiser, / what then? I am not changed towards you."
그게 무슨 문제인데? 당신에 대한 감정은 변하지 않았잖아."

She shook her head.
그녀는 머리를 흔들었다.

"Am I?"
"변했단 말인가?"

"Our contract is an old one. It was made / when we were
"우리 약속은 옛일이에요.   약속이었죠

both poor and content to be so, / until, in good season,
우리 둘 다 가난하고 가난에 만족했던 때의,   좋은 시절이 올 때까지,

/ we could improve our worldly fortune / by our patient
    우리도 잘 살 수 있는   참고 부지런히 일해서.

industry. You are changed. When it was made, / you
                 당신은 변했어요.   우리가 약속했을 때,

were another man."
당신은 다른 사람이었어요."

"I was a boy," / he said impatiently.
"그땐 어린 아이였소,"   그는 조바심 내며 대답했다.

"Your own feeling tells you / that you were not / what
"당신 자신도 알고 있어요   예전에는 달랐다고   지금의

you are," / she returned. "I am. That which promised
당신 모습과,"   그녀가 대답했다.   "난 같아요. 우리가 약속했던 행복은

happiness / when we were one in heart, / is fraught with
                우리의 마음이 하나였을 때,   지금은 고통으로 가득할

misery now / that we are two. How often and how keenly
뿐이에요   우리의 마음이 둘이 되었으니. 얼마나 자주 그리고 얼마나 심각하게

/ I have thought of this, / I will not say. It is enough / that
   이 일을 생각했는지는,   말하지 않을게요.   충분해요

I have thought of it, / and can release you."
그 문제에 대해 생각했던 것으로,   그러니 당신을 놓아 줄 수 있어요."

"Have I ever sought release?"
"내가 언제 자유롭게 되기를 바랐소?"

"In words. No. Never."
"말로 하지 않았죠. 아뇨. 결코 말하지 않았어요."

"In what, / then?"
"뭐 때문에 이러는 거요,   그럼?"

"In a changed nature; / in an altered spirit; / in another
"달라진 성격;   바뀐 영혼;

atmosphere of life; / another Hope / as its great end. In
또 다른 분위기;   다른 희망이에요   예전과는 완전히 반대인.

everything / that made my love of any worth or value / in
모든 것이죠   내 사랑을 가치 있고 소중하게 만들었던

your sight. If this had never been between us," / said the
당신이 보기에. 만약 우리 사이에 이런 일이 일어나지 않았더라면." 그녀는 말했지만,

girl, / looking mildly, / but with steadiness, / upon him;
부드럽게 쳐다보면서, 확고했다. 그에게;

/ "tell me, / would you seek me out / and try to win me
"말해 봐요. 나를 찾아나서고 나를 차지하기 위해 노력할

now? Ah, / no!"
건가요? 아, 아니겠죠!"

He seemed to yield / to the justice of this supposition, / in
그는 굴복한 듯 보였다 이 가정이 맞다고,

spite of himself. But he said with a struggle, / "You think
어쩔 수 없이. 하지만 그는 애써 말했다. "그렇게 생각하

not."
지 마시오."

"I would gladly think otherwise / if I could," / she
"나도 달리 생각하고 싶어요 할 수만 있다면,"

answered, "Heaven knows! When I have learned a Truth
그녀가 대답했다. "맹세코! 이런 진리를 깨닫게 되었을 때,

like this, / I know / how strong and irresistible / it must
알았죠 얼마나 강하고 저항할 수 없는 진실인지 그것이.

be. But if you were free / today, / tomorrow, / yesterday,
하지만 당신이 자유롭다면 오늘, 내일, 혹은 어제가 됐든,

/ can even I believe / that you would choose a dowerless
내가 과연 믿을 수 있을까요 당신이 지참금이 없는 아가씨를 선택하리라는 것을

girl / — you who, / in your very confidence / with her, /
— 당신이, 확신에 가득 차서 함께하리라고,

weigh everything by Gain: / or, / choosing her, / if for a
수입에 의해 모든 것을 재는: 아니면, 선택하리라고, 설령 순간적으로

moment / you were false enough / to your one guiding
당신이 잘못하여 당신을 이끄는 원칙을

principle / to do so, / do I not know / that your repentance
그렇게 한다 해도, 내가 모를까요 당신에게 후회와 한탄이

and regret / would surely follow? I do; / and I release you.
분명히 따를 것이라는 것을? 난 알아요; 그래서 놓아 드리는 거예요.

---

industry 근면성 | fraught 내포한, 가득한 | supposition 추정 | dowerless 지참금이 없는 | repentance 후회

With a full heart, / for the love of him / you once were."
진심으로, 당신과의 사랑을 위해 예전 모습의."

He was about to speak; / but with her head turned from
그는 말하려고 했지만; 그녀는 스크루지를 외면하고,

him, / she resumed.
계속했다.

"You may / — the memory of what is past / half makes
"아마도 당신은 — 과거의 추억 때문에 바라는 마음이 있죠

me hope / you will — / have pain in this. A very, / very
그랬으면 하고 — 이 일로 마음이 아플지 몰라요. 아주,

brief time, / and you will dismiss the recollection of
아주 짧은 시간에, 그 기억을 떨쳐 버리겠죠

it, / gladly, / as an unprofitable dream, / from which it
기꺼이, 쓸데없는 꿈이니까, 잘 됐다고 생각하겠죠

happened well / that you awoke. May you be happy / in
꿈에서 깨어난 것이. 부디 행복하길 바라요

the life you have chosen!"
당신이 선택한 삶에서!"

She left him, / and they parted.
그녀는 떠났고, 그렇게 그들은 헤어졌다.

"Spirit!" / said Scrooge, / "show me no more! Conduct
"유령님!" 스크루지는 말했다, "더 이상 보여 주지 마세요! 집에 데려다

me home. Why do you delight to torture me?"
주세요. 왜 저를 고문하면서 좋아하시는 겁니까?"

"One shadow more!" / exclaimed the Ghost.
"환영이 하나 더 있다!"   유령은 외쳤다.

"No more!" / cried Scrooge. "No more. I don't wish to
"더 이상 싫습니다!"   스크루지는 울부짖었다.   "그만 하세요.   보고 싶지 않아요.

see it. Show me no more!"
더 이상 보여 주지 마세요!"

But the relentless Ghost pinioned him / in both his arms,
하지만 가차없는 유령은 그를 껴안고   두 팔로.

/ and forced him to observe / what happened next.
강제로 보게 했다   다음에 일어나는 일을.

They were in another scene and place; / a room, / not
그들은 다른 장면과 장소에 있었다;   방이었다.

very large or handsome, / but full of comfort. Near to
크거나 멋지지는 않지만,   안락함이 가득한.

the winter fire / sat a beautiful young girl, / so like that
겨울 난로 가까이에   아름다운 젊은 아가씨가 앉아 있었다.   아까 본 아가씨와 비슷

last / that Scrooge believed / it was the same, / until
해서   스크루지는 생각했다   같은 사람이라고.   다른 여자를 발견

he saw her, / now a comely matron, / sitting opposite
할 때까지.   지금은 아름다운 주부가 된.   그녀의 딸 반대쪽에 앉은.

her daughter. The noise in this room / was perfectly
방에서 나는 소리 때문에   완전히 난장판이었다.

tumultuous, / for there were more children there, / than
거기에는 다른 아이들이 더 있었기 때문이었다.

Scrooge in his agitated state of mind / could count; / and,
흥분 상태의 스크루지가   다 셀 수 없을 정도로; 그리고.

/ unlike the celebrated herd in the poem, / they were not
시에 나오는 축복받은 양떼와 달리.   40명의 아이들이 아니라

forty children / conducting themselves like one, / but
한 명처럼 행동하는.

every child was conducting itself / like forty.
각각의 아이들이 행동했다   제각각 40명처럼.

---

relentless 무정한, 가차없는 | pinion ~을 붙들어 매다 | comely 고운 | matron 기혼녀, 부인 | tumultuous
시끄러운, 소동을 일으키는 | agitate 흔들리고 있는, 동요하고 있는

The consequences were uproarious / beyond belief; / but
결과적으로 아수라장이 되었지만   믿을 수 없을 만큼;

no one seemed to care; / on the contrary, / the mother
아무도 신경 쓰지 않는 듯 했고;   반대로,

and daughter laughed heartily, / and enjoyed it very
엄마와 딸은 즐겁게 웃으며,   그 상황을 굉장히 즐기고 있었다;

much; / and the latter, / soon beginning to mingle in
            그리고 딸은,   곧 그 소동 속에 섞이기 시작해,

the sports, / got pillaged by the young brigands / most
            어린 약탈자들에게 강탈당했다

ruthlessly. What would I not have given / to be one of
무자비하게도.   무엇인들 주지 못하겠는가   그들 중 하나가 될 수

them! Though I never could have been so rude, / no,
있다면!   그렇게 무례할 수는 없겠지만 말이다,   절대로,

/ no! I wouldn't for the wealth of all the world / have
 그럴 수 없다! 세상의 어떤 부를 준다 해도

Key Expression

조동사 have p.p의 의미
앞에서 may/might have p.p에 대해서는 설명했습니다. 이와 같이 다른 조동
사도 뒤에 have p.p를 동반하여 과거를 표현합니다.
또한 조동사 + have p.p 표현에는 가정법의 속뜻이 숨어있다는 점에 주의하
세요.

▶ could have p.p : ~할 수도 있었다 (그러나 하지 못했다는 의미)
▶ should have p.p : ~했어야 했다 (그러나 하지 않았다는 의미)

ex) I couldn't have done it; I should have expected my arm to have grown round
    it for a punishment, and never come straight again.
    난 그것을 할 수 없었을 것이다, 내 팔이 벌을 받아 굽어 버려서 다시는 펴지 못
    하게 되리라고 예상했어야 했다.

crushed that braided hair, / and torn it down; / and for
저 아이의 땋은 머리를 짓밟고, 헝클어뜨리지는 못하리라;

the precious little shoe, / I wouldn't have plucked it off,
그리고 사랑스러운 작은 신발을, 잡아채지는 못하리라,

/ God bless my soul! To save my life. As to measuring
맙소사! 저를 구하소서. 장난으로 저 아이의 허리를

her waist in sport, / as they did, / bold young brood, / I
껴안는 일도, 그들이 하듯이, 대담한 꼬마들인,

couldn't have done it; / I should have expected / my arm
난 하지 못했을 것이며; 될 것이다

to have grown round it / for a punishment, / and never
내 팔이 굽어 버려서 벌을 받아,

come straight again. And yet I should have dearly liked,
다시는 펴지 못하게 될 것이다. 하지만 감히 원하리라,

/ I own, / to have touched her lips; / to have questioned
내 입술에, 그 아이의 입술이 맞닿기를: 질문해서,

her, / that she might have opened them; / to have looked
그 입술을 열게 하기를; 올려다 볼 수 있기를

upon / the lashes of her downcast eyes, / and never raised
내리깐 눈의 속눈썹을, 얼굴을 붉히지 않고;

a blush; / to have let loose waves of hair, / an inch of
구불구불한 머리를 풀어 헤칠 수 있기를, 그 머리카락 1인치라도

which / would be a keepsake / beyond price: / in short,
기념품이 되었으리라: 값을 매길 수 없는 한 마디로,

/ I should have liked, / I do confess, / to have had the
원했을 것이다, 고백하자면, 아이라는 가볍디 가벼운

lightest licence of a child, / and yet to have been man /
허가증을 가진 채, 어른이 되기를

enough to know its value.
그 가치를 잘 아는.

---

uproarious 떠들썩한, 시끄러운 | pillage 약탈하다 | brigand 약탈자 | ruthlessly 무자비하게, 잔인하게 | braid 머리를 땋다 | pluck off 털썩 던지다 | downcast 눈을 내리깐 | keepsake 기념품

But now a knocking at the door was heard, / and such a
하지만 그때 문을 두드리는 소리가 들렸고,   아이들이 갑자기

rush immediately ensued / that she with laughing face /
엄청나게 돌진하며 나가버리자   웃음 띤 얼굴의 소녀는

and plundered dress / was borne towards it / the centre
헝클어진 옷을 입은 채   문 쪽으로 떠밀려 가 버렸다

of a flushed and boisterous group, / just in time / to greet
얼굴이 빨개지고 떠들썩한 아이들 가운데로,   때마침   아빠에게 인

the father, / who came home attended by a man / laden
사를 하러 간,   아버지는 한 남자와 같이 들어왔다

with Christmas toys and presents. Then the shouting
크리스마스 장난감과 선물을 들고 있는.

and the struggling, and the onslaught / that was made on
그러자 소리지르며 버둥거리고 맹공격이 일어났다

the defenceless porter! The scaling him / with chairs for
무방비 상태의 짐꾼에게 행해졌다!   그 짐꾼에게 달려들고   의자를 사다리 삼아 갖다

ladders / to dive into his pockets, / despoil him of brown-
놓고   주머니에 뛰어들었고,   갈색 종이로 싼 꾸러미들을

paper parcels, / hold on tight by his cravat, / hug him
빼앗고,   넥타이를 꽉 잡고,

round his neck, / pommel his back, / and kick his legs
목을 꼭 껴안고,   등을 주먹으로 때리고,   다리를 찼다

/ in irrepressible affection! The shouts of wonder and
감정을 주체할 수 없어서!   놀라움과 기쁨의 환성이 터져 나왔다

delight / with which the development of every package
꾸러미를 모두 받을 때마다!

was received! The terrible announcement / that the baby
끔찍한 소식이 들렸고

had been taken / in the act of putting a doll's frying-
아기를 발견했다는   인형의 프라이팬을 입 속에 넣어버렸다는,

pan into his mouth, / and was more than suspected /
또한 의심된다는 얘기가 들렸다

of having swallowed / a fictitious turkey, / glued on a
삼켰는지   장난감 칠면조를,

wooden platter!
나무 접시 위에 붙어 있는!

ensue 잇달아 일어나다 | plunder 약탈하다 | boisterous 떠들썩한 | onslaught 맹공격, 맹습 | scaling 껍질을
벗기다 | despoil 빼앗다 | pommel 주먹으로 연타하다 | irrepressible 억제할 수 없는 | fictitious 진짜가 아닌

The immense relief / of finding this a false alarm!
그 커다란 안도감이라니   잘못된 경보임을 알았을 때!

The joy, / and gratitude, / and ecstasy! They are all
기쁨과,   감사와,   희열이란!

indescribable alike. It is enough / that by degrees / the
말로 다 표현할 수 없었다.   충분했다   점차로

children and their emotions / got out of the parlor, /
아이들과 그들의 흥분도   거실을 빠져 나갔다,

and by one stair at a time, / up to the top of the house; /
한 번에 한 계단씩,   아이들이 위층으로 올라가면서;

where they went to bed, / and so subsided.
거기에서 그들은 잠자리에 들었으며,   그렇게 가라앉았다.

And now Scrooge looked on / more attentively than ever,
이제 스크루지는 살펴볼 수 있었고   전보다 더 자세히,

/ when the master of the house, / having his daughter
그때 집주인은,   딸을 자신에게 기대게 한 채,

leaning fondly on him, / sat down with her and her
          딸과 부인과 앉았다

mother / at his own fireside; / and when he thought / that
          난롯가에;   그리고 스크루지는 생각하자

such another creature, / quite as graceful and as full of
저런 아이가,   저렇게 우아하고 앞날이 창창한

promise, / might have called him father, / and been a
          자신을 아버지라고 불렀을지도 모르며,   봄날이 되었을지도

spring-time / in the haggard winter of his life, / his sight
모른다고   황량한 겨울같은 자신의 삶에.

grew very dim indeed.
시야가 뿌옇게 흐려졌다.

"Belle," / said the husband, / turning to his wife with a
"여보,"   남편이 말했다,   미소를 띄고 부인을 돌아보며,

smile, / "I saw an old friend of yours / this afternoon."
          "당신의 옛 친구를 보았소   오늘 오후에."

---

immense 굉장한 | by degrees 차츰, 단계적으로 | parlor 거실 | subside 가라앉다 | graceful 우아한 |
haggard 사나운, 초췌한 | in the same breath 동시에

"Who was it?"
"누구요?"

"Guess!"
"맞혀 보구려!"

"How can I? Tut, / don't I know?" / she added in the
"어떻게 알아요? 당신도, 내가 모를 것 같아요?" 그녀는 동시에 덧붙였다,

same breath, / laughing as he laughed. **"Mr. Scrooge."**
그가 웃자 따라 웃으며. "스크루지 씨."

"Mr. Scrooge it was. I passed his office window; / and as
"맞소, 스크루지 씨요. 그 사람 사무실 창가를 지나쳤는데;

it was not shut up, / and he had a candle inside, / I could
문이 닫혀 있지 않고, 안에 촛불을 켜 놔서,

scarcely help seeing him. His partner lies upon the point
볼 수밖에 없었소. 동업자가 죽을 날을 받아놓고 있다고,

of death, / I hear; / and there he sat alone. Quite alone in
들었는데; 그 사람은 거기 혼자 앉아 있었소. 세상에 혼자 남겨진 사람

the world, / I do believe."
같았소 내가 보기에는."

"Spirit!" / said Scrooge in a broken voice, / "remove me
"유령님!" 스크루지는 갈라진 목소리로 말했다,

from this place."
"나를 여기에서 데려가 주세요."

Key Expression 🍂

신체 접촉의 표현
신체 접촉을 표현하는 동사는 '신체접촉 동사 + 사람 + 전치사 + the + 신체부위'
의 형태로 표현합니다. 이때 동사에 따라 사용하는 전치사가 달라집니다.

▶ [잡다] take/catch/seize/hold/grasp/get : by 사용
▶ [치다] strike/hit/pat/tap/touch : on 사용
▶ [보다] look/gaze/stare : in 사용

ex) The scaling him with chairs for ladders to dive into his pockets, despoil him of
brown-paper parcels, hold on tight by his cravat, hug him round his neck.
의자를 사다리 삼아 그의 주머니에 뛰어들어, 갈색 종이로 싼 꾸러미를 빼앗고,
그의 넥타이를 꽉 잡고, 목을 꼭 껴안았다.

"I told you / these were shadows of the things / that have
"내가 말했지   이것들은 환영들이라고   일어났던 일의,"

been," / said the Ghost. "That they are / what they are, /
유령은 말했다.   "그것들은   사실일 뿐이다,

do not blame me!"
나를 원망하지 마라!"

"Remove me!" / Scrooge exclaimed, / "I cannot bear it!"
"나를 내보내 주세요!"   스크루지는 소리쳤다,   "참을 수 없어요!"

He turned upon the Ghost, / and seeing / that it looked
스크루지는 유령을 향해 고개를 돌렸고,   보았다   유령이 자신을 보고 있는

upon him / with a face, / in which in some strange way /
것을   얼굴로,   그 얼굴에는 기묘하게도

there were fragments of all the faces / it had shown him,
모든 얼굴 조각들이   유령이 그에게 보여 주었던,

/ wrestled with it.
얽혀 있었다.

"Leave me! Take me back. Haunt me no longer!"
"나를 내버려 둬! 돌려보내 줘.   더 이상 나타나지 마!"

In the struggle, / if that can be called a struggle / in
싸우면서,   만약 그것을 싸움이라 부를 수 있다면

which the Ghost with no visible resistance / on its own
유령은 전혀 상대를 하지 않고 있는데   그쪽에서는

part / was undisturbed / by any effort of its adversary, /
전혀 흔들리지 않았으니   적군의 어떤 공격에도,

Scrooge observed / that its light was burning high and
스크루지는 보았다   유령의 불빛이 높고 환하게 타오르는 것을;

bright; / and dimly connecting that / with its influence
그 불꽃이 관련이 있을지 모른다고 생각해   유령이 그에게 미치는 힘과,

over him, / he seized the extinguisher-cap, / and by a
스크루지는 불 끄는 모자를 잡아,

sudden action / pressed it down upon its head.
갑작스럽게,   유령의 머리에 눌러 씌웠다.

---

adversary 적수, 상대 | dimly 어둑하게, 희미하게 | reel 비틀거리다, 휘청휘청 걷다

The Spirit dropped beneath it, / so that the extinguisher
유령은 모자 밑으로 떨어져,   소화기가 유령 전체를 덮어 버렸지만;

covered its whole form; / but though Scrooge pressed it
                    스크루지가 모자를 눌러도

down / with all his force, / he could not hide the light:
        온 힘을 다해,   빛을 감출 수 없었다:

/ which streamed from under it, / in an unbroken flood
    그 빛은 모자 밑에서 흘러나왔다,   땅 위에서 흥건한 홍수를 이루며.

upon the ground.

He was conscious of being exhausted, / and overcome by
스크루지는 녹초가 된 것을 깨달았고,

an irresistible drowsiness; / and, / further, / of being in
저항할 수 없는 졸음에 빠져 들었다;   그리고,   또한,

his own bedroom. He gave the cap a parting squeeze, / in
자신의 방에 있었다.   그는 마지막으로 모자를 비틀었다가,

which his hand relaxed; / and had barely time to reel to
손에 힘을 풀었고;   겨우 휘청휘청 침대로 걸어 들어가서,

bed, / before he sank into a heavy sleep.
        깊은 잠에 빠져 들었다.

Key Expression♀

barely : 겨우

barely, hardly, scarcely는 모두 '거의 ~아니다' 혹은 '간신히 ~하다'라는 뜻
으로 쓰이는 부사입니다. 이들 부사는 any, anyone과 같은 단어나 형용사, 동사
와 함께 쓰이고, 그 위치는 조동사와 본동사 사이에 옵니다. 또한 부정적인 뜻을 가
진 단어이므로 다른 부정어와 함께 쓰이지 않습니다.
한편 hardly와 scarcely는 '거의 ~하지 않다'라는 뜻으로도 쓰이지만, barely
는 이런 의미로는 쓰이지 않습니다.

ex) He gave the cap a parting squeeze, in which his hand relaxed; and had
    barely time to reel to bed, before he sank into a heavy sleep.
    그는 마지막으로 모자를 비틀었다가 손의 힘을 푼 뒤, 휘청거리며 겨우 침대로
    걸어 들어가서, 깊은 잠에 빠져 들었다.

mini test 4

A. 다음 문장을 해석해 보세요.

(1) Although they had but that moment / left the school behind them, / they were now / in the busy thoroughfares of a city.
→

(2) New top couple starting off again, / as soon as they got there; / all top couples at last, / and not a bottom one to help them!
→

(3) But if they had been twice as many / — ah, four times — / old Fezziwig would have been a match for them, / and so would Mrs. Fezziwig.
→

(4) I should have expected / my arm to have grown / round it / for a punishment, / and never come straight / again.
→

B. 다음 주어진 문구가 알맞은 문장이 되도록 순서를 맞춰 보세요.

(1) 그들은 다른 장면과 장소에 있었다; <u>크거나 멋지진 않지만 안락함이 가득한 방이었다.</u>
(very / but / or / comfort / full / large / not / of / handsome,)
They were in another scene and place; a room,

(2) 그는 이제 좀 더 나이가 들어서; <u>인생의 황금기에 있는 남자였다.</u>
(the / of / man / a / in / life / prime)
He was older now;

A. (1) 학교를 두고 떠난 지 얼마 지나지 않았지만, 그들은 이제 도시의 복잡한 큰 길에 있었다. (2) 새로 리드하는 커플이 다시 시작하여, 선두 자리에 서자마자; 결국은 모두 리드하는 커플이 되어, 뒤따라서 리드를 도와야 하는 커플이 하나도 없었다! (3) 하지만 두 배는 많은 사람이 있다 해도 — 아, 네 배나 많이 —페

(3) 세상에 가난처럼 힘든 것은 아무것도 없다.
(is / it / poverty / nothing / is / There / on which / hard / as so)
→

(4) <u>예전의 당신은 지금 당신 모습이 아니었다고</u> 자신도 느끼고 있어요.
(what / are / were / not / you / you)
Your own feeling tells you that _____.

C. 다음 주어진 문장이 본문의 내용과 맞으면 T, 틀리면 F에 동그라미 하세요.

(1) Scrooge had a bad memory about old Fezziwig.
[T / F]

(2) While Scrooge was looking at his past, he acted like a crazy man.
[T / F]

(3) Scrooge abandoned his first lover.
[T / F]

(4) Scrooge made the spirit disappeared by using his cap.
[T / F]

D. 의미가 비슷한 것끼리 서로 연결해 보세요.

(1) snug   ▶   ◀ ① sink

(2) plunge   ▶   ◀ ② inflexible

(3) rigid   ▶   ◀ ③ opponent

(4) adversary   ▶   ◀ ④ comfortable

5

THE SECOND OF THE THREE SPIRITS I
두 번째 유령 I

Awaking / in the middle of a prodigiously tough snore,
잠에서 깨어나   엄청나게 코를 골던 중,

/ and sitting up in bed / to get his thoughts together,
침대 위에 앉아서   생각을 정리하기 위해,

/ Scrooge had no occasion / to be told / that the bell
스크루지는 경황이 없었다   들었던 것을 떠올릴

was again upon the stroke of One. He felt / that he was
시계가 다시 1시를 칠 것이라고.   그는 생각했다

restored to consciousness / in the right nick of time,
정신을 차렸다고   아슬아슬하게 때를 맞춰,

/ for the especial purpose / of holding a conference /
그 특별한 일을 하기 위해   만남을 갖는다는

with the second messenger despatched to him / through
자신에게 파견될 두 번째 전령과

Jacob Marley's intervention. But finding that he turned
제이콥 말리의 주선으로.   하지만 불안으로 등골이 오싹해져서

uncomfortably cold / when he began to wonder / which
궁금해하기 시작하자

of his curtains this new spectre would draw back, / he
이 새로운 유령은 어느 쪽 커튼을 들어 올릴지,

put them every one aside / with his own hands; / and
그는 커튼을 모두 한쪽으로 젖혀 놓고   직접;

lying down again, / established a sharp look-out / all
다시 드러누워,   날카롭게 훑어 보았다

round the bed. For he wished to challenge the Spirit / on
침대 주위를.   그는 유령과 맞서고 싶었고

the moment of its appearance, / and did not wish to be
나타나는 순간,   깜짝 놀라고 싶지 않았기 때문이다,

taken by surprise, / and made nervous.
긴장하거나.

prodigiously 터무니없게 | dispatch 파견하다, 보내다 | intervention 중재, 주선 | free-and-easy 격식을
차리지 않는, 소탈한 | plume ~으로 우쭐대다 | time-of-day 실정, 진상 | pitch-and-toss 돈 던지기 놀이 |
manslaughter 살인 | tolerably 상당히, 웬만큼 | rhinoceros 코뿔소

Gentlemen of the free-and-easy sort, / who plume
이른 바 소탈한 신사들은,   우쭐대는

themselves / on being acquainted / with a move or two, /
          잘 알고   한두 가지에,

and being usually equal to the time-of-day, / express the
그리고 세상 물정을 잘 안다면서,

wide range of their capacity / for adventure / by observing
폭넓은 능력을 과시하곤 한다   모험을 강행하며   말하면서

/ that they are good for anything / from pitch-and-toss to
무엇이든 잘한다고   동전 던지기에서 살인까지;

manslaughter; / between which opposite extremes, / no
           이 양 극단의 모험 사이에는,   의심할

doubt, / there lies a tolerably wide and comprehensive
바 없이,   상당히 넓고 포괄적인 문제들이 자리잡고 있기는 하다.

range of subjects. Without venturing / for Scrooge / quite
모험도 없으니   스크루지에게는

as hardily as this, / I don't mind calling on you to believe
이 정도로 대단한,   여러분에게 믿어 달라고 요구할 생각은 없다

/ that he was ready / for a good broad field of strange
그는 준비되어 있었고,   온갖 종류의 기묘한 존재의

appearances, / and that nothing between a baby and
출현을 맞이하기 위해,   아이에서 코뿔소까지 무엇이 나타나도

rhinoceros / would have astonished him very much.
그를 아주 많이 놀라게 하지는 않을 거라고.

131

Now, / being prepared for almost anything, / he was
이제, 거의 어떤 모습의 유령이라도 맞을 준비가 되어 있었지만,

not by any means prepared / for nothing; / and, /
스크루지도 전혀 준비하지 못했다 실체가 없는 존재에 대해; 그리고,

consequently, / when the Bell struck One, / and no shape
마침내, 종이 1시를 치고, 아무것도 나타나지

appeared, / he was taken with a violent fit of trembling.
않자, 격심한 떨림이 그를 사로잡았다.

Five minutes, / ten minutes, / a quarter of an hour went
오 분, 십 분, 15분이 흘렀지만,

by, / yet nothing came. All this time, / he lay upon his
아무것도 오지 않았다. 그 동안 내내, 그는 침대에 누워 있었다,

bed, / the very core and centre of a blaze of ruddy light, /
불그스름한 램프 불빛의 중심이,

which streamed upon it / when the clock proclaimed the
침대를 비추는 상황에서 시계가 1시를 알렸을 때;

hour; / and which, being only light, / was more alarming
단지 불빛일 뿐이었지만, 십여 명의 유령보다

/ than a dozen ghosts, / as he was powerless to make out
더욱 무서웠다, 알 길이 없었으므로

/ what it meant, / or would be at; / and was sometimes
그것이 뭘 의미하고, 어디를 향해 비치는지를; 또한 걱정스럽기도 했다

apprehensive / that he might be at that very moment / an
자신이 바로 그런 순간에 있는 것은 아닌지

interesting case of spontaneous combustion, / without
자연발화라는 흥미로운 사례의,

having the consolation of knowing it. At last, / however,
그 사실을 알고 있는 누군가의 위로도 받지 못한 채 마침내, 그러나,

/ he began to think / — as you or I would have thought at
그는 생각하기 시작했다 — 여러분이나 나라면 처음부터 생각했겠지만;

first; / for it is always / the person not in the predicament
언제나 그런 법이다 궁지에 빠지지 않은 사람이라면

/ who knows / what ought to have been done in it, / and
알고 있고 어떻게 해야 할지,

would unquestionably have done it too / — at last, / I say,
또 의심할 바 없이 역시 그렇게 했겠지만 말이다 — 마침내, 말하자면,

/ he began to think / that the source and secret of this
그는 생각하기 시작했다   이 괴상한 빛의 출처와 비밀이

ghostly light / might be in the adjoining room, / from
옆 방에 있을지도 모른다고.

whence, / on further tracing it, / it seemed to shine. This
거기에서부터,   좀 더 생각해 보니,   빛나는 것 같았다.

idea taking full possession of his mind, / he got up softly
이런 생각에 사로잡히자,   그는 가만히 일어나

/ and shuffled in his slippers to the door.
슬리퍼를 끌며 문으로 향했다.

The moment Scrooge's hand was on the lock, / a strange
스크루지의 손이 열쇠에 닿는 순간,

voice called him by his name, / and bade him enter. He
낯선 목소리가 그의 이름을 부르며,   들어오라 했다.

obeyed.
그는 시키는 대로 했다.

It was his own room. There was no doubt / about that.
그 방은 스크루지 자신의 방이었다. 의심의 여지가 없었다   그 사실에 대해서는.

But it had undergone a surprising transformation. The
하지만 그 방은 놀라운 변화를 겪은 듯 했다.

walls and ceiling were so hung with living green, / that
벽과 천정에 살아있는 식물들이 덮여 있어,

it looked a perfect grove; / from every part of which, /
방은 완전히 작은 숲처럼 보였고;   사방에,

bright gleaming berries glistened. The crisp leaves / of
밝게 빛나는 열매들이 반짝였다.   빳빳한 잎들이   호랑가

holly, / mistletoe, / and ivy / reflected back the light, / as
시나무,   겨우살이나무,   담쟁이 등이   빛을 반사하여,

if so many little mirrors had been scattered there; / and
수많은 작은 거울이 방 안에 흩어져 있는 것처럼 보였고;

such a mighty blaze went roaring / up the chimney, / as
강한 불꽃이 활활 타올랐다   굴뚝까지,

apprehensive 염려하는, 불안한 | spontaneous 자발적인 | combustion 연소 | consolation 위안, 위로 |
predicament 궁지 | whence 어디서 | shuffle 발을 질질 끌며 걷다 | grove 작은 숲 | mistletoe 겨우살이

that dull petrification of a hearth had never known / in
화석같던 난로에서 한 번도 본 적이 없었던 모습으로

Scrooge's time, / or Marley's, / or for many and many a
스크루지의 평생 동안,   말리의 평생 동안,   또한 수많은 겨울을 나는 동안,

winter season gone. Heaped up on the floor, / to form a
바닥에는 쌓여 있었다,

kind of throne, / were turkeys, / geese, / game, / poultry,
왕좌같은 모습으로,   칠면조,   거위,   들짐승,   가금류,

/ brawn, / great joints of meat, / sucking-pigs, / long
삶은 돼지고기,   커다란 고기 덩어리들,   통돼지 구이,

wreaths of sausages, / mince-pies, / plum-puddings, /
기다란 소시지들,   고기 파이,   자두 푸딩,

barrels of oysters, / red-hot chestnuts, / cherry-cheeked
굴이 들어 있는 통,   빨갛게 익은 밤,   체리빛 사과,

apples, / juicy oranges, / luscious pears, / immense
즙 많은 오렌지,   달콤한 배,   커다란 주현절 케이크

twelfth-cakes, / and seething bowls of punch, / that made
들이,   보글보글 끓는 펀치 그릇은,

the chamber dim / with their delicious steam. In easy
방을 온통 흐릿하게 만드는   맛있는 냄새의 연기로.   편한 자세로

state / upon this couch, / there sat a jolly Giant, / glorious
이 왕좌에,   쾌활한 거인이 앉아 있다가,   위풍당당해

to see; / who bore a glowing torch, / in shape not unlike
보이는;   밝게 타오르는 횃불을 들고,   '풍요의 뿔'처럼 보이는,

Plenty's horn, / and held it up, / high up, / to shed its light
횃불을 쳐들어,   아주 높이,   스크루지에게 비추었다,

on Scrooge, / as he came peeping round the door.
문간에서 방 안을 살펴보자.

"Come in!" / exclaimed the Ghost. "Come in! And know
"들어오라!"   유령이 소리쳤다.   "들어오라!   그리고 나를 더

me better, / man!"
자세히 보라,   인간이여!"

petrification 석화, 화석 | hearth 난로 | heap 쌓아 올리다 | game 사냥한 고기 | brawn 삶아서 소금에 절인
돼지 고기 | sucking-pig 통구이용 젖먹이 돼지 | red-hot 새빨갛게 단 | luscious 달콤한 | seething 끓는 |
shed 발산하다, 떨어지다 | dogged 고집센

Scrooge entered timidly, / and hung his head / before this
스크루지는 멈칫거리며 들어가서,　　　머리를 조아렸다　　　유령 앞에.

Spirit. He was not the dogged Scrooge / he had been; /
　　　스크루지는 더 이상 완고한 사람이 아니었기 때문에　예전처럼;

and though the Spirit's eyes were clear and kind, / he did
유령의 눈은 맑고 상냥했으나,

not like to meet them.
그는 유령의 눈을 보고 싶지 않았다.

"I am the Ghost of Christmas Present," / said the Spirit.
"나는 현재 크리스마스 유령이다,"　　　　　　　　유령은 말했다.

"Look upon me!"
"고개를 들어 나를 보아라!"

Scrooge reverently did so. It was clothed in / one
스크루지는 공손하게 그렇게 했다.　유령은 입고 있었다

simple green robe, or mantle, / bordered with white
단순하게 생긴 녹색 외투나 망토같은 것만을,　하얀 모피로 가장자리를 댄.

fur. This garment hung so loosely on the figure, / that
이 옷은 아주 헐렁하게 몸에 걸쳐 있어,

its capacious breast was bare, / as if disdaining / to
유령의 넓은 가슴이 드러나 있었다,　업신여기기라도 하는 듯이

be warded or concealed / by any artifice. Its feet, /
감싸거나 숨기는 일을　일부러.　유령의 발은,

observable beneath the ample folds of the garment,
넓은 옷자락 밑으로 보이는,

/ were also bare; / and on its head / it wore no other
역시 맨발이었고;　머리에는　아무것도 쓰고 있지 않았다

covering / than a holly wreath, / set here and there with
호랑가시나무 화관 말고는,　여기 저기에 반짝이는 고드름이 달린.

shining icicles. Its dark brown curls were long and free; /
구불거리는 짙은 밤색 머리는 길게 자유 분방하게 흩어져 있었다;

free as its genial face, / its sparkling eye, / its open hand,
친절해 보이는 얼굴,　반짝이는 눈,　활짝 편 손,

/ its cheery voice, / its unconstrained demeanor, / and
쾌활한 목소리,　거침없는 태도와　명랑한

its joyful air. Girded round its middle / was an antique
분위기와 마찬가지로. 허리에 차고 있었지만　골동품같은 칼집을;

scabbard; / but no sword was in it, / and the ancient
칼은 들어있지 않고,

sheath was eaten up with rust.
그 낡은 칼집에는 녹이 슬어 있었다.

"You have never seen the like of me / before!" /
"나같은 유령은 본 적이 없을 것이다　전에!"

exclaimed the Spirit.
유령이 외쳤다.

---

reverently 공경하여 | mantle 망토, 외투 | disdaining 멸시하다, 업신여기다 | warded 피하다 | artifice 책략,
술책 | observable 관찰할 수 있는, 눈길을 끄는 | ample 광대한, 넓은 | genial 친절한, 다정한 | unconstrained
구속을 받지 않는, 자유로운 | demeanor 태도, 행동 | girded 졸라매다, 묶다 | scabbard 칼집 | sheath 칼집

"Never," / Scrooge made answer to it.
"절대 없죠," 스크루지는 대답했다.

"Have never walked forth / with the younger members
"돌아다닌 적도 없나 내 가족 중 젊은 축에 속하는 유령들과도;

of my family; / meaning / (for I am very young) / my
말하자면 (나는 아주 어리니)

elder brothers / born in these later years?" / pursued the
나의 형들과도 요 몇 년 사이에 태어난?"

Phantom.
유령은 계속해서 물었다.

"I don't think / I have," / said Scrooge. "I am afraid / I
"없던 것 같습니다 그런 적이," 스크루지는 말했다. "유감입니다 그런

have not. Have you had many brothers, / Spirit?"
적이 없어서. 형제가 많으신가요, 유령님?"

"More than eighteen hundred," / said the Ghost.
"1,800명도 넘는다," 유령이 말했다.

"A tremendous family / to provide for!" / muttered
"엄청난 대가족이군 먹여 살리기에는!"

Scrooge.
스크루지가 중얼거렸다.

The Ghost of Christmas Present rose.
현재 크리스마스 유령은 일어섰다.

"Spirit," / said Scrooge submissively, / "conduct me /
"유령님," 스크루지는 공손하게 말했다. "인도해 주십시오

where you will. I went forth last night on compulsion, /
가려는 곳으로. 어젯밤 저는 강제로 끌려 다녔고,

and I learnt a lesson / which is working now. Tonight, / if
교훈을 배웠습니다. 지금 제게 효과를 발휘하고 있는. 오늘 밤,

you have aught to teach me, / let me profit by it."
저를 가르쳐야 한다면, 많이 배우게 해 주십시오."

"Touch my robe!"
"내 옷을 잡아라!"

Scrooge did as he was told, / and held it fast.
스크루지는 들은 대로 했고,   바로 옷을 잡았다.

Holly, / mistletoe, / red berries, / ivy, / turkeys, / geese,
호랑가시나무, 겨우살이나무,   붉은 열매,   담쟁이,   칠면조,   거위,

/ game, / poultry, / brawn, / meat, / pigs, / sausages,
들짐승,   가금류,   삶은 돼지고기, 고기,   돼지,   소시지,

/ oysters, / pies, / puddings, / fruit, / and punch, / all
굴,   파이,   푸딩,   과일,   그리고 펀치 등은,

vanished instantly. So did the room, / the fire, / the
순식간에 사라졌다.   방도 사라졌고,   불도,

ruddy glow, / the hour of night, / and they stood in the
붉은 불길도,   컴컴한 밤도 그랬다,   그리고 나서 그들은 도시의 길 위에

city streets / on Christmas morning, / where / (for the
서 있었다   크리스마스 아침의,   그곳에는

weather was severe) / the people made / a rough, but
(날씨가 많이 추웠다)   사람들이 소리를 냈다

brisk and not unpleasant kind of music, / in scraping the
거칠지만, 활기차고 유쾌한 종류의 음악같은,   눈을 쓸어내면서

snow / from the pavement / in front of their dwellings, /
거리에서   살고있는 집 앞의,

and from the tops of their houses, / whence it was mad
또 지붕 위에서,   아이들에게는 아주 신나는 일이었다

delight to the boys / to see it come / plumping down into
눈을 구경하는 것은   길 아래로 털썩 떨어져서,

the road below, / and splitting into artificial little snow-
조그만 가짜 눈보라가 사방으로 튀는.

storms.

submissively 복종하게, 유순하게 | on compulsion 강요되어 | brisk 활발한, 기운찬

The house fronts looked black enough, / and the windows
집은 칙칙하게 보였고,   창문은 더 칙칙하게 보였다.

blacker, / contrasting / with the smooth white sheet of
대조되어   지붕 위의 부드럽고 하얀 눈과

snow upon the roofs, / and with the dirtier snow upon the
길 위의 좀 더 더러워진 눈과;

ground; / which last deposit had been ploughed up / in
길 위의 눈은 파헤쳐져 있었다

deep furrows / by the heavy wheels of carts and waggons;
깊은 바퀴 자국으로   짐차와 마차의 무거운 바퀴들로 인해;

/ furrows that crossed and re-crossed each other /
서로 얽힌 바퀴 자국은

hundreds of times / where the great streets branched off;
수백 번이나   큰 길이 갈라지는 곳에서;

/ and made intricate channels, / hard to trace / in the thick
얽히고 설킨 고랑을 만들어,   자취를 찾을 수 없었다

yellow mud and icy water. The sky was gloomy, / and the
두터운 황토빛 진흙과 살얼음 웅덩이에서.   하늘은 잔뜩 흐렸고,

shortest streets were choked up / with a dingy mist, / half
아주 가까운 길조차 가려져 있었다   우중충한 안개로,

thawed, / half frozen, / whose heavier particles descended
반은 녹고,   반은 얼어 있던,   안개의 무거운 입자는 쏟아져 내렸다

/ in a shower of sooty atoms, / as if all the chimneys in
거무스름한 먼지와 섞인 비가 되어,   마치 대영제국의 모든 굴뚝이,

Great Britain had, / by one consent, / caught fire, / and
모두 동의하여,   불을 지피고,

were blazing away / to their dear hearts' content. There
날려 보내는 것처럼   굴뚝 속 내용물을.

was nothing very cheerful / in the climate or the town, /
별로 즐거워할 만한 일은 없었지만   날씨나 도시 풍경에서,

and yet was there an air of cheerfulness abroad / that the
쾌활한 분위기가 가득 차 있었다

clearest summer air and brightest summer sun / might
제 아무리 청명한 여름 공기와 밝게 빛나는 여름 햇살도

have endeavored to diffuse / in vain.
발산하려고 애써봐야 헛수고가 될 것처럼.

For, / the people who were shovelling away / on the
왜냐하면, 삽으로 퍼내는 사람들이

housetops / were jovial and full of glee; / calling out
지붕에 있는 눈을   즐거워하며 기쁨에 차 있기 때문이었다;

to one another from the parapets, / and now and then
지붕 난간에서 서로 서로 소리쳐 부르다가,   가끔씩

/ exchanging a facetious snowball / — better-natured
장난스럽게 눈뭉치를 서로 던져서   — 더 좋은 무기인

missile / far than many a wordy jest — / laughing heartily
말로 하는 수많은 장난보다 —   눈뭉치에 맞으면 신나서 웃고

if it went right / and not less heartily if it went wrong.
맞지 않아도 마찬가지로 신나게 웃으며.

The poulterers' shops were still half open, / and the
닭이나 칠면조를 파는 푸줏간은 아직 반쯤 열려 있고

fruiterers' were radiant in their glory. There were great, /
과일 가게는 제철을 뽐내는 광채로 빛나고 있었다.   크고,

round, / pot-bellied baskets of chestnuts, / shaped like the
둥근,   배가 불뚝 튀어 나온 밤 바구니들은,

waistcoats of jolly old gentlemen, / lolling at the doors,
쾌활한 노신사의 조끼처럼 생긴,   문간에 널브러져 있다가,

/ and tumbling out into the street / in their apoplectic
길 위에 굴러다니기도 했다   다양한 모습으로.

opulence. There were ruddy, / brown-faced, / broad-
혈색 좋고,   다갈색 얼굴에,   넓적한 띠를 두른

girthed / Spanish Onions, / shining in the fatness of their
스페인 양파는,   살이 올라 빛났고

growth / like Spanish Friars, / and winking from their
스페인 탁발 수사들처럼,   선반에서 윙크를 던지며

shelves / in wanton slyness / at the girls / as they went by,
음란하게   아가씨들에게   지나가는,

/ and glanced demurely / at the hung-up mistletoe.
점잔을 빼며 슬쩍 쳐다보았다   걸려 있는 겨우살이나무를.

plough up (차 따위가) [도로, 지면]을 파헤치다 | furrow 자취, 바퀴자국 | intricate 뒤얽힌, 얽히고 설킨 | choke
up 막다 | particle 작은 조각 | sooty 검댕의, 그을은 | atom 파편 | consent 묵인, 허가 | diffuse 발산하다 |
parapet 난간 | facetious 익살맞은 | better-nature 양심, 좋은 쪽의 성질 | in one's glory 전성기에 | loll
축 늘어지다, 빈둥거리다 | apoplectic 중풍의 | opulence 풍부, 다양 | friar 탁발 수도사 | wanton 음란한 |
demurely 점잔 빼며

There were pears and apples, / clustered high / in
배와 사과는, 높이 쌓여 있었고

blooming pyramids; / there were bunches of grapes, /
멋있는 피라미드 모양으로; 포도 송이는,

made, / in the shopkeepers' benevolence / to dangle from
매달려 있어, 가게 주인의 자비심 때문인지 눈에 잘 띄는 고리에,

conspicuous hooks, / that people's mouths might water
사람들의 입에 군침을 돌게 했다

gratis / as they passed; / there were piles of filberts,
지나갈 때; 개암나무 열매 더미는,

/ mossy and brown, / recalling, / in their fragrance,
이끼가 낀 갈색의, 기억을 떠올리게 했다, 그 향기로,

/ ancient walks among the woods, / and pleasant
옛날 나무 사이를 걷던 때의,

shufflings ankle deep through withered leaves; / there
시든 낙엽에 발목까지 빠져 즐겁게 지척거리며;

were Norfolk Biffins, / squat and swarthy, / setting off
노퍽산 사과는, 검붉은 모습으로 웅크린 채,

the yellow of the oranges and lemons, / and, in the great
오렌지와 레몬의 노란빛을 돋보이게 하면서,

compactness of their juicy persons, / urgently entreating
과육이 풍부하고 속이 꽉 차 있어서,

and beseeching / to be carried home in paper bags /
간절히 간청하고 애원했다 종이봉투에 담겨 집에 데려가서

and eaten after dinner. The very gold and silver fish, /
저녁 식사 후에 먹어 달라고. 금색 은색의 잉어들은,

set forth among these choice fruits in a bowl, / though
이 과일들 사이의 어항에 담겨 있던,

members of a dull and stagnant-blooded race, / appeared
비록 둔하고 느릿느릿한 종족이지만, 알고 있는 듯이

to know / that there was something going on; / and, to a
보였다 무슨 일인가 벌어질 거라고; 물고기에게,

fish, / went gasping round and round / their little world /
숨을 할딱이며 빙빙 돌고 있었다 자신들의 작은 세계 안에서

in slow and passionless excitement.
느리고 침착한 흥분에 사로잡혀.

The Grocers'! Oh, the Grocers'! Nearly closed, / with
식품점! 아, 식품점이 보였다! 거의 닫혀 있거나,

perhaps two shutters down, / or one; / but through those
아마도 덧문 두 개를 열어 놓거나, 아니면 한 개만;

gaps such glimpses! It was not alone / that the scales
덧문 틈 사이로 보이는 광경이란! 한 가지가 아니었다

descending on the counter / made a merry sound, / or
계산대 위에서 내려 놓는 저울이 즐거운 소리를 내거나,

that the twine and roller parted company so briskly,
노끈 타래에서 노끈은 기운차게 작별을 고했고,

/ or that the canisters were rattled up and down / like
혹은 통조림 깡통들은 위아래로 덜컥거렸고

juggling tricks, / or even that the blended scents of tea
곡예라도 하듯, 심지어 차와 커피가 섞인 향기는

and coffee / were so grateful to the nose, / or even that
코를 엄청 향기롭게 자극했고,

the raisins were so plentiful and rare, / the almonds so
건포도는 아주 많고 최상급이었으며, 아몬드는 엄청 흰색이었으며,

extremely white, / the sticks of cinnamon so long and
막대 계피는 아주 길고 곧았고,

straight, / the other spices so delicious, / the candied
다른 향신료들도 굉장히 맛있는 것이었으며,

fruits so caked and spotted with molten sugar / as to
설탕에 절인 과일은 잘 굳고 녹인 설탕이 풍성하게 묻어 있어

make the coldest lookers-on / feel faint and subsequently
가장 무관심할 듯 한 구경꾼마저 정신을 아찔하게 하고 급기야 속을 뒤집었다.

bilious. Nor was it that the figs were moist and pulpy,
무화과는 촉촉하고 말랑말랑 했고,

/ or that the French plums blushed in modest tartness /
프랑스 자두는 적당히 새콤하게 얼굴을 붉히고 있었으며

cluster 떼지어 뒤덮다, 송이를 이루다 | blooming 번영하는, 융성하는 | benevolence 자비심, 자선 | conspicuous 잘 보이는, 눈에 잘 띄는 | gratis 무료로, 공짜로 | filbert 개암나무 열매 | shuffling 발을 끌며 걷는 | wither 시들다 | biffin 검붉은 요리용 사과 | squat 쪼그리고 앉은 | swarthy 까무잡잡한 | set off 돋보이게 하다 | entreat 애원하다 | beseech 간청하다 | stagnant 침체해 있는 | twine 노끈 | canister 깡통 | rattle 덜걱덜걱하다 | molten 열로 녹은, 용해된 | looker-on 방관자, 구경꾼 | bilious 담즙을 너무 많이 분비하는 | fig 무화과 | pulpy 연한, 걸쭉한 | tartness 시큼함

from their highly-decorated boxes, / or that everything
화려하게 장식된 상자 안에서,   모든 것이 먹음직스러워 보이고

was good to eat / and in its Christmas dress; / but the
크리스마스에 어울리게 치장하고 있었다;

customers were all so hurried / and so eager / in the
손님들은 모두 서두르고   기대에 부풀어,

hopeful promise of the day, / that they tumbled up
크리스마스에 대한 희망으로,   서로 부딪치고 넘어지거나

against each other / at the door, / crashing their wicker
문 가에서,   시장 바구니를 부딪쳐 찌그러뜨리기도

baskets wildly, / and left their purchases upon the
했고,   구입한 물건을 계산대에 두고 나와,

counter, / and came running back to fetch them, / and
물건을 가지러 허둥지둥 돌아가는 등,

committed hundreds of the like mistakes, / in the best
수백 번이나 실수를 저질렀다,

humour possible; / while the Grocer and his people were
기분이 잔뜩 들든 상태로;   상점 주인과 점원들은 솔직하고 생기 넘쳐서

so frank and fresh / that the polished hearts / with which
반짝이는 하트 모양의 단추가

they fastened their aprons behind / might have been their
앞치마를 뒤로 여미는   자기 심장처럼 보이기도 했다

own, / worn outside for general inspection, / and for
구경 삼아 밖에 내어놓아,

Christmas daws to peck at / if they chose.
갈가마귀보고 쪼아 먹도록 한   원한다면.

Key Expression

so ~ that … : 너무 ~ 해서 …하다

so + 형용사/부사 + that…는 '너무 ~해서 …하다'라는 의미로 결과를 나타내는 구문이에요. so 대신 much를 사용기도 하며, 형용사나 부사가 아닌 명사를 넣을 경우에는 so 대신 such + (a)를 사용합니다.

ex) Customers were all so hurried and so eager in the hopeful promise of the
    day, that they tumbled up against each other at the door.
    손님들은 모두 크리스마스에 대한 희망으로 서두르고 기대에 부풀어, 문 가에서
    서로 부딪치고 넘어졌다.

But soon / the steeples called good people all, / to
하지만 곧　교회의 뾰족탑의 종이 선한 사람들 모두를 부르자,

church and chapel, / and away they came, / flocking
교회와 예배당으로,　사람들이 왔다.　떼지어 거리로

through the streets / in their best clothes, / and with
가장 좋은 옷을 입고,

their gayest faces. And at the same time / there emerged
가장 즐거운 표정을 지으며.　그와 동시에　나타났다

/ from scores of bye-streets, / lanes, / and nameless
수많은 샛길,　골목길,　그리고 이름 모를 길모퉁이에서,

turnings, / innumerable people, / carrying their dinners
수많은 사람들이,　저녁거리를 들고 빵집으로 가기 위해.

to the bakers' shops. The sight of these poor revellers /
이 가난한 사람들의 흥청거리는 모습이

appeared to interest the Spirit very much, / for he stood
유령에게는 굉장히 흥미 있는 모습인 듯했다.

with Scrooge beside him / in a baker's doorway, / and
왜냐하면 유령은 스크루지를 옆에 세우고　빵집 문 앞에 서서,

taking off the covers / as their bearers passed, / sprinkled
뚜껑을 열어　빵을 가진 사람이 지나갈 때마다,　향료를 흩뿌렸으

incense / on their dinners / from his torch. And it was a
니까　사람들의 저녁거리에　유령의 횃불에서.

very uncommon kind of torch, / for once or twice / when
그것은 무척이나 범상치 않은 횃불이어서,　한두 번

there were angry words / between some dinner-carriers /
말다툼이 일어날 때에도　만찬을 나르던 사람들 사이에

who had jostled each other, / he shed a few drops of water
서로 떠밀려버린,　유령이 몇 방울의 물을 뿌리자

/ on them / from it, / and their good humour was restored
그들에게　횃불에서,　즐거운 기분은 바로 되살아났다.

directly. For they said, / it was a shame / to quarrel upon
그들은 말했다.　부끄러운 일이라고　크리스마스에 싸움을 하다니.

Christmas Day. And so it was! God love it, so it was!
부끄러운 일이었다!　하나님께 축복을!

wicker 고리버들 세공품 | daw 갈가마귀 | peck 쪼다, 쪼아서 파다 | steeple 뾰족탑 | score of 많은 | revel
한껏 즐기다, 흥청대다 | sprinkle 흩뿌리다, 끼얹다 | incense 향, 향료 | jostle (난폭하게) 떠밀다

In time the bells ceased, / and the bakers were shut up;
종소리가 그칠 무렵, 빵집도 문을 닫았지만;

/ and yet there was a genial shadowing forth / of all
따뜻한 환영이 보였다

these dinners / and the progress of their cooking, / in the
이 모든 만찬과 만찬을 준비하는 과정을 보여 주는,

thawed blotch of wet / above each baker's oven; / where
얼룩덜룩 녹은 얼룩에 각 빵집의 오븐 위의;

the pavement smoked / as if its stones were cooking too.
오븐에서는 자갈이 김을 뿜었다 돌도 함께 구워지고 있는 듯이.

"Is there a peculiar flavor / in what you sprinkle from
"무슨 특별한 향료라도 있습니까 햇불에서 가져와 뿌린 물에는?"

your torch?" / asked Scrooge.
스크루지가 물었다.

"There is. My own."
"그렇다. 나만의 향료다."

"Would it apply / to any kind of dinner / on this day?" /
"어울리는 향료입니까 저녁으로 먹는 어떤 음식에나 오늘 저녁에?"

asked Scrooge.
스크루지가 물었다.

"To any kindly given. To a poor one most."
"정성스럽게 준비된 음식에는. 가난한 자의 음식에 가장 잘 맞는다."

"Why to a poor one most?" / asked Scrooge.
"왜 가난한 자의 음식에 가장 잘 어울리죠?" 스크루지는 물었다.

"Because it needs it most."
"가난한 자의 음식이 향료를 가장 필요로 하기 때문이다."

"Spirit," / said Scrooge, / after a moment's thought, /
"유령님," 스크루지는 말했다, 잠시 생각한 후에,

"I wonder / you, / of all the beings in the many worlds
"궁금합니다 당신이, 우리가 속한 수많은 세계의 존재 가운데서,

about us, / should desire to cramp / these people's
빼앗고 싶어 하는지 이 사람들이 기회를

opportunities / of innocent enjoyment."
순수한 즐거움을 맛볼."

"I!" / cried the Spirit.
"내가!" 유령은 소리쳤다.

"You would deprive them / of their means of dining /
"당신은 그들에게서 앗아가시려 합니다   저녁 먹을 기회를

every seventh day, / often the only day / on which they
매주 주일날에,   종종 유일한 날인데

can be said to dine at all," / said Scrooge. "Wouldn't you?"
저녁다운 저녁을 먹을 수 있는."   스크루지는 말했다.   "안 그렇습니까?"

"I!" / cried the Spirit.
"내가!" 유령이 소리쳤다.

"*You seek to close these places / on the Seventh Day?"
"유령님은 이 가게들이 닫기를 원하시잖아요   주일에?"

/ said Scrooge. "And it comes to the same thing."
스크루지는 말했다.   "그리고 그것이 바로 같은 얘기지요."

"I seek!" / exclaimed the Spirit.
"내가 원했다고!" 유령은 고함을 질렀다.

"Forgive me / if I am wrong. It has been done in your
"용서하십시오   만약 제가 틀렸다면.   주일에 가게를 닫는 것은 유령님의 이름으로 행해

name, / or at least in that of your family," / said Scrooge.
져 왔습니다, 아니면 적어도 유령님 가족의 이름으로요."   스크루지는 말했다.

"There are some upon this earth of yours," / returned
"너희 인간 세상에는 그런 사람들이 있다."   유령이 대답했다.

the Spirit, / "who lay claim to know us, / and who do
"우리를 잘 안다고 주장하면서,   행하곤 하지

their deeds / of passion, / pride, / ill-will, / hatred, / envy,
욕망,   교만,   악의,   증오,   질투,

/ bigotry, / and selfishness / in our name, / who are as
편협,   그리고 이기심을   우리의 이름으로,   그러나 그들은 낯선

strange / to us and all our kith and kin, / as if they had
자들이다   우리는 물론이고 모든 일가 친척에게도   마치 그들이 세상에 살았던

never lived. Remember that, / and charge their doings on
적이 없었던 듯이.   그것을 기억해라,   그리고 그들이 한 짓에 대해 그들을 비난하라,

themselves, / not us."
우리가 아니라."

* 영국의 청교도는 주일 성수를 시행하며 주일에는 가게문을 닫도록 했다.

Scrooge promised / that he would; / and they went on,
스크루지는 약속했고   그러겠다고;   그들은 계속 갔다,

/ invisible, / as they had been before, / into the suburbs
보이지 않는 모습으로, 전에도 그래왔듯이,   도시 근교로.

of the town. It was a remarkable quality of the Ghost
유령은 놀라운 재주를 가지고 있어서

/ (which Scrooge had observed at the baker's), / that
(스크루지가 빵집에서 목격했듯이),

notwithstanding his gigantic size, / he could accommodate
거대한 덩치에도 불구하고,   몸을 맞추어 들어갈 수 있었고

himself / to any place / with ease; / and that he stood
어느 장소에서나   쉽게;   서 있을 수 있었다

/ beneath a low roof / quite as gracefully / and like a
낮은 지붕 밑에서도   우아한 자세로

supernatural creature, / as it was possible / he could have
초자연적인 존재답게,   가능할 것 같은   지붕이 높은 홀에서나.

done in any lofty hall.

And perhaps it was the pleasure / the good Spirit had /
아마 기쁨이었거나   선한 유령이 가지고 있는

in showing off this power of his, / or else it was his own
자신의 힘을 과시하는 것이,   또는 그 자신의 친절하고,

kind, / generous, / hearty nature, / and his sympathy / with
관대하고,   따뜻한 천성이거나,   동정이었을지도 모른다   모든 가

all poor men, / that led him straight to Scrooge's clerk's; /
난한 사람에 대한,   스크루지를 그의 서기 집으로 곧바로 데려간 것은;

for there he went, / and took Scrooge with him, / holding
유령은 갔고,   스크루지를 데리고,   유령의 옷을

to his robe; / and on the threshold of the door / the Spirit
잡고 있는;   집 문간에서   웃으며,

smiled, / and stopped / to bless Bob Cratchit's dwelling /
잠깐 멈췄다   밥 크래칫의 집을 축복하기 위해

notwithstanding ~임에도 불구하고 | goodly 양질의, 고급의 | confer 수여하다, 주다 | gallantly 당당하게 |
yearn 동경하다, 그리워하다

148   A Christmas Carol

with the sprinkling of his torch. Think of that! Bob had
햇불의 불꽃을 튀기게 해서.   생각해 보라!

but fifteen "*Bob" a-week himself; / he pocketed / on
밥은 일주일에 15 "밥"밖에 벌지 못한다: 주머니에 넣을 뿐이지만

Saturdays / but fifteen copies of his Christian name; / and
매주 토요일마다   자신의 기독교식 이름과 똑같은 동전 15개를:

yet the Ghost of Christmas Present blessed / his four-
그런데 현재 크리스마스 유령은 축복을 내린 것이다

roomed house!
그의 방 네 칸짜리 집에!

Then up rose Mrs. Cratchit, / Cratchit's wife, / dressed out
이때 크래칫 부인이 나타났다.   크래칫의 아내인,   초라하게 입은 모습

but poorly / in a twice-turned gown, / but brave in ribbons,
으로   천을 두 번이나 뒤집어 만든 가운을,   리본만은 화려한,

/ which are cheap / and make a goodly show for sixpence;
싸구려지만   6펜스 주고 산 옷치고는 꽤 볼 만한 옷이었다:

/ and she laid the cloth, / assisted by Belinda Cratchit, /
그의 부인은 식탁보를 깔았다.   벨린다 크래칫의 도움을 받아,

second of her daughters, / also brave in ribbons; / while
둘째 딸인,   역시 화려한 리본이 달린 옷을 입은:

Master Peter Cratchit plunged a fork / into the saucepan of
그 동안 피터 크래칫은 포크로 찔러보고 있었다   감자를 넣은 냄비 안을,

potatoes, / and getting the corners of his monstrous shirt
커다란 셔츠의 깃을 잡고서

collar / (Bob's private property, / conferred upon his son
(밥의 셔츠였는데,   대를 이을 아들에게 물려준 옷이었다

and heir / in honour of the day) / into his mouth, / rejoiced
크리스마스를 기념하여)   자꾸 입 속으로 들어갔지만,

to find himself so gallantly attired, / and yearned to show
이렇게 당당하게 차려 입을 것을 기뻐하며,   린넨 셔츠를 자랑하고 싶어 했다

his linen / in the fashionable Parks. And now two smaller
멋쟁이들이 가는 공원에 가서.   그리고 이때 더 어린 크래칫 남매가,

Cratchits, / boy and girl, / came tearing in, / screaming
사내 아이와 여자 아이인, 뛰어 들어왔다.   소리지르며

* Bob : '밥'은 1실링을 가리키는 런던 사투리

149

/ that outside the baker's they had smelt the goose, /
빵집 밖에서 거위 요리 냄새를 맡았는데,

and known it for their own; / and basking in luxurious
자기네 것인 줄 알았다며; 세이지와 양파를 먹는다는 호사스러운

thoughts of sage and onion, / these young Cratchits
생각에 행복에 겨워, 이 어린 크래칫 남매는 춤추며

danced / about the table, / and exalted Master Peter
식탁 주위를 돌았고, 피터 크래칫을 추켜 세웠다

Cratchit / to the skies, / while he / (not proud, / although
하늘 끝까지, 한편 피터는 (우쭐대지 않았다. 비록 그의 셔츠

his collars nearly choked him) / blew the fire, / until
깃이 그를 거의 질식시킬 지경이었지만) 화덕에 바람을 불러대며,

the slow potatoes bubbling up, / knocked loudly at the
감자가 부글부글 끓어 오를 때까지, 냄비 뚜껑을 야단스럽게 두드렸다

saucepan-lid / to be let out and peeled.
꺼내서 껍질을 벗겨 달라고.

"What has ever got your precious father then?" / said
"도대체 귀하신 네 아빠에게 무슨 일이 생긴 걸까?"

Mrs. Cratchit. "And your brother, / Tiny Tim! And
크래칫 부인이 말했다. "그리고 네 동생, 꼬맹이 팀은!"

Martha warn't as / late last Christmas Day / by half-an-
또 마사도 이렇게 늦지 않았지 작년 크리스마스에는 30분 정도?"

hour?"

"Here's Martha, / mother!" / said a girl, / appearing as
"여기 마사가 있어요, 엄마!" 한 소녀가 말했다,

she spoke.
말하면서 들어왔다.

"Here's Martha, / mother!" / cried the two young
"마사 누나가 왔어요, 엄마!" 어린 남매가 소리쳤다.

Cratchits. "Hurrah! There's such a goose, / Martha!"
"우와! 진짜 근사한 거위야, 마사 누나!"

"Why, / bless your heart alive, / my dear, / how late you
"세상에, 신이 축복하시길, 귀여운 내 딸, 늦었구나!"

are!" / said Mrs. Cratchit, / kissing her a dozen times,
크래칫 부인이 말했다, 딸에게 열두 번도 더 입을 맞추고는,

/ and taking off her shawl and bonnet for her / with
숄과 모자를 벗겨 주며

officious zeal.
부산을 떨면서.

"We'd a deal of work / to finish up / last night," /
"일이 많았어요 끝냈어야 하는 어젯밤에,

replied the girl, / "and had to clear away this morning, /
딸이 대답했다. "그리고 오늘 아침에 청소를 하느라 늦었어요,

mother!"
엄마!"

"Well! Never mind so long as you are come," / said Mrs.
"그래! 집에 온 이상 신경 쓰지 마라," 크래칫 부인이

Cratchit. "Sit ye down / before the fire, / my dear, / and
말했다. "앉아서 난로 앞에, 귀여운 내 딸,

have a warm, / Lord bless ye!"
불 좀 쬐렴, 신이 축복하시길!"

"No, no! There's father coming," / cried the two young
"아니, 아니야! 아빠가 오고 계세요," 어린 남매가 외쳤다.

Cratchits, / who were everywhere at once. "Hide, /
동에 번쩍 서에 번쩍하던. "숨어,

Martha, / hide!"
마사 누나, 숨어!"

bask 행복한 처지에 있다 | sage 세이지(살비아라고도 하며 카레나 돼지고기 요리의 향신료로 사용됨) | exalt
칭찬하다, 찬미하다 | officious 주제넘은 | zeal 열중, 열의

So Martha hid herself, / and in came little Bob, / the
마사가 숨고 나서, 왜소한 밥이 들어왔다, 아빠인,

father, / with at least three feet of comforter / exclusive
3피트는 족히 되는 목도리를 하고 술 장식을 제외

of the fringe, / hanging down before him; / and his
하더라도, 앞쪽에 늘어뜨린;

threadbare clothes / darned up and brushed, / to look
낡은 옷을 입고 기우고 잘 솔질한, 크리스마스답게

seasonable; / and Tiny Tim upon his shoulder. Alas for
보이려고; 팀을 무등 태우고.

Tiny Tim, / he bore a little crutch, / and had his limbs
가엾은 팀, 팀은 작은 목발을 갖고 있었고, 몸뚱이를 지탱하고 있었다

supported / by an iron frame!
철로 된 의족으로!

"Why, / where's our Martha?" / cried Bob Cratchit, /
"그런데, 우리 마사는 어디 있지?" 밥 크래칫이 외쳤다,

looking round.
방 안을 둘러보며.

"Not coming," / said Mrs. Cratchit.
"오지 않았어요," 크래칫 부인이 말했다.

"Not coming!" / said Bob, / with a sudden declension /
"오지 않았다고!" 밥이 말했다, 갑자기 꺾이면서

in his high spirits; / for he had been Tim's blood horse /
들뜬 기분이; 그는 팀의 순종 말 역할을 하면서

all the way from church, / and had come home rampant.
교회에서 오는 동안 내내, 집으로 활기차게 왔는데.

"Not coming upon Christmas Day!"
"크리스마스인데 안 왔다고!"

Martha didn't like to see him disappointed, / if it were
마사는 아빠가 실망하시는 모습을 보고 싶지 않아서,

only in joke; / so she came out prematurely / from behind
아무리 장난일지라도; 계획보다 빨리 뛰어 나와 옷장 문 뒤에서,

the closet door, / and ran into his arms, / while the two
아빠의 품 속으로 뛰어 들었다,

young Cratchits hustled Tiny Tim, / and bore him off
어린 남매는 팀에게 달려가, 부엌으로 데려갔다.

into the wash-house, / that he might hear the pudding
팀이 푸딩의 부글부글 노래하는 소리를 들을 수 있도록

singing / in the copper.
구리 냄비 속에서.

"And how did little Tim behave?" / asked Mrs. Cratchit, /
"팀은 어땠어요?" 크래칫 부인이 물었다,

when she had rallied Bob on his credulity, / and Bob had
밥이 남의 말을 너무 쉽게 믿는다고 놀리고,

hugged his daughter / to his heart's content.
그가 딸을 껴안고 나서 따뜻하게.

"As good as gold," / said Bob, / "and better. Somehow
"정말 착했지." 밥이 말했다, "아니 그 이상이었지.

he gets thoughtful, / sitting by himself so much, / and
아무래도 생각에 잠겨 있더니, 혼자 오랫동안 앉아서,

thinks the strangest things / you ever heard. He told me,
아주 희한한 생각을 해 냈다오 당신이 들어 본 적이 없는. 팀이 내게 말했어요,

/ coming home, / that he hoped / the people saw him in
집에 오면서, 바란다고 교회 안에 있는 사람들이 자기를 봤기를.

the church, / because he was a cripple, / and it might be
자기가 절름발이이니까, 아마 사람들이 자기를 보고

pleasant to them / to remember upon Christmas Day, /
기뻐했을 거라고 크리스마스에 기억해 낼 수 있을 테니,

who made lame beggars walk, / and blind men see."
앉은뱅이를 걷게 하고, 장님의 눈을 뜨게 한 분을."

Bob's voice was tremulous / when he told them this, /
밥의 목소리는 떨리고 있었고 이 말을 할 때,

and trembled more / when he said / that Tiny Tim was
심지어 더 떨렸다 말할 때

growing strong and hearty.
팀이 강하고 튼튼하게 자라고 있다고.

threadbare 닳아서 실밥이 보이는, 낡은 | darn 깁다 | crutch 목발 | declension 격변 | rampant 맹렬한 |
wash-house 세탁장 | rally ~을 놀리다 | credulity 너무 쉽게 믿는 성질 | lame 절름발이의

His active little crutch was heard upon the floor, / and
팀의 작고 활기찬 목발 소리가 위층에서 들렸고,

back came Tiny Tim / before another word was spoken,
팀은 되돌아 왔다   엄마 아빠가 이야기를 더 나누기 전에

/ escorted by his brother and sister / to his stool before
누나와 형의 부축을 받아   난롯가에 있는 그의 의자로;

the fire; / and while Bob, / turning up his cuffs / — as
그리고 밥은,   소맷자락을 걷어 올리고   — 마치,

if, / poor fellow, / they were capable of being made more
불쌍한 친구,   더 초라한 꼴이 될 수 있다고 보여 주기라도 하듯이

shabby / — compounded some hot mixture / in a jug /
— 뜨거운 음료에 섞어서

with gin and lemons, / and stirred it round and round
진과 레몬을,   휘휘 저은 후

/ and put it on the hob / to simmer; / Master Peter, /
벽난로의 시렁 위에 올려 놓았다 끓이려고;   피터와,

and the two ubiquitous young Cratchits / went to fetch
동에 번쩍 서에 번쩍 하는 꼬마 남매는   거위를 가지러 갔고,

the goose, / with which they soon returned / in high
거위와 함께 곧 다시 돌아왔다   당당하게 행진하며.

procession.

Such a bustle ensued / that you might have thought / a
그런 소동이 계속 일어나는 것을 보고 여러분은 생각했을지도 모른다

goose the rarest of all birds; / a feathered phenomenon,
거위가 세상에서 가장 진귀한 새라도 된다고;   이 깃털 달린 짐승에는,

/ to which a black swan was a matter of course / — and
그런 짐승에서는 흑고니가 대단한 존재이지만   — 그리고

in truth / it was something very like it in that house.
사실   거위는 이 집에서 흑고니만큼의 대접을 받았다.

---

shabby 초라한 | compound 뒤섞다, 혼합하다 | jug 주전자 | hob 벽난로 안쪽의 시렁 | simmer (요리 따위가)
부글부글 끓다 | ubiquitous 도처에 존재하는 | in procession 행렬을 지어 | bustle 야단 법석, 소동 | ensue
계속되다, 잇달아 일어나다 | dust 먼지를 닦아내다 | cram 억지로 밀어 넣다 | shriek 날카로운 소리를 지르다 |
grace 감사 기도 | carving-knife (고기 써는 데 쓰는) 대형 나이프 | gush 솟아 나오다

Mrs. Cratchit made the gravy / (ready beforehand in
크래칫 부인은 육수를 끓였다 (작은 냄비에 미리 준비해 둔)

a little saucepan) / hissing hot; / Master Peter mashed
아주 뜨겁게; 피터는 감자를 으깼다

the potatoes / with incredible vigour; / Miss Belinda
믿을 수 없을 만큼 힘차게;

sweetened up the apple-sauce; / Martha dusted the hot
벨린다는 사과 소스에 설탕을 넣었고; 마사는 뜨거운 접시를 닦았다;

plates; / Bob took Tiny Tim beside him / in a tiny corner
밥이 팀을 옆자리에 앉혔다 식탁의 한 구석에 있는;

at the table; / the two young Cratchits set chairs for
어린 남매는 식구들이 앉을 의자를 준비하고,

everybody, / not forgetting themselves, / and mounting
자기 자리를 잊지 않고,

guard upon their posts, / crammed spoons into their
자기 자리에서 망을 보며, 숟가락으로 입을 누르고 있었다.

mouths, / lest they should shriek for goose / before their
거위를 달라고 소리치지 않도록

turn came to be helped. At last / the dishes were set on,
자신들의 차례가 오기 전에. 마침내 접시가 준비되었고,

/ and grace was said. It was succeeded by a breathless
감사 기도를 올렸다. 숨죽인 순간이 이어졌다,

pause, / as Mrs. Cratchit, / looking slowly all along the
크래칫 부인은, 고기 써는 칼을 찬찬히 살펴본 후,

carving-knife, / prepared to plunge it in the breast; /
거위의 가슴에 찌를 준비를 했다;

but when she did, / and when the long expected gush of
그녀가 칼을 찔러 넣고, 오랫동안 기다렸던 거위 속을 채운 재료가 밖으로 솟아 나오자,

stuffing issued forth, / one murmur of delight arose / all
기쁨의 속삭임이 맴돌았으며

round the board, / and even Tiny Tim, / excited by the
식탁 주위에, 심지어 팀까지도,

two young Cratchits, / beat on the table with the handle
어린 남매를 따라 덩달아 신이 나서, 나이프의 손잡이를 잡고 식탁을 두드렸고,

of his knife, / and feebly cried Hurrah!
가냘프게 만세하고 외쳤다!

There never was such a goose. Bob said / he didn't
이렇게 훌륭한 거위는 처음이었다.   밥은 말했다   믿을 수 없다고

believe / there ever was such a goose cooked. Its
이렇게 훌륭하게 요리된 거위가 또 있을지.

tenderness and flavour, / size and cheapness, / were the
거위 고기의 부드러움과 향미,   크기와 싼 가격은,

themes of universal admiration. Eked out by apple-sauce
모든 식구의 감탄의 대상이었다.

and mashed potatoes, / it was a sufficient dinner / for the
사과 소스와 으깬 감자를 보충하니,   충분한 저녁이 되었다

whole family; / indeed, / as Mrs. Cratchit said with great
모든 식구에게;   정말로,   크래칫 부인이 아주 기뻐하며 말했다

delight / (surveying one small atom of a bone / upon the
즐겁게 (조금밖에 되지 않는 뼈를 바라보면서   접시 위의),

dish), / they hadn't ate it all at last! Yet everyone had
결국은 다 먹지도 못했다고!   그러나 모두 배부르게 먹었고,

had enough, / and the youngest Cratchits in particular,
                특히 어린 남매는,

/ were steeped in sage and onion / to the eyebrows! But
  세이지와 양파에 푹 빠져 있었다   눈썹에 붙일 정도로!   하지만

now, / the plates being changed by Miss Belinda, / Mrs.
이제,   벨린다가 접시를 바꾸자,

Cratchit left the room alone / — too nervous / to bear
크래칫 부인은 홀로 방을 나가   — 매우 긴장하여

witnesses — / to take the pudding up and bring it in.
누군가 볼까 봐 —   푸딩을 갖고 들어왔다.

Suppose / it should not be done enough! Suppose / it
만약   푸딩이 잘 익지 않았다면!   만약

should break in turning out! Suppose / somebody should
꺼내다가 모양을 망치기라도 한다면!   만약   누군가 벽을 타고 넘어와

have got over the wall / of the back-yard, / and stolen it, /
                        뒤뜰의,   푸딩을 훔쳐간다면,

universal 전체의 | eke out ～의 부족을 메우다 | an atom of 소량의 | steep ～을 담그다, 적시다 |
supposition 상상, 추측, 가정 | livid 잿빛의, 창백한 | laundress 세탁부 | flush 얼굴 붉힘 | speckle
얼룩덜룩하게 하다 | cannon-ball 포탄 | ignite 불을 붙이다, 점화하다 | bedight 꾸미다, 장식하다

while they were merry with the goose / — a supposition
그들이 거위를 먹으며 기뻐하고 있는 동안   — 그런 가정이 사실이라면

at which / the two young Cratchits became livid! All
두 어린 남매는 얼굴이 새파래질 텐데!

sorts of horrors were supposed.
모든 종류의 끔찍한 일을 상상했다.

Hallo! A great deal of steam! The pudding was out of
우와!   무럭무럭 피어나는 김!   푸딩을 구리 냄비에서 꺼냈다.

the copper. A smell like a washing-day! That was the
빨래하는 날 같은 냄새!   그것은 빨래 냄새였다.

cloth. A smell / like an eating-house and a pastrycook's
냄새였다   마치 식당과 빵집 옆에 나란히 붙어 있는,

next door to each other, / with a laundress's next door
그 옆집 세탁부에게서 나는 냄새였다!

to that! That was the pudding! In half a minute / Mrs.
그것이 푸딩이었다!   잠시 후

Cratchit entered / — flushed, but smiling proudly — /
크래칫 부인이 들어갔다   — 상기됐지만, 자랑스럽게 미소지으며 —

with the pudding, / like a speckled cannon-ball, / so hard
푸딩을 들고,   알록달록한 포탄같이 생긴,   아주 단단하

and firm, / blazing in half of half-a-quartern of ignited
게 굳은,   브랜디를 아주 조금 끼얹어 불을 붙이고,

brandy, / and bedight with Christmas holly stuck / into
호랑나무가시 잎으로 장식해 놓았다

the top.
꼭대기에는.

Oh, a wonderful pudding! Bob Cratchit said, / and
아, 이 근사한 푸딩이군!   밥 크래칫이 말했다,

calmly too, / that he regarded it / as the greatest success
역시 침착하게,   생각한다고   최고의 걸작이라고

/ achieved by Mrs. Cratchit / since their marriage. Mrs.
크래칫 부인이 만든 것 중   결혼 이후로.

Cratchit said / that now the weight was off her mind, / she
크래칫 부인은 말하며   이제 마음의 짐이 사라졌다고,

would confess / she had had her doubts about the quantity
고백했다   밀가루 분량에 좀 걱정을 하고 있었다고.

of flour. Everybody had something to say about it, / but
모두 그 푸딩에 대해 한 마디씩 했지만,

nobody said or thought / it was at all a small pudding for a
아무도 말하거나 생각하지 않았다   이런 대가족이 먹기에는 너무 작은 푸딩이라고.

large family. It would have been flat heresy / to do so. Any
분명히 이단자가 되었으리라   그렇게 했다면.

Cratchit would have blushed / to hint at such a thing.
크래칫 가족 누구라도 부끄럽게 생각했을 것이다   그런 얘기를 비치는 것만으로도.

At last the dinner was all done, / the cloth was cleared, /
마침내 만찬이 끝나자,   식탁보를 걷고,

the hearth swept, / and the fire made up. The compound
난로 주위를 치우고,   불을 지폈다.

in the jug being tasted, / and considered perfect, / apples
주전자 안의 혼합주 맛을 보니,   완벽했고,

and oranges were put upon the table, / and a shovel-full
사과와 오렌지를 식탁에 올려 놓고,   밤 한 삽을 난로에 넣었다.

of chestnuts on the fire. Then all the Cratchit family drew
그리고는 크래칫 가족 모두 난로 주위에 모여 앉았고,

round the hearth, / in what Bob Cratchit called a circle, /
밥 크래칫은 원 모양이라고 했지만,

meaning half a one; / and at Bob Cratchit's elbow stood /
사실은 반원 모양으로;   밥 크래칫의 팔꿈치에 놓여 있었다

the family display of glass. Two tumblers, / and a custard-
가족이 가진 유리잔 모두가.   큰 잔 두 개와,

cup without a handle.
손잡이가 없는 커스터드 잔 하나.

These held the hot stuff from the jug, / however, / as well
이 잔들에 주전자 안의 음료를 담자. 그러나,

as golden goblets would have done; / and Bob served it out
황금 술잔만큼의 역할을 했고; 밥은 식구들에게 나누어 주었다

/ with beaming looks, / while the chestnuts on the fire /
기쁨에 넘치는 표정으로, 난롯불 위의 밤이

sputtered and cracked noisily. Then Bob proposed:
타닥타닥 소리를 내며 요란스럽게 갈라지는 동안. 그리고 나서 밥은 말했다:

"A Merry Christmas to us all, / my dears. God bless us!"
"모두 메리 크리스마스, 내 사랑하는 가족들. 하나님의 은총이 가득하길!"

Which all the family re-echoed.
그 말에 모두들 되풀이 해서 대답했다.

"God bless us every one!" / said Tiny Tim, / the last of all.
"하나님의 은총이 우리 모두에게 가득하길!" 팀이 말했다. 마지막으로.

He sat very close to his father's side / upon his little stool.
팀은 아빠 곁에 바짝 붙어 앉아 있었다 작은 의자 위에서.

Bob held his withered little hand in his, / as if he loved the
밥은 팀의 야윈 작은 손을 잡고 있었다. 그 아이를 사랑하고,

child, / and wished to keep him by his side, / and dreaded
곁에 두고 싶어 하고, 염려된다는 듯이

/ that he might be taken from him.
누군가 빼앗아갈까 봐.

"Spirit," / said Scrooge, / with an interest / he had never
"유령님." 스크루지가 말했다. 관심을 가지며 한 번도 느낀 적 없는,

felt before, / "tell me / if Tiny Tim will live."
"말해 주세요 팀이 살 수 있을지."

"I see a vacant seat," / replied the Ghost, / "in the poor
"빈 의자가 보인다." 유령이 대답했다.

chimney-corner, / and a crutch without an owner, /
"저 초라한 굴뚝 모퉁이에, 주인 없는 목발과 함께,

carefully preserved. If these shadows remain unaltered /
소중히 보존되어 있는. 만약 이 환영들이 바뀌지 않는다면

by the Future, / the child will die."
미래에, 저 아이는 죽을 것이다."

---

heresy 이단 | sputter 탁탁 튀다 | dread 염려하다, 걱정하다

"No, no," / said Scrooge. "Oh, no, / kind Spirit! / say / he
"안 됩니다, 안 돼요," 스크루지가 말했다. "아, 안 돼요, 자비로우신 유령님! 말해 주세요

will be spared."
저 아이가 살 수 있을 거라고."

"If these shadows remain unaltered / by the Future, /
"만약 이 환영들이 바뀌지 않는다면 미래에,

none other of my race," / returned the Ghost, / "will find
우리 중 누구도," 유령은 대답했다, "저 애를 여기에서

him here. What then? If he be like to die, / he had better
볼 수 없을 것이다. 무슨 상관인가? 만약 저 애가 죽기로 되어 있다면, 죽는 것이 낫지 않은가,

do it, / and decrease the surplus population."
인구 과잉도 줄어들 테고."

Scrooge hung his head / to hear his own words quoted
스크루지는 고개를 떨구고 자신이 했던 말을 인용하는 것을 들으며

/ by the Spirit, / and was overcome with penitence and
유령이, 뉘우침과 비탄에 휩싸였다.

grief.

"Man," / said the Ghost, / "if man you be in heart, / not
"인간아," 유령이 말했다, "만약 네가 심장이 들어 있는 인간이라면, 단단한

adamant, / forbear that wicked cant / until you have
돌이 아니라, 그런 고약한 말은 삼가라 발견할 때까지

discovered / What the surplus is, / and Where it is. Will
인구과잉이 무엇인지, 그리고 그것이 어디에 있는지.

you decide / what men shall live, / what men shall die?
네가 결정하겠는가 어떤 사람들이 살아야 하고, 어떤 사람들이 죽어야 하는지?

It may be, / that in the sight of Heaven, / you are more
보일 것이다, 하늘에서 보면,

worthless and less fit to live / than millions / like this
네가 쓸모없고 살 가치가 없는 인간으로 수백만 명보다

poor man's child. Oh God! To hear the Insect on the leaf
이 가난한 사내의 아이들보다. 오 신이시여! 나뭇잎에 붙은 벌레가 말하는 것을 들어야 하다니

pronouncing / on the too much life / among his hungry
너무 많은 생명이라고

brothers in the dust!"
굶주리고 있는 제 형제들 사이에서!"

penitence 회개, 뉘우침 | adamant 단단한 돌 | forbear 삼가다, 보류하다 | wicked 사악한, 행실이 고약한, 심술궂은 | cant 위선적인 말 | pronounce 단언하다 | in the dust 굴욕을 당하여

Scrooge bent before the Ghost's rebuke, / and trembling
스크루지는 유령의 호된 꾸지람에 고개를 숙이고,   벌벌 떨며 눈을 떨구었다

cast his eyes / upon the ground. But he raised them
        땅 위로.   하지만 그는 재빨리 고개를 들었다,

speedily, / on hearing his own name.
            자기 이름이 나오는 소리를 듣고.

"Mr. Scrooge!" / said Bob; / "I'll give you Mr. Scrooge, /
"스크루지 씨!"   밥이 말했다;   "스크루지 씨를 위해 건배하자,

the Founder of the Feast!"
이 향연을 베풀어 주신!"

"The Founder of the Feast indeed!" / cried Mrs. Cratchit,
"참도도 이 향연을 베풀어 주셨군요!"   크래칫 부인이 소리쳤다,

/ reddening. "I wish / I had him here. I'd give him a piece
얼굴이 벌개져서.   "좋겠군요   그 사람이 여기 있다면.   내 속에 있는 말 좀 해서

of my mind / to feast upon, / and I hope he'd have a good
속이 후련하게,   욕으로 배 좀 부르라고요."

appetite for it."

"My dear," / said Bob, / "the children! Christmas Day."
"여보,"   밥이 말했다.   "아이들이 들어요!   크리스마스잖소."

"It should be Christmas Day, / I am sure," / said she, /
"크리스마스가 틀림없군요,   분명히 말하지만," 그녀는 말했다.

"on which one drinks the health / of such an odious, /
"건배를 들자고 하다니   그런 추악하고,

stingy, / hard, man / as Mr. Scrooge. You know / he is,
인색하며,   냉혹한 사람을 위해 스크루지 씨 같은.   알잖아요   그 사람을,

/ Robert! Nobody knows it better than you do, / poor
로버트!   당신만큼 잘 아는 사람도 없죠

fellow!"
불쌍한 양반!'

---

rebuke 비난, 책망 | cast (눈을) 돌리다 | redden 얼굴을 붉히다 | feast 눈, 귀를 즐겁게 하다 | health 건배, 축배
| odious 추악한 | toast 건배하다 | twopence 조금도, 전연 | ogre 추한 사람, 사람 잡아먹는 귀신 | dispel 쫓아
버리다

"My dear," / was Bob's mild answer, / "Christmas Day."
"여보," 밥이 부드럽게 대답했다. "크리스마스잖소."

"I'll drink his health / for your sake and the Day's," / said
"영감님의 건강을 위해 건배하죠 당신과 크리스마스를 위해."

Mrs. Cratchit, / "not for his. Long life to him! A merry
크래칫 부인은 말했다. "그 사람이 아니죠. 그 사람이 오래 살기를!

Christmas and a happy new year! He'll be very merry
메리 크리스마스 그리고 해피 뉴 이어! 영감님은 즐겁고 행복하겠지요,

and very happy, / I have no doubt!"
의심할 바 없어!"

The children drank the toast after her. It was the first of
아이들이 부인 다음에 건배했다. 이 축배가 처음이었다

their proceedings / which had no heartiness. Tiny Tim
마지못해 진행했던 일은.

drank it last of all, / but he didn't care twopence for it.
팀이 마지막으로 건배했지만, 조금도 신경 쓰지 않았다.

Scrooge was the Ogre of the family. The mention of his
스크루지는 가족에게 싫은 존재였다. 그의 이름을 거론하는 것만으로도

name / cast a dark shadow on the party, / which was not
파티에 어두운 그림자가 드리워졌다.

dispelled for full five minutes.
5분 동안이나 사라지지 않는.

Key Expression 🎵

배수 비교 표현하기

'~보다 몇 배, ~의 몇 배'를 나타내는 배수 비교는 원급과 비교급의 두 가지로 표현할 수 있습니다.

▶ 배수 + as + 형용사/부사 + as +비교할 대상
▶ 배수 + 형용사/부사의 비교급 + than + 비교할 대상
  * 배수의 자리에는 twice(2배), three times(3배), half(절반) 등의 단어를 넣어 표현합니다.

ex) After it had passed away, they were ten times merrier than before.
    그것이 사라진 후, 그들은 전보다 10배나 더 즐거워했다.

163

After it had passed away, / they were ten times merrier /
사악한 그림자가 사라진 후,　　　　가족들은 10배 더 즐거워졌다

than before, / from the mere relief / of Scrooge the Baleful
전보다,　　　약간의 안도감에　　　고약한 스크루지에게 해야 할 것을

being done with. Bob Cratchit told them / how he had a
했다는.　　　밥 크래칫은 가족에게 말했다

situation in his eye for Master Peter, / which would bring
피터를 위한 일자리가 있는데,　　　그 일로 벌 수 있다고,

in, / if obtained, / full five-and-sixpence weekly. The
만약 취직이 된다면,　일주일에 5실링 반은 충분히.

two young Cratchits laughed tremendously / at the idea
어린 크래칫 남매는 신나게 웃어 젖혔고

of Peter's being a man of business; / and Peter himself
피터가 일을 하게 된다는 생각에;　　　피터 자신은 생각에 잠긴 듯이

looked thoughtfully / at the fire / from between his collars,
보였다　　　난로를 바라봤다　옷깃에 파묻혀,

/ as if he were deliberating / what particular investments
심사숙고라도 하는 듯이　　　어떤 특별한 투자를 해야 할지

he should favour / when he came into the receipt / of that
받게 된다면

bewildering income. Martha, / who was a poor apprentice
그렇게 엄청난 수입을.　　　마사는,　　　숙녀용 모자 가게에서 일하는 가난한

at a milliner's, / then told them / what kind of work she
견습공인,　　　가족들에게 말했고　　　어떤 일들을 해야만 했는지,

had to do, / and how many hours she worked / at a stretch,
얼마나 오랜 시간 동안 일했는지　　　쉬지 않고,

/ and how she meant to lie abed / tomorrow morning / for
그리고 얼마나 오래 침대에 누워 있을 생각인지　내일 아침에　　　길고

a good long rest; / tomorrow being a holiday / she passed
달콤한 휴식을 취하기 위해;　내일은 휴일이니까　　　집에서 시간을 보낼

at home. Also how she had seen / a countess and a lord
것이다.　또 마사가 어떻게 보았으며　　　백작 부인과 그 아들을

/ some days before, / and how the lord "was much about
며칠 전에,　　　그 아들이 "키가 피터만 했다"고 얘기했고,

as tall as Peter;" / at which Peter pulled up his collars so
그 말에 피터는 옷깃을 너무 높이 세워

high / that you couldn't have seen his head / if you had
얼굴을 볼 수 없었을 것이다   여러분이 그 자리에

been there. All this time / the chestnuts and the jug went
있었다면.   이런 이야기가 오가는 동안 밤과 주전자가 몇 번이나 돌고 돌았고;

round and round; / and by-and-bye they had a song, /
                        이윽고 그들은 노래를 불렀다.

about a lost child travelling in the snow, / from Tiny
눈 속에서 길을 잃고 헤매는 아이에 대한,   팀은,

Tim, / who had a plaintive little voice, / and sang it very
가냘픈 작은 목소리를 가진,   그 노래를 정말로 잘 불렀다.

well indeed.

There was nothing of high mark in this. They were not
이 가족에게는 특별한 점이 없었다.

a handsome family; / they were not well dressed; / their
외모가 훌륭한 집안도 아니었고;   옷을 잘 차려 입은 것도 않았다:

shoes were far from being water-proof; / their clothes
신발은 방수가 되지 않았고;   옷은 허름했으며;

were scanty; / and Peter might have known, / and very
            피터는 알고 있는 듯 했다.

likely did, / the inside of a pawnbroker's. But, / they
진짜 그랬다,   전당포 출입을 많이 해서.   하지만,

were happy, / grateful, / pleased with one another, / and
그들은 행복했고,   감사했고,   서로 즐거워하며,

contented with the time; / and when they faded, / and
그 시간에 만족했다;   그리고 그들의 모습이 사라져갈 때,

looked happier yet / in the bright / sprinklings of the
더욱 행복해 보였다   반짝임 속에서   유령의 횃불에서 뿌려진

Spirit's torch / at parting, / Scrooge had his eye upon
              헤어질 때,   스크루지는 시선을 그들에게 고정했다,

them, / and especially on Tiny Tim, / until the last.
특히 팀에게,   마지막까지.

---

baleful 악의가 있는, 사악한 | situation 지위, 일자리 | obtained 목적을 달성하다 | deliberate 심사숙고하다
| bewilder 당혹케 하는 | milliner 여성 모자 판매인 | abed 침대에, 잠자리에 | countess 백작부인 | by-and-
bye 이윽고, 곧 | plaintive 구슬픈, 가련한 | scanty 옹색한 | pawnbroker 전당포

A. 다음 문장을 해석해 보세요.

(1) Now, / being prepared for almost anything, / he was not by any means / prepared for nothing.
→

(2) The very gold and silver fish, / set forth among these choice fruits in a bowl, / though members of a dull and stagnant-blooded race, / appeared to know / that there was something going on.
→

(3) Because he was a cripple, / and it might be pleasant to them / to remember upon Christmas Day, / who made lame beggars walk, / and blind men see.
→

(4) The two young Cratchits set chairs for everybody, / not forgetting themselves, / and mounting guard upon their posts, / crammed spoons into their mouths, / lest they should shriek for goose / before their turn came to be helped.
→

B. 다음 주어진 문장이 되도록 빈칸에 써서 넣으세요.

(1) 그는 딱 알맞은 때에 의식이 돌아왔다고 느꼈다.

He felt that he was restored to consciousness ＿＿＿＿＿＿
＿＿＿＿＿＿＿＿＿＿＿ .

(2) 팀이 살 수 있을지 말해 주세요.

→

(3) 그 사람이 여기 있다면 좋겠는데.

→

(4) 그것이 사라진 후, <u>그들은 전보다 10배나 더 즐거워 했다</u>.

After it had passed away, ▯▯▯▯▯▯▯▯▯▯▯▯▯▯▯▯▯▯▯▯▯▯▯▯▯▯▯▯▯

▯▯▯▯▯▯▯ .

C. 다음 주어진 문구가 알맞은 문장이 되도록 순서를 맞춰 보세요.

(1) 집에 온 이상 신경 쓰지 마라.
   (as / mind / come / so / Never / are / you / long)
   →

(2) 이렇게 훌륭한 거위는 없었다.
   (never / a / There / was / goose / such)
   →

(3) 결국은 다 먹지도 못했다.
   (hadn't / They / it / ate / last / all / at)
   →

(4) 당신보다 더 잘 아는 사람은 없다.
   (than / knows / Nobody / it / better / do / you)
   →

D. 다음 단어에 대한 맞는 설명과 연결해 보세요.

(1) spontaneous ▶   ◀ ① not planned or arranged

(2) artifice   ▶   ◀ ② speak severely

(3) beseech   ▶   ◀ ③ clever use of tricks and devices

(4) rebuke   ▶   ◀ ④ ask very eagerly and anxiously

기쁨이 될 수도 있다. 크리스마스의 주인공은 앉은뱅이를 걷게 하고, 장님의 눈을 뜨게 했으니까. (4) 두 꼬
마 크래칫 남매는 자신들의 자리를 잊지 않고 식구들이 앉을 의자를 준비했으며, 자기 초소에서 망을 보며,
자신들의 맘껏 먹을 차례가 오기 전에 거위를 달라고 소리치지 않도록 숟가락으로 입을 틀어막았다. | B. (1)
in the right nick of time (2) if Tiny Tim will live (3) I wish I had him here. (4) they were ten times merrier
than before | C. (1) Never mind so long as you are come. (2) There never was such a goose. (3) they
hadn't ate it all at last. (4) Nobody knows it better than you do. | D. (1) ① (2) ③ (3) ④ (4) ②

THE SECOND OF THE THREE SPIRITS II
두 번째 유령 II

By this time it was getting dark, / and snowing pretty
이때쯤 날이 어두워져 갔고,   함박눈이 펑펑 내렸다;

heavily; / and as Scrooge and the Spirit went along the
스크루지와 유령은 길을 걸어갈 때,

streets, / the brightness of the roaring fires / in kitchens,
타오르는 듯한 밝은 불길은   부엌,

/ parlors, / and all sorts of rooms, / was wonderful. Here,
거실,   그리고 모든 방에서 새어 나오는,   대단했다.   여기에서,

/ the flickering of the blaze showed / preparations for
어른거리는 불길은 보여 주었고   아늑한 저녁을 준비하는 모습을,

a cosy dinner, / with hot plates baking / through and
뜨거운 접시를 데우며   난로마다,

through before the fire, / and deep red curtains, / ready
짙은 붉은색의 커튼은,   드리워질

to be drawn / to shut out cold and darkness. There all the
준비가 되어 있었다   추위와 어둠을 막기 위해.

children of the house / were running out into the snow
집 안의 모든 아이들은   눈 위로 뛰어 나왔다

/ to meet / their married sisters, brothers, / cousins, /
맞이하며   결혼한 형제 자매,   사촌,

uncles, / aunts, / and be the first to greet them. Here, /
삼촌,   숙모들과,   가장 먼저 인사하기 위해.   여기,

again, / were shadows / on the window-blind / of guests
다시,   그림자가 비쳤고   블라인드가 내려진 창문에

assembling; / and there a group of handsome girls, /
모여 있는 손님들의;   어여쁜 아가씨 한 무리가,

all hooded and fur-booted, / and all chattering at once,
모두 모자를 쓰고 털부츠를 신은 채,   한꺼번에 수다를 떨다가,

---

through and through 모조리, 속속들이 | woe 비난, 비통 | in a glow 얼굴이 벌겋게 달아 올라 | exult 크게
기뻐하다, 환희하다 | outpour 흘려 보내다, 유출하다 | mirth 명랑, 유쾌한 법석 | dot 산재하다 | dusky 어스레한
| speck 반점 | ken 알다, 이해하다

/ tripped lightly off / to some near neighbor's house; /
경쾌하게 몰려갔다　　이웃집으로;

where, / woe upon the single man / who saw them enter
그 집에는,　고민에 빠진 총각이 있었다　아가씨들이 들어오는 걸 보고

/ — artful witches, / well they knew it — / in a glow!
— 앙큼한 마녀들,　다 알고 있었다 —　얼굴이 벌개진!

But, / if you had judged from the numbers of people /
하지만,　사람들 숫자만으로 판단한다면

on their way to friendly gatherings, / you might have
정겨운 모임에 가고 있는,　생각했을지도 모른다

thought / that no one was at home / to give them welcome
집에 아무도 없을 거라고　손님을 맞이하는

/ when they got there, / instead of every house expecting
그들이 도착했을 때,　집집마다 손님들을 기다리며,

company, / and piling up its fires half-chimney high.
굴뚝 가까이까지 장작을 쌓아 놓고 기다리기는 커녕.

Blessings on it, / how the Ghost exulted! How it bared
그곳에 축복을 내리며,　유령이 얼마나 기뻐했는지!

its breadth of breast, / and opened its capacious palm,
넓은 가슴을 드러내고,　널찍한 손바닥을 벌려,

/ and floated on, / outpouring, / with a generous hand,
떠다니든지,　자비롭게 축복하며,　자비로운 손으로,

/ its bright and harmless mirth / on everything within
그 빛나고 이로운 축복을　손에 닿는 것이면 무엇이든!

its reach! The very lamplighter, / who ran on before, /
그 점등원은,　달려가다가,

dotting the dusky street with specks of light, / and who
어슴프레한 거리에 불을 밝히며,

was dressed / to spend the evening somewhere, / laughed
옷을 차려 입고서　어디선가 저녁 시간을 보내려는지,　크게 소리 내

out loudly / as the Spirit passed, / though little kenned the
어 웃었다　유령이 지나갈 때,　하지만 점등원은 몰랐으리라

lamplighter / that he had any company / but Christmas!
길동무가 있다는 사실을　크리스마스 외에는!

And now, / without a word of warning from the Ghost,
이제, 유령에게서 어떤 경고의 말도 없이,

/ they stood upon a bleak and desert moor, / where
그들은 황량하고 버려진 황무지에 서 있었다,

monstrous masses of rude stone were cast about, / as
그곳에는 거친 바위 덩어리가 널려 있고,

though it were the burial-place of giants; / and water
마치 거인의 묘지처럼; 물이 제멋대로

spread itself / wheresoever it listed, / or would have done
흘러가며 어디에나 고랑을 만들었고, 혹은 그렇게 흘러갔으리라,

so, / but for the frost / that held it prisoner; / and nothing
서리만 없었다면 죄수처럼 가둔; 아무것도 자라지 않는,

grew / but moss and furze, and coarse rank grass. Down
이끼와 가시금작화와 잡초 외에. 서쪽 하늘

in the west / the setting sun had left a streak of fiery red,
에서는 지는 해가 타는 듯한 붉은 광선을 남기며,

/ which glared upon the desolation / for an instant, / like
황야를 노려보다가 한 순간,

a sullen eye, / and frowning / lower, lower, lower yet, /
성난 눈처럼, 찌푸리고 아래로, 아래로, 더 아래로,

was lost in the thick gloom of darkest night.
어두운 밤의 우울 속으로 사라졌다.

Key Expression

but for : ~이 없다면

but for는 '~이 없다면, ~이 아니라면'이라는 의미로 if 없이 가정법을 표현하는 특수 구문입니다. but for 대신 without으로 바꾸어 쓸 수 있습니다. but for 가정법 구문은 주절의 시제에 따라 문장의 시제가 정해집니다. 주절에 would + 동사원형이 쓰이면 '~이 없다면', would + have p.p가 쓰이면 '~이 없었다면'의 뜻이 됩니다.

ex) Water spread itself wheresoever it listed, or would have done so, but for the frost that held it prisoner.
물은 제멋대로 흘러가며 어디에나 고랑을 만들었고, 혹은 서리가 죄수처럼 가둬 두지만 않았더라면 그렇게 했을 것이다.

bleak 황량한 | moor 황무지 | wheresoever 어디에서나(whereever의 강조형) | list ~에 이랑을 만들다 | furze 가시금작화 | coarse 하등의 | streak 줄, 층 | fiery 타는 듯한 | desolation 황량한 장소 | sullen 시무룩한, 골난 | deck 꾸미다, 치장하다 | howling 울부짖는 | barren 불모인 | blithe 즐거운, 유쾌한 | vigour 활기, 활력

"What place is this?" / asked Scrooge.
"여기는 어디입니까?" 스크루지가 물었다.

"A place where Miners live, / who labor in the bowels
"광부들이 사는 곳이다, 지구의 창자에서 일하는,"

of the earth," / returned the Spirit. "But they know me.
유령이 대답했다. "하지만 그들은 나를 알고 있다.

See!"
보아라!"

A light shone from the window of a hut, / and swiftly
오두막집 창문에서 불빛이 새어 나왔고,

they advanced towards it. Passing through the wall
그들은 재빨리 그쪽으로 다가갔다. 진흙과 돌로 만들어진 담을 통과하자,

of mud and stone, / they found a cheerful company
들뜬 사람들이 모여 있는 것이 보였다

assembled / round a glowing fire. An old, old man
이글거리는 불가에. 아주 늙은 노부부와,

and woman, / with their children / and their children's
그들의 자녀 그리고 그 자녀의 자녀,

children, / and another generation beyond that, / all
또한 그 다음 세대가,

decked out gaily / in their holiday attire. The old man,
모두 치장한 채였다 크리스마스 옷차림으로. 노인은,

/ in a voice / that seldom rose / above the howling of
목소리로 거의 들리지 않는 울부짖는 바람 소리에 묻혀

the wind / upon the barren waste, / was singing them a
황무지에 부는, 자손들에게 크리스마스 노래를

Christmas song / — it had been a very old song / when
불러 주고 있었고 — 아주 오래된 노래였다

he was a boy — / and from time to time / they all joined
노인이 어릴 때 부르던 — 때때로 모두 합창했다.

in the chorus. So surely as they raised their voices, / the
사람들의 목소리가 높아지는 만큼,

old man got quite blithe and loud; / and so surely as they
노인은 즐거워져 큰 소리로 불렀고; 사람들이 노래를 멈추면,

stopped, / his vigour sank again.
노인의 활기찬 목소리도 다시 가라앉았다.

The Spirit did not tarry here, / but bade Scrooge hold
유령은 여기에서 머무르지 않고, 스크루지에게 옷을 잡게 하더니,

his robe, / and passing on above the moor, / sped / —
황무지 위를 지나가며, 속도를 냈다 — 어디로

whither? Not to sea? To sea. To Scrooge's horror, /
가는 것일까? 설마 바다는 아니겠지? 바다였다. 스크루지가 깜짝 놀라서,

looking back, / he saw / the last of the land, / a frightful
뒤를 돌아보니, 보였고, 육지의 끝과,

range of rocks, / behind them; / and his ears were
무시무시한 바위 산맥이, 그들 뒤에; 귀가 먹먹해졌다

deafened / by the thundering of water, / as it rolled and
천둥같은 파도 소리에, 돌진하고 포효하면서,

roared, / and raged among the dreadful caverns / it had
으스스한 동굴 사이에서 울부짖으며 파도에 깎인,

worn, / and fiercely tried to undermine the earth.
맹렬하게 대지를 파고 들려 하는.

Key Expression

in itself : 그 자체로

in itself는 '그 자체로, 본질적으로'라는 의미를 지닌 숙어입니다.
이처럼 재귀대명사는 다양한 전치사와 결합하여 새로운 의미를 지닌 숙어가 됩니다.

▶ by oneself : 홀로, 단독으로
▶ by itself : 저절로, 홀로
▶ for oneself : 스스로, 혼자 힘으로
▶ of oneself : 저절로, 제 스스로
▶ to oneself : 혼자 (독차지하는)
▶ in itself : 그 자체로, 원래, 본질적으로

ex) One of them: the elder, too, with his face all damaged and scarred with hard
weather, as the figure-head of an old ship might be: struck up a sturdy song
that was like a Gale in itself.
역시 연장자인 그들 중 한 명은 낡은 배의 뱃머리 장식물처럼 모진 날씨로 얼굴
에 상처 입고 흉터가 생긴 모습으로 원래 거센 바람인 듯 힘찬 노래를 부르기
시작했다.

Built upon a dismal reef of sunken rocks, / some league
기울어진 바위의 우울한 암초 위에 지어진,   해안에서 몇 리그 정도

or so from shore, / on which the waters chafed and
떨어진,   파도가 부딪쳐 부서져 내리는,

dashed, / the wild year through, / there stood a solitary
1년 내내 험난하게,   등대 하나가 외롭게 서 있었다.

lighthouse. Great heaps of sea-weed clung to its base,
커다란 해초 더미가 등대 아래쪽에 들러 붙어 있고,

/ and storm-birds — / born of the wind / one might
바다새들은 —   바람 속에서 태어났다고   누군가는 생각할지도 모른다,

suppose, / as sea-weed of the water / — rose and fell
바다 속의 해초처럼   — 등대 주위를 오르락내리락

about it, / like the waves / they skimmed.
하고 있었다,   파도처럼,   그들이 스치듯 날아간.

But even here, / two men / who watched the light / had
하지만 여기에서도,   두 남자가   빛을 지키는

made a fire, / that through the loophole / in the thick
불을 지폈고,   그 불빛은 작은 창문을 통과하여   두터운 돌벽에 있는

stone wall / shed out a ray of brightness / on the awful
밝은 빛줄기를 비췄다   거친 바다 위로.

sea. Joining their horny hands / over the rough table
굳은 살이 박힌 손을 맞잡고   둥근 테이블 위로

/ at which they sat, / they wished each other Merry
그들이 앉아 있는,   서로에게 크리스마스 인사를 나누었다

Christmas / in their can of grog; / and one of them: / the
그로그주를 나누며;   그리고 그들 중 한 명이:

elder, too, / with his face / all damaged and scarred with
역시, 연장자인,   얼굴 모습의   모진 풍파에 시달려 상처 입고 흉터가 생긴,

hard weather, / as the figure-head of an old ship might be:
뱃머리 장식물처럼:

/ struck up a sturdy song / that was like a Gale in itself.
힘찬 노래를 부르기 시작했다   거센 바람과 같은.

tarry 머무르다 | whither 어디로 | range 산맥 | cavern 동굴 | undermine ~의 밑을 파다 | league 리그 (
거리의 단위) | chafed 쓸려 벗겨지게 하다 | skim 스치듯 날아가다 | loophole 작은 창문 | horny 못이 박힌 |
grog 그로그주(럼주에 물을 탄 것) | figure-head 선수상(船首像, 뱃머리에 부착한 장식용 조각) | sturdy 억센 |
gale 매우 센 바람

173

Again the Ghost sped on, / above the black and heaving
다시 유령은 속력을 내서, 검고 요동치는 바다 위를 날아가더니

sea / — on, and on — / until, being far away, / as he
— 계속해서 — 아주 멀리까지, 유령이 스크루지

told Scrooge, / from any shore, / they lighted on a ship.
에게 말했던 대로, 바다 한가운데로부터, 배 위에 내렸다.

They stood / beside the helmsman at the wheel, / the
그들은 다가섰다 타륜을 잡은 조타수,

look-out in the bow, / the officers who had the watch;
이물에서 망보는 보초, 경계를 서던 선원들 옆에;

/ dark, ghostly figures / in their several stations; / but
시커먼 유령같은 모습으로 서 있던, 각자의 거리에서;

every man among them / hummed a Christmas tune, /
하지만 모든 사람들은 크리스마스 노래를 흥얼거리거나,

or had a Christmas thought, / or spoke below his breath
크리스마스에 관한 생각을 하거나, 나직하게 말했다

/ to his companion / of some bygone Christmas Day, /
동료에게 크리스마스의 추억 이야기를,

with homeward hopes belonging to it. And every man
집으로 향하는 바람을 담아. 배에 타고 있는 모든 사람은,

on board, / waking or sleeping, / good or bad, / had had
깨어 있든 자고 있든, 착하든 나쁘든, 더욱 다정한

a kinder word for another / on that day / than on any
말을 주고 받았고 평소보다 추억했고 그 날에는

day in the year; / and had shared to some extent in its
평소보다; 축제 분위기를 함께 즐겼으며;

festivities; / and had remembered / those he cared for /
추억했고 사랑하는 사람들과

at a distance, / and had known / that they delighted to
멀리 떨어진, 알고 있었다 그들도 자기들을 떠올리며 기뻐하리란 것

remember him.
을.

---

heaving 상하 요동 | light 내리다 | helmsman 조타수, 지도자 | wheel (배의) 타륜 | bow 이물, 선수 |
homeward 집으로 향하는 | solemn 장엄한 | abyss 심연, 심해 | profound 고상한, 심원한 | affability 상냥함,
싹싹한 태도 | cultivate 우정 따위를 돈독히 하려고 애를 쓰다

It was a great surprise to Scrooge, / while listening to
스크루지에게는 엄청난 놀라움이었다. 바람의 신음 소리를 들으며,

the moaning of the wind, / and thinking / what a solemn
생각하는 것이 얼마나 장엄한 일인지

thing it was / to move on through the lonely darkness /
고독한 어둠을 뚫고 지나가는 것은

over an unknown abyss, / whose depths were secrets / as
미지의 심연 위로, 깊은 곳에 비밀을 간직한

profound as Death: / it was a great surprise to Scrooge,
죽을 만큼 심오한: 또한 스크루지에게는 대단히 놀라웠다.

/ while thus engaged, / to hear a hearty laugh. It was a
이런 생각에 잠겨 있는 동안, 호탕한 웃음 소리가 들려온 것도.

much greater surprise / to Scrooge / to recognise it as
더욱 놀라운 것은 스크루지에게 그 웃음 소리가 조카가 낸 것임을

his own nephew's / and to find himself / in a bright, /
알아차리고 자신의 모습을 발견한 것이다 밝고,

dry, / gleaming room, / with the Spirit / standing smiling
눅눅하지 않고, 눈부시게 빛나는 방에서, 유령과 함께 미소지으며 서 있는

/ by his side, / and looking at that same nephew / with
나란히, 조카를 바라보고 있는 것을

approving affability!
만족스럽고 따뜻한 표정을 지으며!

"Ha, ha!" / laughed Scrooge's nephew. "Ha, ha, ha!"
"하, 하!" 스크루지의 조카가 웃었다. "하, 하, 하!"

If you should happen, / by any unlikely chance, / to
여러분이 혹시, 그럴 리는 없겠지만,

know a man / more blest in a laugh / than Scrooge's
사람을 알고 있다면 더 호탕하게 웃는 스크루지의 조카보다,

nephew, / all I can say is, / I should like to know
내가 말할 수 있는 것은, 그 사람을 알고 싶다는 것이다.

him too. Introduce him to me, / and I'll cultivate his
내게 그 사람을 소개시켜 달라, 알고 지내고 싶으니.

acquaintance.

It is a fair, / even-handed, / noble adjustment / of things,
정당하고,   공평하고,   숭고한 이치인가   세상 만물의,

/ that while there is infection / in disease and sorrow, /
전염성이 있지만   병이나 슬픔에도,

there is nothing in the world / so irresistibly contagious
세상에 없으니   이토록 아주 전염성이 강한 것이

/ as laughter and good-humor. When Scrooge's nephew
웃음이나 유쾌한 기분만큼.   조카가 웃자

laughed / in this way: / holding his sides, / rolling his
이런 식으로: 옆구리를 잡고,   머리를 흔들며,

head, / and twisting his face into the most extravagant
얼굴을 아주 이상한 모습으로 일그러뜨리자:

contortions: / Scrooge's niece, by marriage, / laughed as
조카 며느리도,   남편만큼 유쾌하게

heartily as he. And their assembled friends / being not a
웃었다.   그리고 모여 있던 친구들도   조금도 뒤지지 않고,

bit behindhand, / roared out lustily.
호탕하게 큰 소리로 웃어댔다.

"Ha, ha! Ha, ha, ha, ha!"
"하, 하!   하, 하, 하, 하!"

Key Expression 🎯

as I live : 아주 확실하게, 틀림없이

as I live는 '틀림없이, 절대로, 결단코'라는 의미로 강조를 위해 감탄사처럼 쓰이는 관용구문입니다.

이 구문은 AS I live (and breathe)에서 나온 것인데, 사람이 숨쉬고 살아가는 일이 당연한 것처럼 확실하다는 의미입니다.

ex) He said that Christmas was a humbug, as I live!
그분은 크리스마스가 헛소리라고 말씀하셨어, 틀림없다고!

---

contagious 전염성의, 옮기 쉬운 | extravagant 지나친, 터무니없는 | contortions 뒤틀림, 찌그러짐 | behindhand 뒤져, 못하여 | lust 열의, 열정 | indignantly 분개하여 | capital 훌륭한, 뛰어난 | provoking 도발하는

contagious 전염성의, 옮기 쉬운 | extravagant 지나친, 터무니없는 | contortions 뒤틀림, 찌그러짐 | behindhand 뒤져, 못하여 | lust 열의, 열정 | indignantly 분개하여 | capital 훌륭한, 뛰어난 | provoking 도발하는

"He said / that Christmas was a humbug, / as I live!" /
"말씀하시더라고 크리스마스가 헛소리라고, 틀림없이!"

cried Scrooge's nephew. "He believed it too!"
조카가 소리쳤다. "삼촌은 그렇게 믿고 계시더라!"

"More shame for him, / Fred!" / said Scrooge's niece, /
"더욱 부끄러운 일이군요, 프레드!" 조카 며느리가 말했다,

indignantly. Bless those women; / they never do anything
분개하여. 이런 여인들에게 축복 있으라; 결코 무슨 일이든 적당히 하지 않는다.

by halves. They are always in earnest.
언제나 성의를 다한다.

She was very pretty: / exceedingly pretty. With a
그녀는 아주 예뻤다: 뛰어나게 예뻤다. 보조개가 지고,

dimpled, / surprised-looking, / capital face; / a ripe little
놀란 듯한 표정에, 뛰어난 미모였다; 농익은 작은 입술,

mouth, / that seemed made to be kissed / — as no doubt
입맞추고 싶어지는 — 정말 그러했다;

it was; / all kinds of good little dots / about her chin, /
작고 귀여운 점들과 턱 언저리에 있는,

that melted into one another / when she laughed; / and
또 다른 하나의 점처럼 합쳐지는 그녀가 웃을 때;

the sunniest pair of eyes / you ever saw in any little
태양처럼 빛나는 눈동자 어린 아이의 얼굴에서나 볼 수 있는,

creature's head. Altogether she was / what you would
모든 면에서 그녀는 도발적이라고 부를 수도 있는

have called provoking, / you know; / but satisfactory, too.
모습이었지만, 알다시피; 또한 더할 나위 없이 아름다웠다.

Oh, perfectly satisfactory.
아, 더할 나위 없이 완벽한 아름다움.

"He's a comical old fellow," / said Scrooge's nephew, /
"외삼촌은 재미있는 양반이야," 조카가 말했다,

"that's the truth: / and not so pleasant / as he might be.
"그건 사실이야: 그다지 즐거워 하는 법이 없으셔 그럴 만한데도.

However, / his offences carry their own punishment, /
그래도, 그런 공격적인 성격 때문에 벌을 받고 계시니,

and I have nothing to say against him."
내가 그다지 삼촌에게 나쁘게 말할 건 없지."

"I'm sure he is very rich, / Fred," / hinted Scrooge's
"확실히 그 분은 부자죠, 프레드," 조카 며느리가 넌지시 물었다.

niece. "At least you always tell me so."
"적어도 당신은 항상 그렇게 얘기했잖아요."

"What of that, / my dear!" / said Scrooge's nephew. "His
"무슨 소용이오, 여보!" 조카가 말했다.

wealth is of no use to him. He don't do any good with
"삼촌이 부자인들 아무 소용이 없는 걸. 그 돈으로 좋은 일도 하지 않으시지.

it. He don't make himself comfortable with it. He hasn't
편안하게 살지도 않으시고.

the satisfaction of thinking / — ha, ha, ha! — / that he is
생각을 하고 계시지도 않고 — 하, 하, 하! —

ever going to benefit US with it."
우리를 도와주려는."

"I have no patience with him," / observed Scrooge's
"난 그런 사람을 참을 수 없어요," 조카 며느리가 말했다.

niece. Scrooge's niece's sisters, / and all the other ladies,
조카 며느리의 여동생들과, 다른 모든 여자들도

/ expressed the same opinion.
같은 생각이라고 말했다.

"Oh, I have!" / said Scrooge's nephew. "I am sorry for
"아, 난 참을 수 있소!" 조카가 말했다. "난 그분이 불쌍해;

him; / I couldn't be angry with him / if I tried. Who
화를 낼 수 없소 그러려고 해도. 삼촌의 고약한

suffers by his ill whims! Himself, / always. Here, / he
성미 탓에 누가 고통을 당하겠소! 그분 자신이지, 언제나. 자,

takes it into his head to dislike us, / and he won't come
삼촌은 우리를 싫어한다는 생각을 머리 속에 집어 넣고, 저녁 먹으러 오지도 않겠다고

and dine with us. What's the consequence? He don't lose
하시더군. 결과는 어떻게 되었지?

much of a dinner."
대단한 만찬을 놓치는 것은 아니지만."

---

whim 일시적 기분 | cluster 떼지어 뒤덮다 | wretch 가엾은 사람 | outcast 따돌림을 받은 사람, 추방자 |
whereat 무엇에 대하여 | plump 풍만한, 통통한 | tucker 장식 주름

"Indeed, / I think / he loses a very good dinner," /
"정말로, 난 생각해요 그분이 아주 훌륭한 만찬을 놓친 거라고,"

interrupted Scrooge's niece. Everybody else said the
조카 며느리가 끼어들었다. 모두 같은 의견이라고 말했고,

same, / and they must be allowed to have been competent
그들 모두는 유능한 심판이 될 수 있었다,

judges, / because they had just had dinner; / and, with
막 만찬을 끝내고;

the dessert upon the table, / were clustered round the fire,
식탁 위에 디저트를 올려 놓고, 난로 주위에 둘러 앉아 있기 때문에,

/ by lamplight.
등불 옆에.

"Well! I'm very glad to hear it," / said Scrooge's
"그렇다면! 그렇다니 기쁘군," 조카가 말했다,

nephew, / "because I haven't great faith / in these young
"왜냐하면 그다지 믿지 않았거든

housekeepers. What do you say, / Topper?"
이 젊은 주부들을. 어떻게 생각하나, 토퍼?"

Topper had clearly got his eye / upon one of Scrooge's
토퍼는 시선을 고정한 것이 분명했다 조카 며느리의 여동생 중 한 명에게,

niece's sisters, / for he answered / that a bachelor was
왜냐하면 대답했으니까 총각은 가엾게도 따돌림을 당했으니,

a wretched outcast, / who had no right / to express an
권리가 없다고 의견을 말할

opinion / on the subject. Whereat Scrooge's niece's sister
그런 문제에 대해. 그 말에 조카 며느리의 여동생은

/ — the plump one with the lace tucker: / not the one
— 레이스 깃을 단 통통한 아가씨는: 장미꽃을 단 아가씨가

with the roses — / blushed.
아니라 — 얼굴을 붉혔다.

"Do go on, / Fred," / said Scrooge's niece, / clapping her
"계속해 보세요, 프레드," 조카 며느리가 말했다, 손뼉을 치며.

hands. "He never finishes / what he begins to say! He is
"이 사람은 결코 끝내지 않아요 시작했던 말을!

such a ridiculous fellow!"
아주 엉뚱한 사람이죠!'

Scrooge's nephew revelled in another laugh, / and as it
조카는 다시 한 번 웃음을 터뜨렸고,

was impossible / to keep the infection off; / though the
불가능했기에   전염이 되지 않는 것은;

plump sister tried hard to do it / with aromatic vinegar; /
통통한 처제는 웃지 않으려고 했지만   향이 나는 식초 냄새를 맡으며;

his example was unanimously followed.
모두들 예외 없이 따라 웃고 말았다.

"I was only going to say," / said Scrooge's nephew, / "that
"내가 하려던 말은,"   조카가 말했다.

the consequence / of his taking a dislike to us, / and not
"결과는   삼촌이 우리를 싫어하고,   우리와 즐겁게

making merry with us, is, / as I think, / that he loses
지내지 않음으로써 생기는,   내가 생각하기에는,

some pleasant moments, / which could do him no harm.
즐거운 시간을 잃고 있다는 거야.   그게 삼촌에게 해가 되지는 않지만.

I am sure / he loses pleasanter companions / than he can
확신해   삼촌이 더욱 유쾌한 친구들을 잃어버린 것은

find in his own thoughts, / either in his mouldy old office,
혼자 사색에 잠겨 있는 것 보다.   곰팡내 나는 낡은 사무실이나,

/ or his dusty chambers. I mean to give him the same
먼지 나는 집에서.   난 똑같은 기회를 드릴 생각이야

chance / every year, / whether he likes it or not, / for I
매년,   삼촌이 좋아하시든 말든,

pity him. He may rail at Christmas / till he dies, / but he
가여우니까.   크리스마스에 악담을 퍼부을지 모르지만   돌아가실 때까지,

can't help thinking better of it / — I defy him — / if he
더 좋게 생각할 수밖에 없을 걸   — 어디 한 번 해 보자고 —

finds me going there, / in good temper, / year after year, /
만약 내가 가는 걸 보신다면,   공손하게,   매년,

and saying Uncle Scrooge, / how are you? If it only puts
그리고 인사 드린다면,   안녕하세요?라고.   만약 삼촌이 생각하게

him in the vein / to leave his poor clerk fifty pounds, /
된다면   그 불쌍한 서기에게 50파운드라도 남기겠다고.

that's something; / and I think / I shook him yesterday."
그것만 해도 대단한 일이고;   난 생각해   어제 삼촌을 좀 움직였다고."

revel 한껏 즐기다, 열중하다 | unanimously 만장일치로, 이의 없이 | mouldy 곰팡이 난 | rail at 욕하다,
악담하다 | I defy ~할 수 있으면 해 봐라 | in the vein ~하고 싶은 기분이 들어

It was their turn to laugh now / at the notion of his
이제 다른 사람들이 웃음을 터뜨릴 차례였다   그가 삼촌을 움직였다는 소리에.

shaking Scrooge. But being thoroughly good-natured,
하지만 천성이 좋은 사람이었기 때문에,

/ and not much caring / what they laughed at, / so that
별로 신경 쓰지 않고   그들이 웃는 이유에,

they laughed at any rate, / he encouraged them in their
어찌 되었든 사람들이 웃었으므로,   그들을 더 즐겁게 만들며,

merriment, / and passed the bottle joyously.
유쾌하게 술병을 돌렸다.

After tea, / they had some music. For they were a
차를 마시고 나서, 그들은 노래를 불렀다.   그들은 음악적인 가족이었고,

musical family, / and knew / what they were about, /
알고 있었다,   어떻게 해야 할지,

when they sung a Glee or Catch, / I can assure you: /
합창곡이나 돌림 노래를 부를 때,   분명히:

especially Topper, / who could growl away in the bass
특히 토퍼는,   저음을 잘 내면서도

/ like a good one, / and never swell the large veins in
가수처럼,   결코 이마에 핏줄이 서거나,

his forehead, / or get red in the face over it. Scrooge's
얼굴이 빨개지지도 않았다.

niece played well upon the harp; / and played among
조카 며느리는 하프를 잘 켰고;   아주 간단한 곡들을 연주했다

other tunes a simple little air / (a mere nothing: / you
(쉬운 곡들:

might learn to whistle it / in two minutes), / which had
배워서 휘파람을 불 수도 있는   이 분 안에),

been familiar to the child / who fetched Scrooge from
그 아이가 잘 알고 있었던 노래였다   기숙학교로 스크루지를 데리러 왔던,

the boarding-school, / as he had been reminded / by
스크루지가 다시 생각하게 된

the Ghost of Christmas Past. When this strain of music
과거 크리스마스 유령 덕에.   이 음악 선율이 들리자,

sounded, / all the things / that Ghost had shown him, /
모든 것들이   유령이 보여 줬던,

came upon his mind; / he softened more and more; / and
스크루지의 마음속에 다시 떠올랐고; 그는 점점 더 온화해져서;

thought / that if he could have listened to it often, / years
생각했다   이 노래를 자주 들을 수 있었더라면,   몇 년 전에,

ago, / he might have cultivated the kindnesses of life /
친절함을 베풀 수 있었을 것이라고

for his own happiness / with his own hands, / without
자신의 행복을 위해   자기 스스로,

resorting to the sexton's spade / that buried Jacob Marley.
묘지 일꾼의 삽을 쓰지 않고   제이콥 말리를 묻은.

But they didn't devote the whole evening to music. After
하지만 사람들은 저녁 내내 음악에만 빠져 있던 것은 아니었다.

a while / they played at forfeits; / for it is good to / be
잠시 후에   그들은 벌금 돌이를 했다;   좋은 일이고   동심의 세계로

children / sometimes, / and never better than at Christmas,
돌아가는 것은   때때로,   크리스마스보다 더 좋은 기회는 없으므로,

/ when its mighty Founder was a child himself. Stop!
크리스마스를 만든 것도 바로 어린 아이였으니까.   잠깐!

Key Expression ♪

more and more : 점점 더
'비교급 + and + 비교급'은 '점점 더 ~한(하게)'란 뜻을 가진 구문입니다.
grow, become, get과 같은 상태 변화를 나타내는 2형식 동사와 함께 쓰여
'점점 더 ~해지다'라는 의미로 쓰이는 경우가 많아요.

ex) He softened more and more; and thought that if he could have listened to it
    often, years ago.
    그는 점점 더 온화해져서, 몇 년 전에 이 노래를 자주 들었더라면 좋았을 것이라
    고 생각했다.

at any rate 어찌 되었건, 하여간 | merriment 유쾌한 파티, 웃고 떠듦 | joyously 즐겁게, 유쾌하게 | glee 무반주
합창곡 | catch 돌림노래 | growl 소리를 내다 | sexton 무덤 파는 일꾼 | forfeit 벌금 놀이

There was first a game at blind-man's buff. Of course
우선 장님 놀이가 있었다.   물론 그렇다.

there was. And I no more believe / Topper was really
그러나 나는 더 이상 믿지 않고   토퍼가 정말 장님이라고

blind / than I believe / he had eyes in his boots. My
차라리 믿겠다   그의 신발에 눈이 달렸다고.

opinion is, / that it was a done thing / between him and
내 생각에는,   미리 계획된 일이었고   토퍼와 스크루지 조카 사이에;

Scrooge's nephew; / and that the Ghost of Christmas
현재 크리스마스 유령은 그것을 알고 있었다는 것이다.

Present knew it. The way he went after that plump sister
그가 통통한 여동생을 쫓아 다니는 모습을 보면

/ in the lace tucker, / was an outrage on the credulity of
레이스 깃을 단,   인간의 본성이란 믿을 게 못 되었다.

human nature. Knocking down the fire-irons, / tumbling
난로 부지깽이를 넘어뜨리고,

over the chairs, / bumping against the piano, / smothering
의자에 걸려 넘어지고,   피아노에 부딪히고,

himself among the curtains, / wherever she went, / there
커튼에 감겨 숨이 막히면서도,   그녀가 가는 곳은 어디든지,

went he! He always knew / where the plump sister was.
따라다녔다!   그는 언제나 알았다   그 통통한 여동생이 어디에 있는지.

He wouldn't catch anybody else. If you had fallen up
다른 사람은 잡으려 들지 않았다.   만약 여러분이 토퍼 위에 넘어졌다 해도

against him / (as some of them did), / on purpose, / he
(그들 중 몇몇은 실제로 그리 했다),   의도적으로,

would have made a feint / of endeavoring to seize you, /
그는 시늉만 하고   여러분을 잡으려고 애쓰는 척,

which would have been an affront to your understanding,
이미 속을 빤히 알고 있는 여러분을 모욕하며,

/ and would instantly have sidled off / in the direction
곧바로 옆걸음질쳤을 것이다   그 통통한 여동생이 있는

of the plump sister. She often cried out / that it wasn't
쪽으로.   그녀는 종종 소리쳤고   불공평하다고;

outrage 불법 행위 | smother 숨막히게 하다 | feint 가장, 시늉 | affront 모욕, 치욕 | sidle 옆걸음질치다 |
rustle 바스락거리다, 사각거리다 | execrable 밉살스러운 | vile 몹시 나쁜, 비도덕적인

fair; / and it really was not. But when at last, / he caught
실제로 불공평했다.   하지만 마침내,   그가 그녀를 잡았

her; / when, in spite of all her silken rustlings, / and her
을 때;   그때, 비단옷을 사각거리며,

rapid flutterings past him, / he got her into a corner /
재빨리 그의 곁을 지나가려 함에도 불구하고, 그는 그녀를 구석으로 몰아 넣었고

whence there was no escape; / then his conduct was the
빠져나갈 공간이 없는;   그의 행동은 어느 때보다도 밉살스러웠다.

most execrable. For his pretending not to know her; / his
              그녀인지 모르는 척하면서;

pretending / that it was necessary / to touch her head-
연기를 했으니   필요하다고   그녀의 머리 장식을 만져봐야 하며,

dress, / and further to assure himself of her identity / by
누구인지 확실히 알아내야 한다고

pressing / a certain ring upon her finger, / and a certain
더듬어서   손가락에 끼워진 반지와,   목에 한 목걸이를;

chain about her neck; / was vile, / monstrous! No doubt
              나쁜 행동이었다, 짐승같으니라고!   의심할 바 없이 그

she told him / her opinion of it, / when, another blind-
녀는 그에게 말했을 것이다 그 행동에 관한 자신의 생각을, 다른 사람이 장님이 되어 게임이

man being in office, / they were so very confidential
계속되는 동안,   두 사람이 함께 숨게 되었을 때,

together, / behind the curtains.
커튼 뒤에.

Key Expression

in spite of ~ : ~에도 불구하고
in spite of는 '~에도 불구하고'라는 뜻으로 양보의 의미를 가진 전치사구입니다.
despite라는 한 단어로 바꾸어 쓸 수 있으며, 전치사구이므로 뒤에는 명사나 동
명사가 와야 합니다.

▶ in spite of[despite] + 명사[명사구] : ~에도 불구하고 (전치사)
▶ in spite of[despite] the fact that + 절 : ~에도 불구하고 (접속사처럼 쓰임)

ex) In spite of all her silken rustlings, and herrapid flutterings past him, he got her
into a corner whence there was no escape.
비단옷의 사각거리며 그의 옆을 재빨리 지나가려는 움직임에도 불구하고, 그는
그녀를 빠져나갈 공간이 없는 구석으로 몰아넣었다.

Scrooge's niece was / not one of the blind-man's buff
조카 며느리는 　　　　　　　장님 놀이 일행에 끼지 않고,

party, / but was made comfortable / with a large chair
편히 쉬고 있었다　　　　　　큰 의자에 앉아 발판에 발을

and a footstool, / in a snug corner, / where the Ghost and
올려 놓은 채,　　　　포근한 구석에서,

Scrooge were close behind her. But she joined in the
유령과 스크루지가 그녀 뒤편 가까운 곳에 있었던.　하지만 그녀는 마음을 빼앗겨,

forfeits, / and loved her love / to admiration with all the
자신의 열정을 사랑하게 됐다

letters of the alphabet. Likewise / at the game / of How,
알파벳 글자들에 감탄하는.　　마찬가지로　　놀이에서도　　'어떻게, 언제,

When, and Where, / she was very great, / and to the
어디에서'라는,　　　그녀는 매우 잘했으며,

secret joy of Scrooge's nephew, / beat her sisters hollow:
스크루지 조카가 은밀하게 기뻐할 정도로,　　자매들보다 월등히 뛰어났다:

/ though they were sharp girls too, / as Topper could
자매들 또한 영리한 소녀들이었음에도 불구하고,　토퍼가 말했듯이,

have told you. There might have been twenty people
그곳에는 20명이 있었는데,

there, / young and old, / but they all played, / and so did
남녀노소의,　　모두 게임에 참여했고,　　스크루지도 그랬다;

Scrooge; / for wholly forgetting / in the interest he had /
왜냐하면 완전히 잊어버려서　　자신이 가졌던 관심을

in what was going on, / that his voice made no sound / in
무슨 일이 일어나고 있는지에 대한,　자신의 목소리는 들리지 않는데도

their ears, / he sometimes came out with his guess / quite
그들의 귀에는,　스크루지는 자신이 추측한 답을 이야기 하거나　　　　꽤 큰 목

loud, / and very often guessed quite right, / too; / for the
소리로,　종종 맞추기도 했다.　　　　　　또한;

sharpest needle, / best *Whitechapel, / warranted not to
가장 날카로운 바늘도,　화이트채플에서 최고인,　　바늘귀가 부러지지 않는다고

cut in the eye, / was not sharper than Scrooge; / blunt / as
보장된,　　스크루지보다 날카롭지 못했으며;　　무뎌졌다 그가

he took it / in his head to be.
추측을 떠올릴 때　머리 속에서.

* 화이트채플(영국 런던 교외의 도시로 중세시대 바늘 등 금속 세공업으로 유명했다)

The Ghost was greatly pleased / to find him in this
유령은 매우 기뻐하며   그가 이렇게 들뜬 것을 보고,

mood, / and looked upon him / with such favor, / that
             스크루지를 바라보았다   매우 호의적으로,   그러자 스크

he begged like a boy / to be allowed to stay / until the
루지는 아이처럼 애원했다   머무르도록 허락해 달라고

guests departed. But this the Spirit said / could not be
손님들이 떠날 때까지.   하지만 유령은 말했다   그렇게는 될 수 없다고.

done.

"Here is a new game," / said Scrooge. "One half hour, /
"이건 새로운 게임이에요,"   스크루지가 말했다.   "한 시간 반만요,

Spirit, / only one!"
유령님,   단 한 번만요!"

It was a Game called Yes and No, / where Scrooge's
그것은 '예와 아니오'라고 불리는 게임이었는데,

nephew had to think of something, / and the rest must
스크루지의 조카가 뭔가를 생각해 내면,   나머지 사람들이 그것이 무엇인지

find out what; / he only answering to their questions yes
알아내는 게임이었다;   그는 사람들의 질문에 '예' 또는 '아니오'로만 대답할 수 있다.

or no, / as the case was. The brisk fire of questioning /
각 경우에서.   속사포같은 질문에

to which he was exposed, / elicited from him / that he
그는 노출되었고,   그에게서 끌어냈다

was thinking of an animal, / a live animal, / rather a
그가 동물을 생각하고 있다는 사실을,   살아있는 동물이며,

disagreeable animal, / a savage animal, / an animal that
꽤 혐오스러운 동물이고,   맹수이며,

growled and grunted sometimes, / and talked sometimes,
때때로 으르렁거리고 꿀꿀대는 동물이고,   때로는 말도 하며,

/ and lived in London, / and walked about the streets, /
런던에 살고,   거리를 걸어다니지만,

and wasn't made a show of, / and wasn't led by anybody,
쇼를 하지는 않고,   누군가에게 끌려 다니지도 않으며,

---

buff -광, 애호가 | beat a person hollow 남을 완전히 패배시키다, 남보다 월등히 뛰어나다 warrant 보증하다 |
blunt 무딘, 뭉툭한 | with favor 호의적으로, 찬성하여 | brisk (차갑지만) 상쾌한 | elicit 끌어내다

/ and didn't live in a menagerie, / and was never killed /
동물원에 살지도 않고,   도살당하지도 않으며

in a market, / and was not a horse, / or an ass, / or a cow,
시장에서,   말도 아니고,   당나귀도,   소도,

/ or a bull, / or a tiger, / or a dog, / or a pig, / or a cat, / or
황소도,   호랑이도,   개도,   돼지도,   고양이도,   곰도

a bear. At every fresh question / that was put to him, /
아니었다.   새로운 질문마다   그에게 쏟아진,

this nephew burst into a fresh roar of laughter; / and was
조카는 큰 웃음을 터뜨렸고;   매우 표현하기

so inexpressibly tickled, / that he was obliged to get up
어려울 정도로 재미있어 하며,   어쩔 수 없이 소파에서 일어나 발을 동동 구르기도

off the sofa and stamp. At last the plump sister, / falling
했다.   마침내 통통한 처제가,

into a similar state, / cried out: /
형부와 비슷한 상황에 빠져,   외쳤다:

"I have found it out! I know what it is, / Fred! I know
"알았어요!   그게 뭔지 알았어요,   프레드 형부!

what it is!"
그게 뭔지 알았다고요!"

"What is it?" / cried Fred.
"뭔데?"   프레드가 말했다.

"It's your Uncle Scro-o-o-o-oge!"
"형부의 삼촌 스크루-우-우-우-우지요!"

Which it certainly was. Admiration was the universal
정답이었다.   모두에게서 감탄이 터져나왔다.

sentiment, / though some objected / that the reply to "Is
일부는 항의했지만   "곰이에요?"라는 질문에 대한

it a bear?" / ought to have been "Yes;" / inasmuch as an
답변이   "예"였어야 한다고;

answer in the negative / was sufficient to have diverted
그의 대답이 부정적이었기 때문에   바꾸게 되었다면서,

/ their thoughts from Mr. Scrooge, / supposing they had
스크루지라는 추측을,

ever had any tendency that way.
진작에 그쪽으로 생각하고 있었으면서.

"He has given us plenty of merriment, / I am sure," /
"삼촌이 무척 즐거운 시간을 안겨 주었어, 정말로,"

said Fred, / "and it would be ungrateful / not to drink his
프레드가 말했다, "그러니 배은망덕한 일이지 그의 건강에 건배하지 않

health. Here is a glass of mulled wine / ready to our hand
는 것은. 여기 데운 포도주가 있군 우리 손에 준비된

/ at the moment; / and I say, 'Uncle Scrooge!' "
적당한 때에; 제가 말할게요, '스크루지 삼촌을 위해!"

"Well! Uncle Scrooge!" / they cried.
"자! 스크루지 아저씨를 위해!" 사람들은 소리쳤다.

"A Merry Christmas / and a Happy New Year / to the
"메리 크리스마스 그리고 새해 복 많이 받으시길

old man, / whatever he is!" / said Scrooge's nephew.
영감님이, 그분이 어떤 분이든!" 조카가 말했다.

"He wouldn't take it from me, / but may he have it, /
"그분은 내게 받으려고 하지 않으시겠지만, 축복을 받으시길,

nevertheless. Uncle Scrooge!"
그래도. 스크루지 삼촌을 위해!"

Uncle Scrooge had imperceptibly become so gay
스크루지는 눈에 띄지 않게 매우 기뻐하며 마음이 가벼워져서,

and light of heart, / that he would have pledged / the
축배를 들고

unconscious company / in return, / and thanked them / in
자신을 알아보지 못하는 친구들에게 보답으로, 그리고 그들에게 감사했을지 모른다

an inaudible speech, / if the Ghost had given him time.
들리지 않는 말로, 만약 유령이 그에게 시간을 주었다면.

But the whole scene passed off / in the breath of the last
하지만 모든 장면은 사라졌고 마지막 말이 나옴과 동시에

word / spoken by his nephew; / and he and the Spirit
조카가 말한; 그리고 스크루지와 유령은 다시 한 번

were again / upon their travels.
여행길에 올랐다.

---

menagerie (동물쇼 등을 위해 모아 놓은) 야생 동물들, 동물원 | inexpressibly 표현하기 어려울 정도로, 대단히 |
tickle (흥미를) 돋우다 | inasmuch ~이므로, ~인 점을 고려하면 | imperceptibly 눈에 안 띌 정도로

Much they saw, / and far they went, / and many homes
많은 것을 보았고, 멀리까지 다녔으며, 수많은 집들을 방문했지만,

they visited, / but always with a happy end. The Spirit
항상 행복한 결말로 끝났다. 유령이 병든 사람의

stood beside sick beds, / and they were cheerful; /
침대 곁에 서 있으면, 환자들은 활력을 되찾았고:

on foreign lands, / and they were close at home; / by
타향에서 지내는 사람은, 집에 있는 것처럼 느꼈으며;

struggling men, / and they were patient / in their greater
괴로움을 겪는 사람들은, 인내심을 가지게 되었고 더 큰 희망을 품으며;

hope; / by poverty, / and it was rich. In almshouse,
가난한 사람들은, 부자가 되었다. 구호소, 병원, 그리고 감옥에서,

hospital, and jail, / in misery's every refuge, / where vain
비참한 사람들의 피난처마다,

man in his little brief authority / had not made fast the
하찮은 권위를 가지고 과시하는 사람들이 문을 꽁꽁 닫아놓지 않고,

door, / and barred the Spirit out, / he left his blessing, /
유령을 쫓아내지도 않았다. 유령은 축복을 내리며 떠났고,

and taught Scrooge his precepts.
스크루지에게 교훈을 가르쳐 주었다.

Key Expression

시간 표현
영어에서 시간을 표현할 때 quarter를 사용하여 15분을, half를 사용하여
30분을 나타냅니다.
또한 전치사를 사용하여 '~전'(to, before)과 '~후'(past, after)는 다음과
같이 표현합니다.
▶ ~분/quarter/half + to/before + 시 : ~시 ~분 전
▶ ~분/quarter/half + part/after + 시 : ~시 ~분

ex) The chimes were ringing the three quarters past eleven at that moment.
그 순간 11시 45분을 가리키는 종소리가 울리고 있었다.

almshouse (옛날 영국의) 빈민 구호소 | refuge 피난처 | vain 자만심이 강한, 허영심을 가진 | fast 굳게 닫힌 |
precept 교훈 | condensed 응축한, 요약한 | unaltered 변하지 않은
hark 잘 들어라(명령문으로만 쓰이던 옛글투) | chime 차임, (교회) 종

It was a long night, / if it were only a night; / but Scrooge
긴 밤이었다,   그것이 단 하룻밤의 일이었다면;   하지만 스크루지는

had his doubts of this, / because the Christmas Holidays
하룻밤이었는지 의심이 들었다,   왜냐하면 크리스마스 휴일 기간이 압축되어 있었기 때

appeared to be condensed / into the space of time /
문에   시간 안에

they passed together. It was strange, / too, / that while
그들이 함께 보낸.   이상했다,   또한,

Scrooge remained unaltered / in his outward form, / the
스크루지가 변하지 않은 채 그대로인 반면,   겉모습에서,

Ghost grew older, / clearly older. Scrooge had observed
유령은 늙어가고 있다는 것이,   분명히 더 늙은.   스크루지는 이 변화를 알아챘지만,

this change, / but never spoke of it, / until they left a
                      말하지는 않았다,

children's *Twelfth Night party, / when, / looking at the
아이들의 주현절 파티장을 떠날 때까지.   그때,   유령을 바라보다가

Spirit / as they stood together / in an open place, / he
      함께 서 있을 때   공터에,   그는

noticed / that its hair was grey.
알아챘다   유령의 머리가 백발이 되었음을.

"Are spirits' lives so short?" / asked Scrooge.
"유령님의 수명은 그렇게 짧은가요?"   스크루지가 물었다.

"My life upon this globe, / is very brief," / replied the
"이승에서의 내 수명은,   매우 짧아,"   유령이 대답했다.

Ghost. "It ends to-night."
      "오늘 밤에 끝나지."

"To-night!" / cried Scrooge.
"오늘 밤이라뇨!"   스크루지가 소리쳤다.

"To-night at midnight. Hark! The time is drawing near."
"오늘 밤 자정이야.   들어라!   시간이 다가오고 있어."

The chimes were ringing / the three quarters past eleven
종소리가 울리고 있었다   11시 45분을 가리키는

/ at that moment.
    그 순간.

* 주현절(교회에서 예수가 세상 사람들 앞에 나타났던 일을 축하하는 경축일로 1월 6일이다. 영국 등에서는 이
축제일을 예수 탄생 후 12일째 되는 날이라 하여 '십이야'라고 부른다)

"Forgive me / if I am not justified / in what I ask," / said
"용서하세요   제가 정당하지 않다면   이런 질문을 하는 것이,"   스크루지

Scrooge, / looking intently / at the Spirit's robe, / "but I
가 말했다.   뚫어지게 쳐다보며   유령의 옷자락을,

see something strange, / and not belonging to yourself, /
"하지만 이상한 게 보이네요,   당신의 것이 아닌 것이,

protruding from your skirts. Is it a foot or a claw?" /
스커트 자락 밖으로 빠져나온.   그것은 발인가요 아니면 발톱인가요?"

"It might be a claw, / for the flesh there is upon it," / was
"발톱이겠지.   살이 붙어 있으니까,"

the Spirit's sorrowful reply. "Look here."
유령이 슬픈 목소리로 대답했다.   "여기를 보아라."

From the foldings of its robe, / it brought two children;
옷자락으로부터,   유령은 두 명의 아이들을 끌어냈다:

/ wretched, abject, frightful, hideous, miserable. They
불쌍하고, 절망적이며, 놀랍고, 끔찍하고, 비참한 모습이었다.   아이들은

knelt down at its feet, / and clung upon the outside of its
무릎을 꿇은 채,   옷자락을 꼭 붙잡고 있었다.

garment.

"Oh, Man! Look here. Look, look, / down here!" /
"이보게!   여기를 보아라.   봐, 보라고,   여기 아래야!"

exclaimed the Ghost.
유령이 소리쳤다.

Key Expression

부정주어를 사용한 최상급
부정주어와 원급/비교급을 사용해서 최상급을 표현할 수 있습니다.
▶부정어 ~ so[as] 원급 as … : …만큼 ~한 것은 없다
▶부정어 ~ 비교급 than any other 단수명사 : …보다 더 ~한 것은 없다

ex) No change, no degradation, no perversion of humanity, in any grade, through
all the mysteries of wonderful creation, has monsters half so horrible and
dread.
어떤 변화도, 어떤 수모도, 인간성에 대한 어떤 왜곡도, 위대한 창조의 모든 신비
로운 과정을 통한 어떤 단계에서도, 그토록 끔찍하고 흉악한 악마같은 존재를
만들어내지 못했다 .
There is nothing in the world so irresistibly contagiousas laughter and good-
humor.
세상에는 웃음이나 유쾌한 기분만큼 저항할 수 없이 옮기 쉬운 것도 없다.

They were a boy and girl. Yellow, meagre, ragged,
남자 아이와 여자 아이였다. 얼굴은 누렇게 뜨고, 비쩍 마른 데다, 누더기를 걸치고,

/ scowling, wolfish; / but prostrate, / too, / in their
찡그린 채, 늑대같은 눈빛이었다; 하지만 적개심이 보였다, 또한, 겸손한 모습 안에는.

humility. Where graceful youth / should have filled
우아한 젊음은 어디로 갔을까 저 아이들의 얼굴에 가득했어야 하는,

their features out, / and touched them / with its freshest
아이들을 어루만지고 싱싱한 기운으로,

tints, / a stale and shrivelled hand, / like that of age, /
더럽고 쭈글쭈글한 손이, 나이든 것처럼,

had pinched, / and twisted them, / and pulled them into
꼬집고, 비틀어, 아이들을 갈기갈기 찢어놓은 듯 했다.

shreds. Where angels might have sat enthroned, / devils
천사들이 자리했어야 할 곳에, 악마들이

lurked, / and glared out menacing. No change, / no
숨어들어, 위협하며 노려보았다. 어떤 변화도,

degradation, / no perversion of humanity, / in any grade,
어떤 수모도, 인간성에 대한 어떤 왜곡도, 어떤 단계에서도,

/ through all the mysteries of wonderful creation, / has
위대한 창조의 모든 신비로운 과정을 통해, 악마같은

monsters half / so horrible and dread.
존재를 만들어 내지 못했다 이토록 끔찍하고 흉악한.

Scrooge started back, / appalled. Having them shown
스크루지는 뒷걸음쳤다, 간담이 서늘해져서. 그에게 아이들을 보여 주었으니

to him / in this way, / he tried to say / they were fine
이런 방식으로, 그는 말하려 했지만 귀여운 아이들이라고,

children, / but the words choked themselves, / rather than
그 말이 목에 걸려 나오지 않았다,

be parties to a lie of such enormous magnitude.
그런 엄청난 거짓말에 참여하기 보다는.

---

justified 당연한, 정당한, (그럴 만한) 이유가 있는 | protrude 튀어나오다, 돌출되다 | wretched 비참한, 불쌍한
| abject 극도로 비참한, 절망적인 | hideous 흉측한, 끔찍한 | miserable 비참한 | cling 꼭 붙잡다, 매달리다
| garment 의복, 옷 | ragged 누더기를 걸친 | scowling 찡그린 | wolfish 늑대같은 | prostrate 엎드린 |
humility 겸손 | tint 색조 | stale 생기가 없는 | pinch 꼬집다 | enthrone 왕좌에 앉히다 | lurk 숨어 있다 |
glare 노려보다 | menace 위협하다 | degradation 비하, 수모 | perversion 왜곡 | appalled 간담이 서늘한,
끔찍해 하는 | magnitude (엄청난) 규모

"Spirit! Are they yours?" / Scrooge could say no more.
"유령님! 당신의 아이들인가요?" 스크루지는 더 이상 말을 하지 못했다.

"They are Man's," / said the Spirit, / looking down upon
"인간의 아이들이지." 영혼이 말했다. 아이들을 내려다보며.

them. "And they cling to me, / appealing from their
"그리고 내게 매달려서, 아버지를 구해 달라고 애원하고 있어.

fathers. This boy is Ignorance. This girl is Want. Beware
남자 아이의 이름은 '무지'야. 여자 아이의 이름은 '결핍'이지.

them both, / and all of their degree, / but most of all /
이 둘을 경계하게. 그리고 이들과 비슷한 모든 것들도, 하지만 무엇보다도

beware this boy, / for on his brow / I see that written /
남자 아이를 경계하라. 왜냐하면 그의 이마에 적혀 있는 게 보이니까

which is Doom, / unless the writing be erased. Deny it!" /
'파멸'이라고, 그 글자가 지워지지 않는다면. 그것을 물리쳐라!"

cried the Spirit, / stretching out its hand / towards the city.
유령이 소리쳤다. 손을 뻗으며 도시를 향해.

"Slander those who tell it ye! Admit it / for your factious
"너희에게 그것을 말하는 사람들을 비난해라! 그것을 받아들여라 당파의 목적을 위해.

purposes, / and make it worse. And bide the end!"
그러면 무지는 더욱 악화될 것이다. 그리하여 종말을 맞이할 것이다!"

"Have they no refuge or resource?" / cried Scrooge.
"아이들에게 피난처나 도와줄 자원은 없나요?" 스크루지가 물었다.

"Are there no prisons?" / said the Spirit, / turning on him
"감옥이 없느냐고?" 유령이 말했다. 그에게 되돌려 주며

/ for the last time / with his own words. "Are there no
지난번에 했던 마지막 말을. "아니면 구빈원이 없느냐고?"

workhouses?"

The bell struck twelve.
종소리가 12시를 울렸다.

Scrooge looked about him / for the Ghost, / and saw it
스크루지는 주변을 돌아보며 유령을 찾았는데, 보이지 않았다.

not. As the last stroke ceased to vibrate, / he remembered
마지막 종소리가 떨림을 멈추자,

want 결핍, 빈곤 | slander 비방하다 | factious 당파적인 | bide 살다, 머무르다 | workhouses (과거 영국의)
구빈원 | cease 중단되다, 그치다 | vibrate 떨다, 흔들리다, 진동하다 | prediction 예측, 예견 | beheld 바라보다 |
drape (옷을 느슨하게) 걸치다

the prediction of old Jacob Marley, / and lifting up his
그는 제이콥 말리의 예언을 기억해 내며,   눈을 들었고,

eyes, / beheld a solemn Phantom, / draped and hooded, /
              근엄한 모습의 유령이 보였다,   옷을 걸치고 두건을 쓴 채,

coming, / like a mist along the ground, / towards him.
다가오는,   땅에서 퍼지는 안개처럼,   자신을 향해.

 mini test 6

A. 다음 문장을 해석해 보세요.

(1) The old man, / in a voice / that seldom rose / above the howling of the wind / upon the barren waste, / was singing them a Christmas song.
→

(2) So surely as they raised their voices, / the old man got quite blithe and loud; / and so surely as they stopped, / his vigour sank again.
→

(3) In spite of all her silken rustlings, / and herrapid flutterings past him, / he got her into a corner / whence there was no escape.
→

(4) No change, / no degradation, / no perversion of humanity, / in any grade, / through all the mysteries of wonderful creation, / has monsters half / so horrible and dread.
→

B. 다음 주어진 문구가 알맞은 문장이 되도록 순서를 맞춰 보세요.

(1) 그들은 결코 무슨 일이든 적당히 하지 않는다.
(halves / anything / never / they / by / do)
→

(2) 삼촌이 부자인들 아무 소용이 없는 걸.
(him / of / wealth / use / His / to / is / no)
→

 Answer

A. (1) 노인은, 황무지에서 울부짖는 바람 소리에 묻혀 거의 들리지 않는 목소리로, 그들에게 크리스마스 노래를 불러 주고 있었다. (2) 아주 확실히 그들이 목소리를 높이면, 노인은 아주 즐거워져 크게 부르고; 마찬가지로 그들이 노래를 멈추면, 노인의 활력도 다시 가라앉았다. (3) 비단옷의 사각거리는 소리와 그의 옆을

(3) 난 그 사람을 참을 수 없어요.
(patience / I / have / no / him / with)
→

(4) 그녀가 가는 곳이면 어디든지, 그곳에 그도 갔다!
(there / she / went / went, / Wherever / he)
→

C. 다음 주어진 문장이 본문의 내용과 맞으면 T, 틀리면 F에 동그라미 하세요.

(1) Scrooge and the Spirit visited miners and soldiers.
(T / F)

(2) Scrooge's nephew hate Scrooge very much.
(T / F)

(3) The Spirit hid two kids inside his robe.
(T / F)

(4) Scrooge remained as he was, but the Ghost grew older.
(T / F)

D. 의미가 비슷한 것끼리 서로 연결해 보세요.

(1) bleak   ▶   ◀ ① dismal

(2) defy   ▶   ◀ ② wicked

(3) vile   ▶   ◀ ③ regret

(4) precept   ▶   ◀ ④ instruction

재빨리 지나가려는 움직임에도 불구하고, 그는 그녀를 빠져나갈 공간이 없는 구석으로 몰아넣었다. (4)
어떤 변화도, 어떤 수모도, 인간성에 대한 어떤 왜곡도, 위대한 창조의 모든 신비로운 과정을 통한 어
떤 단계에서도, 그토록 끔찍하고 흉악한 악마같은 존재를 만들어내지 못했다. | B. (1) They never do
anything by halves. (2) His wealth is of no use to him. (3) I have no patience with him. (4) Wher-
ever she went, there went he! | C. (1) F (2) F (3) F (4) T | D. (1) ① (2) ④ (3) ② (4) ①

7

THE LAST OF THE SPIRITS
마지막 유령

The Phantom slowly, gravely, silently, approached. When
유령은 천천히, 근엄하고, 소리없이 다가왔다.

it came near him, / Scrooge bent down upon his knee; /
유령이 가까이 오자,   스크루지는 무릎을 꿇었다;

for in the very air / through which this Spirit moved / it
바로 그 공기 속에서   유령이 뚫고 온

seemed to scatter gloom and mystery.
우울하고 신비한 기운이 흩어지는 듯 보였기 때문이었다.

It was shrouded / in a deep black garment, / which
유령은 덮여 있었고   시커먼 옷으로,

concealed its head, its face, its form, / and left nothing
머리, 얼굴, 몸 전체를 가리고 있어서,   아무것도 보이지 않았다

of it visible / save one outstretched hand. But for this / it
쭉 뻗은 팔 하나를 제외하고는.   이것마저 없었다면

would have been difficult / to detach its figure from the
힘들었을 것이다   그 모습과 어두운 밤을 구별하고,

night, / and separate it from the darkness / by which it
유령과 어둠을 구분하는 것이

was surrounded.
둘러 싸고 있는.

He felt / that it was tall and stately / when it came beside
느껴졌다   키가 크고 위풍당당한 모습이   유령이 그의 옆에 다가왔을 때,

him, / and that its mysterious presence / filled him with a
그리고 그 신비스러운 존재에   엄숙한 두려움으로 가득

solemn dread. He knew no more, / for the Spirit neither
찼다.   그는 더 이상 알 수 없었다,   유령이 말도 하지 않고 움직이지도

spoke nor moved.
않았기 때문에.

---

gravely 근엄하게, 진지하게 | scatter 흩어지다 | shroud 뒤덮다, 가리다, 가리개 | conceal 감추다, 숨기다
| outstretched 죽 뻗은 | detach 분리하다 | surround 둘러싸다, 에워싸다 | stately 위풍당당한 | pursue
계속하다 | contract 줄어들다 | incline 고개를 끄덕이다

"I am in the presence of the Ghost of Christmas / Yet To
"제가 지금 크리스마스 유령 앞에 있는 것이군요

Come?" / said Scrooge.
미래의?"   스크루지가 말했다.

The Spirit answered not, / but pointed onward / with its
유령은 대답하지 않았지만,   앞을 가리켰다   그

hand.
손으로.

"You are about to show me / shadows of the things / that
"당신은 제게 보여 주려는 것이군요   일들의 그림자를

have not happened, / but will happen / in the time before
아직 일어나지 않았지만,   일어나게 될   미래에."

us," / Scrooge pursued. "Is that so, / Spirit?"
      스크루지는 말을 계속했다.   "그렇죠,   유령님?"

The upper portion of the garment was contracted / for
옷의 윗부분이 줄어들며

an instant / in its folds, / as if the Spirit had inclined its
잠시동안   주름이 잡혔다.   마치 유령이 고개를 끄덕이는 듯.

head. That was the only answer / he received.
그것이 유일한 답변이었다   그가 얻어낸.

Key Expression 🎯

be about to : 막 ~하려고 하다
be about to는 '막 ~하려고 하다, ~할 참이다'라는 뜻을 나타내는 숙어입니
다. 강조를 위해 just를 넣어 be just about to라고 쓰기도 합니다.

ex) You are about to show me shadows of the things that have not happened,
but will happen in the time before us.
당신은 제게 아직 일어나지 않았지만 미래에 일어나게 될 일들의 그림자를 보여
주려는 것이군요.

Although well used to ghostly company / by this time,
유령과 동행하는데 익숙해졌음에도 불구하고, 지금까지,

/ Scrooge feared the silent shape so much / that his legs
스크루지는 유령이 침묵하는 모습에 매우 공포감을 느껴서

trembled beneath him, / and he found that he could
다리까지 떨릴 정도였고, 거의 서 있을 수도 없을 지경이었다

hardly stand / when he prepared to follow it. The Spirit
유령을 따라가려고 준비할 때,

paused a moment, / as observing his condition, / and
유령은 잠시 멈춰 서서, 그의 모습을 보자,

giving him time to recover.
회복할 시간을 주었다.

But Scrooge was all the worse / for this. It thrilled him
하지만 스크루지의 상태는 더욱 악화됐다 이 유령을 보고, 소름끼쳤고

/ with a vague uncertain horror, / to know / that behind
모호하고 불확실한 두려움으로, 알고 나서

the dusky shroud, / there were ghostly eyes / intently
시커먼 장막 뒤에, 유령의 눈이 있다는 것을

fixed upon him, / while he, / though he stretched his own
자신을 뚫어지게 쳐다보는, 그는, 고개를 최대한 들었지만,

to the utmost, / could see nothing / but a spectral hand
아무것도 보이지 않았다

and one great heap of black.
유령의 손과 크고 검은 형체 외에는.

"Ghost of the Future!" / he exclaimed, / "I fear you /
"미래의 유령님!" 스크루지가 소리쳤다, "유령님이 두려워요

more than any spectre / I have seen. But as I know / your
어느 유령보다도 지금까지 본. 하지만 알고 있으니까

purpose is to do me good, / and as I hope to live / to be
제게 도움을 주려고 온 것을, 그리고 살고 싶으니까

another man / from what I was, / I am prepared / to bear
다른 사람이 되어 과거의 제가 아닌, 전 준비되어 있어요

you company, / and do it with a thankful heart. Will you
유령님과 동행할, 감사하는 마음으로 함께하려는.

not speak to me?"
제게 말씀해 주시겠어요?"

It gave him no reply. The hand was pointed straight
유령은 대답하지 않았다.   그의 손이 곧장 앞쪽을 가리켰을 뿐이다.

before them.

"Lead on!" / said Scrooge. "Lead on! The night is
"인도해 주세요!"   스크루지가 말했다.   "인도해 주세요!

waning fast, / and it is precious time to me, / I know.
밤은 금방 흘러가요.   그리고 제게는 귀중한 시간입니다.   알고 있어요.

Lead on, / Spirit!"
인도해 주세요,   유령님!"

The Phantom moved away / as it had come towards him.
유령은 움직였다   그에게 다가왔을 때처럼.

Scrooge followed / in the shadow of its dress, / which
스크루지가 따라가자   유령 옷자락의 그림자 속으로,   그림자는

bore him up, / he thought, / and carried him along.
그를 들어올려,   그가 생각하기에,   데려가는 것 같았다.

They scarcely seemed to enter the city; / for the city /
그들은 도시로 들어간 것 같지 않았다;   왜냐하면 도시가

rather seemed to spring up about them, / and encompass
오히려 그들 주변에 솟아올라,

them of its own act. But there they were, / in the heart
그들을 감싼 듯 했기 때문이다.   하지만 그들은 있었다,   도시의 한복판에;

of it; / on 'Change, / amongst the merchants; / who
동전들이,   상인들 사이에;

hurried up and down, / and chinked the money / in their
바삐 오르내리며,   돈을 짤랑거리고

pockets, / and conversed / in groups, / and looked at their
주머니 속에서,   이야기를 나누며   모여서,   시계를 들여다 보거나,

watches, / and trifled thoughtfully / with their great gold
진지하게 장난치거나   시계의 금색 인장을 갖고;

seals; / and so forth, / as Scrooge had seen them often.
등의 행동을 했다,   스크루지가 종종 보아왔듯이.

---

vague 희미한, 모호한 | utmost 최대한, 극도의 | spectral 유령의, 귀신의 | spectre 유령, 귀신 | wane 줄어들다,
달이 이지러지다 | spring 튀다 | encompass 둘러싸다 | amongst ~의 가운데(=among) | chink 쟁그랑거리다 |
converse 대화를 나누다 | trifle 하찮은 것, 하찮게 보다 | seal 인장

The Spirit stopped / beside one little knot of business
유령은 멈춰 섰다   모여 있는 몇몇 상인들 옆에.

men. Observing that the hand was pointed to them, /
          유령의 손이 그들을 가리키는 것을 보자,

Scrooge advanced / to listen to their talk.
스크루지는 그들에게 다가가서   대화에 귀를 기울였다.

"No," / said a great fat man / with a monstrous chin, / "I
"아니,"   매우 뚱뚱한 남자가 말했다   큰 턱을 가진,

don't know much about it, / either way. I only know he's
"난 그것에 대해 잘 몰라,   어느 쪽인지.   그가 죽었다는 것만 알

dead."
뿐이지."

"When did he die?" / inquired another.
"언제 죽었는데?"   다른 남자가 물었다.

"Last night, / I believe."
"어젯밤에,   내 생각에는."

"Why, / what was the matter with him?" / asked a third, /
"저런,   무슨 일인데?"   세 번째 남자가 물었다,

taking a vast quantity of snuff / out of a very large snuff-
코담배를 잔뜩 꺼내며   커다란 담배갑에서.

box. "I thought he'd never die."
      "그는 죽지 않을 거라고 생각했는데."

"God knows," / said the first, / with a yawn.
"누가 알겠어,"   첫 번째 남자가 말했다, 하품을 하며.

"What has he done / with his money?" / asked a red-
"어떻게 했대   그의 돈은?"   붉은 얼굴의 신사가 물었다

faced gentleman / with a pendulous excrescence / on the
                  늘어진 혹을 가진

end of his nose, / that shook like the gills of a turkey-
코 끝에,   그 혹이 칠면조 수컷의 턱살처럼 흔들렸다.

cock.

---

monstrous 무시무시하게 큰 | snuff 코담배 | pendulous 축 늘어져 대롱거리는 | excrescence 혹, 사마귀 |

gills (복수형) 아가미 | turkey-cock 칠면조의 수컷 | pleasantry 사교적인 인사말

"I haven't heard," / said the man with the large chin, /
"못 들었네."　　　　　　　큰 턱을 가진 남자가 말했다.

yawning again. "Left it to his company, / perhaps. He
다시 하품하며.　　　　　"회사에 남겼겠지.　　　아마도.

hasn't left it to me. That's all I know."
나한텐 한 푼도 안 남겼어.　　내가 아는 건 그게 전부야."

This pleasantry was received / with a general laugh.
이런 인사말이 오갔다　　　　　　한바탕 웃음이 터지며.

"It's likely to be a very cheap funeral," / said the same
"아주 저렴한 장례식이 될 것 같군."　　　　　같은 남자가 말했다;

speaker; / "for upon my life / I don't know of anybody to
"내 인생에서　　　　　가겠다는 사람이 아무도 없으니.

go to it. Suppose we make up a party and volunteer?"
우리가 무리지어 자발적으로 간다면?"

"I don't mind going / if a lunch is provided," / observed
"가도 괜찮아　　　　점심이 나온다면야"

the gentleman / with the excrescence on his nose. "But I
신사가 말했다　　코에 혹이 난.　　　　　　　　　"하지만

must be fed, / if I make one."
반드시 먹을 거야.　　일행에 낀다면."

Another laugh.
다시 웃음이 터져 나왔다.

"Well, / I am the most disinterested among you, / after
"음,　　　내가 가장 관심없는 사람이군,

all," / said the first speaker, / "for I never wear black
결국."　　첫 번째 남자가 말했다.　　　　"난 절대 검은 장갑도 끼지 않고,

gloves, / and I never eat lunch. But I'll offer to go, / if
　　　　점심도 먹지 않을 거니까.　　　　하지만 가겠네

anybody else will. When I come to think of it, / I'm not
누군가 함께 간다면.　　　　생각해 보니.

at all sure / that I wasn't his most particular friend; / for
확실치 않지만　　내가 그의 가장 특별한 친구가 아니었는가 싶군;

we used to stop and speak / whenever we met. Bye, bye!"
멈춰 서서 이야기도 나눴느니　　　마주치게 되면.　　　그럼, 잘 가게나!"

Speakers and listeners strolled away, / and mixed with
이야기를 나누던 뻘뻘이 흩어져서,   다른 무리 속에 섞였다.

other groups. Scrooge knew the men, / and looked
스크루지는 그 사람들을 알고 있었기에,   유령을 쳐다보았다

towards the Spirit / for an explanation.
유령을 바라며,

The Phantom glided on / into a street. Its finger pointed
유령은 미끄러져 갔다   거리 속으로.   그의 손가락은 가리켰다

/ to two persons meeting. Scrooge listened again, /
두 사람이 만나고 있는 모습을.   스크루지는 다시 귀를 기울였다,

thinking / that the explanation might lie here.
생각하면서   이곳에서 설명을 들을 수 있을까 싶어서.

He knew these men, / also, / perfectly. They were men
스크루지는 이들도 알고 있었다.   역시,   아주 잘.   그들은 사업가들이었다:

of business: / very wealthy, / and of great importance.
매우 부유하고,   중요한 사람들이었다.

He had made a point always / of standing well in their
그는 항상 중요하게 여겼다   좋은 평판을 얻는 것을:

esteem: / in a business point of view, / that is; / strictly /
사업적인 측면에서,   말하자면: 엄격하게

in a business point of view.
사업적인 측면에서였다.

"How are you?" / said one.
"잘 지내셨어요?"   한 사람이 말했다.

"How are you?" / returned the other.
"잘 지내셨어요?"   다른 사람이 대답했다.

"Well!" / said the first. "Old Scratch has got his own / at
"음!"   첫 번째 사람이 말했다.   "스크루지 영감이 돌아가셨다네요

last, / hey?"
결국,   그렇죠?"

"So I am told," / returned the second. "Cold, / isn't it?"
"저도 그렇게 들었어요,"   두 번째 사람이 대답했다.   "춥네요,   그렇죠?"

"Seasonable for Christmas time. You're not a skater, / I
"크리스마스 시즌에 어울리는 날씨네요.   스케이트를 안 타시나 봐요,

suppose?"
그런가요?"

"No. No. Something else to think of. Good morning!"
"네. 안 타요. 다른 볼 일이 생각나서. 안녕히 가세요!"

Not another word. That was their meeting, / their
다른 말은 없었다. 그것이 그들의 만남이었고,

conversation, / and their parting.
대화였으며, 작별이었다.

Scrooge was / at first / inclined to be surprised / that
스크루지는 처음에 놀랐다

the Spirit should attach importance to conversations /
유령이 대화에 중요한 의미를 두는 것에

apparently so trivial; / but feeling assured / that they
분명히 사소해 보이는; 하지만 확신이 느껴져서

must have some hidden purpose, / he set himself to
숨겨진 의도가 있는 것이 분명하다는, 그는 곰곰이 생각했다

consider / what it was likely to be. They could scarcely
그것이 무엇일지.

be supposed to have any bearing / on the death of Jacob,
그 대화가 어떤 의미를 내포하고 있을 리는 없지만 제이콥의 죽음에 대해,

/ his old partner, / for that was Past, / and this Ghost's
그의 오랜 동업자인, 그것은 과거의 유령이 한 말이고, 이 유령이 관여하는 영역은

province was the Future. Nor could he think of any one /
미래이기 때문이었다. 그는 아무도 생각해 낼 수 없었다

immediately / connected with himself, / to whom he could
바로 자신과 관련된, 그 대화에 적용할 만한.

apply them. But nothing doubting that / to whomsoever
하지만 의심할 바 없이 그 대화에 관련된 사람이

they applied / they had some latent moral / for his own
누구든 숨겨져 있는 교훈이 있다는 것이 분명하기에

improvement, / he resolved to treasure up / every word
자신의 발전을 위한, 그는 간직하기로 결심했다 자신이 들었던 모든

he heard, / and everything he saw; / and especially to
이야기와, 보았던 모든 것을;

observe the shadow of himself / when it appeared. For he
그리고 특히 자신의 환영을 관찰하겠다고 나타나면. 왜냐하면

had an expectation / that the conduct of his future self /
기대를 가졌기 때문이었다 미래의 자신이 하는 행동이

would give him the clue he missed, / and would render
과거에 놓친 단서를 제공해 줄 것이며,

the solution of these riddles easy.
이런 수수께끼를 해결해 줄 것이라고.

He looked about / in that very place / for his own image;
그는 둘러보았다   바로 그 자리에서   자신의 환영을 찾으며;

/ but another man stood / in his accustomed corner, / and
하지만 다른 사람이 서 있었다   익숙했던 자리에는,

though the clock pointed / to his usual time of day for
또한 시계가 가리키고 있었지만   자신이 평소 그곳에 나타났던 시간을,

being there, / he saw no likeness of himself / among the
          자신과 비슷한 사람을 볼 수 없었다

multitudes / that poured in / through the Porch. It gave
사람들 중에서   밀려 들어오는   현관을 통과하여.   그 광경에 스크

him little surprise, / however; / for he had been revolving
루지는 그다지 놀라지 않았다.   그러나;   왜냐하면 그는 계속해서

/ in his mind / a change of life, / and thought and hoped /
마음속에서   삶의 변화를 겪었고,   생각하며 바랐기 때문이다

he saw / his new-born resolutions carried out / in this.
보게 되기를   새로운 결심이 실행되는 것을   이 장면에서.

Quiet and dark, / beside him stood the Phantom, / with
조용하고 어두운 가운데,   그의 옆에는 유령이 서 있었다

its outstretched hand. When he roused himself / from
손을 쭉 뻗은 채.   정신을 차렸을 때

his thoughtful quest, / he fancied / from the turn of the
깊은 생각에 빠져 있다가,   그는 생각했다   손의 방향이 바뀐 것을 보고,

hand, / and its situation in reference to himself, / that the
          그리고 자신에 대한 유령의 위치로.

Unseen Eyes were looking at him keenly. It made him
보이지 않는 눈이 자신을 날카롭게 바라보고 있다고.   그로 인해 몸이 떨리고,

shudder, / and feel very cold.
          오싹함을 느꼈다.

---

latent 잠재하는, 잠복해 있는 | moral 교훈 | resolve 결심하다 | treasure up 모아두다, 간직하다 | multitude
아주 많은 수, 다수 | porch 현관 | revolve 회전하다 | quest 탐구, 탐색 | fancy 생각하다, 상상하다 | in
reference to ~에 관하여 | keenly 날카롭게 | shudder 몸을 떨다, 전율하다

They left the busy scene, / and went into an obscure
그들은 분주한 광경을 떠나,   마을의 어둑한 부분으로 들어갔다,

part of the town, / where Scrooge had never penetrated
                          스크루지가 지나간 적이 없었던

/ before, / although he recognised / its situation, / and its
이전에,   알고 있었지만,   그 위치와,

bad repute. The ways were foul and narrow; / the shops
그곳에 대한 악명도. 길은 더럽고 좁았으며;

and houses wretched; / the people half-naked, drunken,
상점과 주택은 끔찍했고;   사람들은 헐벗고, 술에 취한 채,

/ slipshod, ugly. Alleys and archways, / like so many
남루한 옷에, 흉측했다. 골목길과 아치형 입구는,   시궁창이나 다름없는,

cesspools, / disgorged / their offences of smell, / and dirt,
                쏟아냈다   냄새나는 범죄와,   오물과,

/ and life, / upon the straggling streets; / and the whole
삶을,   멋대로 뻗어있는 거리로;   그리고 모든 구역에서

quarter reeked / with crime, / with filth, / and misery.
악취가 풍겼다   범죄와,   오물과,   빈곤의.

Far in this den of infamous resort, / there was a low-
이 악명 높은 깊숙한 소굴에,   입구가 낮은,

browed, / beetling shop, / below a pent-house roof, /
        튀어나온 상점이 있었다   팬트하우스 지붕 아래,

---

obscure 모호한, 희미한 | penetrate 뚫고 들어가다, 관통하다 | recognise 인식하다, 알아보다(=recognize) |
repute 평판, 명성 | foul 더러운, 악취 나는 | wretched 끔찍한, 형편없는 | slipshod 엉성한, 대충 한 | alley
골목길, 좁은 뒷길 | archway 아치 지붕이 덮인 길, 아치형 입구 | cesspool 오수 구덩이, 시궁창 | disgorge 쏟아
내다, 토해 내다 | offence 범죄, 모욕, 불쾌한 행위 | straggling 흩어져 있는, 멋대로 뻗은 | quarter (도시 내의)
구역, 지구 | reek 지독한 악취를 풍기다 | filth 오물, 쓰레기 | misery 고통, 빈곤 | den 굴, 소굴 | low-browed (
바위가) 튀어나온, (건물) 입구가 낮은 | beetling (눈썹·벼랑 등이) 돌출한 | pent-house 펜트하우스(고층 건물 맨
위층에 자리한 고급 아파트) | rag 걸레 | greasy 기름 투성이의 | offal (동물의) 내장 | rusty 녹슨, 녹 투성이의 |
hinge 경첩 | file (매끈하게 다듬는 데 쓰는) 줄 | scale 큰 저울 | weight (고정시키는데 쓰이는) 추 | refuse 폐물
| scrutinise 세심히 살피다(=scrutinize) | unseemly 꼴 사나운 | corrupted 변질된, 부패된 | sepulchre 무덤 |
ware 제품, 기물, 물품 | charcoal 숯, 석탄 | rascal 악한, 악당 | frousy 곰팡내 나는, 너저분한(=frowzy) | tatters
누더기, 넝마

where iron, / old rags, / bottles, / bones, / and greasy
그곳에서는 쇠붙이,   낡은 걸레,   빈 병,   뼈다귀,   기름투성이의 내장을,

offal, / were bought. Upon the floor within, / were piled
팔고 있었다.   안으로 들어가면,   쌓여 있었다

up / heaps of rusty keys, / nails, / chains, / hinges, / files,
수많은 녹슨 열쇠와,   못과,   사슬,   경첩,   줄,

/ scales, / weights, / and refuse iron of all kinds. Secrets
저울,   추,   그리고 온갖 종류의 고철들이.

that few would like to scrutinise / were bred and hidden /
아무도 살피고 싶어하지 않는 비밀들이   숨어 자라났다

in mountains / of unseemly rags, / masses of corrupted fat,
산더미 속에서   볼품없는 걸레 조각과,   부패된 비계 덩어리와,

/ and sepulchres of bones. Sitting in among the wares / he
뼈 무덤의.   물건들 사이에 앉아서   그가

dealt in, / by a charcoal stove, / made of old bricks, / was a
다루고 있는,   석탄 난로 옆에,   낡은 벽돌로 만들어진,   머리가 희

grey-haired rascal, / nearly seventy years of age; / who had
끗한 건달 노인이 있었다,   70세쯤 된;

screened himself / from the cold air without, / by a frousy
그는 가려놓고   차가운 공기가 들어오지 않도록,

curtaining of miscellaneous tatters, / hung upon a line; /
넝마 조각으로 만든 너저분한 천막으로,   줄을 지어 걸려 있는,

and smoked his pipe / in all the luxury of calm retirement.
그리고 파이프 담배를 피웠다   조용한 은퇴 생활을 누리면서.

Key Expression

be followed by 의 해석

follow는 '따라가다'라는 뜻을 가진 동사입니다. 이를 수동태로 사용하여 be followed by가 되면 '뒤이어 ~가 생겨나다, 뒤따라 ~가 들어오다'라는 의미로 해석합니다.

ex) She was closely followed by a man in faded black, who was no less startled by the sight of them, than they had been upon the recognition of each other.
빛 바랜 검은 옷을 입은 한 남자가 여자의 바로 뒤를 따라 들어왔고, 그는 두 여자를 보자 두 여자가 서로를 알아보고 놀란 것 만큼 깜짝 놀랐다.

Scrooge and the Phantom came / into the presence of this
스크루지와 유령은 안으로 들어갔다   이 남자에게,

man, / just as a woman / with a heavy bundle / slunk into
바로 그때 한 여자가   무거운 짐을 든   상점 안으로 살금

the shop. But she had scarcely entered, / when another
살금 들어갔다. 하지만 그녀가 미처 들어오기도 전에,   다른 여자가,

woman, / similarly laden, / came in too; / and she was
똑같이 짐을 잔뜩 든,   역시 들어왔고   여자의 바로 뒤를 따라

closely followed / by a man / in faded black, / who was no
들어왔다   한 남자가   빛 바랜 검은 옷을 입은,

less startled / by the sight of them, / than they had been /
그는 깜짝 놀랐고   두 여자를 보고,   두 여자가 놀란 것 만큼

upon the recognition of each other. After a short period of
서로를 알아보고.   잠시 놀라서 멍해 있다가,

blank astonishment, / in which the old man with the pipe
파이프를 문 노인이 끼어 들자,

had joined them, / they all three burst into a laugh.
세 사람 모두 웃음을 터뜨렸다.

"Let the charwoman alone to be the first!" / cried she
"청소부가 첫 번째예요!"

who had entered first. "Let the laundress alone to be the
가장 먼저 들어온 여자가 소리쳤다.   "세탁부가 두 번째;

second; / and let the undertaker's man alone to be the
장의사가 세 번째예요.

third. Look here, / old Joe, / here's a chance! If we haven't
보세요,   조 영감님,   이런 우연이 있네요!   우리 셋이 이곳에서

all three met here / without meaning it!"
만나지 못했다면요   그런 의도가 없이."

"You couldn't have met / in a better place," / said old
"만날 수 없을 테니까   더 좋은 장소는,"   조 영감이 대답했다.

Joe, / removing his pipe from his mouth. "Come into the
파이프를 입에서 떼며.   "응접실로 들어오게.

parlour. You were made free of it long ago, / you know; /
오래 전부터 이곳에서 편하게 지냈잖아,   당신도 알다시피;

and the other two an't strangers. Stop till I shut the door
다른 두 사람도 낯선 이들은 아니고.   가게 문을 닫고 올 때까지 기다리게.

of the shop. Ah! How it skreeks! There an't such a rusty bit
아! 너무 삐걱거리는군! 녹슨 쇠붙이는 없을 거야

of metal / in the place / as its own hinges, / I believe; / and
이곳에서 이 경첩만큼, 틀림없이;

I'm sure / there's no such old bones / here, / as mine.
그리고 확실히 그렇게 오래된 뼈다귀도 없지 이곳에서, 내 것만큼.

Ha, ha! We're all suitable / to our calling, / we're well
하, 하! 모두 어울리는 군 각자의 직업에, 우리는 참 잘 맞지.

matched. Come into the parlor. Come into the parlor."
응접실로 오게. 어서 들어오게."

The parlor was the space / behind the screen of rags. The
응접실이 있었다 넝마 천막 뒤에.

old man raked the fire together / with an old stair-rod, / and
노인은 화로를 헤쳐 정리하고 양탄자 누르개로,

having trimmed his smoky lamp / (for it was night), / with
등잔 심지를 다듬은 후 (밤이 되었으므로),

the stem of his pipe, / put it in his mouth again.
파이프 설대로, 다시 파이프를 입에 물었다.

While he did this, / the woman who had already spoken /
노인이 이러는 동안, 조금 전 말한 여성은

threw her bundle on the floor, / and sat down in a flaunting
짐을 바닥에 던져 놓고, 거만한 자세로 앉았다

manner / on a stool; / crossing her elbows on her knees, /
의자에; 무릎 위에 팔짱 낀 팔을 놓은 채,

and looking with a bold defiance / at the other two.
반항적인 눈빛으로 바라보았다 다른 두 사람을.

"What odds then! What odds, / Mrs. Dilber?" / said
"그래서 뭐가 이상하다는 거야! 뭐가 이상한데, 딜버 부인?"

the woman. "Every person has a right / to take care of
여자가 말했다. "모두 권리가 있죠 자신을 돌볼.

themselves. He always did."
그는 항상 그랬어요."

---

slink 살금살금 움직이다, 슬그머니 움직이다 | laden 잔뜩 든 | faded 시든, 빛깔이 바랜 | burst into 갑자기
터뜨리다 | charwoman 청소부 | parlour 응접실 | skreek 울다(=skrike) | rake 헤치다, 긁어 모으다 | stair-rod
양탄자 누르개(양탄자를 누르는 금속 막대) | trim 다듬다, 잘라 내다 | stem 담배 설대 | flaunting 과시하는 |
defiance 반항

"That's true, / indeed!" / said the laundress. "No man
"그건 그래요, 맞아요!" 세탁부가 말했다.

more so."
"더 지독한 사람은 없을 거예요."

"Why then, / don't stand staring / as if you was afraid, /
"그렇다면, 쳐다보며 서 있지 말라고요 불안해 하는 듯이,

woman; / who's the wiser? We're not going to pick holes
부인; 누가 더 똑똑한가요? 우리가 구멍을 찾아내려는 게 아니잖아요

/ in each other's coats, / I suppose?"
각자의 코트에서 내 생각엔?"

"No, / indeed!" / said Mrs. Dilber and the man together.
"아니지, 그럼!" 딜버 부인과 남자가 함께 말했다.

"We should hope not."
"그러면 안 되지."

"Very well, / then!" / cried the woman. "That's enough.
"좋아, 그럼 됐어!" 여자가 소리쳤다. "그거면 충분해.

Who's the worse / for the loss of a few things like these?
누가 더 나빠지겠어 이따위 물건 몇 개 잃는다고?

Not a dead man, / I suppose."
죽은 사람이라도 안 그럴 걸, 내 생각에는."

"No, / indeed," / said Mrs. Dilber, / laughing.
아닐 거야, 그렇고 말고," 딜버 부인이 말했다, 웃으면서.

"If he wanted to keep 'em / after he was dead, / a wicked
"그 양반이 계속 갖고 있길 원했다면 죽은 뒤에도, 못된 영감이,

old screw," / pursued the woman, / "why wasn't he
못된 영감이, 여자가 말을 이었다, "왜 제대로 하지 않은 거람

natural / in his lifetime? If he had been, / he'd have had
살아있는 동안? 그랬다면, 누군가 돌봐줬겠지

somebody to look after him / when he was struck with
갑자기 죽음을 맞이했을 때,

Death, / instead of lying gasping out his last there, /
그곳에서 마지막 숨을 거두는 대신,

alone by himself."
홀로."

wicked 못된, 사악한 | screw 교도관, 간수 | pursue 계속하다 | gasp out 마지막 숨을 거두다 | depend upon
~에 의존하다, ~에 달려있다, ~에 따라 다르다 | plain 솔직한, 있는 그대로의 | help oneself 마음대로 집어먹다,
마음대로 쓰다, 훔치다

"It's the truest word / that ever was spoke," / said Mrs.
"가장 맞는 말이군   지금까지 들어본."   딜버 부인이 말했다.

Dilber. "It's a judgment on him."
"그에 대한 심판인 거야."

"I wish it was a little heavier judgment," / replied the
"더 심한 벌을 받았으면 좋았을 것을."   여자가 대답했다:

woman; / "and it should have been, / you may depend
"그랬어야 했는데,   당신들도 달라졌을지 모르지,

upon it, / if I could have laid my hands on anything else.
내가 다른 것을 들고 나왔다면.

Open that bundle, / old Joe, / and let me know the value
짐 좀 열어 봐요,   조 영감님,   그리고 값어치가 얼마나 되는지 알려 줘요.

of it. Speak out plain. I'm not afraid to be the first, / nor
솔직히 말해 줘요.   내 것이 처음이라도 두려울 것 없고,

afraid for them to see it. We know pretty well / that we
저 사람들이 내 짐을 봐도 괜찮아요.   우리는 매우 잘 알고 있으니까

were helping ourselves, / before we met here, / I believe.
마음껏 훔쳤다는 걸,   여기에서 만나기 전에,   분명히.

It's no sin. Open the bundle, / Joe."
그건 죄도 아니죠. 꾸러미를 열어 봐요,   조 영감님."

Key Expression ✏

pretty : 매우, 꽤

pretty는 '예쁜, 귀여운'이라는 뜻의 형용사로 알려져 있지만 형용사나 부사 앞에 쓰일 때에는 '매우, 꽤'라는 의미를 가진 부사가 됩니다. '예쁜'이라는 의미의 부사는 prettily(예쁘게)입니다.
이처럼 그 자체로 부사의 의미를 가지면서 -ly 형태의 부사도 존재하는 단어들이 있습니다.

▶ pretty	(형)예쁜, (부)매우	– prettily	(부)예쁘게
▶ high	(형)높은, (부)높이	– highly	(부)매우
▶ late	(형)늦은, (부)늦게	– lately	(부)최근에
▶ short	(형)짧은, (부)짧게	– shortly	(부)곧
▶ free	(형)무료의, (부)무료로	– freely	(부)자유롭게
▶ near	(형)가까운, (부)가까이	– nearly	(부)거의
▶ bad	(형)나쁜	– badly	(부)나쁘게, (부)몹시
▶ hard	(형)어려운, 단단한, (부)열심히	– hardly	(부)거의 ~않다
▶ rare	형)드문	– rarely	(부)드물게, (부)좀처럼 ~않다

ex) We know pretty well that we were helping ourselves, before we met here, I believe.
분명히 우리가 여기에서 만나기 전에 마음껏 훔쳤다는 걸 매우 잘 알고 있어.

But the gallantry of her friends would not allow of this; /
하지만 정중한 친구들은 이를 허락하지 않았고;

and the man in faded black, / mounting the breach first,
색 바랜 옷을 입은 남자가, 먼저 틈새를 치고 들어와,

/ produced his plunder. It was not extensive. A seal or
약탈품을 꺼내 보였다. 그건 별 것 아니었다. 도장 한두 개,

two, / a pencil-case, / a pair of sleeve-buttons, / and a
필통 하나, 소매 단추 한 벌,

brooch of no great value, / were all. They were severally
값나가지 않는 브로치 하나, 그게 전부였다.

examined and appraised / by old Joe, / who chalked the
물건들은 각자 검사되고 평가되었고 조 영감에 의해, 그는 가격을 분필로 썼다

sums / he was disposed to give for each, / upon the wall,
자신이 각 물건에 매기고자 하는, 벽 위에,

/ and added them up into a total / when he found / there
그리고 그 값을 모두 더했다 알게 되자

was nothing more to come.
더 이상 나올 물건이 없음을.

"That's your account," / said Joe, / "and I wouldn't give
"이것이 당신 물건 값이야," 조 영감이 말했다, "그리고 6펜스를 더 줄 수는 없네,

another sixpence, / if I was to be boiled / for not doing it.
끓는 물에 던져진다 해도 더 주지 않는다고.

Who's next?"
다음은 누구지?"

Mrs. Dilber was next. Sheets and towels, / a little
딜버 부인이 다음 차례였다. 침대보와 수건,

wearing apparel, / two old-fashioned silver teaspoons, /
옷 한 벌, 구식 은스푼 두 개,

a pair of sugar-tongs, / and a few boots. Her account was
설탕 집게 하나, 그리고 신발 몇 켤레였다. 그녀의 물건값도 적혔다

stated / on the wall / in the same manner.
벽에 같은 방법으로.

"I always give too much to ladies. It's a weakness of
"난 숙녀에게는 항상 더 많이 쳐 주지. 그게 내 약점이야,

mine, / and that's the way I ruin myself," / said old Joe.
그래서 내가 망한다니까," 조 영감이 말했다.

"That's your account. If you asked me for another penny,
"이것이 당신 물건 값이오. 더 달라고 요구하거나,

/ and made it an open question, / I'd repent of being so
물건 값을 의심한다면, 후하게 쳐 준 걸 후회하고

liberal / and knock off half-a-crown."
반 크라운 깎아버릴 테야."

"And now undo my bundle, / Joe," / said the first woman.
"그럼 이제 내 짐을 풀어 보세요, 조 영감님," 첫 번째 여자가 말했다.

Joe went down on his knees / for the greater convenience
조는 무릎을 꿇고 편하게 꾸러미를 열기 위해,

of opening it, / and having unfastened a great many knots,
여러 번 묶은 매듭을 풀고,

/ dragged out a large and heavy roll of some dark stuff.
돌돌 말린 크고 무겁고 검은 물건을 꺼냈다.

"What do you call this?" / said Joe. "Bed-curtains!"
"이게 뭐지?" 조가 말했다. "침대 커튼이잖아!"

"Ah!" / returned the woman, / laughing and leaning
"아!" 여자가 대답했고, 웃으면서 몸을 앞으로 숙였다

forward / on her crossed arms. "Bed-curtains!"
팔짱을 낀 채. "침대 커튼이에요!"

"You don't mean to say / you took 'em down, / rings and
"말하려는 건 아니겠지 꺼내 왔다고, 고리까지 전부,

all, / with him lying there?" / said Joe.
그 영감이 거기 누워 있는데?" 조가 말했다.

"Yes I do," / replied the woman. "Why not?"
"네 그랬어요," 여자가 대답했다. "뭐 어때요?"

"You were born to make your fortune," / said Joe, / "and
"당신은 부자가 될 팔자로군," 조가 말했다,

you'll certainly do it."
"틀림없이 그럴 거야."

---

gallantry (남성이 여성에게 보이는) 정중한 관심 | mount (~을 조직하여) 시작하다 | breach 틈, 구멍 | produce
꺼내 보이다, 보여 주다 | plunder 약탈품 | severally 각자, 각기 | appraise 살피다, 평가하다 | chalk 분필(로
쓰다) | be disposed to ~을 (좋게·나쁘게) 생각하는 | account 계좌, 장부, 거래, 설명 | sheet 시트(침대에 까는
얇은 천) | apparel 의류 | sugar-tongs 각설탕 집게(식탁용) | open question 미결 문제, 의문의 여지 | repent
후회하다 | liberal 아끼지 않는, 후한 | knock off 해치우다, 중단하다, 가치를 떨어뜨리다 | half-a-crown 반
크라운(영국 구 화폐 단위. 2실링 6펜스의 백동화)

"I certainly shan't hold my hand, / when I can get
"물론 손을 멈출 리 없죠.   뭐든지 가질 수 있는데

anything in it / by reaching it out, / for the sake of such
           손만 뻗으면,   그런 남자를 위해서

a man / as He was, / I promise you, / Joe," / returned the
      그 영감같은,   물론이죠,   조 영감님"

woman coolly. "Don't drop that oil / upon the blankets, /
여자는 차갑게 말했다.   "기름을 떨어뜨리지 마세요   담요에.

now."
지금요."

"His blankets?" / asked Joe.
"그 영감의 담요인가?"   조가 물었다.

"Whose else's do you think?" / replied the woman. "He
"아니라면 누구 것이겠어요?"   여자가 대답했다.

isn't likely to take cold / without 'em, / I dare say."
"그 영감은 감기도 걸리지 않을 거예요   그게 없어도,   아마."

"I hope he didn't die of anything catching? Eh?" / said
"그 영감이 전염병으로 죽은 것이 아니었으면 좋겠는데?   그렇지?"   조 영감이

old Joe, / stopping in his work, / and looking up.
말했다.   일을 멈추고,   올려다 보며.

"Don't you be afraid of that," / returned the woman. "I
"그런 걱정은 마세요,"   여자가 대답했다.

an't so fond of his company / that I'd loiter about him /
"그 영감이랑 어울리는 건 싫으니   주변에 얼씬거리지 않았겠죠

for such things, / if he did. Ah! You may look through
이런 걸 가져오려고,   그가 그렇게 죽었다면. 아! 그 셔츠 좀 잘 살펴보세요

that shirt / till your eyes ache; / but you won't find a hole
           눈이 아플 만큼;   그래도 구멍 하나 찾지 못할 걸요

/ in it, / nor a threadbare place. It's the best he had, / and
   그것에서.   올이 빠진 부분도.   그건 그 영감이 가진 가장 좋은 옷이에요,

a fine one too. They'd have wasted it, / if it hadn't been
고급이기도 하구요.   없어졌을 거예요   내가 없었다면."

for me."

"What do you call wasting of it?" / asked old Joe.
"없어지다니?"   조 영감이 말했다.

loiter 어정거리다 | threadbare (낡아서) 올이 다 드러난

"Putting it on him / to be buried in, / to be sure," /
"그 영감이 입고   땅 속에 묻혔을 테니까요,   분명히,"

replied the woman with a laugh. "Somebody was fool
여자가 웃으며 대답했다.   "누군가 멍청하게도 그렇게 입혀

enough to do it, / but I took it off again. If calico an't
놓았기에   내가 다시 벗겨 왔죠.   옥양목으로 충분하지 않다면

good enough / for such a purpose, / it isn't good enough
           그런 사람에게 입히기에,   다른 뭐가 충분하겠어요.

for anything. It's quite as becoming to the body. He can't
        죽은 사람에겐 옥양목이 어울려요.   더 추해 보이

look uglier / than he did in that one."
는 것도 아니고   그렇게 입힌다고 해서."

Scrooge listened to this dialogue / in horror. As they
스크루지는 이 대화를 들었다   공포를 느끼며.

sat grouped about their spoil, / in the scanty light /
그들이 전리품 주변에 무리 지어 앉아 있을 때,   희미한 불빛 속에

afforded by the old man's lamp, / he viewed them / with
노인의 램프에서 나오는,   그는 그들을 지켜보았다

a detestation and disgust, / which could hardly have
혐오감과 역겨움을 느끼며,   그 혐오감은 더 클 수 없었을 것이다,

been greater, / though they had been obscene demons, /
          그들이 음란한 악마라 하더라도,

marketing the corpse itself.
시체 그 자체를 놓고 흥정하는.

"Ha, ha!" / laughed the same woman, / when old Joe,
"하, 하!"   같은 여자가 웃었다.   조 영감이,

/ producing a flannel bag / with money in it, / told out
플란넬 주머니를 꺼내어   돈으로 가득 찬,

their several gains / upon the ground. "This is the end of
각자의 몫을 챙기자   바닥에서.   "이제 끝이구나

it, / you see! He frightened every one away from him /
   봐요!   그 영감은 모든 사람을 겁 줘서 쫓아버리더니

when he was alive, / to profit us / when he was dead! Ha,
살아있는 동안,   도움을 주는군요   죽고 나서!

ha, ha!"
하하하!"

"Spirit!" / said Scrooge, / shuddering from head to foot.
"유령님!"　　　스크루지가 말했다　　온몸을 부들부들 떨면서.

"I see, I see. The case of this unhappy man / might be
"알겠어요, 알겠다고요. 이 불행한 사내가 겪는 일이　　　　　내 일이 될 수도

my own. My life tends that way, / now. Merciful Heaven,
있군요.　　내 인생도 저런 식이군요.　　　이제.　자비로우신 하나님,

/ what is this!"
이게 대체 무슨 일이랍니까!"

He recoiled in terror, / for the scene had changed, / and
그는 놀라서 움찔했다.　　　　장면이 바뀌었고,

now he almost touched a bed: / a bare, uncurtained
침대에 부딪힐 뻔 했기 때문에:　　이불도 없고, 커튼도 없는 침대였다:

bed: / on which, / beneath a ragged sheet, / there lay a
그 위에,　　　낡은 시트 밑에,

something covered up, / which, / though it was dumb, /
뭔가 놓여 있었다.　　　　그것은,　아무 소리도 나지 않았지만,

announced itself / in awful language.
그 자체로 말해 주고 있었다　섬뜩한 말로.

The room was very dark, / too dark to be observed / with
방은 매우 어두웠다.　　　　　너무 어두워서 보이지 않을 정도였다

any accuracy, / though Scrooge glanced round it / in
정확히,　　　　스크루지가 방을 힐끗 둘러보았지만

obedience to a secret impulse, / anxious to know / what
은밀한 충동에 사로잡혀,　　　　　간절히 알고 싶어서

kind of room it was. A pale light, / rising in the outer air,
방이 어떻게 생겼는지.　　희미한 불빛이,　　밖에서부터 들어온,

/ fell straight / upon the bed; / and on it, / plundered and
똑바로 떨어졌고　침대 위로;　　　그리고 그 위에,　약탈 당하고 아무것도

bereft, / unwatched, unwept, uncared for, / was the body
없는,　　지켜보는 이도, 울어주는 이도, 돌봐주는 이도 없이,

of this man.
시체가 놓여 있었다.

calico 옥양목 | dialogue 대화 | group (무리를 지어) 모이다 | spoil 약탈품, 전리품 | scanty 얼마 안 되는,
빈약한 | afford 제공하다 | detestation 혐오, 증오 | disgust 혐오감, 역겨움 | obscene 음란한, 터무니없는 |
demon 악령, 악마 | flannel 플란넬(면이나 양모를 섞어 만든 가벼운 천) | recoil 움찔하다 | glance 흘깃 보다
| in obedience to ~을 따라서, ~에 복종하여 | impulse 충동 | anxious to ~하고 싶은 생각이 간절한 |
plunder 약탈하다 | bereft ~이 전무한, ~을 상실한

Scrooge glanced towards the Phantom. Its steady hand
스크루지는 유령을 흘낏 쳐다보았다. 유령의 흔들림 없는 손이

was pointed to the head. The cover was so carelessly
머리 쪽을 가리켰다. 이불이 아무렇게나 덮여 있어서

adjusted / that the slightest raising of it, / the motion of
살짝 들어 올리기만 해도,

a finger upon Scrooge's part, / would have disclosed the
스크루지가 손가락을 까딱하여, 얼굴이 드러날 것 같았다.

face. He thought of it, / felt how easy it would be to do, /
스크루지는 생각했다. 얼마나 쉽게 들어 올릴 수 있을지를 생각하며,

and longed to do it; / but had no more power / to withdraw
그렇게 하고 싶은 마음이 있었다; 하지만 더 이상 힘이 없었다 이불을 걷어낼 만한

the veil / than to dismiss the spectre / at his side.
유령을 쫓아내는 것이 힘든 만큼 옆에 서 있던.

Oh cold, cold, rigid, dreadful Death, / set up thine altar
아 차디 차고, 엄격하고, 두려운 죽음이여, 이곳에 서 것의 제단을 차리고,

here, / and dress it with such terrors / as thou hast at thy
공포로 장식하라 네 명령으로 부리는:

command: / for this is thy dominion! But of the loved,
이는 네 영토일지니!

revered, and honored head, / thou canst not turn one hair
하지만 사랑받고, 존경받고, 존중받는 머리는, 머리카락 한 올도 건드려서는 안 된다

/ to thy dread purposes, / or make one feature odious. It
네 무서운 의도에 따라, 또한 모습을 혐오스럽게 만들어서도 안 된다.

is not that the hand is heavy and will fall down / when
그 손은 무거워서 떨어지지 않으며

released; / it is not that the heart and pulse are still; / but
내려 놓을 때; 심장과 맥박이 멈추지 않으며;

that the hand was open, generous, and true; / the heart
그 손을 열려 있고, 관대하며, 진실하다;

brave, warm, and tender; / and the pulse a man's. Strike,
심장은 용감하고, 따뜻하고, 부드럽다; 맥박은 인간의 것이다.

Shadow, strike! And see his good deeds / springing from
쳐라, 환영이여, 쳐라! 그리고 그의 선행을 보아라 상처에서 샘솟아 올라,

the wound, / to sow the world with life immortal!
세상에 불멸의 삶을 뿌리는!

No voice pronounced these words / in Scrooge's ears, /
아무 목소리도 이렇게 말하지 않았지만   스크루지의 귀에 대고,

and yet he heard them / when he looked upon the bed. He
그러나 스크루지는 들었다   침대를 내려다볼 때.

thought, / if this man could be raised up now, / what would
그는 생각했다,   만약 이 사람이 지금 일어날 수만 있다면,

be his foremost thoughts? Avarice, hard-dealing, griping
가장 먼저 드는 생각은 무엇일까?   탐욕, 야박한 흥정, 배 아픈 근심일까?

cares? They have brought him to a rich end, / truly!
          그것들이 이 부자에게 종말을 선사한 것은 아닌가,   정말로!

He lay, / in the dark empty house, / with not a man, a
시체는 누워 있다, 어둡고 텅 빈 집 안에,   남자도, 여자도, 아이도 없이,

woman, or a child, / to say that he was kind to me in this
          그가 이런 저런 식으로 친절했다고 말해 주는 사람이나,

or that, / and for the memory of one kind word / I will be
또 친절한 말 한 마디의 기억을 갖고   친절하게 대해야

kind to him. A cat was tearing / at the door, / and there
한다고 말하는 사람도. 고양이 한 마리가 울고 있었다 문 가에서,

was a sound of gnawing rats / beneath the hearth-stone.
그리고 신경을 긁는 쥐의 찍찍 소리가   벽난로 바닥 밑에서 들렸다.

What they wanted / in the room of death, / and why they
저놈들은 무엇을 원하는 건가   죽음의 방 안에서,

were so restless and disturbed, / Scrooge did not dare to
왜 저렇게 불안하고 불행해 할까,   스크루지는 감히 생각도 할 수 없었다.

think.

"Spirit!" / he said, / "this is a fearful place. In leaving it, / I
"유령님!"   스크루지가 말했다, "이곳은 무서운 곳입니다.   이곳을 떠난 후,

shall not leave its lesson, / trust me. Let us go!"
나는 이 교훈을 절대 잊지 않겠어요,   믿어 주세요.   이제 갑시다!"

Still the Ghost pointed / with an unmoved finger / to the
하지만 유령은 가리켰다   미동도 하지 않는 손가락으로

head.
그 머리를.

"I understand you," / Scrooge returned, / "and I would do
"알고 있습니다."   스크루지가 대답했다.   "그렇게 하겠습니다.

it, / if I could. But I have not the power, / Spirit. I have not
할 수만 있다면.   하지만 제겐 힘이 없어요,   유령님.

the power."
전 힘이 없다고요."

Again / it seemed to look upon him.
다시 한 번   유령이 스크루지를 쳐다보았다.

"If there is any person / in the town, / who feels emotion
"누군가 있다면   이 마을에,

caused by this man's death," / said Scrooge quite agonised,
이 사람의 죽음으로 감정을 느낀 사람이,"   스크루지가 고통스러워하며 말했다.

/ "show that person to me, / Spirit, / I beseech you!"
"그 사람을 제게 보여 주세요,   유령님,   부탁합니다!"

The Phantom spread its dark robe / before him / for a
유령이 검은 옷자락을 펼쳤다가   그의 앞에서   잠시,

moment, / like a wing; / and withdrawing it, / revealed a
          날개처럼;   옷자락을 접으니,   방이 나타났다

room / by daylight, / where a mother and her children were.
햇살이 비추는,   그곳에는 엄마와 아이들이 있었다.

She was expecting some one, / and with anxious eagerness;
그녀는 누군가를 기다리고 있었다.   걱정하며 애타게;

/ for she walked up and down the room; / started at every
방을 왔다갔다 하며;   소리가 날 때마다 깜짝 놀라고;

sound; / looked out from the window; / glanced at the
          창 밖을 쳐다보고;   시계를 흘낏 보았다

clock; / tried, / but in vain, / to work with her needle; / and
          시도했으나, 허사였다,   바느질을 하려고;

could hardly bear / the voices of the children in their play.
그러나 참을 수 없었다   아이들이 노는 소리를.

At length / the long-expected knock was heard. She
마침내   오랫동안 기다려온 노크 소리가 들렸다.

hurried to the door, / and met her husband; / a man
그녀는 급히 문으로 달려가,   남편을 맞이했다;

whose face was careworn and depressed, / though he
초췌하고 우울해 보이는 얼굴의 남자였다,   젊은 나이였지만.

was young. There was a remarkable expression in it now;
지금 놀랄 만한 표정을 지었다;

/ a kind of serious delight / of which he felt ashamed, /
매우 기뻐하면서도   부끄러워하며,

and which he struggled to repress.
이를 애써 감추려 했다.

Key Expression !

I dare say : 아마 ~일 것이다

dare는 '~할 용기가 있다, 감히 ~하다, ~할 엄두를 내다'라는 뜻의 동사입니다.
하지만 그 외에도 다양한 의미로 사용됩니다.

▶ not dare to + 동사원형 : 감히 ~하지 못하다 (흔히 부정문에서 쓰임)
▶ daren't + 동사원형 : 감히 ~하지 못하다 (영국 영어에서 dare를 조동사 취급)
▶ dare to + 동사원형 : 겁내지 않고 ~하다 (긍정문에서 not be afraid to의 의미)
▶ I dare say : 아마 ~일 것이다
▶ how dare you : 어떻게 감히 네가 (분노를 표현)
▶ don't you dare! : 그러기만 했단 봐! (하지 말라고 강력하게 요구)

ex) He isn't likely to take cold without 'em, I dare say.
    그 영감은 아마 그게 없어도 감기에 걸리지 않을 거예요.
    Scrooge did not dare to think.
    스크루지는 감히 생각도 할 수 없었다.

agonised 고뇌에 찬(=agonized) | beseech 간청하다, 애원하다 | eagerness 열의, 열심, 열망 | careworn 근심
걱정으로 초췌한 | ashamed 부끄러운, 창피한, 수치스러운 | repress (감정을) 참다, 억누르다

He sat down to the dinner / that had been hoarding for
남편은 저녁 식탁에 앉았다   그를 위해 차려 놓은

him / by the fire; / and when she asked him faintly / what
난롯가의;   부인이 힘없이 묻자   무슨 소

news / (which was not until after a long silence), / he
식인지   (오랜 침묵 끝에),

appeared embarrassed / how to answer.
그는 난처해 했다   어떻게 대답해야 할지 몰라.

"Is it good?" / she said, / "or bad?" / — to help him.
"좋은 소식인가요?" 부인이 물었다. "아니면 나쁜 소식?" — 남편을 돕기 위해.

"Bad," / he answered.
"나쁜 소식이오," 남편이 대답했다.

"We are quite ruined?"
"우린 망한 건가요?"

"No. There is hope yet, / Caroline."
"아니.   아직 희망은 있어,   캐롤라인."

"If he relents," / she said, / amazed, / "there is! Nothing
"만약 그분이 누그러진다면," 부인이 말했다. 놀라면서,   "희망이 있죠! 가망 없는 건

is past hope, / if such a miracle has happened."
아니니까요,   그런 기적이 일어나기만 한다면."

"He is past relenting," / said her husband. "He is dead."
"누그러지기엔 늦었소,"   남편이 말했다.   "그분은 죽었으니."

She was a mild and patient creature / if her face spoke
그녀는 온화하고 참을성 있는 사람이었다   얼굴 표정이 진실을 말해 주는

truth; / but she was thankful / in her soul / to hear it,
것이라면; 하지만 그녀는 다행이라 생각하며 마음속으로   그 말을 듣고,

/ and she said so, / with clasped hands. She prayed
그렇게 말했다,   손뼉을 치면서.   용서를 빌고

forgiveness / the next moment, / and was sorry; / but the
다음 순간,   후회했지만;

first was the emotion of her heart.
처음 감정이 그녀의 진심이었다.

---

hoard 비축하다 | relent 동의하다, 누그러지다 | mild 온화한, 포근한 | clasp 움켜쥐다 | merciless 무자비한,
인정사정 없는 | successor 후임자, 계승자 | hushed 조용한, 숨죽인 | clustered 무리를 이룬

"What the half-drunken woman / whom I told you of /
"그 반쯤 술 취한 여자가   당신한테 애기했던

last night, / said to me, / when I tried to see him / and
어젯밤에,   뭐라 했는지 아시오, 영감님을 찾아가서

obtain a week's delay; / and what I thought was / a mere
일주일만 연기해 달라고 했을 때;   생각했었는데   단순한 핑계

excuse / to avoid me; / turns out to have been quite true.
일 거라고   나를 피하기 위한;   사실로 밝혀졌소.

He was not only very ill, / but dying, / then."
영감님은 몹시 아팠을 뿐만 아니라,   죽어가고 있었던 거요, 그때."

"To whom / will our debt be transferred?"
"누구에게   우리 빚이 넘어가는 거죠?"

"I don't know. But before that time / we shall be ready
"모르겠소.   하지만 그 전에   돈을 마련해야겠지;

with the money; / and even though we were not, / it
          그리고 마련하지 못하더라도,

would be a bad fortune indeed / to find so merciless a
정말로 불운한 일이 되겠지   매우 인정없는 사람이

creditor / in his successor. We may sleep to-night / with
          영감님 뒤를 잇는다면.   오늘 밤은 잠들 수 있겠어

light hearts, / Caroline!"
가벼운 마음으로,   캐롤라인!"

Yes. Soften it as they would, / their hearts were lighter.
그랬다. 감정을 누르려고 해도,   그들의 마음은 더 가벼워졌다.

The children's faces, / hushed and clustered round to
아이들의 표정도,   숨죽인 채 모여 앉아 듣고 있던

hear / what they so little understood, / were brighter; /
들으려고   잘 알아듣지도 못하는 말을,   더 밝아졌다;

and it was a happier house / for this man's death! The
그리고 가족은 더 행복해졌다   이 남자의 죽음으로!

only emotion / that the Ghost could show him, / caused
유일한 감정은   유령이 스크루지에게 보여 줄 수 있었던,

by the event, / was one of pleasure.
이 사건으로 인한,   기쁨 뿐이었다.

"Let me see some tenderness / connected with a death,"
"다정한 모습을 보여 주세요   죽음과 관련된,"

/ said Scrooge; / "or that dark chamber, / Spirit, / which
스크루지가 말했다;   "아니면 그 어두운 방이,   유령님,

we left just now, / will be forever present to me."
누리가 방금 전 떠나 온,   내게 영원히 남아있을 거예요."

The Ghost conducted him / through several streets /
유령은 스크루지를 안내했다   여러 거리를

familiar to his feet; / and as they went along, / Scrooge
스크루지에게 낯익은;   돌아다니는 동안,

looked here and there / to find himself, / but nowhere
스크루지는 이곳 저곳을 보며   자신의 모습을 찾았지만,   어디에도 보이지 않았다.

was he to be seen. They entered poor Bob Cratchit's
                  그들은 불쌍한 밥 크래칫의 집으로 들어갔다;

house; / the dwelling he had visited before; / and found
house;   스크루지도 전에 가 본 적 있는 집이었는데;

the mother and the children seated / round the fire.
엄마와 아이들이 앉아 있는 것이 보였다   난로 주위에.

Quiet. Very quiet. The noisy little Cratchits were / as
조용했다. 매우 조용했다.   시끄러운 크래칫 꼬마들은

still as statues / in one corner, / and sat looking up at
동상처럼 꼼짝하지 않고   한쪽 구석에,   피터를 쳐다보며 앉아 있었다,

Peter, / who had a book before him. The mother and her
Peter,   앞에 책을 두고 있는.

daughters were engaged in sewing. But surely they were
부인과 딸들은 바느질을 하고 있었다.   하지만 확실히 그들도 매우 조용했다!

very quiet!

" 'And He took a child, / and set him in the midst of
"그리고 그분은 한 아이를 데려와,   그들 가운데 세우셨고,;"

them.' "

---

tenderness 친절, 다정, 애정 | chamber 방 | conduct 안내하다 | threshold 문지방 | falter (자신이 없어
목소리가) 흔들리다, 더듬거리다

Where had Scrooge heard those words? He had not
저 말을 어디에서 들었던가?   꿈 속에서 들은 것은

dreamed them. The boy must have read them out, / as he
아니었다.   소년은 소리 내어 읽고 있었던 것이 분명했다.

and the Spirit crossed the threshold. Why did he not go on?
스크루지가 유령과 문지방을 넘어올 때.   왜 계속 읽지 않았을까?

The mother laid her work / upon the table, / and put her
부인은 바느질감을 놓고   탁자 위에.

hand up to her face.
손으로 얼굴을 감쌌다.

"The color hurts my eyes," / she said.
"색깔 때문에 눈이 아프구나,"   부인이 말했다.

The color? Ah, poor Tiny Tim!
색깔이라고?   아, 불쌍한 팀!

"They're better now again," / said Cratchit's wife. "It
"이제 다시 괜찮아졌어,"   크래칫 부인이 말했다.   "바느질을

makes them weak / by candle-light; / and I wouldn't show
했더니 눈이 약해졌구나   촛불 옆에서;   네 아빠에게 침침한 눈을 보이고

weak eyes to your father / when he comes home, / for the
싶지 않은데   집에 돌아오셨을 때,   제발.

world. It must be near his time."
              거의 오실 시간이 되었구나."

"Past it rather," / Peter answered, / shutting up his book.
"벌써 지났어요,"   피터가 대답했다,   책을 덮으며.

"But I think / he has walked a little slower / than he used, /
"하지만 제 생각에   아버지는 좀 더 느리게 걸어오시나 봐요   평소보다.

these few last evenings, / mother."
요즘 저녁마다,   어머니."

They were very quiet again. At last / she said, / and in a
그들은 다시 조용해졌다.   마침내   부인이 말했다,

steady, cheerful voice, / that only faltered once: /
차분하고 밝은 목소리로,   한 번 더듬거렸다가:

"I have known him walk with / — I have known him walk
"아빠의 걸음을 알고 있지   — 알고 있어

/ with Tiny Tim upon his shoulder, / very fast indeed."
팀을 어깨에 태웠을 때는,   정말 빠르셨는데."

"And so have I," / cried Peter. "Often."
"저도 알아요." 피터가 소리쳤다. "자주 그러셨죠."

"And so have I," / exclaimed another. So had all.
"저도 알아요." 다른 아이가 소리쳤다. 모두 알고 있었다.

"But he was very light to carry," / she resumed, / intent
"하지만 팀은 매우 가벼웠으니까," 부인이 말을 이었다.

upon her work, / "and his father loved him so, / that it was
바느질에 열중하며, "그리고 팀을 매우 사랑하셨으니까, 문제가 아니었지:

no trouble: / no trouble. And there is your father / at the
아무렇지 않았어. 아빠가 오셨구나

door!"
문 앞에!"

She hurried out / to meet him; / and little Bob / in his
부인은 서둘러서 남편을 맞이했다; 그리고 꼬마 밥이

comforter / — he had need of it, / poor fellow — / came in.
목도리를 두른 채 — 그 애에게는 그것이 필요했다. 불쌍한 녀석 — 들어왔다.

His tea was ready for him / on the hob, / and they all tried
크래칫의 차가 준비되어 있었다 화덕에는, 그리고 모두 노력했다

/ who should help him to it most. Then / the two young
아빠를 최대한 도우려고. 그때

Cratchits got upon his knees and laid, / each child a little
두 꼬마가 아빠의 무릎에 앉아, 뺨을 댔다,

cheek, / against his face, / as if they said, / "Don't mind it, /
아빠의 얼굴에, 마치 말하는 듯, "괜찮아요,

father. Don't be grieved!"
아빠, 슬퍼하지 마세요!"라고.

Bob was very cheerful with them, / and spoke pleasantly /
밥은 아이들 덕분에 매우 쾌활해져서, 기쁘게 말했다

to all the family. He looked at the work / upon the table, /
가족들에게. 바느질감을 보고 탁자 위에 놓여 있던,

and praised the industry and speed of Mrs. Cratchit and the
부인과 딸들의 솜씨와 빠른 속도를 칭찬했다.

girls. They would be done / long before Sunday, / he said.
끝낼 수 있을 거라고 일요일이 되기 훨씬 전에, 그는 말했다.

resume 다시 시작하다 | intent 몰두, 열중하는 | hob (냄비를 데우기 위해 올려놓는) 요리판 | reconcile (체념하고) 받아들이다

"Sunday! You went today, / then, / Robert?" / said his
"일요일이요! 당신 오늘 갔었군요, 그러고 보니, 로버트?"

wife.
부인이 말했다.

"Yes, / my dear," / returned Bob. "I wish you could have
"그래요, 여보," 밥이 대답했다. "당신도 갔으면 좋았을 텐데.

gone. It would have done you good to see / how green a
보았으면 좋았을 텐데 그곳이 얼마나 푸른지.

place it is. But you'll see it often. I promised him / that I
하지만 자주 보게 될 거요. 약속했으니까

would walk there / on a Sunday. My little, little child!" /
그곳에 가겠다고 일요일마다. 불쌍한 내 아들!"

cried Bob. "My little child!"
밥이 울먹였다. "불쌍한 내 아들!"

He broke down / all at once. He couldn't help it. If he
그는 무너져 버렸다 갑자기. 어쩔 수 없었다.

could have helped it, / he and his child would have been
할 수 있었다면, 그와 아들은 헤어지기 쉬웠을지도 모른다

farther apart / perhaps / than they were.
아마도 이미 했던 것보다.

He left the room, / and went up-stairs into the room
그는 방을 떠나, 위층 방으로 올라갔다.

above, / which was lighted cheerfully, / and hung with
그곳은 불이 환히 켜 있고, 크리스마스 장식이 걸려

Christmas. There was a chair / set close beside the child,
있었다. 의자가 하나 있었는데 아이 곁에 가까이 놓았던.

/ and there were signs / of some one having been there,
흔적이 있었다 누군가 그곳에 있었던,

/ lately. Poor Bob sat down in it, / and when he had
최근까지. 불쌍한 밥은 그 의자에 앉아,

thought a little and composed himself, / he kissed the
잠시 생각에 잠겨 자신을 추스르게 되자, 아이의 얼굴에 입맞췄다.

little face. He was reconciled to / what had happened, /
그는 받아들이고 일어난 일을,

and went down again quite happy.
다시 행복해진 마음으로 내려왔다.

They drew about the fire, / and talked; / the girls
가족들은 난롯가에 모여, 이야기를 나눴다; 딸들과 어머니는

and mother working still. Bob told them / of the
아직도 바느질을 하고 있었다. 밥을 그들에게 말했다

extraordinary kindness of Mr. Scrooge's nephew, / whom
스크루지 영감의 조카가 아주 친절하다고,

he had scarcely seen but once, / and who, / meeting him
한 번 밖에 본 적이 없지만, 그는, 자신을 만났을 때

/ in the street / that day, / and seeing / that he looked
거리에서 그 날, 알아차리더니 자신이 조금

a little / — "just a little down / you know," / said Bob,
— "조금 우울해 보인다고 하더군 당신도 알다시피," 밥이 말했다,

/ inquired what had happened to distress him. "On
무슨 걱정거리라도 있는지 물었다고 했다. "그 질문에,"

which," / said Bob, / "for he is the pleasantest-spoken
밥이 말했다, "그는 아주 다정하게 말하는 신사니까

gentleman / you ever heard, / I told him. 'I am heartily
당신도 들었다시피, 내가 말했소. '정말 안 됐군요,

sorry for it, / Mr. Cratchit,' / he said, / 'and heartily sorry
크래칫 씨,' 그가 말하더군,

for your good wife.' By the bye, / how he ever knew that,
'착한 부인도 정말 안 되셨군요.' 그런데, 그가 어떻게 그 사실을 알았는지,

/ I don't know."
모르겠단 말이야."

"Knew what, / my dear?"
"뭘 알고 있었는데요, 여보?"

"Why, / that you were a good wife," / replied Bob.
"음, 당신이 착한 아내라는 사실 말이야," 밥이 말했다.

"Everybody knows that!" / said Peter.
"모두 알고 있어요!" 피터가 말했다.

"Very well observed, / my boy!" / cried Bob. "I hope
"말 한 번 잘했구나, 아들아!" 밥이 소리쳤다. "사람들이 알았으

they do. 'Heartily sorry,' / he said, / 'for your good wife.
면 좋겠구나. '진심으로 안 됐어요,' 그가 말했지, '착한 부인께.

by the bye 그런데, 말이 났으니 말이지(=by the way) | get along with you 저리 가, 썩 꺼져 | retort 쏘아붙이다,
대꾸하다

If I can be of service to you / in any way,' / he said, /
도움이 될 수 있다면　　　　　　　　어떤 식으로든,'　　그가 말했지,

giving me his card, / 'that's where I live. Pray come
명함을 주면서,　　　　　'이곳이 내가 사는 곳이에요. 저를 찾아오세요.'라고.

to me.' Now, / it wasn't," / cried Bob, / "for the sake of
있잖아,　　그게,"　　밥이 말했다,　　"뭔가를 위해서가 아니라

anything / he might be able to do for us, / so much as
　　　　　그가 우리에게 해 줄 수 있는,

for his kind way, / that this was quite delightful. It really
그의 친절한 마음씨가,　　정말 고마웠어.

seemed / as if he had known our Tiny Tim, / and felt
정말로　　그는 우리 팀을 알고 있는 듯 했고,　　　　　우리를 마음 써

with us."
주는 듯 했어."

"I'm sure he's a good soul!" / said Mrs. Cratchit.
"정말 좋은 분이네요!"　　　　　크래칫 부인이 말했다.

"You would be surer of it, / my dear," / returned Bob,
"정말 그렇게 느낄 거야,　　　여보,"　　　밥이 대답했다,

/ "if you saw and spoke to him. I shouldn't be at all
　　"당신도 그를 만나 이야기 해 본다면,　　그리 놀라지 않을 거야

surprised / — mark what I say! — / if he got Peter a
　　　　　— 내 말 들어봐! —　　　그가 피터에게 더 좋은 자리를

better situation."
마련해 준다 해도."

"Only hear that, / Peter," / said Mrs. Cratchit.
"잘 들어라,　　　피터,"　　크래칫 부인이 말했다.

"And then," / cried one of the girls, / "Peter will be
"그렇게 되면,"　　딸 아이 한 명이 소리쳤다,

keeping company with someone, / and setting up for
"피터 오빠는 누군가랑 결혼해서,　　　　　독립하겠네."

himself."

"Get along with you!" / retorted Peter, / grinning.
"그만해!　　　　　　　　피터가 쏘아붙였다,　　씩 웃으면서.

"It's just as likely as not," / said Bob, / "one of these
불가능한 일은 아니지." 밥이 말했다. "언젠가는:

days; / though there's plenty of time for that, / my dear.
그러기엔 시간이 아직 많이 남았지만, 얘야.

But however and whenever we part from one another, / I
하지만 우리가 언젠가는 각자 헤어지게 되더라도,

am sure / we shall none of us forget poor Tiny Tim / —
나는 믿는다 우리가 불쌍한 팀을 잊지 않을 거라고

shall we — / or this first parting / that there was among
— 그럴 거지 — 그리고 이 첫 번째 이별을 우리에게 일어난?"

us?"

"Never, / father!" / cried they all.
"물론이죠, 아빠!" 아이들이 모두 소리쳤다.

"And I know," / said Bob, / "I know, / my dears, / that
"그리고 알고 있단다." 밥이 말했다. "알고 있어, 얘들아,

when we recollect / how patient and how mild he was; /
우리가 다시 회상하면 그 애가 얼마나 착하고 참을성이 많았는지;

although he was a little, little child; / we shall not quarrel
비록 작고, 어린 아이였지만;

easily among ourselves, / and forget poor Tiny Tim in
우리는 서로 다투지 않을 것이고, 불쌍한 팀을 잊어버리지도 않을 것이라고."

doing it."

"No, never, / father!" / they all cried again.
"절대 잊지 않을게요, 아빠!" 아이들은 다시 한 번 소리쳤다.

"I am very happy," / said little Bob, / "I am very happy!"
"정말 행복하구나," 왜소한 밥이 말했다. "난 정말 행복해!"

Mrs. Cratchit kissed him, / his daughters kissed him,
크래칫 부인이 남편에게 입을 맞추자, 딸들도 입을 맞췄고,

/ the two young Cratchits kissed him, / and Peter and
두 어린 꼬마들도 입을 맞췄다.

himself shook hands. Spirit of Tiny Tim, / thy childish
그리고 피터와 밥은 악수를 나눴다. 꼬마 팀의 영혼이여,

essence was from God!
신으로부터 받은 어린 아이의 순수함일지니!

"Spectre," / said Scrooge, / "something informs me / that
"영혼님," 스크루지가 말했다, "뭔가 제게 알려 주는군요

our parting moment is at hand. I know it, / but I know not
우리가 헤어질 순간이 다가왔다고. 알겠어요, 하지만 어떻게 할지 모

how. Tell me / what man that was / whom we saw lying
르겠어요. 말해 주세요 그 사람이 누구인지 우리가 봤던 누워 있는 시체가?"

dead?"

The Ghost of Christmas Yet To Come conveyed him, /
미래의 크리스마스 유령은 그를 데려갔다,

as before / — though at a different time, / he thought: /
아까처럼 — 하지만 다른 시간으로, 그가 생각하기에:

indeed, / there seemed no order / in these latter visions, /
정말 그랬다, 순서가 없는 듯 했다 이 마지막 장면에는,

save that they were in the Future / — into the resorts of
그들이 미래에 있다는 것 말고는 — 상인들이 보였던 곳으로,

business men, / but showed him not himself. Indeed, / the
하지만 그 자신의 모습을 보여 주지 않았다. 정말로,

Spirit did not stay for anything, / but went straight on, / as
유령은 어느 곳에도 머무르지 않고, 곧장 나아가기만 했다,

to the end just now desired, / until besought by Scrooge /
지금 당장 가려는 목적지로, 그러자 스크루지가 애원했다

to tarry for a moment.
잠시 멈춰 달라고.

"This court," / said Scrooge, / "through which we hurry
"이 거리는," 스크루지가 말했다, "우리가 지금 서둘러 지나고 있는,

now, / is where my place of occupation is, / and has been
내 사무실이 있는 곳이에요.

for a length of time. I see the house. Let me behold / what
오랫동안 있던 곳이에요. 그 집이 보이네요. 보여 주세요 제가

I shall be, / in days to come!"
어떤 모습일지, 다가올 미래에!"

The Spirit stopped; / the hand was pointed elsewhere.
유령은 멈춰 서서; 손으로 어딘가를 가리켰다.

"The house is yonder," / Scrooge exclaimed. "Why do
"건물은 저기 있는데."   스크루지가 소리쳤다.

you point away?"
"왜 다른 쪽을 가리키시나요?"

The inexorable finger underwent no change.
변함없는 손가락은 변화가 없었다.

Scrooge hastened to the window of his office, / and
스크루지는 서둘러 사무실 창가로 가서,

looked in. It was an office still, / but not his. The
안을 들여다보았다. 여전히 사무실이었지만,   그의 것은 아니었다.

furniture was not the same, / and the figure in the chair
가구도 같지 않았고,   의자에 앉은 사람의 모습도 자신이 아니었다.

was not himself. The Phantom pointed / as before.
                유령은 가리켰다   전과 같은 방향을.

Key Expression ●

save : ~는 제외하고

save는 동사로 '구출하다, 저축하다, 절약하다, 피하다' 등의 다양한 뜻을 가지고 있습니다.
하지만 이 외에도 전치사로 '~ 외에', 접속사로 '~를 제외하고'라는 의미로도 쓰입니다.

ex) There seemed no order in these latter visions, save that they were in the
Future. (접속사)
그들이 미래에 있다는 점을 제외하고 이 마지막 장면에는 순서가 없는 듯 했다.
It was shrouded in a deep black garment, which concealed its head, its face,
its form, and left nothing of it visible save one outstretched hand. (전치사)
유령은 머리와 얼굴, 몸 전체를 가린 시커먼 옷으로 덮여 있어서 쭉 뻗은 팔 하나 외에 아무것도 보이지 않았다.

tarry 지체하다, 머무르다 | court 코트(아파트 건물이나 거리 이름에 쓰임) | yonder 저기 있는, 보이는 |
inexorable 멈출 수 없는, 거침없는 | undergo 겪다 | hasten 서둘러 하다

He joined it once again, / and wondering / why and
스크루지는 다시 유령에게 돌아와서,   궁금해 하며

whither he had gone, / accompanied it / until they
자신이 왜 어디로 간 것인지를,   유령을 따라 갔다   철문에 도착할 때까지.

reached an iron gate. He paused to look round / before
그는 멈춰 서서 주위를 돌아보았다

entering.
들어가기 전에.

A churchyard. Here, / then; / the wretched man / whose
교회 묘지였다.   이곳은,   그때;   비참한 남자가

name he had now to learn, / lay underneath the ground.
이제서야 그 이름을 알게 된,   땅 밑에 누워 있었다.

It was a worthy place. Walled in by houses; / overrun
그곳은 훌륭한 장소였다.   집들로 둘러싸여 있고;

by grass and weeds, / the growth of vegetation's death,
잔디와 잡초가 무성하며,   죽은 식물을 먹고 자란,

/ not life; / choked up with too much burying; / fat with
살아있지 않은: 너무 많은 묘지들로 숨이 턱턱 막히고;   엄청난 식욕으

repleted appetite. A worthy place!
로 기름진 땅이었다.   훌륭한 곳이었다!

The Spirit stood among the graves, / and pointed
유령은 무덤 가운데 서서,   한 무덤을 가리켰다.

down to One. He advanced towards it / trembling. The
스크루지는 그곳으로 갔다   덜덜 떨면서.

Phantom was exactly / as it had been, / but he dreaded /
유령은 정확히   지금까지의 모습과 같지만, 스크루지는 두려워했다

that he saw new meaning / in its solemn shape.
새로운 의미를 발견하고   유령의 엄숙한 모습에서.

"Before I draw nearer to that stone / to which you point,"
"제가 저 묘비로 가기 전에   유령님이 가리키는,"

/ said Scrooge, / "answer me one question. Are these
스크루지가 말했다,   "한 가지만 대답해 주세요.

the shadows of the things / that Will be, / or are they
이 환영들은   미래에 일어날 일인가요,

shadows of things / that May be, / only?"
아니면 보여 준 건가요   일어날 수도 있는 일을,   단지?"

Still the Ghost pointed downward / to the grave / by
그러나 유령은 가리켰다   무덤을

which it stood.
자신의 옆에 있는.

"Men's courses will foreshadow certain ends, / to which,
"사람들의 행로는 어떤 종착점을 예견할 수도 있고,   그곳에,

/ if persevered in, / they must lead," / said Scrooge. "But
참고 계속 간다면,   이끌어 줄 것입니다."   스크루지가 말했다.

if the courses be departed from, / the ends will change.
"하지만 그 행로에서 벗어나면,   종착점도 바뀌겠지요.

Say it is thus / with what you show me!"
그런 거라고 말해 주세요 제게 보여 주신 것도!"

The Spirit was immovable / as ever.
유령은 꿈쩍도 하지 않았다   이전처럼.

Scrooge crept towards it, / trembling / as he went; /
스크루지는 무덤을 향해 기어갔다.   벌벌 떨면서   가는 동안;

and following the finger, / read / upon the stone of the
그리고 손가락이 가리키는 대로,   읽었다 버려진 무덤 묘비에 쓰여진

neglected grave / his own name, / Ebenezer Scrooge.
              자신의 이름을,   '에브니저 스크루지'라는.

"Am I that man / who lay upon the bed?" / he cried, /
"저 사람이 저인가요   그 침대에 누워 있던?"   스크루지가 소리쳤다.

upon his knees.
무릎을 꿇고.

The finger pointed from the grave / to him, / and back
손가락은 무덤을 가리켰다가   스크루지를 향하더니,

again.
다시 무덤을 가리켰다.

"No, Spirit! Oh no, no!"
"싫어요, 유령님!   오 안 돼요, 안 돼요!"

---

whither 어디로 | accompany 동반하다, 동행하다 | churchyard 교회 경내(흔히 묘지로 쓰임) | wretched
비참한 | worthy 훌륭한 | overrun 급속히 퍼지다, 가득 차다 | vegetation 초목, 식물 | choke 숨이 막히다 |
repleted 포식을 한, 몹시 배가 부른(=replete) | appetite 식욕 | persevere 인내하며 계속하다 | depart 떠나다,
출발하다. 그만두다

The finger still was there.
손가락은 여전히 그곳을 가리켰다.

"Spirit!" / he cried, / tight clutching at its robe, / "hear
"유령님!"   그가 소리쳤다,   유령의 옷자락을 꽉 움켜잡으며,   "제 말을 들어

me! I am not the man I was. I will not be the man / I
보세요! 저는 과거의 제가 아니에요.   그런 사람이 되지 않을 거예요

must have been / but for this intercourse. Why show me
되었을지 모르는   유령들과의 교류가 없었다면.   왜 제게 이걸 보여 주시는

this, / if I am past all hope!"
건가요,   제게 희망이 없다면!"

For the first time / the hand appeared to shake.
처음으로   유령의 손이 떨리는 것처럼 보였다.

"Good Spirit," / he pursued, / as down upon the ground
"자비로운 유령님,"   스크루지가 애원했다, 땅에 쓰러져 엎드리며

he fell / before it: / "Your nature intercedes for me, /
           유령 앞에: "유령님의 성품으로 저를 구해 주세요,

and pities me. Assure me / that I yet may change / these
불쌍히 여겨 주세요.   제게 약속해 주세요 아직은 바꿀 수 있다고

shadows you have shown me, / by an altered life!"
유령님이 보여 준 이 환영들을,   변화된 삶을 산다면!"

The kind hand trembled.
유령의 친절한 손이 떨렸다.

"I will honor Christmas / in my heart, / and try to keep it
"크리스마스를 기릴 것이고   진심으로,   잊지 않도록 하겠습니다

/ all the year. I will live / in the Past, the Present, and the
일 년 내내.   살겠어요   과거와 현재와 미래의 유령님 뜻대로.

Future. The Spirits of all Three shall strive within me. I
세 분 유령님은 제 안에 살아 계실 거예요.

will not shut out the lessons / that they teach. Oh, tell me
그 교훈들을 잊지 않겠어요   여러분이 가르쳐 주신.   오, 말해 주세요

/ I may sponge away the writing / on this stone!"
제가 저 이름을 지울 수 있다고   이 묘비에 쓰인!"

---

clutch 움켜잡다 | intercourse 교류, 소통 | intercede 탄원하다, 선처를 호소하다 | strive 분투하다 | agony
고통, 괴로움 | entreaty 간청, 애원 | detain 붙들다 | repulse 물리치다, 거부하다 | shrink 줄어들다 | collapse
붕괴되다, 무너지다 | dwindle (점점) 줄어들다 | bedpost 침대 기둥

In his agony, / he caught the spectral hand. It sought
괴로워하며,   스크루지는 유령의 손을 잡았다.   유령은 손을 빼려

to free itself, / but he was strong / in his entreaty, / and
했지만,   스크루지가 꽉 잡고   간절하게,

detained it. The Spirit, / stronger yet, / repulsed him.
놓아 주지 않았다. 유령은,   더욱 강했기에,   스크루지를 물리쳤다.

Holding up his hands / in a last prayer / to have his fate
손을 모으고   마지막 기도를 드리며   운명이 바뀌게 해 달라고,

reversed, / he saw / an alteration in the Phantom's hood
        그는 봤다   유령의 두건과 옷이 변하는 모습을.

and dress. It shrunk, / collapsed, / and dwindled down /
        줄어들며,   무너지고,   작아지더니

into a bedpost.
침대 기둥이 되어 버렸다.

A. 다음 문장을 해석해 보세요.

(1) It was shrouded / in a deep black garment, / which concealed its head, its face, its form, / and left nothing of it visible / save one outstretched hand.
→

(2) But for this / it would have been difficult / to detach its figure from the night, / and separate it from the darkness / by which it was surrounded.
→

(3) If you asked me for another penny, / and made it an open question, / I'd repent of being so liberal / and knock off half-a-crown.
→

(4) The room was very dark, . too dark to be observed / with any accuracy.
→

B. 다음 주어진 문장이 되도록 빈칸에 써 넣으세요.

(1) 나는 <u>지금까지 본 어떤 유령보다도</u> 당신이 두려워요.

I fear you _____.

(2) 나는 <u>과거의 제가 아닌 다른 사람이 되어</u> 살고 싶어요.

I hope to live _____.

(3) 빛 바랜 검은 옷을 입은 한 남자가 <u>여자의 바로 뒤를 따라 들어왔다</u>.

_____ a man in faded black.

A. (1) 그것은 시커먼 옷으로 덮여 있었고, 그 옷이 머리와 얼굴, 몸 전체를 가리고 있어서, 쭉 뻗은 팔 하나를 제외하고는 아무것도 보이지 않았다. (2) 이것마저 없었다면 그 모습과 어두운 밤을 구별하고, 그것을 둘러 싸고 있는 어둠과 구분하는 것이 힘들었을 것이다. (3) 더 달라고 요구하거나, 물건 값을 의심한다면,

240 **A Christmas Carol**

(4) 더 심한 벌을 받았으면 좋았을 것을.

→

C. 다음 주어진 문구가 알맞은 문장이 되도록 순서를 맞춰 보세요.

(1) 청소부가 첫 번째예요!
(be / charwoman / alone / the / Let / first / the / to)
→

(2) 당신은 부자가 될 팔자로 태어났군.
(were / You / to / fortune / your / born / make)
→

(3) 그래서 내가 망한다니까.
(way / That's / I / the / myself / ruin)
→

(4) 스크루지는 감히 생각도 할 수 없었다.
(not / think / did / Scrooge / to / dare)
→

D. 다음 단어에 대한 맞는 설명과 연결해 보세요.

(1) encompass ▶   ◀ ① shake with fear

(2) shudder ▶   ◀ ② extremely strong desire

(3) avarice ▶   ◀ ③ become smaller, weaker, or less in number

(4) dwindle ▶   ◀ ④ completely surround or cover

후하게 쳐 준 걸 후회하고 반 크라운 깎아버릴 테야. (4) 방은 매우 어두웠고, 너무 어두워서 정확히 보이지 않을 정도였다. | B. (1) more than any spectre I have seen (2) to be another man from what I was (3) She was closely followed by (4) I wish it was a little heavier judgment. | C. (1) Let the charwoman alone to be the first! (2) You were born to make your fortune. (3) That's the way I ruin myself. (4) Scrooge did not dare to think. | D. (1) ④ (2) ① (3) ② (4) ③

THE END OF IT
이야기의 끝

Yes! And the bedpost was his own. The bed was his own,
그랬다! 침대 기둥은 스크루지의 것이었다.   침대도 그의 침대였고,

/ the room was his own. Best and happiest of all, / the
방도 그의 방이었다.   최고로 행복했던 점은,

Time before him was his own, / to make amends in!
그의 앞에 시간이 남아 있다는 사실이었다.   바로 잡을 수 있는!

"I will live / in the Past, the Present, and the Future!"
"살겠습니다   과거, 현재, 그리고 미래 유령님의 뜻대로!"

/ Scrooge repeated, / as he scrambled out of bed. "The
스크루지는 거듭 말했다,   침대 밖으로 나오며.

Spirits of all Three shall strive within me. Oh Jacob
"세 분 유령님은 제 마음속에 계실 거예요.   이봐 제이콥 말리!

Marley! Heaven, / and the Christmas Time be praised for
하나님을,   그리고 크리스마스를 이렇게 찬양하고 있네!

this! I say it / on my knees, / old Jacob; / on my knees!"
말하지   무릎을 꿇고,   제이콥;   무릎을 꿇고 말이야!"

Key Expression ❢

라오콘에 대해서

라오콘(Laocoon)은 그리스 신화에 나오는 트로이의 아폴로 신전의 사제입니다. 트로이 전쟁 때 그리스군이 '트로이의 목마' 계략을 알아채고 트로이성 안에 목마를 들이는 것을 반대했지요. 이로 인해 신의 노여움을 사서 두 아들과 함께 바다의 신 포세이돈이 보낸 두 마리의 큰 뱀에게 칭칭 감겨 살해당했습니다. 큰 뱀에게 칭칭 감겨서 막 질식당해 죽으려는 라오콘과 두 아들의 모습을 표현한 조각상이 로마의 바티칸 미술관에 전시되어 있습니다.

ex) …cried Scrooge, laughing and crying in the same breath; and making a
  perfect Laocoon of himself with his stockings.
  스크루지는 소리쳤다, 동시에 울고 웃으며, 그리고 양말을 가지고 라오콘을 완벽
  하게 흉내 내면서. (양말을 뱀으로 삼아 목 졸리는 모습을 흉내 낸 모습을 표현)

---

amend 수정하다 ┃ scramble 재빨리 움직이다 ┃ flutter 두근거리다 ┃ glowing 극찬하는, 상기된 ┃ mislay
제자리에 두지 않다 ┃ extravagance 낭비 과도 ┃ giddy 어지러운, 아찔한 들뜬

He was so fluttered and so glowing / with his good
스크루지는 두근거리고 상기되어   선한 의도로,

intentions, / that his broken voice would scarcely answer / to
목소리가 갈라져 거의 대답할 수 없을 것 같았다   누가

his call. He had been sobbing violently / in his conflict with
부른다 해도. 그는 격렬하게 흐느껴서   유령과의 갈등으로,

the Spirit, / and his face was wet with tears.
그의 얼굴은 눈물 범벅이 되었다.

"They are not torn down," / cried Scrooge, / folding one of
"찢어지지 않았어,"   스크루지가 소리쳤다,

his bed-curtains / in his arms, / "they are not torn down, /
침대 커튼을 붙잡고   팔로,   "찢어지지 않았다고,

rings and all. They are here / — I am here — / the shadows
고리도 모두 있고. 여기에 있다고   — 난 여기에 있어 —

of the things / that would have been, / may be dispelled.
환영들은   여기 있었던,   쫓아버리겠어.

They will be. I know they will!"
그렇게 될 거야. 그렇게 될 거라는 걸 알아!"

His hands were busy with his garments / all this time; /
스크루지의 손은 옷을 갖고 바쁘게 움직였다   줄곧;

turning them inside out, / putting them on upside down, /
옷을 뒤집었다가,   거꾸로 입었다가,

tearing them, / mislaying them, / making them parties / to
찢기도 했으며,   엉뚱한 곳에 두었다가,   옷을 갖고

every kind of extravagance.
여러 가지 과도한 짓을 했다.

"I don't know / what to do!" / cried Scrooge, / laughing and
"모르겠어   뭘 해야 할지!"   스크루지는 소리쳤다,   울고 웃으며

crying / in the same breath; / and making a perfect Laocoön
동시에;   라오콘을 완벽하게 흉내 내며

of himself / with his stockings. "I am as light as a feather, /
양말로.   "난 새털처럼 가벼워,

I am as happy as an angel, / I am as merry as a schoolboy.
천사처럼 행복해,   아이처럼 즐겁지.

I am as giddy as a drunken man. A merry Christmas to
술 취한 사람처럼 들떠 있어.   여러분 메리 크리스마스!

everybody! A happy New Year to all the world. Hallo
모두 새해 복 많이 받으세요.   어이, 여기요!

here! Whoop! Hallo!"
와!   이것 보세요!"

He had frisked into the sitting-room, / and was now
그는 거실로 뛰어들어가며,   그곳에 섰다:

standing there: / perfectly winded.
완전히 숨이 찬 모습으로.

"There's the saucepan / that the gruel was in!" / cried
"냄비가 있었지   귀리 죽이 들어 있는!"   스크루지가

Scrooge, / starting off again, / and going round the
소리쳤다,   다시 뛰어 다니기 시작하며,   난로 주위로 갔다.

fireplace. "There's the door, / by which the Ghost of
"문이 있군,   제이콥 말리의 유령이 저 문으로 들어왔지!

Jacob Marley entered! There's the corner / where the
저 구석이야

Ghost of Christmas Present, / sat! There's the window /
현재의 크리스마스 유령이 있던 곳은,   앉아 있었지! 창문도 있군

where I saw the wandering Spirits! It's all right, / it's all
떠돌아다니는 유령을 보았던!   모두 맞아,   모두 사실

true, / it all happened. Ha ha ha!"
이야,   모두 일어났던 거야.   하하하!"

Really, / for a man / who had been out of practice / for so
정말,   사람치고는   연습을 하지 않았던

many years, / it was a splendid laugh, / a most illustrious
오랫동안,   멋진 웃음이었다   매우 대단한 웃음이었다.

laugh. The father of a long, long line of brilliant laughs!
오래오래 이어져 온 멋진 웃음의 아버지라고 할 수 있었다!

"I don't know / what day of the month it is!" / said
"모르겠어   오늘이 며칠인지!"   스크루지가

Scrooge. "I don't know / how long I've been among the
말했다.   "모르겠어   내가 얼마나 오랫동안 유령들과 있었는지.

Spirits. I don't know anything. I'm quite a baby. Never
아무것도 모르겠어.   아기나 마찬가지로군.

mind. I don't care. I'd rather be a baby. Hallo! Whoop!
상관없어. 괜찮아.   차라리 아기였으면.   이봐!   와우!

Hallo here!"
어이 여기요!

He was checked in his transports / by the churches /
스크루지는 도취되었다가 정신을 차렸다   교회 종 소리에

ringing out the lustiest peals / he had ever heard. Clash,
가장 활기차게 울리는   지금까지 들어보았던.

clang, hammer; / ding, dong, / bell. Bell, / dong, ding; /
쨍, 쨍그랑, 쿵: 딩, 동,   땡, 땡,   동, 딩;

hammer, clang, clash! Oh, glorious, glorious!
쿵, 쨍그랑, 쨍!   오, 참으로 영광스럽도다!

Running to the window, / he opened it, / and put out his
창가로 달려가서,   그는 창문을 열고,   고개를 내밀었다.

head. No fog, no mist; / clear, bright, jovial, / stirring,
안개도, 가랑비도 없었고;   맑고, 밝고, 상쾌하며,   마음을 뒤흔드는,

cold; / cold, piping for the blood to dance to; / Golden
추운 날씨였다; 피가 요동칠 정도로 추웠다;

sunlight; / Heavenly sky; / sweet fresh air; / merry bells.
황금색 태양빛;   천국같은 하늘;   달콤하고 상쾌한 공기;   즐거운 종소리.

Oh, glorious! Glorious!
오, 영광스럽도다!   참으로 영광스럽도다!

"What's today!" / cried Scrooge, / calling downward to
"오늘이 며칠이지!"   스크루지가 소리쳤다,   걸어 내려오는 소년을 부르며

a boy / in Sunday clothes, / who perhaps had loitered in /
주일 복장으로,   소년을 어슬렁거리다

to look about him.
스크루지를 쳐다 보았다.

"Eh?" / returned the boy, / with all his might of wonder.
"네?"   소년이 대답했다,   어리둥절해 하며.

Whoop (기쁨으로) 와 하는 함성 I frisk 뛰어 다니다 I winded 숨이 찬 I saucepan (긴 손잡이와 뚜껑이 달린)
냄비 I wandering 돌아다니는, 방랑하는, 헤매는 I illustrious 저명한, 걸출한 I transport (문예체) 도취 I lusty
건장한, 튼튼한, 활기찬 I peal 큰 소리 종소리 I clash (두 개의 금속 물체가 부딪쳐 나는) 쨍하는 소리 I clang (
금속이 부딪치며 울리듯) 쨍그랑, 땡그랑 하는 소리를 내다 I hammer 쿵쿵치다, 쾅쾅 치다 I mist 엷은 안개,
스프레이 I stirring 마음을 뒤흔드는, 신나는

"What's today, / my fine fellow?" / said Scrooge.
"며칠이지,   착한 꼬마야?"   스크루지가 말했다.

"Today!" / replied the boy. "Why, / Christmas Day."
"오늘이요!"   소년이 대답했다.   "저런,   크리스마스잖아요."

"It's Christmas Day!" / said Scrooge to himself. "I
"크리스마스라고!"   스크루지가 중얼거렸다.

haven't missed it. The Spirits have done it all / in one
"놓치지 않았어.   유령들은 그 모든 일을 한 거야   하룻밤 만에.

night. They can do anything / they like. Of course they
밤에.   뭐든지 할 수 있으니까   하려는 일은.   물론 할 수 있지.

can. Of course they can. Hallo, / my fine fellow!"
물론 할 수 있어.   이봐,   꼬마야!"

"Hallo!" / returned the boy.
"네!"   소년이 대답했다.

"Do you know the Poulterer's, / in the next street but
"양계장 주인을 알고 있니,   다음 골목 말고 그 다음 골목에 있는,

one, / at the corner?" / Scrooge inquired.
모퉁이에?"   스크루지가 물었다.

"I should hope I did," / replied the lad.
"물론 알죠,"   소년이 대답했다.

"An intelligent boy!" / said Scrooge. "A remarkable boy!
"똑똑한 아이구나!"   스크루지가 말했다.   "영리한 아이구나!

Do you know / whether they've sold the prize Turkey /
알고 있니   거기에서 최상급 칠면조가 팔렸는지

that was hanging up there? — Not the little prize Turkey:
걸려 있던?   — 작은 칠면조가 아니라:

/ the big one?"
큰 것 말이야?"

"What, / the one as big as me?" / returned the boy.
"뭐라고요,   저만큼 큰 칠면조 말인가요?"   소년이 대답했다.

"What a delightful boy!" / said Scrooge. "It's a pleasure
"정말 똑똑한 아이구나!"   스크루지가 말했다.   "네게 말해서 다행이구나.

to talk to him. Yes, / my buck!"
그래,   그놈 말이야!"

poulterer 가금류 판매상, 양계장 | buck (비격식) 젊은 남자, 총각(여기서는 칠면조 수컷을 일컫는 말) | walk-er
영국 영어로, 'Are you serious'라는 뜻임

246 A Christmas Carol

"It's hanging there now," / replied the boy.
"지금도 걸려 있어요,"   소년이 대답했다.

"Is it?" / said Scrooge. "Go and buy it."
"그래?"   스크루지가 말했다.   "가서 그것 좀 사다 주렴."

"Walk-er!" / exclaimed the boy.
"진심이세요!"   소년이 소리쳤다.

"No, no," / said Scrooge, / "I am in earnest. Go and buy
"그럼, 그럼."   스크루지가 말했다.   "진심이란다.   가서 그놈을 사서,

it, / and tell 'em to bring it here, / that I may give them
여기로 가져다 달라고 말해 주렴,   위치를 알려 줄게

the direction / where to take it. Come back with the man,
어디로 배달해야 할지.   주인을 데리고 돌아오렴,

/ and I'll give you a shilling. Come back with him / in
그러면 네게 1실링을 주마.   그를 데리고 돌아오면

less than five minutes / and I'll give you half-a-crown!"
5분 안에   반 크라운을 더 줄게!"

The boy was off like a shot. He must have had a steady
소년은 쏜살같이 사라졌다.   방아쇠에 손가락을 걸고 있다가

hand / at a trigger / who could have got a shot off / half
총을   쏜 사람이라도

so fast.
속도가 절반 밖에 안 되었을 것이 분명했다.

Key Expression ♪

감탄문의 표현
영어의 감탄문은 how와 what으로 시작하는 두 가지가 있어요. how는 형용사나 부사의 문장에, what은 명사가 있는 문장에 사용합니다.

▶ What + (a / an) + 형용사 + 명사 + (주어 + 동사)!
▶ How + 형용사 / 부사 + (주어 + 동사)!

ex) What a delightful boy!
    정말 똑똑한 아이구나!
    How his niece by marriage started!
    조카 며느리가 얼마나 놀라던지!

"I'll send it to Bob Cratchit's!" / whispered Scrooge,
"그것을 밥 크래칫의 집에 보내야지!" 스크루지가 중얼거렸다.

/ rubbing his hands, / and splitting with a laugh. "He
손을 비벼대고, 웃음이 터져 나오면서.

sha'n't know / who sends it. It's twice the size of Tiny
"모를 거야 누가 보냈는지. 크기가 꼬맹이 팀의 두 배는 될 걸.

Tim. Joe Miller never made such a joke / as sending it /
조 밀러라도 농담조차 못했겠지 그것을 보낼 거라고

to Bob's will be!"
밥의 집에!"

The hand / in which he wrote the address / was not a
손이 주소를 쓰고 있던

steady one, / but write it he did, / somehow, / and went
덜덜 떨렸지만, 그는 썼다. 어떻게든 그리고 아랫층으로

down-stairs / to open the street door, / ready for the
내려가 거리로 통하는 현관을 열고,

coming of the poulterer's man. As he stood there, /
양계장 주인을 맞이할 준비를 했다. 스크루지는 그곳에 서서,

waiting his arrival, / the knocker caught his eye.
그가 오기를 기다리는데, 문고리가 시선을 사로잡았다.

"I shall love it, / as long as I live!" / cried Scrooge, /
"이것도 아껴줘야지 내가 살아있는 한!" 스크루지가 소리쳤다,

patting it / with his hand. "I scarcely ever looked at it
쓰다듬으며 손으로. "거의 쳐다본 적도 없었어

/ before. What an honest expression it has / in its face!
전에는. 정말 정직하게 생겼구나 모양이!

It's a wonderful knocker! — Here's the Turkey! Hallo!
멋진 문고리야! — 칠면조가 왔군! 여기요!

Whoop! How are you! Merry Christmas!"
어이! 안녕하시오! 메리 크리스마스!"

It was a Turkey! He never could have stood / upon his
칠면조였다! 그것은 살아있지 못할 정도로 뚱뚱했다 제 다리로,

legs, / that bird. He would have snapped 'em short off /
그 새는. 다리를 부러뜨리고 말았을 것이다

in a minute, / like sticks of sealing-wax.
1분 만에, 봉랍 막대처럼.

snap 부러뜨리다 | sealing-wax 봉랍

"Why, / it's impossible / to carry that to Camden Town," /
"아이고, 불가능하겠군 캠던 타운까지 갖고 가는 것은."

said Scrooge. "You must have a cab."
스크루지가 말했다. "마차가 있어야겠어."

The chuckle with which he said this, / and the chuckle
스크루지는 이 말을 하면서 싱긋 웃었고,

with which he paid for the Turkey, / and the chuckle with
칠면조 값을 지불하며 싱긋 웃었으며,

which he paid for the cab, / and the chuckle with which he
마차값을 지불하며 싱긋 웃었고, 소년에게 심부름 값을 주면서 싱긋 웃었는데,

recompensed the boy, / were only to be exceeded by the
너무 많이 웃어서

chuckle / with which he sat down breathless / in his chair
숨이 차서 앉아버렸다 다시 의자에,

again, / and chuckled till he cried.
그리고 눈물이 나오도록 웃었다.

Shaving was not an easy task, / for his hand continued to
면도도 쉬운 일이 아니었다, 계속해서 손이 심하게 떨렸기 때문이다;

shake very much; / and shaving requires attention, / even
그리고 면도는 주의를 기울여야 하는 일이기에,

when you don't dance / while you are at it. But if he had
춤을 출 수도 없을 정도로 면도를 하는 동안에는.

cut the end of his nose off, / he would have put a piece of
하지만 코 끝을 베었다고 해도, 그는 반창고나 하나 붙이고,

sticking-plaister over it, / and been quite satisfied.
만족했을 것이다.

He dressed himself "all in his best," / and at last / got out
스크루지는 "가장 좋은 옷을" 입고, 마침내

into the streets. The people were by this time pouring
거리로 나갔다. 때맞춰 사람들이 쏟아져 나오고 있었다,

forth, / as he had seen them / with the Ghost of Christmas
보았던 것처럼 현재의 크리스마스 유령과;

Present; / and walking with his hands behind him, /
그리고 뒷짐을 지고 걸어다니면서,

Scrooge regarded every one / with a delighted smile. He
스크루지는 모두를 보았다   기쁜 미소를 지으며.

looked so irresistibly pleasant, / in a word, / that three or
그는 참을 수 없이 즐거워 보였고,   한 마디로,

four good-humored fellows said, / "Good morning, sir!
기분이 좋았던 서너 명은 말했다.   "안녕하세요, 선생님!

A merry Christmas to you!" And Scrooge said often /
메리 크리스마스!"   그리고 스크루지는 종종 말했다

afterwards, / that of all the blithe sounds / he had ever
나중에,   그것이 매우 즐거운 말이었다고   지금까지 들어보았던,

heard, / those were the blithest / in his ears.
그 말은 아주 즐겁게 들렸다고   그의 귀에.

He had not gone far, / when coming on towards him / he
얼마 가지 않았을 때,   스크루지 쪽으로 다가오는

beheld the portly gentleman, / who had walked into his
뚱뚱한 신사가 보였다.   그는 스크루지의 회계사무소에 찾아와서

counting-house / the day before, / and said, / "Scrooge
전 날,   말했었다.   "스크루지와 말리

and Marley's, / I believe?" It sent a pang across his heart
사무소죠,   맞습니까?" 라고.   가슴 속에 갑자기 고통이 느껴졌다

/ to think / how this old gentleman would look upon him
생각하니   이 노신사가 자신을 어떻게 쳐다볼까를

/ when they met; / but he knew / what path lay straight /
둘이 마주쳤을 때;   하지만 알고 있었기에   어떤 길이 펼쳐져 있는지

before him, / and he took it.
자신의 앞에,   그 길을 택했다.

"My dear sir," / said Scrooge, / quickening his pace, /
"선생님,"   스크루지가 말했다.   발걸음을 재촉하여,

and taking the old gentleman / by both his hands.
노신사의 손을 잡으며   두 손으로.

"How do you do? I hope you succeeded yesterday. It was
"안녕하십니까?   어제 성공하셨기를 바랍니다.   친절하게

very kind of you. A merry Christmas to you, sir!"
대해 주셔서 감사했습니다.   즐거운 크리스마스 보내세요, 선생님!"

---

chuckle 싱긋 웃다 | plaster 반창고 | regard (특히 어떤 감정을 갖고) ~을 보다 | irresistibly 저항할 수 없는,
거부할 수가 없는 | portly 약간 뚱뚱한 | pang (갑자기 격렬하게 일어나는) 아픔

"Mr. Scrooge?"
"스크루지 씨인가요?"

"Yes," / said Scrooge. "That is my name, / and I fear
"네." 스크루지가 말했다. "그것이 제 이름입니다. 그리고 제 이름을

it may not be pleasant to you. Allow me to ask your
듣고 불쾌하시지 않았을까 걱정이네요. 용서해 주세요.

pardon. And will you have the goodness" / — here
그리고 부디"

Scrooge whispered / in his ear.
— 이때 스크루지가 속삭였다 노신사의 귀에 대고.

"Lord bless me!" / cried the gentleman, / as if his breath
"맙소사!" 노신사가 소리쳤다, 숨이 넘어갈 듯이.

were taken away.

"My dear Mr. Scrooge, / are you serious?"
"스크루지 씨. 진심이십니까?"

"If you please," / said Scrooge. "Not a farthing less. A
"제발 부탁입니다." 스크루지가 말했다. "한 푼도 빠짐없이요.

great many back-payments are included in it, / I assure
그 동안 밀린 큰돈이 그 안에 포함되어 있어요, 정말입니다.

you. Will you do me that favor?"
부탁을 들어주실 건가요?"

"My dear sir," / said the other, / shaking hands with him.
"선생님." 노신사가 말했다, 스크루지의 손을 흔들며.

"I don't know / what to say to such munifi —"
"모르겠군요 왜 그런 큰 돈을 —"

"Don't say anything, / please," / retorted Scrooge. "Come
"아무 말씀 마세요, 제발." 스크루지가 말을 막았다. "

and see me. Will you come and see me?"
제게 들러 주세요. 와 주실 건가요?"

"I will!" / cried the old gentleman. And it was clear he
"가겠습니다!" 노신사가 소리쳤다. 그의 말투로 보아 분명했다.

meant to do it.

"Thank'ee," / said Scrooge. "I am much obliged to you. I
"감사합니다," 스크루지가 말했다. "정말 감사합니다.

thank you fifty times. Bless you!"
50번이라도 감사합니다. 신의 은총을 빕니다!"

He went to church, / and walked about the streets, / and
스크루지는 교회에 갔고, 거리를 걸어다녔으며,

watched the people hurrying to and fro, / and patted
바삐 오가는 사람들을 지켜보고,

children on the head, / and questioned beggars, / and
아이의 머리를 쓰다듬기도 하고, 거지에게 질문을 하거나,

looked down into the kitchens of houses, / and up to the
여러 집 부엌을 들여다 보고, 창문을 올려 보면서,

windows, / and found / that everything could yield him
알았다 모든 것이 자신에게 행복을 줄 수 있다는 사실을.

pleasure. He had never dreamed / that any walk / — that
꿈에도 생각하지 못했다 산책이

anything — / could give him so much happiness. In the
— 고작 그런 것이 — 자신에게 그토록 큰 행복을 안겨 주리라고는.

afternoon / he turned his steps / towards his nephew's
오후가 되자 그는 발걸음을 돌려 조카의 집으로 향했다.

house.

He passed the door / a dozen times, / before he had the
스크루지는 문을 지나갔다 십 수 번이나, 마침내 용기를 내어

courage / to go up and knock. But he made a dash, / and
올라가 노크를 하기 전까지. 하지만 급하게 서둘러서,

did it:
노크했다:

"Is your master at home, / my dear?" / said Scrooge to the
"주인 아저씨는 집에 계시니, 애야?" 스크루지가 소녀에게 말했다.

girl. Nice girl! Very.
친절한 소녀였다! 매우.

---

farthing 파딩(구 페니의 4분의 1에 해당하던 영국의 옛 화폐) | back-payment 밀린 돈 | obliged (감사를
표하거나 정중한 부탁을 할 때) 고마운, 감사한

"Yes, sir."
예, 선생님.

"Where is he, / my love?" / said Scrooge.
"어디 계시니,   애야?"   스크루지가 말했다.

"He's in the dining-room, / sir, / along with mistress. I'll
"식당에 계세요,   선생님,   마님과 함께.

show you up-stairs, / if you please."
위층으로 안내하겠습니다,   괜찮으시다면."

"Thank'ee. He knows me," / said Scrooge, / with his
"고맙구나.   날 알거든,"   스크루지가 말했다,

hand already / on the dining-room lock. "I'll go in here, /
그의 손은 이미   식당 문고리를 잡은 채로.   "그러니 내가 들어갈게,

my dear."
애야."

He turned it gently, / and sidled his face in, / round the
그는 문고리를 부드럽게 돌렸고,   얼굴을 들이밀었다,   문 사이로.

door. They were looking at the table / (which was spread
그들은 식탁을 바라보고 있었다   (놓여 있던

out / in great array); / for these young housekeepers are
줄 지어);   젊은 주부들은 항상 신경 쓰고

always nervous / on such points, / and like to see / that
그런 점에,   알고 싶어 하곤 한다

everything is right.
모든 것이 제대로 되어 있는지.

"Fred!" / said Scrooge.
"프레드!"   스크루지가 말했다.

Dear heart alive, / how his niece by marriage started!
가슴이 철렁했다,   조카 며느리가 얼마나 놀랐던지!

Scrooge had forgotten, / for the moment, / about her
스크루지는 잊고 있었다,   잠시 동안,   조카 며느리가 앉아 있

sitting / in the corner with the footstool, / or he wouldn't
다는 사실을 발판 귀퉁이에,

have done it, / on any account.
알았다면 그렇게 하지는 않았을 텐데,   무슨 일이 있어도.

"Why bless my soul!" / cried Fred, / "who's that?"
"맙소사!"   프레드가 외쳤다,   "누구신가요?"

"It's I. Your uncle Scrooge. I have come to dinner. Will
"나야.　　네 삼촌 스크루지.　　　　　　저녁 먹으러 왔다.

you let me in, / Fred?"
들어가도 되겠니,　프레드?"

Let him in! It is a mercy / he didn't shake his arm off.
들어가도 되냐!　다행이었다　　　　프레드가 삼촌의 팔을 잡고 흔들지 않은 것만으로도.

He was at home / in five minutes. Nothing could be
스크루지는 마음이 편해졌다 5분 만에.　　　　아무것도 더 따뜻할 수 없으리라.

heartier. His niece looked just the same. So did Topper /
　　　　조카 며느리는 똑같아 보였다.　　　　토퍼도 똑같았다

when he came. So did the plump sister / when she came.
도착했을 때.　　통통한 처제도 똑같았고,　　　도착했을 때.

So did every one / when they came. Wonderful party, /
모두 똑같았다　　도착했을 때.　　　멋진 파티에,

wonderful games, / wonderful unanimity, / won-der-ful
즐거운 게임,　　　한 마음이 되어,

happiness!
정말 행복했다!

Key Expression

if only : ~하기만 한다면 좋을 텐데
if 가정법에 only를 추가하면 '~하기만 한다면 좋을 텐데'라는 의미로 주절이 없이 소망을 나타냅니다.
반면 위치가 바뀌어 only if의 형태가 되면 '~할 경우에 한해서, ~하지 않는 한'이라는 의미되는 것에 주의하세요.

ex) If he could only be there first, and catch Bob Cratchit coming late!
자신이 첫 번째로 도착하여 늦게 들어오는 밥 크래칫을 잡을 수만 있으면 좋을 텐데!

But he was early at the office / next morning. Oh, he was
하지만 스크루지는 사무실에 일찍 나왔다   다음 날 아침.   정말, 이른 시간에

early there. If he could only be there first, / and catch
그곳에 있었다.   자신이 첫 번째로 도착하면 좋을텐데,   밥 크래칫을 잡을

Bob Cratchit / coming late! That was the thing / he had
수만 있으면   늦게 들어오는!   그것이 바로

set his heart upon.
그가 마음속에 품었던 생각이었다.

And he did it; / yes, he did! The clock struck nine. No
그리고 그렇게 했다;   그랬다, 그렇게 했다! 시계가 9시를 쳤다.   밥은 오지

Bob. A quarter past. No Bob. He was full eighteen
않았다. 15분이 지났다.   그래도 오지 않았다.

minutes and a half / behind his time. Scrooge sat / with
밥은 18분 30초에 나타났다   출근 시간을 지나.   스크루지는 앉아 있었다

his door wide open, / that he might see him come into
문을 활짝 열어놓은 채,   밥이 사무실로 들어오는 것을 보려고.

the Tank.

His hat was off, / before he opened the door; / his
밥은 모자를 벗고,   문을 열기 전에;

comforter too. He was on his stool / in a jiffy; / driving
목도리도 풀었다.   밥은 의자에 앉았다   즉시;

away with his pen, / as if he were trying to overtake nine
부지런히 펜을 움직였다,   마치 9시 이후 지난 시간을 보충하려는 듯.

o'clock.

"Hallo!" / growled Scrooge, / in his accustomed voice,
"어이!"   스크루지가 툴툴거렸다,   익숙한 목소리로,

/ as near as he could feign it. "What do you mean / by
최대한 꾸미며.   "무슨 일인가

coming here / at this time of day?"
출근하다니   이 시간에?"

---

behind time 늦게 | jiffy 순간 | overtake 따라잡다 | feign 가장하다, ~인 척하다

"I am very sorry, sir," / said Bob. "I am behind my time."
"죄송합니다." 밥이 말했다. "늦었습니다."

"You are?" / repeated Scrooge. "Yes. I think you are.
"그런가?" 스크루지가 다시 말했다. "그래. 그렇군.

Step this way, sir, / if you please."
이리로 오게, 괜찮다면."

"It's only once a year, sir," / pleaded Bob, / appearing
"1년에 한 번 뿐입니다." 밥이 애원했다. 사무실에서 나오며.

from the Tank. "It shall not be repeated. I was making
"다시는 이런 일 없을 겁니다.

rather merry yesterday, sir."
어제 너무 즐겼나 봅니다, 사장님"

"Now, / I'll tell you what, / my friend," / said Scrooge, /
"그래, 말하지 친구여." 스크루지가 말했다.

"I am not going to stand this sort of thing / any longer.
"이런 일을 참을 수 없네 더 이상은.

And therefore," / he continued, / leaping from his stool,
그래서." 그는 말을 이었다. 의자에서 일어나.

/ and giving Bob such a dig / in the waistcoat / that he
밥을 쿡 찌르며 조끼를 입은 그래서 밥은

staggered back / into the Tank again; / "and therefore / I
비틀거리며 돌아갔다 다시 사무실로; "그래서' 말이지

am about to raise your salary!"
자네 급료를 올려 주려 하네!"

Bob trembled, / and got a little nearer / to the ruler. He
밥은 벌벌 떨며, 가까이 다가갔다 막대 자 쪽으로.

had a momentary idea / of knocking Scrooge down /
순간 생각이 떠올랐다 스크루지를 때려 눕혀서

with it, / holding him, / and calling to the people / in the
그 자로, 그를 잡은 뒤, 사람들을 불러 거리에 있는

court / for help and a strait-waistcoat.
도움과 구속복을 청해야겠다고.

---

plead 애원하다 | dig (손가락이나 팔꿈치로) 쿡 찌르기 | waistcoat 조끼 | stagger 비틀거리다, 휘청거리다 |
ruler 통치자, 지배자, 자 | strait-waistcoat 구속복(정신 이상자와 같이 폭력적인 사람의 행동을 제압하기 위해
입히는 것)(=straitjacket) | bishop 비숍(레몬과 설탕을 가미한 따뜻한 포도주) | coal-scuttle (난로 옆에 두는) 석탄통

"A merry Christmas, Bob!" / said Scrooge, / with an
"메리 크리스마스, 밥!"   스크루지가 말했다,

earnestness / that could not be mistaken, / as he clapped
진지하게   틀림없이,

him on the back. "A merrier Christmas, / Bob, / my good
밥의 등을 두드리며.   "더 즐거운 크리스마스 보내게,   밥,

fellow, / than I have given you, / for many a year! I'll
좋은 동료여,   내가 자네에게 주었던 것 보다,   오랫동안!

raise your salary, / and endeavor to assist your struggling
급료를 올려 주고,   자네 가족을 도울 생각이네,

family, / and we will discuss your affairs / this very
그리고 자네 일을 의논해 보세   오늘 오후,

afternoon, / over a Christmas bowl of smoking bishop, /
김이 나는 크리스마스용 비숍을 한 사발 마시며.

Bob! Make up the fires, / and buy another coal-scuttle /
밥!   불을 피우게,   석탄을 더 사고

before you dot another i, / Bob Cratchit!"
글자 하나 더 쓰기 전에,   밥 크래칫!"

Scrooge was better / than his word. He did it all, / and
스크루지는 더 많이 베풀었다   말한 것보다.   모든 일을 했고,

infinitely more; / and to Tiny Tim, / who did not die, /
훨씬 더 많이;   그리고 팀에게는,   죽지 않았던,

he was a second father. He became as good a friend, /
양부가 되어 주었다.   스크루지는 좋은 친구이자,

as good a master, / and as good a man, / as the good old
너그러운 주인이며,   착한 사람이 되었다.   멋지고 오래된 도시나,

city knew, / or any other good old city, town, or borough,
다른 도시, 마을, 자치구에서도.

/ in the good old world. Some people laughed / to see
훌륭하고 오래된 세계의.   어떤 사람들은 웃었지만

the alteration in him, / but he let them laugh, / and little
그의 달라진 모습을 보고,   그는 웃도록 내버려 두었고,

heeded them; / for he was wise enough to know / that
신경 쓰지 않았다;   왜냐하면 그는 알만큼 현명했기 때문이었다

nothing ever happened / on this globe, / for good, / at
아무 일도 일어나지 않는다는 것을   이 세계에,   영원히,

which / some people did not have their fill of laughter /
그것에 대해 그 세계에서 사람들의 끝없는 비웃음을 사지 않고서는

in the outset; / and knowing / that such as these would
처음에는;   그리고 알고 있었다   그런 비웃음은 눈감아 버릴 수 있다는 것을,

be blind anyway, / he thought / it quite as well / that they
그는 생각했다   그것이 낫다고

should wrinkle up their eyes / in grins, / as have the
그들에게 주름이 생겨 버리는 것이   웃어서,   병이 생기는 것 보다는

malady / in less attractive forms. His own heart laughed:
별로 아름답지 않은 모습으로.   스크루지의 마음이 웃고 있었고;

/ and that was quite enough for him.
그에게는 그것으로 충분했다.

borough 자치구, 도시 | alteration 변화 | heed 주의를 기울이다 | outset 착수, 시초 | malady 병, 병폐 |
intercourse 교류

He had no further intercourse / with Spirits, / but lived
스크루지는 더 이상 교류가 없었지만   유령들과,

upon the Total Abstinence Principle, / ever afterwards;
"완벽한 금욕주의"를 지키며 살았다.   이후 언제까지나.

/ and it was always said of him, / that he knew / how to
그리고 언제나 그에 대해 말했다.   그가 알고 있다고   크리스마스를

keep Christmas well, / if any man alive possessed the
어떻게 잘 보내야 하는지.   살아있는 누군가 그 이야기를 꺼낼 때면.

knowledge. May that be truly said of us, / and all of us!
진심으로 바라건대,   우리 모두 그렇게 되기를!

And so, / as Tiny Tim observed, / God bless Us, / Every
마찬가지로,   팀이 말했듯이,   우리에게도 신의 가호가 있기를,

One!
모든 이에게!

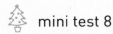 mini test 8

A. 다음 문장을 해석해 보세요.

(1) Best and happiest of all, / the Time before him was his own, / to make amends in!
→

(2) He must have had a steady hand / at a trigger / who could have got a shot off / half so fast.
→

(3) If he could only be there first, / and catch Bob Cratchit / coming late!
→

(4) He had no further intercourse with Spirits, / but lived upon the Total Abstinence Principle, / ever afterwards.
→

B. 다음 주어진 문구가 알맞은 문장이 되도록 순서를 맞춰 보세요.

(1) 그의 조카 며느리가 얼마나 놀라던지!
(marriage / niece / How / his / started / by)
→

(2) 정말 감사합니다.
(you / to / much / I / obliged / am)
→

(3) 아무것도 더 따뜻할 수 없으리라.
(heartier / be / could / Nothing)
→

(4) 그는 그들이 웃도록 내버려 두었고, 신경 쓰지 않았다.
(let / He / little / them / and / laugh, / them / heeded)
→

A. (1) 최고로 행복했던 점은, 그의 앞에 바로 잡을 수 있는 시간이 남아 있다는 사실이었다! (2) 방아쇠에 손가락을 걸고 있다가 총을 쏜 사람이라도 속도가 절반 밖에 안 되었을 게 분명했다. (3) 자신이 첫 번째로 도착하여 늦게 들어오는 밥 크래칫을 잡을 수만 있으면 좋을 텐데! (4) 그는 유령들과 더 이상 교류가 없

C. 다음 주어진 문장이 본문의 내용과 맞으면 T, 틀리면 F에 동그라미 하세요.

(1) Afret Scrooge waked up, it was the day after Christmas.
   [T / F]

(2) Scrooge was very happy because he had time to change his life.
   [T / F]

(3) Scrooge presented a big turkey to his nephew.
   [T / F]

(4) Scrooge had a chance to meet the Spirits once again.
   [T / F]

D. 의미가 비슷한 것끼리 서로 연결해 보세요.

(1) amend   ▶   ◀ ① vibrate
(2) flutter ▶   ◀ ② appeal
(3) plead   ▶   ◀ ③ reform
(4) heed   ▶   ◀ ④ impolite

A Christmas Carol을 다시 읽어 보세요.

 MARLEY'S GHOST I

Marley was dead: to begin with. There is no doubt whatever about that. The register of his burial was signed by the clergyman, the clerk, the undertaker, and the chief mourner. Scrooge signed it: and Scrooge's name was good upon 'Change, for anything he chose to put his hand to. Old Marley was as dead as a door-nail.

Mind! I don't mean to say that I know, of my own knowledge, what there is particularly dead about a door-nail. I might have been inclined, myself, to regard a coffin-nail as the deadest piece of ironmongery in the trade. But the wisdom of our ancestors is in the simile; and my unhallowed hands shall not disturb it, or the Country's done for.

You will therefore permit me to repeat, emphatically, that Marley was as dead as a door-nail.

Scrooge knew he was dead? Of course he did. How could it be otherwise? Scrooge and he were partners for I don't know how many years. Scrooge was his sole executor, his sole administrator, his sole assign, his sole residuary legatee, his sole friend, and sole mourner. And even Scrooge was not so dreadfully cut up by the sad event, but that he was an excellent man of business on the very day of the funeral, and solemnized it with an undoubted bargain.

The mention of Marley's funeral brings me back to the point I started from. There is no doubt that Marley was dead. This must be distinctly understood, or nothing wonderful can come of the story I am going to relate. If we were not perfectly convinced that Hamlet's Father died before the play began, there would be nothing more remarkable in his taking a stroll at night, in an easterly wind, upon his own ramparts, than there would be in any other middle-aged gentleman rashly turning out after dark in a breezy spot — say Saint Paul's Churchyard for instance — literally to astonish his son's weak mind.

Scrooge never painted out Old Marley's name. There it stood, years afterwards, above the warehouse door: Scrooge and Marley. The firm was known as Scrooge and Marley. Sometimes people new to the business called Scrooge Scrooge, and sometimes Marley, but he answered to both names. It was all the same to him.

Oh! But he was a tight-fisted hand at the grindstone, Scrooge! A squeezing, wrenching, grasping, scraping, clutching, covetous, old sinner! Hard and sharp as flint, from which no steel had ever struck out generous fire; secret, and self-contained, and solitary as an oyster. The cold within him froze his old features, nipped his pointed nose, shrivelled his cheek, stiffened his gait; made his eyes red, his thin lips blue; and spoke out shrewdly in his grating voice. A frosty rime was on his head, and on his eyebrows, and his wiry chin. He carried his own low temperature always about with him; he iced his office in the dog-days; and didn't thaw it one degree at Christmas.

External heat and cold had little influence on Scrooge. No warmth could warm, no wintry weather chill him. No wind that blew was bitterer than he, no falling snow was more intent upon its purpose, no pelting rain less open to entreaty. Foul weather didn't know where to have him. The heaviest rain, and snow, and hail, and sleet, could boast of the advantage over him in only one respect. They often "came down" handsomely, and Scrooge never did.

Nobody ever stopped him in the street to say, with gladsome looks, "My dear Scrooge, how are you? When will you come to see me?" No beggars implored him to bestow a trifle, no children asked him what it was o'clock, no man or woman ever once in all his life inquired the way to such and such a place, of Scrooge. Even the blind men's dogs appeared to know him; and when they saw him coming on, would tug their owners into doorways and up courts; and then would wag their tails as though they said, "No eye at all is better than an evil eye, dark master!"

But what did Scrooge care! It was the very thing he liked. To edge his way along the crowded paths of life, warning all human sympathy to keep its distance, was what the knowing ones call "nuts" to Scrooge. Once upon a time — of all the good days in the year, on Christmas Eve

— old Scrooge sat busy in his counting-house. It was cold, bleak, biting weather: foggy withal: and he could hear the people in the court outside, go wheezing up and down, beating their hands upon their breasts, and stamping their feet upon the pavement stones to warm them. The city clocks had only just gone three, but it was quite dark already — it had not been light all day — and candles were flaring in the windows of the neighboring offices, like ruddy smears upon the palpable brown air. The fog came pouring in at every chink and keyhole, and was so dense without, that although the court was of the narrowest, the houses opposite were mere phantoms. To see the dingy cloud come drooping down, obscuring everything, one might have thought that Nature lived hard by, and was brewing on a large scale.

The door of Scrooge's counting-house was open that he might keep his eye upon his clerk, who in a dismal little cell beyond, a sort of tank, was copying letters. Scrooge had a very small fire, but the clerk's fire was so very much smaller that it looked like one coal. But he couldn't replenish it, for Scrooge kept the coal-box in his own room; and so surely as the clerk came in with the shovel, the master predicted that it would be necessary for them to part. Wherefore the clerk put on his white comforter, and tried to warm himself at the candle; in which effort, not being a man of a strong imagination, he failed.

"A merry Christmas, uncle! God save you!" cried a cheerful voice. It was the voice of Scrooge's nephew, who came upon him so quickly that this was the first intimation he had of his approach.

"Bah!" said Scrooge, "Humbug!"

He had so heated himself with rapid walking in the fog and frost, this nephew of Scrooge's, that he was all in a glow; his face was ruddy and handsome; his eyes sparkled, and his breath smoked again.

"Christmas a humbug, uncle!" said Scrooge's nephew. "You don't mean that, I am sure?"

"I do," said Scrooge. "Merry Christmas! What right have you to be merry? What reason have you to be merry? You're poor enough."

"Come, then," returned the nephew gaily. "What right have you to be dismal? What reason have you to be morose? You're rich enough."

Scrooge having no better answer ready on the spur of the moment, said, "Bah!" again; and followed it up with "Humbug."

"Don't be cross, uncle!" said the nephew.

"What else can I be," returned the uncle, "when I live in such a world of fools as this? Merry Christmas! Out upon merry Christmas! What's Christmas time to you but a time for paying bills without money; a time for finding yourself a year older, but not an hour richer; a time for balancing your books and having every item in 'em through a round dozen of months presented dead against you? If I could work my will," said Scrooge indignantly, "every idiot who goes about with 'Merry Christmas' on his lips, should be boiled with his own pudding, and buried with a stake of holly through his heart. He should!"

"Uncle!" pleaded the nephew.

"Nephew!" returned the uncle sternly, "keep Christmas in your own way, and let me keep it in mine."

"Keep it!" repeated Scrooge's nephew. "But you don't keep it."

"Let me leave it alone, then," said Scrooge. "Much good may it do you! Much good it has ever done you!"

"There are many things from which I might have derived good, by which I have not profited, I dare say," returned the nephew. "Christmas among the rest. But I am sure I have always thought of Christmas time, when it has come round — apart from the veneration due to its sacred name and origin, if anything belonging to it can be apart from that — as a good time; a kind, forgiving, charitable, pleasant time; the only time I know of, in the long calendar of the year, when men and women seem by one consent to open their shut-up hearts freely, and to think of people below them as if they really were fellow-passengers to the grave, and not another race of creatures bound on other journeys. And therefore, uncle, though it has never put a scrap of gold or silver in my pocket, I believe that it has done me good, and will do me good; and I say, God bless it!"

The clerk in the Tank involuntarily applauded. Becoming immediately sensible of the impropriety, he poked the fire, and extinguished the last frail spark forever.

"Let me hear another sound from you," said Scrooge, "and you'll keep your Christmas by losing your situation! You're quite a powerful speaker, sir," he added, turning to his nephew. "I wonder you don't go into Parliament."

"Don't be angry, uncle. Come! Dine with us tomorrow."

Scrooge said that he would see him — yes, indeed he did. He went the whole length of the expression, and said that he would see him in that extremity first.

"But why?" cried Scrooge's nephew. "Why?"

"Why did you get married?" said Scrooge.

"Because I fell in love."

"Because you fell in love!" growled Scrooge, as if that were the only one thing in the world more ridiculous than a merry Christmas. "Good afternoon!"

"Nay, uncle, but you never came to see me before that happened. Why give it as a reason for not coming now?"

"Good afternoon," said Scrooge.

"I want nothing from you; I ask nothing of you; why cannot we be friends?"

"Good afternoon," said Scrooge.

"I am sorry, with all my heart, to find you so resolute. We have never had any quarrel, to which I have been a party. But I have made the trial in homage to Christmas, and I'll keep my Christmas humor to the last. So A Merry Christmas, uncle!"

"Good afternoon!" said Scrooge.

"And A Happy New Year!"

"Good afternoon!" said Scrooge.

His nephew left the room without an angry word, notwithstanding. He stopped at the outer door to bestow the greetings of the season on the clerk, who, cold as he was, was warmer than Scrooge; for he returned them cordially.

"There's another fellow," muttered Scrooge; who overheard him: "my clerk, with fifteen shillings a week, and a wife and family, talking about a merry Christmas. I'll retire to Bedlam."

This lunatic, in letting Scrooge's nephew out, had let two other people in. They were portly gentlemen, pleasant to behold, and now stood, with their hats off, in Scrooge's office. They had books and papers in their hands, and bowed to him.

"Scrooge and Marley's, I believe," said one of the gentlemen, referring to his list. "Have I the pleasure of addressing Mr. Scrooge, or Mr. Marley?"

"Mr. Marley has been dead these seven years," Scrooge replied. "He died seven years ago, this very night."

"We have no doubt his liberality is well represented by his surviving partner," said the gentleman, presenting his credentials.

It certainly was; for they had been two kindred spirits. At the ominous word "liberality," Scrooge frowned, and shook his head, and handed the credentials back.

"At this festive season of the year, Mr. Scrooge," said the gentleman, taking up a pen, "it is more than usually desirable that we should make some slight provision for the Poor and destitute, who suffer greatly at the present time. Many thousands are in want of common necessaries; hundreds of thousands are in want of common comforts, sir."

"Are there no prisons?" asked Scrooge.

"Plenty of prisons," said the gentleman, laying down the pen again.

"And the Union workhouses?" demanded Scrooge. "Are they still in operation?"

"They are. Still," returned the gentleman, "I wish I could say they were not."

"The Treadmill and the Poor Law are in full vigor, then?" said Scrooge.

"Both very busy, sir."

"Oh! I was afraid, from what you said at first, that something had occurred to stop them in their useful course," said Scrooge. "I'm very glad to hear it."

"Under the impression that they scarcely furnish Christian cheer of mind or body to the multitude," returned the gentleman, "a few of us are endeavoring to raise a fund to buy the Poor some meat and drink, and means of warmth. We choose this time, because it is a time, of all others, when Want is keenly felt, and Abundance rejoices. What shall I put you down for?"

"Nothing!" Scrooge replied.

"You wish to be anonymous?"

"I wish to be left alone," said Scrooge. "Since you ask me what I wish, gentlemen, that is my answer. I don't make merry myself at Christmas and I can't afford to make idle people merry. I help to support the establishments I have mentioned — they cost enough; and those who are badly off must go there."

"Many can't go there; and many would rather die."

"If they would rather die," said Scrooge, "they had better do it, and decrease the surplus population. Besides — excuse me — I don't know that."

"But you might know it," observed the gentleman.

"It's not my business," Scrooge returned. "It's enough for a man to understand his own business, and not to interfere with other people's. Mine occupies me constantly. Good afternoon, gentlemen!"

Seeing clearly that it would be useless to pursue their point, the gentlemen withdrew. Scrooge resumed his labors with an improved opinion of himself, and in a more facetious temper than was usual with him.

Meanwhile the fog and darkness thickened so, that people ran about with flaring links, proffering their services to go before horses in carriages, and conduct them on their way. The ancient tower of a church, whose gruff old bell was always peeping slily down at Scrooge out of a Gothic window in the wall, became invisible, and struck the hours and quarters in the clouds, with tremulous vibrations afterwards as if its teeth were chattering in its frozen head up there. The cold became intense. In the main street, at the corner of the court, some laborers were repairing the gas-pipes, and had lighted a great fire in a brazier, round which a party of ragged men and boys were gathered: warming their hands and winking their eyes before the blaze in rapture. The water-plug being left in solitude, its overflowings sullenly congealed, and turned to misanthropic ice. The brightness of the shops where holly sprigs and berries crackled in the lamp heat of the windows, made pale faces ruddy as they passed. Poulterers' and grocers' trades became a splendid joke: a glorious pageant, with which it was next to impossible to believe that such dull principles as bargain and sale had anything to do.

The Lord Mayor, in the stronghold of the mighty Mansion House, gave orders to his fifty cooks and butlers to keep Christmas as a Lord Mayor's household should; and even the little tailor, whom he had fined five shillings on the previous Monday for being drunk and bloodthirsty in the streets, stirred up tomorrow's pudding in his garret, while his lean wife and the baby sallied out to buy the beef.

Foggier yet, and colder. Piercing, searching, biting cold. If the good Saint Dunstan had but nipped the Evil Spirit's nose with a touch of such weather as that, instead of using his familiar weapons, then indeed he would have roared to lusty purpose. The owner of one scant young nose, gnawed and mumbled by the hungry cold as bones are gnawed by dogs, stooped down at Scrooge's keyhole to regale him with a Christmas carol: but at the first sound of "God bless you, merry gentleman! May nothing you dismay!"

Scrooge seized the ruler with such energy of action, that the singer fled in terror, leaving the keyhole to the fog and even more congenial frost.

At length the hour of shutting up the counting-house arrived. With an ill-will Scrooge dismounted from his stool, and tacitly admitted the fact to the expectant clerk in the Tank, who instantly snuffed his candle out, and put on his hat.

"You'll want all day to-morrow, I suppose?" said Scrooge.

"If quite convenient, sir."

"It's not convenient," said Scrooge, "and it's not fair. If I was to stop half-a-crown for it, you'd think yourself ill-used, I'll be bound?"

The clerk smiled faintly.

"And yet," said Scrooge, "you don't think me ill-used, when I pay a day's wages for no work."

The clerk observed that it was only once a year.

"A poor excuse for picking a man's pocket every twenty-fifth of December!" said Scrooge, buttoning his great-coat to the chin. "But I suppose you must have the whole day. Be here all the earlier next morning."

The clerk promised that he would; and Scrooge walked out with a growl. The office was closed in a twinkling, and the clerk, with the long ends of his white comforter dangling below his waist (for he boasted no great-coat), went down a slide on Cornhill, at the end of a lane of boys, twenty times, in honor of its being Christmas Eve, and then ran home to Camden Town as hard as he could pelt, to play at blindman's-buff.

 **MARLEY'S GHOST II**

Scrooge took his melancholy dinner in his usual melancholy tavern; and having read all the newspapers, and beguiled the rest of the evening with his banker's-book, went home to bed. He lived in chambers which had once belonged to his deceased partner. They were a gloomy suite of rooms, in a lowering pile of building up a yard, where it had so little business to be, that one could scarcely help fancying it must have run there when it was a young house, playing at hide-and-seek with other houses, and forgotten the way out again. It was old enough now, and dreary enough, for nobody lived in it but Scrooge, the other rooms being all let out as offices. The yard was so dark that even Scrooge, who knew its every stone, was fain to grope with his hands.

The fog and frost so hung about the black old gateway of the house, that it seemed as if the Genius of the Weather sat in mournful meditation on the threshold.

Now, it is a fact, that there was nothing at all particular about the knocker on the door, except that it was very large. It is also a fact, that Scrooge had seen it, night and morning, during his whole residence in that place; also that Scrooge had as little of what is called fancy about him as any man in the city of London, even including — which is a bold word — the corporation, aldermen, and livery. Let it also be borne in mind that Scrooge had not bestowed one thought on Marley, since his last mention of his seven years' dead partner that afternoon. And then let any man explain to me, if he can, how it happened that Scrooge, having his key in the lock of the door, saw in the knocker, without its undergoing any intermediate process of change — not a knocker, but Marley's face.

Marley's face. It was not in impenetrable shadow as the other objects in the yard were, but had a dismal light about it, like a bad lobster in a dark cellar. It was not angry or ferocious, but looked at Scrooge as Marley used to look: with ghostly spectacles turned up on its ghostly forehead. The hair was curiously stirred, as if by breath or hot air; and, though the eyes were wide open, they were perfectly motionless. That, and its livid colour, made it horrible; but its horror seemed to be in spite of the face and beyond its control, rather than a part of its own expression.

As Scrooge looked fixedly at this phenomenon, it was a knocker again. To say that he was not startled, or that his blood was not conscious of a terrible sensation to which it had been a stranger from infancy, would be untrue. But he put his hand upon the key he had relinquished, turned it sturdily, walked in, and lighted his candle.

He did pause, with a moment's irresolution, before he shut the door; and he did look cautiously behind it first, as if he half expected to be terrified with the sight of Marley's pigtail sticking out into the hall. But there was nothing on the back of the door, except the screws and nuts that held the knocker on, so he said "Pooh, pooh!" and closed it with a bang.

The sound resounded through the house like thunder. Every room above, and every cask in the wine-merchant's cellars below, appeared to have a separate peal of echoes of its own. Scrooge was not a man to be frightened by echoes. He fastened the door, and walked across the hall, and up the stairs; slowly too: trimming his candle as he went.

You may talk vaguely about driving a coach-and-six up a good old flight of stairs, or through a bad young Act of Parliament; but I mean to say you might have got a hearse up that staircase, and taken it broadwise, with the splinter-bar towards the wall and the door towards the balustrades: and done it easy. There was plenty of width for that, and room to spare; which is perhaps the reason why Scrooge thought he saw a locomotive hearse going on before him in the gloom. Half-a-dozen gas-lamps out of the street wouldn't have lighted the entry too well, so you may suppose that it was pretty dark with Scrooge's dip.

Up Scrooge went, not caring a button for that. Darkness is cheap, and Scrooge liked it. But before he shut his heavy door, he walked through his rooms to see that all was right. He had just enough recollection of the face to desire to do that.

Sitting-room, bedroom, lumber-room. All as they should be. Nobody under the table, nobody under the sofa; a small fire in the grate; spoon and basin ready; and the little saucepan of gruel (Scrooge had a cold in his head) upon the hob. Nobody under the bed; nobody in the closet; nobody in his dressing-gown, which was hanging up in a suspicious attitude against the wall. Lumber-room as usual. Old fire-guard, old shoes, two fish-baskets, washing-stand on three legs, and a poker.

Quite satisfied, he closed his door, and locked himself in; double-locked himself in, which was not his custom. Thus secured against surprise, he took off his cravat; put on his dressing-gown and slippers, and his nightcap; and sat down before the fire to take his gruel.

It was a very low fire indeed; nothing on such a bitter night. He was obliged to sit close to it, and brood over it, before he could extract the least sensation of warmth from such a handful of fuel.

The fireplace was an old one, built by some Dutch merchant long ago, and paved all round with quaint Dutch tiles, designed to illustrate the Scriptures. There were Cains and Abels, Pharaoh's daughters; Queens of Sheba, Angelic messengers descending through the air on clouds like feather-beds, Abrahams, Belshazzars, Apostles putting off to sea in butter-boats, hundreds of figures to attract his thoughts; and yet that face of Marley, seven years dead, came like the ancient Prophet's rod, and swallowed up the whole. If each smooth tile had been a blank at first, with power to shape some picture on its surface from the disjointed fragments of his thoughts, there would have been a copy of old Marley's head on every one.

"Humbug!" said Scrooge; and walked across the room.

After several turns, he sat down again. As he threw his head back in the chair, his glance happened to rest upon a bell, a disused bell, that hung in the room, and communicated for some purpose now forgotten with a chamber in the highest story of the building. It was with great astonishment, and with a strange, inexplicable dread, that as he looked, he saw this bell begin to swing. It swung so softly in the outset that it scarcely made a sound; but soon it rang out loudly, and so did every bell in the house.

This might have lasted half a minute, or a minute, but it seemed an hour. The bells ceased as they had begun, together. They were succeeded by a clanking noise, deep down below; as if some person were dragging a heavy chain over the casks in the wine-merchant's cellar. Scrooge then remembered to have heard that ghosts in haunted houses were described as dragging chains.

The cellar-door flew open with a booming sound, and then he heard the noise much louder, on the floors below; then coming up the stairs; then coming straight towards his door.

"It's humbug still!" said Scrooge. "I won't believe it."

His color changed though, when, without a pause, it came on through the heavy door, and passed into the room before his eyes. Upon its coming in, the dying flame leaped up, as though it cried, "I know him; Marley's Ghost!" and fell again.

The same face: the very same. Marley in his pigtail, usual waistcoat, tights and boots; the tassels on the latter bristling, like his pigtail, and his coat-skirts, and the hair upon his head. The chain he drew was clasped about his middle. It was long, and wound about him like a tail; and it was made (for Scrooge observed it closely) of cash-boxes, keys, padlocks, ledgers, deeds, and heavy purses wrought in steel. His body was transparent; so that Scrooge, observing him, and looking through his waistcoat, could see the two buttons on his coat behind.

Scrooge had often heard it said that Marley had no bowels, but he had never believed it until now.

No, nor did he believe it even now. Though he looked the phantom through and through, and saw it standing before him; though he felt the chilling influence of its death-cold eyes; and marked the very texture of the folded kerchief bound about its head and chin, which wrapper he had not observed before; he was still incredulous, and fought against his senses.

"How now!" said Scrooge, caustic and cold as ever. "What do you want with me?"

"Much!" — Marley's voice, no doubt about it.

"Who are you?"

"Ask me who I was."

"Who were you then?" said Scrooge, raising his voice. "You're particular, for a shade." He was going to say "to a shade," but substituted this, as more appropriate.

"In life I was your partner, Jacob Marley."

"Can you — can you sit down?" asked Scrooge, looking doubtfully at him.

"I can."

"Do it, then."

Scrooge asked the question, because he didn't know whether a ghost so transparent might find himself in a condition to take a chair; and felt that in the event of its being impossible, it might involve the necessity of an embarrassing explanation. But the ghost sat down on the opposite side of the fireplace, as if he were quite used to it.

"You don't believe in me," observed the Ghost.

"I don't," said Scrooge.

"What evidence would you have of my reality beyond that of your senses?"

"I don't know," said Scrooge.

"Why do you doubt your senses?"

"Because," said Scrooge, "a little thing affects them. A slight disorder of the stomach makes them cheats. You may be an undigested bit of beef, a blot of mustard, a crumb of cheese, a fragment of an underdone potato. There's more of gravy than of grave about you, whatever you are!"

Scrooge was not much in the habit of cracking jokes, nor did he feel, in his heart, by any means waggish then. The truth is, that he tried to be smart, as a means of distracting his own attention, and keeping down his terror; for the spectre's voice disturbed the very marrow in his bones. To sit, staring at those fixed glazed eyes, in silence for a moment, would play, Scrooge felt, the very deuce with him. There was something very awful, too, in the spectre's being provided with an infernal atmosphere of its own. Scrooge could not feel it himself, but this was clearly the case; for though the Ghost sat perfectly motionless, its hair, and skirts, and tassels, were still agitated as by the hot vapour from an oven.

"You see this toothpick?" said Scrooge, returning quickly to the charge, for the reason just assigned; and wishing, though it were only for a second, to divert the vision's stony gaze from himself.

"I do," replied the Ghost.

"You are not looking at it," said Scrooge.

"But I see it," said the Ghost, "notwithstanding."

"Well!" returned Scrooge, "I have but to swallow this, and be for the rest of my days persecuted by a legion of goblins, all of my own creation. Humbug, I tell you! humbug!"

At this the spirit raised a frightful cry, and shook its chain with such a dismal and appalling noise, that Scrooge held on tight to his chair, to save himself from falling in a swoon. But how much greater was his horror, when the phantom taking off the bandage round its head, as if it were too warm to wear indoors, its lower jaw dropped down upon its breast!

Scrooge fell upon his knees, and clasped his hands before his face.

"Mercy!" he said. "Dreadful apparition, why do you trouble me?"

"Man of the worldly mind!" replied the Ghost, "do you believe in me or not?"

"I do," said Scrooge. "I must. But why do spirits walk the earth, and why do they come to me?"

"It is required of every man," the Ghost returned, "that the spirit within him should walk abroad among his fellowmen, and travel far and wide; and if that spirit goes not forth in life, it is condemned to do so after death. It is doomed to wander through the world — oh, woe is me! — and witness what it cannot share, but might have shared on earth, and turned to happiness!"

Again the spectre raised a cry, and shook its chain and wrung its shadowy hands.

"You are fettered," said Scrooge, trembling. "Tell me why?"

"I wear the chain I forged in life," replied the Ghost. "I made it link by link, and yard by yard; I girded it on of my own free will, and of my own free will I wore it. Is its pattern strange to you?"

Scrooge trembled more and more.

"Or would you know," pursued the Ghost, "the weight and length of the strong coil you bear yourself? It was full as heavy and as long as this, seven Christmas Eves ago. You have labored on it, since. It is a ponderous chain!"

Scrooge glanced about him on the floor, in the expectation of finding himself surrounded by some fifty or sixty fathoms of iron cable: but he could see nothing.

"Jacob," he said, imploringly. "Old Jacob Marley, tell me more. Speak comfort to me, Jacob!"

"I have none to give," the Ghost replied. "It comes from other regions, Ebenezer Scrooge, and is conveyed by other ministers, to other kinds of men. Nor can I tell you what I would. A very little more is all permitted to me. I cannot rest, I cannot stay, I cannot linger anywhere. My spirit never walked beyond our counting –house — mark me! — in life my spirit never roved beyond the narrow limits of our money-changing hole; and weary journeys lie before me!"

It was a habit with Scrooge, whenever he became thoughtful, to put his hands in his breeches pockets. Pondering on what the Ghost had said, he did so now, but without lifting up his eyes, or getting off his knees.

"You must have been very slow about it, Jacob," Scrooge observed, in a business-like manner, though with humility and deference.

"Slow!" the Ghost repeated.

"Seven years dead," mused Scrooge. "And travelling all the time!"

"The whole time," said the Ghost. "No rest, no peace. Incessant torture of remorse."

"You travel fast?" said Scrooge.

"On the wings of the wind," replied the Ghost.

"You might have got over a great quantity of ground in seven years," said Scrooge.

The Ghost, on hearing this, set up another cry, and clanked its chain so hideously in the dead silence of the night, that the Ward would have been justified in indicting it for a nuisance.

"Oh! Captive, bound, and double-ironed," cried the phantom, "not to know, that ages of incessant labour by immortal creatures, for this earth must pass into eternity before the good of which it is susceptible is all developed. Not to know that any Christian spirit working kindly in its little sphere, whatever it may be, will find its mortal life too short for its vast means of usefulness. Not to know that no space of regret can make amends for one life's opportunity misused! Yet such was I! Oh! Such was I!"

"But you were always a good man of business, Jacob," faltered Scrooge, who now began to apply this to himself.

"Business!" cried the Ghost, wringing its hands again. "Mankind was my business. The common welfare was my business; charity, mercy, forbearance, and benevolence, were, all, my business. The dealings of my trade were but a drop of water in the comprehensive ocean of my business!"

It held up its chain at arm's length, as if that were the cause of all its unavailing grief, and flung it heavily upon the ground again.

"At this time of the rolling year," the spectre said, "I suffer most. Why did I walk through crowds of fellow-beings with my eyes turned down, and never raise them to that blessed Star which led the Wise Men to a poor abode! Were there no poor homes to which its light would have conducted me!"

Scrooge was very much dismayed to hear the spectre going on at this rate, and began to quake exceedingly.

"Hear me!" cried the Ghost. "My time is nearly gone."

"I will," said Scrooge. "But don't be hard upon me! Don't be flowery, Jacob! Pray!"

"How it is that I appear before you in a shape that you can see, I may not tell. I have sat invisible beside you many and many a day."

It was not an agreeable idea. Scrooge shivered, and wiped the perspiration from his brow.

"That is no light part of my penance," pursued the Ghost. "I am here to-night to warn you, that you have yet a chance and hope of escaping my fate. A chance and hope of my procuring, Ebenezer."

"You were always a good friend to me," said Scrooge. "Thank'ee!"

"You will be haunted," resumed the Ghost, "by Three Spirits."

Scrooge's countenance fell almost as low as the Ghost's had done.

"Is that the chance and hope you mentioned, Jacob?" he demanded, in a faltering voice.

"It is."

"I — I think I'd rather not," said Scrooge.

"Without their visits," said the Ghost, "you cannot hope to shun the path I tread. Expect the first tomorrow, when the bell tolls One."

"Couldn't I take 'em all at once, and have it over, Jacob?" hinted Scrooge.

"Expect the second on the next night at the same hour. The third upon the next night when the last stroke of Twelve has ceased to vibrate. Look to see me no more; and look that, for your own sake, you remember what has passed between us!"

When it had said these words, the spectre took its wrapper from the table, and bound it round its head, as before. Scrooge knew this, by the smart sound its teeth made, when the jaws were brought together by the bandage. He ventured to raise his eyes again, and found his supernatural visitor confronting him in an erect attitude, with its chain wound over and about its arm.

The apparition walked backward from him; and at every step it took, the window raised itself a little, so that when the spectre reached it, it was wide open.

It beckoned Scrooge to approach, which he did. When they were within two paces of each other, Marley's Ghost held up its hand, warning him to come no nearer. Scrooge stopped.

Not so much in obedience, as in surprise and fear: for on the raising of the hand, he became sensible of confused noises in the air; incoherent sounds of lamentation and regret; wailings inexpressibly sorrowful and self-accusatory. The spectre, after listening for a moment, joined in the mournful dirge; and floated out upon the bleak, dark night.

Scrooge followed to the window: desperate in his curiosity. He looked out.

The air was filled with phantoms, wandering hither and thither in restless haste, and moaning as they went. Every one of them wore chains like Marley's Ghost; some few (they might be guilty governments) were linked together; none were free. Many had been personally known to Scrooge in their lives. He had been quite familiar with one old ghost, in a white waistcoat, with a monstrous iron safe attached to its ankle, who cried piteously at being unable to assist a wretched woman with an infant, whom it saw below, upon a door-step. The misery with them all was, clearly, that they sought to interfere, for good, in human matters, and had lost the power for ever.

Whether these creatures faded into mist, or mist enshrouded them, he could not tell. But they and their spirit voices faded together; and the night became as it had been when he walked home.

Scrooge closed the window, and examined the door by which the Ghost had entered. It was double-locked, as he had locked it with his own hands, and the bolts were undisturbed. He tried to say "Humbug!" but stopped at the first syllable. And being, from the emotion he had undergone, or the fatigues of the day, or his glimpse of the Invisible World, or the dull conversation of the Ghost, or the lateness of the hour, much in need of repose; went straight to bed, without undressing, and fell asleep upon the instant.

🎄 THE FIRST OF THE THREE SPIRITS I 🎄

When Scrooge awoke, it was so dark, that looking out of bed, he could scarcely distinguish the transparent window from the opaque walls of his chamber. He was endeavoring to pierce the darkness with his ferret eyes, when the chimes of a neighboring church struck the four quarters. So he listened for the hour.

To his great astonishment the heavy bell went on from six to seven, and from seven to eight, and regularly up to twelve; then stopped. Twelve! It was past two when he went to bed. The clock was wrong. An icicle must have got into the works. Twelve!

He touched the spring of his repeater, to correct this most preposterous clock. Its rapid little pulse beat twelve: and stopped.

"Why, it isn't possible," said Scrooge, "that I can have slept through a whole day and far into another night. It isn't possible that anything has happened to the sun, and this is twelve at noon!"

The idea being an alarming one, he scrambled out of bed, and groped his way to the window. He was obliged to rub the frost off with the sleeve of his dressing-gown before he could see anything; and could see very little then. All he could make out was, that it was still very foggy and extremely cold, and that there was no noise of people running to and fro, and making a great stir, as there unquestionably would have been if night had beaten off bright day, and taken possession of the world. This was a great relief, because "three days after sight of this First of Exchange pay to Mr. Ebenezer Scrooge or his order," and so forth, would have become a mere United States' security if there were no days to count by.

Scrooge went to bed again, and thought, and thought, and thought it over and over and over, and could make nothing of it. The more he thought, the more perplexed he was; and the more he endeavored not to think, the more he thought.

Marley's Ghost bothered him exceedingly. Every time he resolved within himself, after mature inquiry, that it was all a dream, his mind flew back again, like a strong spring released, to its first position, and presented the same problem to be worked all through, "Was it a dream or not?"

Scrooge lay in this state until the chime had gone three quarters more, when he remembered, on a sudden, that the Ghost had warned him of a visitation when the bell tolled one. He resolved to lie awake until the hour was passed; and, considering that he could no more go to sleep than go to Heaven, this was perhaps the wisest resolution in his power.

The quarter was so long, that he was more than once convinced he must have sunk into a doze unconsciously, and missed the clock. At length it broke upon his listening ear.

"Ding, dong!"

"A quarter past," said Scrooge, counting.

"Ding, dong!"

"Half-past!" said Scrooge.

"Ding, dong!"

"A quarter to it," said Scrooge.

"Ding, dong!"

"The hour itself," said Scrooge, triumphantly, "and nothing else!"

He spoke before the hour bell sounded, which it now did with a deep, dull, hollow, melancholy One. Light flashed up in the room upon the instant, and the curtains of his bed were drawn.

The curtains of his bed were drawn aside, I tell you, by a hand. Not the curtains at his feet, nor the curtains at his back, but those to which his face was addressed. The curtains of his bed were drawn aside; and Scrooge, starting up into a half-recumbent attitude, found himself face to face with the unearthly visitor who drew them: as close to it as I am now to you, and I am standing in the spirit at your elbow.

It was a strange figure — like a child: yet not so like a child as like an old man, viewed through some supernatural medium, which gave him the appearance of having receded from the view, and being diminished to a child's proportions. Its hair, which hung about its neck and down its back, was white as if with age; and yet the face had not a wrinkle in it, and the tenderest bloom was on the skin. The arms were very long and muscular; the hands the same, as if its hold were of uncommon strength. Its legs and feet, most delicately formed, were, like those upper members, bare. It wore a tunic of the purest white; and round its waist was bound a lustrous belt, the sheen of which was beautiful. It held a branch of fresh green holly in its hand; and, in singular contradiction of that wintry emblem, had its dress trimmed with summer flowers. But the strangest thing about it was, that from the crown of its head there sprung a bright clear jet of light, by which all this was visible; and which was doubtless the occasion of its using, in its duller moments, a great extinguisher for a cap, which it now held under its arm.

Even this, though, when Scrooge looked at it with increasing steadiness, was not its strangest quality. For as its belt sparkled and glittered now in one part and now in another, and what was light one instant, at another time was dark, so the figure itself fluctuated in its distinctness: being now a thing with one arm, now with one leg, now with twenty legs, now a pair of legs without a head, now a head without a body: of which dissolving parts, no outline would be visible in the dense gloom wherein they melted away. And in the very wonder of this, it would be itself again; distinct and clear as ever.

"Are you the Spirit, sir, whose coming was foretold to me?" asked Scrooge.

"I am!"

The voice was soft and gentle. Singularly low, as if instead of being so close beside him, it were at a distance.

"Who, and what are you?" Scrooge demanded.

"I am the Ghost of Christmas Past."

"Long Past?" inquired Scrooge: observant of its dwarfish stature.

"No. Your past."

Perhaps, Scrooge could not have told anybody why, if anybody could have asked him; but he had a special desire to see the Spirit in his cap; and begged him to be covered.

"What!" exclaimed the Ghost, "would you so soon put out, with worldly hands, the light I give? Is it not enough that you are one of those whose passions made this cap, and force me through whole trains of years to wear it low upon my brow!"

Scrooge reverently disclaimed all intention to offend or any knowledge of having wilfully "bonneted" the Spirit at any period of his life. He then made bold to inquire what business brought him there.

"Your welfare!" said the Ghost.

Scrooge expressed himself much obliged, but could not help thinking that a night of unbroken rest would have been more conducive to that end. The Spirit must have heard him thinking, for it said immediately:

"Your reclamation, then. Take heed!"

It put out its strong hand as it spoke, and clasped him gently by the arm. "Rise! And walk with me!"

It would have been in vain for Scrooge to plead that the weather and the hour were not adapted to pedestrian purposes; that bed was warm, and the thermometer a long way below freezing; that he was clad but lightly in his slippers, dressing-gown, and nightcap; and that he had a cold upon him at that time. The grasp, though gentle as a woman's hand, was not to be resisted. He rose: but finding that the Spirit made towards the window, clasped his robe in supplication.

"I am a mortal," Scrooge remonstrated, "and liable to fall."

"Bear but a touch of my hand there," said the Spirit, laying it upon his heart, "and you shall be upheld in more than this!"

As the words were spoken, they passed through the wall, and stood upon an open country road, with fields on either hand. The city had entirely vanished. Not a vestige of it was to be seen. The darkness and the mist had vanished with it, for it was a clear, cold, winter day, with snow upon the ground.

"Good Heaven!" said Scrooge, clasping his hands together, as he looked about him. "I was bred in this place. I was a boy here!"

The Spirit gazed upon him mildly. Its gentle touch, though it had been light and instantaneous, appeared still present to the old man's sense of feeling. He was conscious of a thousand odours floating in the air, each one connected with a thousand thoughts, and hopes, and joys, and cares long, long, forgotten!

"Your lip is trembling," said the Ghost. "And what is that upon your cheek?"

Scrooge muttered, with an unusual catching in his voice, that it was a pimple; and begged the Ghost to lead him where he would.

"You recollect the way?" inquired the Spirit.

"Remember it!" cried Scrooge with fervor; "I could walk it blindfold."

"Strange to have forgotten it for so many years!" observed the Ghost. "Let us go on."

They walked along the road, Scrooge recognising every gate, and post, and tree; until a little market-town appeared in the distance, with its bridge, its church, and winding river. Some shaggy ponies now were seen trotting towards them with boys upon their backs, who called to other boys in country gigs and carts, driven by farmers. All these boys were in great spirits, and shouted to each other, until the broad fields were so full of merry music, that the crisp air laughed to hear it!

"These are but shadows of the things that have been," said the Ghost. "They have no consciousness of us."

The jocund travellers came on; and as they came, Scrooge knew and named them every one. Why was he rejoiced beyond all bounds to see them! Why did his cold eye glisten, and his heart leap up as they went past! Why was he filled with gladness when he heard them give each other Merry Christmas, as they parted at cross-roads and bye-ways, for their several homes! What was merry Christmas to Scrooge? Out upon merry Christmas! What good had it ever done to him?

"The school is not quite deserted," said the Ghost. "A solitary child, neglected by his friends, is left there still."

Scrooge said he knew it. And he sobbed.

They left the high-road, by a well-remembered lane, and soon approached a mansion of dull red brick, with a little weathercock-surmounted cupola, on the roof, and a bell hanging in it. It was a large house, but one of broken fortunes; for the spacious offices were little used, their walls were damp and mossy, their windows broken, and their gates decayed. Fowls clucked and strutted in the stables; and the coach-houses and sheds were over-run with grass. Nor was it more retentive of its ancient state, within; for entering the dreary hall, and glancing through the open doors of many rooms, they found them poorly furnished, cold, and vast. There was an earthy savor in the air, a chilly bareness in the place, which associated itself somehow with too much getting up by candle-light, and not too much to eat.

They went, the Ghost and Scrooge, across the hall, to a door at the back of the house. It opened before them, and disclosed a long, bare, melancholy room, made barer still by lines of plain deal forms and desks. At one of these a lonely boy was reading near a feeble fire; and Scrooge sat down upon a form, and wept to see his poor forgotten self as he used to be.

Not a latent echo in the house, not a squeak and scuffle from the mice behind the panelling, not a drip from the half-thawed water-spout in the dull yard behind, not a sigh among the leafless boughs of one despondent poplar, not the idle swinging of an empty store-house door, no, not a clicking in the fire, but fell upon the heart of Scrooge with a softening influence, and gave a freer passage to his tears.

The Spirit touched him on the arm, and pointed to his younger self, intent upon his reading. Suddenly a man, in foreign garments: wonderfully real and distinct to look at: stood outside the window, with an axe stuck in his belt, and leading by the bridle an ass laden with wood.

"Why, it's Ali Baba!" Scrooge exclaimed in ecstasy. "It's dear old honest Ali Baba! Yes, yes, I know! One Christmas time, when yonder solitary child was left here all alone, he did come, for the first time, just like that. Poor boy! And Valentine," said Scrooge, "and his wild brother, Orson; there they go! And what's his name, who was put down in his drawers, asleep, at the Gate of Damascus; don't you see him! And the Sultan's Groom turned upside down by the Genii; there he is upon his head! Serve him right. I'm glad of it. What business had he to be married to the Princess!"

To hear Scrooge expending all the earnestness of his nature on such subjects, in a most extraordinary voice between laughing and crying; and to see his heightened and excited face; would have been a surprise to his business friends in the city, indeed.

"There's the Parrot!" cried Scrooge. "Green body and yellow tail, with a thing like a lettuce growing out of the top of his head; there he is! Poor Robin Crusoe, he called him, when he came home again after sailing round the island. 'Poor Robin Crusoe, where have you been, Robin

Crusoe?' The man thought he was dreaming, but he wasn't. It was the Parrot, you know. There goes Friday, running for his life to the little creek! Halloa! Hoop! Halloo!"

Then, with a rapidity of transition very foreign to his usual character, he said, in pity for his former self, "Poor boy!" and cried again.

"I wish," Scrooge muttered, putting his hand in his pocket, and looking about him, after drying his eyes with his cuff: "but it's too late now."

"What is the matter?" asked the Spirit.

"Nothing," said Scrooge. "Nothing. There was a boy singing a Christmas Carol at my door last night. I should like to have given him something: that's all."

The Ghost smiled thoughtfully, and waved its hand: saying as it did so, "Let us see another Christmas!"

Scrooge's former self grew larger at the words, and the room became a little darker and more dirty. The panels shrunk, the windows cracked; fragments of plaster fell out of the ceiling, and the naked laths were shown instead; but how all this was brought about, Scrooge knew no more than you do. He only knew that it was quite correct; that everything had happened so; that there he was, alone again, when all the other boys had gone home for the jolly holidays.

He was not reading now, but walking up and down despairingly. Scrooge looked at the Ghost, and with a mournful shaking of his head, glanced anxiously towards the door.

It opened; and a little girl, much younger than the boy, came darting in, and putting her arms about his neck, and often kissing him, addressed him as her "Dear, dear brother."

"I have come to bring you home, dear brother!" said the child, clapping her tiny hands, and bending down to laugh. "To bring you home, home, home!"

"Home, little Fan?" returned the boy.

"Yes!" said the child, brimful of glee. "Home, for good and all. Home, forever and ever. Father is so much kinder than he used to be, that home's like Heaven! He spoke so gently to me one dear night when I was going to bed, that I was not afraid to ask him once more if you might come home; and he said yes, you should; and sent me in a coach to bring you. And you're to be a man!" said the child, opening her eyes, "and are never to come back here; but first, we're to be together all the Christmas long, and have the merriest time in all the world."

"You are quite a woman, little Fan!" exclaimed the boy.

She clapped her hands and laughed, and tried to touch his head; but being too little, laughed again, and stood on tiptoe to embrace him. Then she began to drag him, in her childish eagerness, towards the door; and he, nothing loth to go, accompanied her. A terrible voice in the hall cried, "Bring down Master Scrooge's box, there!" and in the hall appeared the schoolmaster himself, who glared on Master Scrooge with a ferocious condescension, and threw him into a dreadful state of mind by shaking hands with him. He then conveyed him and his sister into the veriest old well of a shivering best-parlor that ever was seen, where the maps upon the wall, and the celestial and terrestrial globes in the windows, were waxy with cold. Here he produced a decanter of curiously light wine, and a block of curiously heavy cake, and administered instalments of those dainties to the young people: at the same time, sending out a meagre servant to offer a glass of "something" to the postboy, who answered that he thanked the gentleman, but if it was the same tap as he had tasted before, he had rather not. Master Scrooge's trunk being by this time tied on to the top of the chaise, the children bade the schoolmaster good-bye right willingly; and getting into it, drove gaily down the garden-sweep: the quick wheels dashing the hoar-frost and snow from off the dark leaves of the evergreens like spray.

"Always a delicate creature, whom a breath might have withered," said the Ghost. "But she had a large heart!"

"So she had," cried Scrooge. "You're right. I will not gainsay it, Spirit. God forbid!"

"She died a woman," said the Ghost, "and had, as I think, children."

"One child," Scrooge returned.

"True," said the Ghost. "Your nephew!"

Scrooge seemed uneasy in his mind; and answered briefly, "Yes."

THE FIRST OF THE THREE SPIRITS II

Although they had but that moment left the school behind them, they were now in the busy thoroughfares of a city, where shadowy passengers passed and repassed; where shadowy carts and coaches battled for the way, and all the strife and tumult of a real city were. It was made plain enough, by the dressing of the shops, that here too it was Christmas time again; but it was evening, and the streets were lighted up.

The Ghost stopped at a certain warehouse door, and asked Scrooge if he knew it.

"Know it!" said Scrooge. "Was I apprenticed here!"

They went in. At sight of an old gentleman in a Welsh wig, sitting behind such a high desk, that if he had been two inches taller he must have knocked his head against the ceiling, Scrooge cried in great excitement: "Why, it's old Fezziwig! Bless his heart; it's Fezziwig alive again!"

Old Fezziwig laid down his pen, and looked up at the clock, which pointed to the hour of seven. He rubbed his hands; adjusted his capacious waistcoat; laughed all over himself, from his shoes to his organ of benevolence; and called out in a comfortable, oily, rich, fat, jovial voice: "Yo ho, there! Ebenezer! Dick!"

Scrooge's former self, now grown a young man, came briskly in, accompanied by his fellow-'prentice.

"Dick Wilkins, to be sure!" said Scrooge to the Ghost. "Bless me, yes. There he is. He was very much attached to me, was Dick. Poor Dick! Dear, dear!"

"Yo ho, my boys!" said Fezziwig. "No more work to-night. Christmas Eve, Dick. Christmas, Ebenezer! Let's have the shutters up," cried old

Fezziwig, with a sharp clap of his hands, "before a man can say Jack Robinson!"

You wouldn't believe how those two fellows went at it! They charged into the street with the shutters — one, two, three — had 'em up in their places — four, five, six — barred 'em and pinned 'em — seven, eight, nine — and came back before you could have got to twelve, panting like race-horses.

"Hilli-ho!" cried old Fezziwig, skipping down from the high desk, with wonderful agility. "Clear away, my lads, and let's have lots of room here! Hilli-ho, Dick! Chirrup, Ebenezer!"

Clear away! There was nothing they wouldn't have cleared away, or couldn't have cleared away, with old Fezziwig looking on. It was done in a minute. Every movable was packed off, as if it were dismissed from public life for evermore; the floor was swept and watered, the lamps were trimmed, fuel was heaped upon the fire; and the warehouse was as snug, and warm, and dry, and bright a ball-room, as you would desire to see upon a winter's night.

In came a fiddler with a music-book, and went up to the lofty desk, and made an orchestra of it, and tuned like fifty stomach-aches. In came Mrs. Fezziwig, one vast substantial smile. In came the three Miss Fezziwigs, beaming and lovable. In came the six young followers whose hearts they broke. In came all the young men and women employed in the business. In came the housemaid, with her cousin, the baker. In came the cook, with her brother's particular friend, the milkman. In came the boy from over the way, who was suspected of not having board enough from his master; trying to hide himself behind the girl from next door but one, who was proved to have had her ears pulled by her mistress. In they all came, one after another; some shyly, some boldly, some gracefully, some awkwardly, some pushing, some pulling; in they all came, anyhow and everyhow. Away they all went, twenty couple at once; hands half round and back again the other way; down the middle and up again; round and round in various stages of affectionate grouping; old top couple always turning up in the wrong place; new top couple starting off again, as soon as they got there; all top couples at last, and not a bottom one to help them! When this result was brought about, old Fezziwig, clapping his hands to stop the dance, cried out, "Well done!" and the fiddler plunged his hot face into a pot of porter, especially provided for that purpose. But scorning rest, upon his reappearance, he instantly began again, though there were no dancers yet, as if the other fiddler had been carried home, exhausted, on a shutter, and he were a bran-new man resolved to beat him out of sight, or perish.

There were more dances, and there were forfeits, and more dances, and there was cake, and there was negus, and there was a great piece of Cold Roast, and there was a great piece of Cold Boiled, and there were mince-pies, and plenty of beer. But the great effect of the evening came after the Roast and Boiled, when the fiddler (an artful dog, mind! The sort of man who knew his business better than you or I could have told it him!) struck up "Sir Roger de Coverley." Then old Fezziwig stood out to dance with Mrs. Fezziwig. Top couple, too; with a good stiff piece of work cut out for them; three or four and twenty pair of partners; people who were not to be trifled with; people who would dance, and had no notion of walking.

But if they had been twice as many — ah, four times — old Fezziwig would have been a match for them, and so would Mrs. Fezziwig. As to her, she was worthy to be his partner in every sense of the term.
If that's not high praise, tell me higher, and I'll use it. A positive light appeared to issue from Fezziwig's calves. They shone in every part of the dance like moons. You couldn't have predicted, at any given time, what would have become of them next. And when old Fezziwig and Mrs. Fezziwig had gone all through the dance; advance and retire, both hands to your partner, bow and curtsey, corkscrew, thread-the-needle, and back again to your place; Fezziwig "cut"— cut so deftly, that he appeared to wink with his legs, and came upon his feet again without a stagger.
When the clock struck eleven, this domestic ball broke up. Mr. and Mrs.

Fezziwig took their stations, one on either side of the door, and shaking hands with every person individually as he or she went out, wished him or her a Merry Christmas. When everybody had retired but the two 'prentices, they did the same to them; and thus the cheerful voices died away, and the lads were left to their beds; which were under a counter in the back-shop.

During the whole of this time, Scrooge had acted like a man out of his wits. His heart and soul were in the scene, and with his former self. He corroborated everything, remembered everything, enjoyed everything, and underwent the strangest agitation. It was not until now, when the bright faces of his former self and Dick were turned from them, that he remembered the Ghost, and became conscious that it was looking full upon him, while the light upon its head burnt very clear.

"A small matter," said the Ghost, "to make these silly folks so full of gratitude."

"Small!" echoed Scrooge.

The Spirit signed to him to listen to the two apprentices, who were pouring out their hearts in praise of Fezziwig: and when he had done so, said,

"Why! Is it not? He has spent but a few pounds of your mortal money: three or four perhaps. Is that so much that he deserves this praise?"

"It isn't that," said Scrooge, heated by the remark, and speaking unconsciously like his former, not his latter, self. "It isn't that, Spirit. He has the power to render us happy or unhappy; to make our service light or burdensome; a pleasure or a toil. Say that his power lies in words and looks; in things so slight and insignificant that it is impossible to add and count 'em up: what then? The happiness he gives, is quite as great as if it cost a fortune."

He felt the Spirit's glance, and stopped.

"What is the matter?" asked the Ghost.

"Nothing particular," said Scrooge.

"Something, I think?" the Ghost insisted.

"No," said Scrooge, "No. I should like to be able to say a word or two to my clerk just now. That's all."

His former self turned down the lamps as he gave utterance to the wish; and Scrooge and the Ghost again stood side by side in the open air.

"My time grows short," observed the Spirit. "Quick!"

This was not addressed to Scrooge, or to any one whom he could see, but it produced an immediate effect. For again Scrooge saw himself. He was older now; a man in the prime of life. His face had not the harsh and rigid lines of later years; but it had begun to wear the signs of care and avarice. There was an eager, greedy, restless motion in the eye, which showed the passion that had taken root, and where the shadow of the growing tree would fall.

He was not alone, but sat by the side of a fair young girl in a mourning-dress: in whose eyes there were tears, which sparkled in the light that shone out of the Ghost of Christmas Past.

"It matters little," she said, softly. "To you, very little. Another idol has displaced me; and if it can cheer and comfort you in time to come, as I would have tried to do, I have no just cause to grieve."

"What Idol has displaced you?" he rejoined.

"A golden one."

"This is the even-handed dealing of the world!" he said. "There is nothing on which it is so hard as poverty; and there is nothing it professes to condemn with such severity as the pursuit of wealth!"

"You fear the world too much," she answered, gently. "All your other hopes have merged into the hope of being beyond the chance of its sordid reproach. I have seen your nobler aspirations fall off one by one, until the master-passion, Gain, engrosses you. Have I not?"

"What then?" he retorted. "Even if I have grown so much wiser, what then? I am not changed towards you."

She shook her head.

"Am I?"

"Our contract is an old one. It was made when we were both poor and content to be so, until, in good season, we could improve our worldly fortune by our patient industry. You are changed. When it was made, you were another man."

"I was a boy," he said impatiently.

"Your own feeling tells you that you were not what you are," she returned. "I am. That which promised happiness when we were one in heart, is fraught with misery now that we are two. How often and how keenly I have thought of this, I will not say. It is enough that I have thought of it, and can release you."

"Have I ever sought release?"

"In words. No. Never."

"In what, then?"

"In a changed nature; in an altered spirit; in another atmosphere of life; another Hope as its great end. In everything that made my love of any worth or value in your sight. If this had never been between us," said the girl, looking mildly, but with steadiness, upon him; "tell me, would you seek me out and try to win me now? Ah, no!"

He seemed to yield to the justice of this supposition, in spite of himself. But he said with a struggle, "You think not."

"I would gladly think otherwise if I could," she answered, "Heaven knows! When I have learned a Truth like this, I know how strong and irresistible it must be. But if you were free today, tomorrow, yesterday, can even I believe that you would choose a dowerless girl — you who, in your very confidence with her, weigh everything by Gain: or, choosing her, if for a moment you were false enough to your one guiding principle to do so, do I not know that your repentance and regret would surely follow? I do; and I release you. With a full heart, for the love of him you once were."

He was about to speak; but with her head turned from him, she resumed. "You may — the memory of what is past half makes me hope you will — have pain in this. A very, very brief time, and you will dismiss the recollection of it, gladly, as an unprofitable dream, from which it happened well that you awoke. May you be happy in the life you have chosen!"

She left him, and they parted.

"Spirit!" said Scrooge, "show me no more! Conduct me home. Why do you delight to torture me?"

"One shadow more!" exclaimed the Ghost.

"No more!" cried Scrooge. "No more. I don't wish to see it. Show me no more!"

But the relentless Ghost pinioned him in both his arms, and forced him to observe what happened next.

They were in another scene and place; a room, not very large or handsome, but full of comfort. Near to the winter fire sat a beautiful young girl, so like that last that Scrooge believed it was the same, until he saw her, now a comely matron, sitting opposite her daughter. The noise in this room was perfectly tumultuous, for there were more children there, than Scrooge in his agitated state of mind could count; and, unlike the celebrated herd in the poem, they were not forty children conducting themselves like one, but every child was conducting itself like forty. The consequences were uproarious beyond belief; but no one seemed to care; on the contrary, the mother and daughter laughed heartily, and enjoyed it very much; and the latter, soon beginning to mingle in the sports, got pillaged by the young brigands most ruthlessly. What would I not have given to be one of them! Though I never could have been so rude, no, no! I wouldn't for the wealth of all the world have crushed that braided hair, and torn it down; and for the precious little shoe, I wouldn't have plucked it off, God bless my soul! To save my life. As to measuring her waist in sport, as they did, bold young brood, I couldn't have done it; I should have expected my arm to have grown round it for a punishment, and never come straight again. And yet I should have dearly liked, I own, to have touched her lips; to have questioned her, that she might have opened them; to have looked upon the lashes of her downcast eyes, and never raised a blush; to have let loose waves of hair, an inch of which would be a keepsake beyond price: in short, I should have liked, I do confess, to have had the lightest licence of a child, and yet to have been man enough to know its value.

But now a knocking at the door was heard, and such a rush immediately ensued that she with laughing face and plundered dress was borne towards it the centre of a flushed and boisterous group, just in time to greet the father, who came home attended by a man laden with Christmas toys and presents. Then the shouting and the struggling, and the onslaught that was made on the defenceless porter! The scaling him with chairs for ladders to dive into his pockets, despoil him of brown-paper parcels, hold on tight by his cravat, hug him round his neck, pommel his back, and kick his legs in irrepressible affection! The shouts of wonder and delight with which the development of every package was received! The terrible announcement that the baby had been taken in the act of putting a doll's frying-pan into his mouth, and was more than suspected of having swallowed a fictitious turkey, glued on a wooden platter! The immense relief of finding this a false alarm! The joy, and gratitude, and ecstasy! They are all indescribable alike. It is enough that by degrees the children and their emotions got out of the parlor, and by one stair at a time, up to the top of the house; where they went to bed, and so subsided. And now Scrooge looked on more attentively than ever, when the master of the house, having his daughter leaning fondly on him, sat down with her and her mother at his own fireside; and when he thought that such another creature, quite as graceful and as full of promise, might have called him father, and been a spring-time in the haggard winter of his life, his sight grew very dim indeed.

"Belle," said the husband, turning to his wife with a smile, "I saw an old friend of yours this afternoon."

"Who was it?"

"Guess!"

"How can I? Tut, don't I know?" she added in the same breath, laughing as he laughed. "Mr. Scrooge."

"Mr. Scrooge it was. I passed his office window; and as it was not shut up, and he had a candle inside, I could scarcely help seeing him. His partner lies upon the point of death, I hear; and there he sat alone. Quite alone in the world, I do believe."

"Spirit!" said Scrooge in a broken voice, "remove me from this place."

"I told you these were shadows of the things that have been," said the Ghost. "That they are what they are, do not blame me!"

"Remove me!" Scrooge exclaimed, "I cannot bear it!"

He turned upon the Ghost, and seeing that it looked upon him with a face, in which in some strange way there were fragments of all the faces it had shown him, wrestled with it.

"Leave me! Take me back. Haunt me no longer!"

In the struggle, if that can be called a struggle in which the Ghost with no visible resistance on its own part was undisturbed by any effort of its adversary, Scrooge observed that its light was burning high and bright; and dimly connecting that with its influence over him, he seized the extinguisher-cap, and by a sudden action pressed it down upon its head. The Spirit dropped beneath it, so that the extinguisher covered its whole form; but though Scrooge pressed it down with all his force, he could not hide the light: which streamed from under it, in an unbroken flood upon the ground.

He was conscious of being exhausted, and overcome by an irresistible drowsiness; and, further, of being in his own bedroom. He gave the cap a parting squeeze, in which his hand relaxed; and had barely time to reel to bed, before he sank into a heavy sleep.

THE SECOND OF THE THREE SPIRITS I

Awaking in the middle of a prodigiously tough snore, and sitting up in bed to get his thoughts together, Scrooge had no occasion to be told that the bell was again upon the stroke of One. He felt that he was restored to consciousness in the right nick of time, for the especial purpose of holding a conference with the second messenger despatched to him through Jacob Marley's intervention. But finding that he turned uncomfortably cold when he began to wonder which of his curtains this new spectre would draw back, he put them every one aside with his own hands; and lying down again, established a sharp look-out all round the bed. For he wished to challenge the Spirit on the moment of its appearance, and did not wish to be taken by surprise, and made nervous. Gentlemen of the free-and-easy sort, who plume themselves on being acquainted with a move or two, and being usually equal to the time-of-day, express the wide range of their capacity for adventure by observing that they are good for anything from pitch-and-toss to manslaughter; between which opposite extremes, no doubt, there lies a tolerably wide and comprehensive range of subjects. Without venturing for Scrooge quite as hardily as this, I don't mind calling on you to believe that he was ready for a good broad field of strange appearances, and that nothing between a baby and rhinoceros would have astonished him very much. Now, being prepared for almost anything, he was not by any means prepared for nothing; and, consequently, when the Bell struck One, and no shape appeared, he was taken with a violent fit of trembling. Five minutes, ten minutes, a quarter of an hour went by, yet nothing came. All this time, he lay upon his bed, the very core and centre of a blaze of ruddy light, which streamed upon it when the clock proclaimed the hour; and which, being only light, was more alarming than a dozen ghosts, as he was powerless to make out what it meant, or would be at; and was sometimes apprehensive that he might be at that very moment an interesting case of spontaneous combustion, without having the consolation of knowing it. At last, however, he began to think — as you or I would have thought at first; for it is always the person not in the predicament who knows what ought to have been done in it, and would unquestionably have done it too — at last, I say, he began to think that the source and secret of this ghostly light might be in the adjoining room, from whence, on further tracing it, it seemed to shine. This idea taking full possession of his mind, he got up softly and shuffled in his slippers to the door.

The moment Scrooge's hand was on the lock, a strange voice called him by his name, and bade him enter. He obeyed.

It was his own room. There was no doubt about that. But it had undergone a surprising transformation. The walls and ceiling were so hung with living green, that it looked a perfect grove; from every part of which, bright gleaming berries glistened. The crisp leaves of holly, mistletoe, and ivy reflected back the light, as if so many little mirrors had been scattered there; and such a mighty blaze went roaring up the chimney, as that dull petrification of a hearth had never known in Scrooge's time, or Marley's, or for many and many a winter season gone. Heaped up on the floor, to form a kind of throne, were turkeys, geese, game, poultry, brawn, great joints of meat, sucking-pigs, long wreaths of sausages, mince-pies, plum-puddings, barrels of oysters, red-hot chestnuts, cherry-cheeked apples, juicy oranges, luscious pears, immense twelfth-cakes, and seething bowls of punch, that made the chamber dim with their delicious steam. In easy state upon this couch, there sat a jolly Giant, glorious to see; who bore a glowing torch, in shape not unlike Plenty's horn, and held it up, high up, to shed its light on Scrooge, as he came peeping round the door.

"Come in!" exclaimed the Ghost. "Come in! And know me better, man!" Scrooge entered timidly, and hung his head before this Spirit. He was not the dogged Scrooge he had been; and though the Spirit's eyes were clear and kind, he did not like to meet them.

"I am the Ghost of Christmas Present," said the Spirit. "Look upon me!" Scrooge reverently did so. It was clothed in one simple green robe, or mantle, bordered with white fur. This garment hung so loosely on the figure, that its capacious breast was bare, as if disdaining to be warded or concealed by any artifice. Its feet, observable beneath the ample folds of the garment, were also bare; and on its head it wore no other covering than a holly wreath, set here and there with shining icicles. Its dark brown curls were long and free; free as its genial face, its sparkling eye, its open hand, its cheery voice, its unconstrained demeanor, and its joyful air. Girded round its middle was an antique scabbard; but no sword was in it, and the ancient sheath was eaten up with rust.

"You have never seen the like of me before!" exclaimed the Spirit.

"Never," Scrooge made answer to it.

"Have never walked forth with the younger members of my family; meaning (for I am very young) my elder brothers born in these later years?" pursued the Phantom.

"I don't think I have," said Scrooge. "I am afraid I have not. Have you had many brothers, Spirit?"

"More than eighteen hundred," said the Ghost.

"A tremendous family to provide for!" muttered Scrooge.

The Ghost of Christmas Present rose.

"Spirit," said Scrooge submissively, "conduct me where you will. I went forth last night on compulsion, and I learnt a lesson which is working now. Tonight, if you have aught to teach me, let me profit by it."

"Touch my robe!"

Scrooge did as he was told, and held it fast.

Holly, mistletoe, red berries, ivy, turkeys, geese, game, poultry, brawn, meat, pigs, sausages, oysters, pies, puddings, fruit, and punch, all vanished instantly. So did the room, the fire, the ruddy glow, the hour of night, and they stood in the city streets on Christmas morning, where (for the weather was severe) the people made a rough, but brisk and not unpleasant kind of music, in scraping the snow from the pavement in front of their dwellings, and from the tops of their houses, whence it was mad delight to the boys to see it come plumping down into the road below, and splitting into artificial little snow-storms.

The house fronts looked black enough, and the windows blacker, contrasting with the smooth white sheet of snow upon the roofs, and with the dirtier snow upon the ground; which last deposit had been ploughed up in deep furrows by the heavy wheels of carts and waggons; furrows that crossed and re-crossed each other hundreds of times where the great streets branched off; and made intricate channels, hard to trace in the thick yellow mud and icy water. The sky was gloomy, and the shortest streets were choked up with a dingy mist, half thawed, half frozen, whose heavier particles descended in a shower of sooty atoms, as if all the chimneys in Great Britain had, by one consent, caught fire, and were blazing away to their dear hearts' content. There was nothing very cheerful in the climate or the town, and yet was there an air of cheerfulness abroad that the clearest summer air and brightest summer sun might have endeavored to diffuse in vain.

For, the people who were shovelling away on the housetops were jovial and full of glee; calling out to one another from the parapets, and now and then exchanging a facetious snowball — better-natured missile far than many a wordy jest — laughing heartily if it went right and not less heartily if it went wrong. The poulterers' shops were still half open, and the fruiterers' were radiant in their glory. There were great, round, pot-bellied baskets of chestnuts, shaped like the waistcoats of jolly old gentlemen, lolling at the doors, and tumbling out into the street in their apoplectic opulence. There were ruddy, brown-faced, broad-girthed Spanish Onions, shining in the fatness of their growth like Spanish Friars, and winking from their shelves in wanton slyness at the girls as they went by, and glanced demurely at the hung-up mistletoe.

There were pears and apples, clustered high in blooming pyramids; there were bunches of grapes, made, in the shopkeepers' benevolence to dangle from conspicuous hooks, that people's mouths might water gratis as they passed; there were piles of filberts, mossy and brown, recalling, in their fragrance, ancient walks among the woods, and pleasant shufflings ankle deep through withered leaves; there were Norfolk Biffins, squat and swarthy, setting off the yellow of the oranges and lemons, and, in the great compactness of their juicy persons, urgently entreating and beseeching to be carried home in paper bags and eaten after dinner. The very gold and silver fish, set forth among these choice fruits in a bowl, though members of a dull and stagnant-blooded race, appeared to know that there was something going on; and, to a fish, went gasping round and round their little world in slow and passionless excitement.

The Grocers'! Oh, the Grocers'! Nearly closed, with perhaps two shutters down, or one; but through those gaps such glimpses! It was not alone that the scales descending on the counter made a merry sound, or that the twine and roller parted company so briskly, or that the canisters were rattled up and down like juggling tricks, or even that the blended scents of tea and coffee were so grateful to the nose, or even that the raisins were so plentiful and rare, the almonds so extremely white, the sticks of cinnamon so long and straight, the other spices so delicious, the candied fruits so caked and spotted with molten sugar as to make the coldest lookers-on feel faint and subsequently bilious. Nor was it that the figs were moist and pulpy, or that the French plums blushed in modest tartness from their highly-decorated boxes, or that everything was good to eat and in its Christmas dress; but the customers were all so hurried and so eager in the hopeful promise of the day, that they tumbled up against each other at the door, crashing their wicker baskets wildly, and left their purchases upon the counter, and came running back to fetch them, and committed hundreds of the like mistakes, in the best humour possible; while the Grocer and his people were so frank and fresh that the polished hearts with which they fastened their aprons behind might have been their own, worn outside for general inspection, and for Christmas daws to peck at if they chose.

But soon the steeples called good people all, to church and chapel, and away they came, flocking through the streets in their best clothes, and with their gayest faces. And at the same time there emerged from scores of bye-streets, lanes, and nameless turnings, innumerable people, carrying their dinners to the bakers' shops. The sight of these poor revellers appeared to interest the Spirit very much, for he stood with Scrooge beside him in a baker's doorway, and taking off the covers as their bearers passed, sprinkled incense on their dinners from his torch. And it was a very uncommon kind of torch, for once or twice when there were angry words between some dinner-carriers who had jostled each other, he shed a few drops of water on them from it, and their good humour was restored directly. For they said, it was a shame to quarrel upon Christmas Day. And so it was! God love it, so it was!

In time the bells ceased, and the bakers were shut up; and yet there was a genial shadowing forth of all these dinners and the progress of their cooking, in the thawed blotch of wet above each baker's oven; where the pavement smoked as if its stones were cooking too.

"Is there a peculiar flavor in what you sprinkle from your torch?" asked Scrooge.

"There is. My own."

"Would it apply to any kind of dinner on this day?" asked Scrooge.

"To any kindly given. To a poor one most."

"Why to a poor one most?" asked Scrooge.

"Because it needs it most."

"Spirit," said Scrooge, after a moment's thought, "I wonder you, of all the beings in the many worlds about us, should desire to cramp these people's opportunities of innocent enjoyment."

"I!" cried the Spirit.

"You would deprive them of their means of dining every seventh day, often the only day on which they can be said to dine at all," said Scrooge. "Wouldn't you?"

"I!" cried the Spirit.

"You seek to close these places on the Seventh Day?" said Scrooge. "And it comes to the same thing."

"I seek!" exclaimed the Spirit.

"Forgive me if I am wrong. It has been done in your name, or at least in that of your family," said Scrooge.

"There are some upon this earth of yours," returned the Spirit, "who lay claim to know us, and who do their deeds of passion, pride, ill-will, hatred, envy, bigotry, and selfishness in our name, who are as strange to us and all our kith and kin, as if they had never lived. Remember that, and charge their doings on themselves, not us."

Scrooge promised that he would; and they went on, invisible, as they had been before, into the suburbs of the town. It was a remarkable quality of the Ghost (which Scrooge had observed at the baker's), that notwithstanding his gigantic size, he could accommodate himself to any place with ease; and that he stood beneath a low roof quite as gracefully and like a supernatural creature, as it was possible he could have done in any lofty hall.

And perhaps it was the pleasure the good Spirit had in showing off this power of his, or else it was his own kind, generous, hearty nature, and his sympathy with all poor men, that led him straight to Scrooge's clerk's; for there he went, and took Scrooge with him, holding to his robe; and on the threshold of the door the Spirit smiled, and stopped to bless Bob Cratchit's dwelling with the sprinkling of his torch. Think of that! Bob had but fifteen "Bob" a-week himself; he pocketed on Saturdays but fifteen copies of his Christian name; and yet the Ghost of Christmas Present blessed his four-roomed house!

Then up rose Mrs. Cratchit, Cratchit's wife, dressed out but poorly in a twice-turned gown, but brave in ribbons, which are cheap and make a goodly show for sixpence; and she laid the cloth, assisted by Belinda Cratchit, second of her daughters, also brave in ribbons; while Master Peter Cratchit plunged a fork into the saucepan of potatoes, and getting the corners of his monstrous shirt collar (Bob's private property, conferred upon his son and heir in honour of the day) into his mouth, rejoiced to find himself so gallantly attired, and yearned to show his linen in the fashionable Parks. And now two smaller Cratchits, boy and girl, came tearing in, screaming that outside the baker's they had smelt the goose, and known it for their own; and basking in luxurious thoughts of sage and onion, these young Cratchits danced about the table, and exalted Master Peter Cratchit to the skies, while he (not proud, although his collars nearly choked him) blew the fire, until the slow potatoes bubbling up, knocked loudly at the saucepan-lid to be let out and peeled.

"What has ever got your precious father then?" said Mrs. Cratchit. "And your brother, Tiny Tim! And Martha warn't as late last Christmas Day by half-an-hour?"

"Here's Martha, mother!" said a girl, appearing as she spoke.

"Here's Martha, mother!" cried the two young Cratchits. "Hurrah! There's such a goose, Martha!"

"Why, bless your heart alive, my dear, how late you are!" said Mrs. Cratchit, kissing her a dozen times, and taking off her shawl and bonnet for her with officious zeal.

"We'd a deal of work to finish up last night," replied the girl, "and had to clear away this morning, mother!"

"Well! Never mind so long as you are come," said Mrs. Cratchit. "Sit ye down before the fire, my dear, and have a warm, Lord bless ye!"

"No, no! There's father coming," cried the two young Cratchits, who were everywhere at once. "Hide, Martha, hide!"

So Martha hid herself, and in came little Bob, the father, with at least three feet of comforter exclusive of the fringe, hanging down before him; and his threadbare clothes darned up and brushed, to look seasonable; and Tiny Tim upon his shoulder. Alas for Tiny Tim, he bore a little crutch, and had his limbs supported by an iron frame!

"Why, where's our Martha?" cried Bob Cratchit, looking round.

"Not coming," said Mrs. Cratchit.

"Not coming!" said Bob, with a sudden declension in his high spirits; for he had been Tim's blood horse all the way from church, and had come home rampant. "Not coming upon Christmas Day!"

Martha didn't like to see him disappointed, if it were only in joke; so she came out prematurely from behind the closet door, and ran into his arms, while the two young Cratchits hustled Tiny Tim, and bore him off into the wash-house, that he might hear the pudding singing in the copper.

"And how did little Tim behave?" asked Mrs. Cratchit, when she had rallied Bob on his credulity, and Bob had hugged his daughter to his heart's content.

"As good as gold," said Bob, "and better. Somehow he gets thoughtful, sitting by himself so much, and thinks the strangest things you ever heard. He told me, coming home, that he hoped the people saw him in the church, because he was a cripple, and it might be pleasant to them to remember upon Christmas Day, who made lame beggars walk, and blind men see."

Bob's voice was tremulous when he told them this, and trembled more when he said that Tiny Tim was growing strong and hearty.

His active little crutch was heard upon the floor, and back came Tiny Tim before another word was spoken, escorted by his brother and sister to his stool before the fire; and while Bob, turning up his cuffs — as if, poor fellow, they were capable of being made more shabby — compounded some hot mixture in a jug with gin and lemons, and stirred it round and round and put it on the hob to simmer; Master Peter, and the two ubiquitous young Cratchits went to fetch the goose, with which they soon returned in high procession.

Such a bustle ensued that you might have thought a goose the rarest of all birds; a feathered phenomenon, to which a black swan was a matter of course — and in truth it was something very like it in that house. Mrs. Cratchit made the gravy (ready beforehand in a little saucepan) hissing hot; Master Peter mashed the potatoes with incredible vigour; Miss Belinda sweetened up the apple-sauce; Martha dusted the hot plates; Bob took Tiny Tim beside him in a tiny corner at the table; the two young Cratchits set chairs for everybody, not forgetting themselves, and mounting guard upon their posts, crammed spoons into their mouths, lest they should shriek for goose before their turn came to be helped. At last the dishes were set on, and grace was said. It was succeeded by a breathless pause, as Mrs. Cratchit, looking slowly all along the carving-knife, prepared to plunge it in the breast; but when she did, and when the long expected gush of stuffing issued forth, one murmur of delight arose all round the board, and even Tiny Tim, excited by the two young Cratchits, beat on the table with the handle of his knife, and feebly cried Hurrah!

There never was such a goose. Bob said he didn't believe there ever was such a goose cooked. Its tenderness and flavour, size and cheapness, were the themes of universal admiration. Eked out by apple-sauce and mashed potatoes, it was a sufficient dinner for the whole family; indeed, as Mrs. Cratchit said with great delight (surveying one small atom of a bone upon the dish), they hadn't ate it all at last! Yet everyone had had enough, and the youngest Cratchits in particular, were steeped in sage and onion to the eyebrows! But now, the plates being changed by Miss Belinda, Mrs. Cratchit left the room alone — too nervous to bear witnesses — to take the pudding up and bring it in.

Suppose it should not be done enough! Suppose it should break in turning out! Suppose somebody should have got over the wall of the back-yard, and stolen it, while they were merry with the goose — a supposition at which the two young Cratchits became livid! All sorts of horrors were supposed.

Hallo! A great deal of steam! The pudding was out of the copper. A smell like a washing-day! That was the cloth. A smell like an eating-house and a pastrycook's next door to each other, with a laundress's next door to that! That was the pudding! In half a minute Mrs. Cratchit entered — flushed, but smiling proudly — with the pudding, like a speckled cannon-ball, so hard and firm, blazing in half of half-a-quartern of ignited brandy, and bedight with Christmas holly stuck into the top. Oh, a wonderful pudding! Bob Cratchit said, and calmly too, that he regarded it as the greatest success achieved by Mrs. Cratchit since their marriage. Mrs. Cratchit said that now the weight was off her mind, she would confess she had had her doubts about the quantity of flour. Everybody had something to say about it, but nobody said or thought it was at all a small pudding for a large family. It would have been flat heresy to do so. Any Cratchit would have blushed to hint at such a thing.

At last the dinner was all done, the cloth was cleared, the hearth swept, and the fire made up. The compound in the jug being tasted, and considered perfect, apples and oranges were put upon the table, and a shovel-full of chestnuts on the fire. Then all the Cratchit family drew round the hearth, in what Bob Cratchit called a circle, meaning half a one; and at Bob Cratchit's elbow stood the family display of glass. Two tumblers, and a custard-cup without a handle.

These held the hot stuff from the jug, however, as well as golden goblets would have done; and Bob served it out with beaming looks, while the chestnuts on the fire sputtered and cracked noisily. Then Bob proposed:

"A Merry Christmas to us all, my dears. God bless us!"

Which all the family re-echoed.

"God bless us every one!" said Tiny Tim, the last of all.

He sat very close to his father's side upon his little stool. Bob held his withered little hand in his, as if he loved the child, and wished to keep him by his side, and dreaded that he might be taken from him.

"Spirit," said Scrooge, with an interest he had never felt before, "tell me if Tiny Tim will live."

"I see a vacant seat," replied the Ghost, "in the poor chimney-corner, and a crutch without an owner, carefully preserved. If these shadows remain unaltered by the Future, the child will die."

"No, no," said Scrooge. "Oh, no, kind Spirit! say he will be spared."

"If these shadows remain unaltered by the Future, none other of my race," returned the Ghost, "will find him here. What then? If he be like to die, he had better do it, and decrease the surplus population."

Scrooge hung his head to hear his own words quoted by the Spirit, and was overcome with penitence and grief.

"Man," said the Ghost, "if man you be in heart, not adamant, forbear that wicked cant until you have discovered What the surplus is, and Where it is. Will you decide what men shall live, what men shall die? It may be, that in the sight of Heaven, you are more worthless and less fit to live than millions like this poor man's child. Oh God! To hear the Insect on the leaf pronouncing on the too much life among his hungry brothers in the dust!"

Scrooge bent before the Ghost's rebuke, and trembling cast his eyes upon the ground. But he raised them speedily, on hearing his own name.

"Mr. Scrooge!" said Bob; "I'll give you Mr. Scrooge, the Founder of the Feast!"

"The Founder of the Feast indeed!" cried Mrs. Cratchit, reddening. "I wish I had him here. I'd give him a piece of my mind to feast upon, and I hope he'd have a good appetite for it."

"My dear," said Bob, "the children! Christmas Day."

"It should be Christmas Day, I am sure," said she, "on which one drinks the health of such an odious, stingy, hard, man as Mr. Scrooge. You know he is, Robert! Nobody knows it better than you do, poor fellow!"

"My dear," was Bob's mild answer, "Christmas Day."

"I'll drink his health for your sake and the Day's," said Mrs. Cratchit, "not for his. Long life to him! A merry Christmas and a happy new year! He'll be very merry and very happy, I have no doubt!"

The children drank the toast after her. It was the first of their proceedings which had no heartiness. Tiny Tim drank it last of all, but he didn't care twopence for it. Scrooge was the Ogre of the family. The mention of his name cast a dark shadow on the party, which was not dispelled for full five minutes.

After it had passed away, they were ten times merrier than before, from the mere relief of Scrooge the Baleful being done with. Bob Cratchit told them how he had a situation in his eye for Master Peter, which would bring in, if obtained, full five-and-sixpence weekly. The two young Cratchits laughed tremendously at the idea of Peter's being a man of business; and Peter himself looked thoughtfully at the fire from between his collars, as if he were deliberating what particular investments he should favour when he came into the receipt of that bewildering income. Martha, who was a poor apprentice at a milliner's, then told them what kind of work she had to do, and how many hours she worked at a stretch, and how she meant to lie abed tomorrow morning for a good long rest; tomorrow being a holiday she passed at home. Also how she had seen a countess and a lord some days before, and how the lord "was much about as tall as Peter;" at which Peter pulled up his collars so high that you couldn't have seen his head if you had been there. All this time the chestnuts and the jug went round and round; and by-and-bye they had a song, about a lost child travelling in the snow, from Tiny Tim, who had a plaintive little voice, and sang it very well indeed.

There was nothing of high mark in this. They were not a handsome family; they were not well dressed; their shoes were far from being water-proof; their clothes were scanty; and Peter might have known, and very likely did, the inside of a pawnbroker's. But, they were happy, grateful, pleased with one another, and contented with the time; and when they faded, and looked happier yet in the bright sprinklings of the Spirit's torch at parting, Scrooge had his eye upon them, and especially on Tiny Tim, until the last.

THE SECOND OF THE THREE SPIRITS II

By this time it was getting dark, and snowing pretty heavily; and as Scrooge and the Spirit went along the streets, the brightness of the roaring fires in kitchens, parlors, and all sorts of rooms, was wonderful. Here, the flickering of the blaze showed preparations for a cosy dinner, with hot plates baking through and through before the fire, and deep red curtains, ready to be drawn to shut out cold and darkness. There all the children of the house were running out into the snow to meet their married sisters, brothers, cousins, uncles, aunts, and be the first to greet them. Here, again, were shadows on the window-blind of guests assembling; and there a group of handsome girls, all hooded and fur-booted, and all chattering at once, tripped lightly off to some near neighbor's house; where, woe upon the single man who saw them enter

— artful witches, well they knew it — in a glow!

But, if you had judged from the numbers of people on their way to friendly gatherings, you might have thought that no one was at home to give them welcome when they got there, instead of every house expecting company, and piling up its fires half-chimney high. Blessings on it, how the Ghost exulted! How it bared its breadth of breast, and opened its capacious palm, and floated on, outpouring, with a generous hand, its bright and harmless mirth on everything within its reach! The very lamplighter, who ran on before, dotting the dusky street with specks of light, and who was dressed to spend the evening somewhere, laughed out loudly as the Spirit passed, though little kenned the lamplighter that he had any company but Christmas!

And now, without a word of warning from the Ghost, they stood upon a bleak and desert moor, where monstrous masses of rude stone were cast about, as though it were the burial-place of giants; and water spread itself wheresoever it listed, or would have done so, but for the frost that held it prisoner; and nothing grew but moss and furze, and coarse rank grass. Down in the west the setting sun had left a streak of fiery red, which glared upon the desolation for an instant, like a sullen eye, and frowning lower, lower, lower yet, was lost in the thick gloom of darkest night.

"What place is this?" asked Scrooge.

"A place where Miners live, who labor in the bowels of the earth," returned the Spirit. "But they know me. See!"

A light shone from the window of a hut, and swiftly they advanced towards it. Passing through the wall of mud and stone, they found a cheerful company assembled round a glowing fire. An old, old man and woman, with their children and their children's children, and another generation beyond that, all decked out gaily in their holiday attire. The old man, in a voice that seldom rose above the howling of the wind upon the barren waste, was singing them a Christmas song — it had been a very old song when he was a boy — and from time to time they all joined in the chorus. So surely as they raised their voices, the old man got quite

blithe and loud; and so surely as they stopped, his vigour sank again.
The Spirit did not tarry here, but bade Scrooge hold his robe, and passing
on above the moor, sped — whither? Not to sea? To sea. To Scrooge's
horror, looking back, he saw the last of the land, a frightful range of
rocks, behind them; and his ears were deafened by the thundering of
water, as it rolled and roared, and raged among the dreadful caverns it
had worn, and fiercely tried to undermine the earth.

Built upon a dismal reef of sunken rocks, some league or so from shore,
on which the waters chafed and dashed, the wild year through, there
stood a solitary lighthouse. Great heaps of sea-weed clung to its base, and
storm-birds — born of the wind one might suppose, as sea-weed of the
water — rose and fell about it, like the waves they skimmed.

But even here, two men who watched the light had made a fire, that
through the loophole in the thick stone wall shed out a ray of brightness
on the awful sea. Joining their horny hands over the rough table at which
they sat, they wished each other Merry Christmas in their can of grog;
and one of them: the elder, too, with his face all damaged and scarred
with hard weather, as the figure-head of an old ship might be: struck up a
sturdy song that was like a Gale in itself.

Again the Ghost sped on, above the black and heaving sea — on, and on
— until, being far away, as he told Scrooge, from any shore, they lighted
on a ship. They stood beside the helmsman at the wheel, the look-out in
the bow, the officers who had the watch; dark, ghostly figures in their
several stations; but every man among them hummed a Christmas tune,
or had a Christmas thought, or spoke below his breath to his companion
of some bygone Christmas Day, with homeward hopes belonging to it.
And every man on board, waking or sleeping, good or bad, had had a
kinder word for another on that day than on any day in the year; and had
shared to some extent in its festivities; and had remembered those he
cared for at a distance, and had known that they delighted to remember
him.

It was a great surprise to Scrooge, while listening to the moaning of the wind, and thinking what a solemn thing it was to move on through the lonely darkness over an unknown abyss, whose depths were secrets as profound as Death: it was a great surprise to Scrooge, while thus engaged, to hear a hearty laugh. It was a much greater surprise to Scrooge to recognise it as his own nephew's and to find himself in a bright, dry, gleaming room, with the Spirit standing smiling by his side, and looking at that same nephew with approving affability!

"Ha, ha!" laughed Scrooge's nephew. "Ha, ha, ha!"

If you should happen, by any unlikely chance, to know a man more blest in a laugh than Scrooge's nephew, all I can say is, I should like to know him too. Introduce him to me, and I'll cultivate his acquaintance.

It is a fair, even-handed, noble adjustment of things, that while there is infection in disease and sorrow, there is nothing in the world so irresistibly contagious as laughter and good-humor. When Scrooge's nephew laughed in this way: holding his sides, rolling his head, and twisting his face into the most extravagant contortions: Scrooge's niece, by marriage, laughed as heartily as he. And their assembled friends being not a bit behindhand, roared out lustily.

"Ha, ha! Ha, ha, ha, ha!"

"He said that Christmas was a humbug, as I live!" cried Scrooge's nephew. "He believed it too!"

"More shame for him, Fred!" said Scrooge's niece, indignantly. Bless those women; they never do anything by halves. They are always in earnest.

She was very pretty: exceedingly pretty. With a dimpled, surprised-looking, capital face; a ripe little mouth, that seemed made to be kissed — as no doubt it was; all kinds of good little dots about her chin, that melted into one another when she laughed; and the sunniest pair of eyes you ever saw in any little creature's head. Altogether she was what you would have called provoking, you know; but satisfactory, too. Oh, perfectly satisfactory.

"He's a comical old fellow," said Scrooge's nephew, "that's the truth: and not so pleasant as he might be. However, his offences carry their own punishment, and I have nothing to say against him."

"I'm sure he is very rich, Fred," hinted Scrooge's niece. "At least you always tell me so."

"What of that, my dear!" said Scrooge's nephew. "His wealth is of no use to him. He don't do any good with it. He don't make himself comfortable with it. He hasn't the satisfaction of thinking — ha, ha, ha! — that he is ever going to benefit US with it."

"I have no patience with him," observed Scrooge's niece. Scrooge's niece's sisters, and all the other ladies, expressed the same opinion.

"Oh, I have!" said Scrooge's nephew. "I am sorry for him; I couldn't be angry with him if I tried. Who suffers by his ill whims! Himself, always. Here, he takes it into his head to dislike us, and he won't come and dine with us. What's the consequence? He don't lose much of a dinner."

"Indeed, I think he loses a very good dinner," interrupted Scrooge's niece. Everybody else said the same, and they must be allowed to have been competent judges, because they had just had dinner; and, with the dessert upon the table, were clustered round the fire, by lamplight.

"Well! I'm very glad to hear it," said Scrooge's nephew, "because I haven't great faith in these young housekeepers. What do you say, Topper?"

Topper had clearly got his eye upon one of Scrooge's niece's sisters, for he answered that a bachelor was a wretched outcast, who had no right to express an opinion on the subject. Whereat Scrooge's niece's sister — the plump one with the lace tucker: not the one with the roses — blushed.

"Do go on, Fred," said Scrooge's niece, clapping her hands. "He never finishes what he begins to say! He is such a ridiculous fellow!"

Scrooge's nephew revelled in another laugh, and as it was impossible to keep the infection off; though the plump sister tried hard to do it with aromatic vinegar; his example was unanimously followed.

"I was only going to say," said Scrooge's nephew, "that the consequence of his taking a dislike to us, and not making merry with us, is, as I think, that he loses some pleasant moments, which could do him no harm. I am sure he loses pleasanter companions than he can find in his own thoughts, either in his mouldy old office, or his dusty chambers. I mean to give him the same chance every year, whether he likes it or not, for I pity him. He may rail at Christmas till he dies, but he can't help thinking better of it — I defy him — if he finds me going there, in good temper, year after year, and saying Uncle Scrooge, how are you? If it only puts him in the vein to leave his poor clerk fifty pounds, that's something; and I think I shook him yesterday."

It was their turn to laugh now at the notion of his shaking Scrooge. But being thoroughly good-natured, and not much caring what they laughed at, so that they laughed at any rate, he encouraged them in their merriment, and passed the bottle joyously.

After tea, they had some music. For they were a musical family, and knew what they were about, when they sung a Glee or Catch, I can assure you: especially Topper, who could growl away in the bass like a good one, and never swell the large veins in his forehead, or get red in the face over it. Scrooge's niece played well upon the harp; and played among other tunes a simple little air (a mere nothing: you might learn to whistle it in two minutes), which had been familiar to the child who fetched Scrooge from the boarding-school, as he had been reminded by the Ghost of Christmas Past. When this strain of music sounded, all the things that Ghost had shown him, came upon his mind; he softened more and more; and thought that if he could have listened to it often, years ago, he might have cultivated the kindnesses of life for his own happiness with his own hands, without resorting to the sexton's spade that buried Jacob Marley. But they didn't devote the whole evening to music. After a while they played at forfeits; for it is good to be children sometimes, and never better than at Christmas, when its mighty Founder was a child himself. Stop! There was first a game at blind-man's buff. Of course there was. And I no more believe Topper was really blind than I believe he had eyes in his boots. My opinion is, that it was a done thing between him and

Scrooge's nephew; and that the Ghost of Christmas Present knew it. The way he went after that plump sister in the lace tucker, was an outrage on the credulity of human nature. Knocking down the fire-irons, tumbling over the chairs, bumping against the piano, smothering himself among the curtains, wherever she went, there went he! He always knew where the plump sister was. He wouldn't catch anybody else. If you had fallen up against him (as some of them did), on purpose, he would have made a feint of endeavoring to seize you, which would have been an affront to your understanding, and would instantly have sidled off in the direction of the plump sister. She often cried out that it wasn't fair; and it really was not. But when at last, he caught her; when, in spite of all her silken rustlings, and her rapid flutterings past him, he got her into a corner whence there was no escape; then his conduct was the most execrable. For his pretending not to know her; his pretending that it was necessary to touch her head-dress, and further to assure himself of her identity by pressing a certain ring upon her finger, and a certain chain about her neck; was vile, monstrous! No doubt she told him her opinion of it, when, another blind-man being in office, they were so very confidential together, behind the curtains.

Scrooge's niece was not one of the blind-man's buff party, but was made comfortable with a large chair and a footstool, in a snug corner, where the Ghost and Scrooge were close behind her. But she joined in the forfeits, and loved her love to admiration with all the letters of the alphabet. Likewise at the game of How, When, and Where, she was very great, and to the secret joy of Scrooge's nephew, beat her sisters hollow: though they were sharp girls too, as Topper could have told you. There might have been twenty people there, young and old, but they all played, and so did Scrooge; for wholly forgetting in the interest he had in what was going on, that his voice made no sound in their ears, he sometimes came out with his guess quite loud, and very often guessed quite right, too; for the sharpest needle, best Whitechapel, warranted not to cut in the eye, was not sharper than Scrooge; blunt as he took it in his head to be.

The Ghost was greatly pleased to find him in this mood, and looked upon him with such favor, that he begged like a boy to be allowed to stay until the guests departed. But this the Spirit said could not be done.

"Here is a new game," said Scrooge. "One half hour, Spirit, only one!"

It was a Game called Yes and No, where Scrooge's nephew had to think of something, and the rest must find out what; he only answering to their questions yes or no, as the case was. The brisk fire of questioning to which he was exposed, elicited from him that he was thinking of an animal, a live animal, rather a disagreeable animal, a savage animal, an animal that growled and grunted sometimes, and talked sometimes, and lived in London, and walked about the streets, and wasn't made a show of, and wasn't led by anybody, and didn't live in a menagerie, and was never killed in a market, and was not a horse, or an ass, or a cow, or a bull, or a tiger, or a dog, or a pig, or a cat, or a bear. At every fresh question that was put to him, this nephew burst into a fresh roar of laughter; and was so inexpressibly tickled, that he was obliged to get up off the sofa and stamp. At last the plump sister, falling into a similar state, cried out:

"I have found it out! I know what it is, Fred! I know what it is!"

"What is it?" cried Fred.

"It's your Uncle Scro-o-o-o-oge!"

Which it certainly was. Admiration was the universal sentiment, though some objected that the reply to "Is it a bear?" ought to have been "Yes;" inasmuch as an answer in the negative was sufficient to have diverted their thoughts from Mr. Scrooge, supposing they had ever had any tendency that way.

"He has given us plenty of merriment, I am sure," said Fred, "and it would be ungrateful not to drink his health. Here is a glass of mulled wine ready to our hand at the moment; and I say, 'Uncle Scrooge!' "

"Well! Uncle Scrooge!" they cried.

"A Merry Christmas and a Happy New Year to the old man, whatever he is!" said Scrooge's nephew. "He wouldn't take it from me, but may he have it, nevertheless. Uncle Scrooge!"

Uncle Scrooge had imperceptibly become so gay and light of heart, that he would have pledged the unconscious company in return, and thanked them in an inaudible speech, if the Ghost had given him time. But the whole scene passed off in the breath of the last word spoken by his nephew; and he and the Spirit were again upon their travels.

Much they saw, and far they went, and many homes they visited, but always with a happy end. The Spirit stood beside sick beds, and they were cheerful; on foreign lands, and they were close at home; by struggling men, and they were patient in their greater hope; by poverty, and it was rich. In almshouse, hospital, and jail, in misery's every refuge, where vain man in his little brief authority had not made fast the door, and barred the Spirit out, he left his blessing, and taught Scrooge his precepts.

It was a long night, if it were only a night; but Scrooge had his doubts of this, because the Christmas Holidays appeared to be condensed into the space of time they passed together. It was strange, too, that while Scrooge remained unaltered in his outward form, the Ghost grew older, clearly older. Scrooge had observed this change, but never spoke of it, until they left a children's Twelfth Night party, when, looking at the Spirit as they stood together in an open place, he noticed that its hair was grey.

"Are spirits' lives so short?" asked Scrooge.

"My life upon this globe, is very brief," replied the Ghost. "It ends to-night."

"To-night!" cried Scrooge.

"To-night at midnight. Hark! The time is drawing near."

The chimes were ringing the three quarters past eleven at that moment.

"Forgive me if I am not justified in what I ask," said Scrooge, looking intently at the Spirit's robe, "but I see something strange, and not belonging to yourself, protruding from your skirts. Is it a foot or a claw?"

"It might be a claw, for the flesh there is upon it," was the Spirit's sorrowful reply. "Look here."

From the foldings of its robe, it brought two children; wretched, abject, frightful, hideous, miserable. They knelt down at its feet, and clung upon the outside of its garment.

"Oh, Man! Look here. Look, look, down here!" exclaimed the Ghost.

They were a boy and girl. Yellow, meagre, ragged, scowling, wolfish; but prostrate, too, in their humility. Where graceful youth should have filled their features out, and touched them with its freshest tints, a stale and shrivelled hand, like that of age, had pinched, and twisted them, and pulled them into shreds. Where angels might have sat enthroned, devils lurked, and glared out menacing. No change, no degradation, no perversion of humanity, in any grade, through all the mysteries of wonderful creation, has monsters half so horrible and dread.

Scrooge started back, appalled. Having them shown to him in this way, he tried to say they were fine children, but the words choked themselves, rather than be parties to a lie of such enormous magnitude.

"Spirit! Are they yours?" Scrooge could say no more.

"They are Man's," said the Spirit, looking down upon them. "And they cling to me, appealing from their fathers. This boy is Ignorance. This girl is Want. Beware them both, and all of their degree, but most of all beware this boy, for on his brow I see that written which is Doom, unless the writing be erased. Deny it!" cried the Spirit, stretching out its hand towards the city. "Slander those who tell it ye! Admit it for your factious purposes, and make it worse. And bide the end!"

"Have they no refuge or resource?" cried Scrooge.

"Are there no prisons?" said the Spirit, turning on him for the last time with his own words. "Are there no workhouses?"

The bell struck twelve.

Scrooge looked about him for the Ghost, and saw it not. As the last stroke ceased to vibrate, he remembered the prediction of old Jacob Marley, and lifting up his eyes, beheld a solemn Phantom, draped and hooded, coming, like a mist along the ground, towards him.

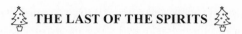
The Phantom slowly, gravely, silently, approached. When it came near him, Scrooge bent down upon his knee; for in the very air through which this Spirit moved it seemed to scatter gloom and mystery.

It was shrouded in a deep black garment, which concealed its head, its face, its form, and left nothing of it visible save one outstretched hand. But for this it would have been difficult to detach its figure from the night, and separate it from the darkness by which it was surrounded.

He felt that it was tall and stately when it came beside him, and that its mysterious presence filled him with a solemn dread. He knew no more, for the Spirit neither spoke nor moved.

"I am in the presence of the Ghost of Christmas Yet To Come?" said Scrooge.

The Spirit answered not, but pointed onward with its hand.

"You are about to show me shadows of the things that have not happened, but will happen in the time before us," Scrooge pursued. "Is that so, Spirit?"

The upper portion of the garment was contracted for an instant in its folds, as if the Spirit had inclined its head. That was the only answer he received.

Although well used to ghostly company by this time, Scrooge feared the silent shape so much that his legs trembled beneath him, and he found that he could hardly stand when he prepared to follow it. The Spirit paused a moment, as observing his condition, and giving him time to recover.

But Scrooge was all the worse for this. It thrilled him with a vague uncertain horror, to know that behind the dusky shroud, there were ghostly eyes intently fixed upon him, while he, though he stretched his own to the utmost, could see nothing but a spectral hand and one great heap of black.

"Ghost of the Future!" he exclaimed, "I fear you more than any spectre

I have seen. But as I know your purpose is to do me good, and as I hope to live to be another man from what I was, I am prepared to bear you company, and do it with a thankful heart. Will you not speak to me?"

It gave him no reply. The hand was pointed straight before them.

"Lead on!" said Scrooge. "Lead on! The night is waning fast, and it is precious time to me, I know. Lead on, Spirit!"

The Phantom moved away as it had come towards him. Scrooge followed in the shadow of its dress, which bore him up, he thought, and carried him along.

They scarcely seemed to enter the city; for the city rather seemed to spring up about them, and encompass them of its own act. But there they were, in the heart of it; on 'Change, amongst the merchants; who hurried up and down, and chinked the money in their pockets, and conversed in groups, and looked at their watches, and trifled thoughtfully with their great gold seals; and so forth, as Scrooge had seen them often.

The Spirit stopped beside one little knot of business men. Observing that the hand was pointed to them, Scrooge advanced to listen to their talk.

"No," said a great fat man with a monstrous chin, "I don't know much about it, either way. I only know he's dead."

"When did he die?" inquired another.

"Last night, I believe."

"Why, what was the matter with him?" asked a third, taking a vast quantity of snuff out of a very large snuff-box. "I thought he'd never die."

"God knows," said the first, with a yawn.

"What has he done with his money?" asked a red-faced gentleman with a pendulous excrescence on the end of his nose, that shook like the gills of a turkey-cock.

"I haven't heard," said the man with the large chin, yawning again. "Left it to his company, perhaps. He hasn't left it to me. That's all I know."

This pleasantry was received with a general laugh.

"It's likely to be a very cheap funeral," said the same speaker; "for upon my life I don't know of anybody to go to it. Suppose we make up a party and volunteer?"

"I don't mind going if a lunch is provided," observed the gentleman with the excrescence on his nose. "But I must be fed, if I make one."

Another laugh.

"Well, I am the most disinterested among you, after all," said the first speaker, "for I never wear black gloves, and I never eat lunch. But I'll offer to go, if anybody else will. When I come to think of it, I'm not at all sure that I wasn't his most particular friend; for we used to stop and speak whenever we met. Bye, bye!"

Speakers and listeners strolled away, and mixed with other groups. Scrooge knew the men, and looked towards the Spirit for an explanation. The Phantom glided on into a street. Its finger pointed to two persons meeting. Scrooge listened again, thinking that the explanation might lie here.

He knew these men, also, perfectly. They were men of business: very wealthy, and of great importance. He had made a point always of standing well in their esteem: in a business point of view, that is; strictly in a business point of view.

"How are you?" said one.

"How are you?" returned the other.

"Well!" said the first. "Old Scratch has got his own at last, hey?"

"So I am told," returned the second. "Cold, isn't it?"

"Seasonable for Christmas time. You're not a skater, I suppose?"

"No. No. Something else to think of. Good morning!"

Not another word. That was their meeting, their conversation, and their parting.

Scrooge was at first inclined to be surprised that the Spirit should attach importance to conversations apparently so trivial; but feeling assured that they must have some hidden purpose, he set himself to consider what it was likely to be. They could scarcely be supposed to have any bearing on the death of Jacob, his old partner, for that was Past, and this Ghost's province was the Future. Nor could he think of any one immediately connected with himself, to whom he could apply them. But nothing doubting that to whomsoever they applied they had some latent moral for his own improvement, he resolved to treasure up every word he heard, and everything he saw; and especially to observe the shadow of himself when it appeared. For he had an expectation that the conduct of his future self would give him the clue he missed, and would render the solution of these riddles easy.

He looked about in that very place for his own image; but another man stood in his accustomed corner, and though the clock pointed to his usual time of day for being there, he saw no likeness of himself among the multitudes that poured in through the Porch. It gave him little surprise, however; for he had been revolving in his mind a change of life, and thought and hoped he saw his new-born resolutions carried out in this. Quiet and dark, beside him stood the Phantom, with its outstretched hand. When he roused himself from his thoughtful quest, he fancied from the turn of the hand, and its situation in reference to himself, that the Unseen Eyes were looking at him keenly. It made him shudder, and feel very cold.

They left the busy scene, and went into an obscure part of the town, where Scrooge had never penetrated before, although he recognised its situation, and its bad repute. The ways were foul and narrow; the shops and houses wretched; the people half-naked, drunken, slipshod, ugly. Alleys and archways, like so many cesspools, disgorged their offences of smell, and dirt, and life, upon the straggling streets; and the whole quarter reeked with crime, with filth, and misery.

Far in this den of infamous resort, there was a low-browed, beetling shop, below a pent-house roof, where iron, old rags, bottles, bones, and greasy offal, were bought. Upon the floor within, were piled up heaps of rusty keys, nails, chains, hinges, files, scales, weights, and refuse iron of all kinds. Secrets that few would like to scrutinise were bred and hidden in mountains of unseemly rags, masses of corrupted fat, and sepulchres of bones. Sitting in among the wares he dealt in, by a charcoal stove, made of old bricks, was a grey-haired rascal, nearly seventy years of age; who had screened himself from the cold air without, by a frousy curtaining of miscellaneous tatters, hung upon a line; and smoked his pipe in all the luxury of calm retirement.

Scrooge and the Phantom came into the presence of this man, just as a woman with a heavy bundle slunk into the shop. But she had scarcely entered, when another woman, similarly laden, came in too; and she was closely followed by a man in faded black, who was no less startled by the sight of them, than they had been upon the recognition of each other. After a short period of blank astonishment, in which the old man with the pipe had joined them, they all three burst into a laugh.

"Let the charwoman alone to be the first!" cried she who had entered first. "Let the laundress alone to be the second; and let the undertaker's man alone to be the third. Look here, old Joe, here's a chance! If we haven't all three met here without meaning it!"

"You couldn't have met in a better place," said old Joe, removing his pipe from his mouth. "Come into the parlour. You were made free of it long ago, you know; and the other two an't strangers. Stop till I shut the door of the shop. Ah! How it skreeks! There an't such a rusty bit of metal in the place as its own hinges, I believe; and I'm sure there's no such old bones here, as mine.

Ha, ha! We're all suitable to our calling, we're well matched. Come into the parlor. Come into the parlor."

The parlor was the space behind the screen of rags. The old man raked the fire together with an old stair-rod, and having trimmed his smoky lamp (for it was night), with the stem of his pipe, put it in his mouth again.

While he did this, the woman who had already spoken threw her bundle on the floor, and sat down in a flaunting manner on a stool; crossing her elbows on her knees, and looking with a bold defiance at the other two.

"What odds then! What odds, Mrs. Dilber?" said the woman. "Every person has a right to take care of themselves. He always did."

"That's true, indeed!" said the laundress. "No man more so."

"Why then, don't stand staring as if you was afraid, woman; who's the wiser? We're not going to pick holes in each other's coats, I suppose?"

"No, indeed!" said Mrs. Dilber and the man together. "We should hope not."

"Very well, then!" cried the woman. "That's enough. Who's the worse for the loss of a few things like these? Not a dead man, I suppose."

"No, indeed," said Mrs. Dilber, laughing.

"If he wanted to keep 'em after he was dead, a wicked old screw," pursued the woman, "why wasn't he natural in his lifetime? If he had been, he'd have had somebody to look after him when he was struck with Death, instead of lying gasping out his last there, alone by himself."

"It's the truest word that ever was spoke," said Mrs. Dilber. "It's a judgment on him."

"I wish it was a little heavier judgment," replied the woman; "and it should have been, you may depend upon it, if I could have laid my hands on anything else. Open that bundle, old Joe, and let me know the value of it. Speak out plain. I'm not afraid to be the first, nor afraid for them to see it. We know pretty well that we were helping ourselves, before we met here, I believe. It's no sin. Open the bundle, Joe."

But the gallantry of her friends would not allow of this; and the man in faded black, mounting the breach first, produced his plunder. It was not extensive. A seal or two, a pencil-case, a pair of sleeve-buttons, and a brooch of no great value, were all. They were severally examined and appraised by old Joe, who chalked the sums he was disposed to give for each, upon the wall, and added them up into a total when he found there was nothing more to come.

"That's your account," said Joe, "and I wouldn't give another sixpence, if I was to be boiled for not doing it. Who's next?"

Mrs. Dilber was next. Sheets and towels, a little wearing apparel, two old-fashioned silver teaspoons, a pair of sugar-tongs, and a few boots. Her account was stated on the wall in the same manner.

"I always give too much to ladies. It's a weakness of mine, and that's the way I ruin myself," said old Joe. "That's your account. If you asked me for another penny, and made it an open question, I'd repent of being so liberal and knock off half-a-crown."

"And now undo my bundle, Joe," said the first woman.

Joe went down on his knees for the greater convenience of opening it, and having unfastened a great many knots, dragged out a large and heavy roll of some dark stuff.

"What do you call this?" said Joe. "Bed-curtains!"

"Ah!" returned the woman, laughing and leaning forward on her crossed arms. "Bed-curtains!"

"You don't mean to say you took 'em down, rings and all, with him lying there?" said Joe.

"Yes I do," replied the woman. "Why not?"

"You were born to make your fortune," said Joe, "and you'll certainly do it."

"I certainly shan't hold my hand, when I can get anything in it by reaching it out, for the sake of such a man as He was, I promise you, Joe," returned the woman coolly. "Don't drop that oil upon the blankets, now."

"His blankets?" asked Joe.

"Whose else's do you think?" replied the woman. "He isn't likely to take cold without 'em, I dare say."

"I hope he didn't die of anything catching? Eh?" said old Joe, stopping in his work, and looking up.

"Don't you be afraid of that," returned the woman. "I an't so fond of his company that I'd loiter about him for such things, if he did. Ah! You may look through that shirt till your eyes ache; but you won't find a hole in it, nor a threadbare place. It's the best he had, and a fine one too. They'd have wasted it, if it hadn't been for me."

"What do you call wasting of it?" asked old Joe.

"Putting it on him to be buried in, to be sure," replied the woman with a laugh. "Somebody was fool enough to do it, but I took it off again.

If calico an't good enough for such a purpose, it isn't good enough for anything. It's quite as becoming to the body. He can't look uglier than he did in that one."

Scrooge listened to this dialogue in horror. As they sat grouped about their spoil, in the scanty light afforded by the old man's lamp, he viewed them with a detestation and disgust, which could hardly have been greater, though they had been obscene demons, marketing the corpse itself.

"Ha, ha!" laughed the same woman, when old Joe, producing a flannel bag with money in it, told out their several gains upon the ground. "This is the end of it, you see! He frightened every one away from him when he was alive, to profit us when he was dead! Ha, ha, ha!"

"Spirit!" said Scrooge, shuddering from head to foot. "I see, I see. The case of this unhappy man might be my own. My life tends that way, now. Merciful Heaven, what is this!"

He recoiled in terror, for the scene had changed, and now he almost touched a bed: a bare, uncurtained bed: on which, beneath a ragged sheet, there lay a something covered up, which, though it was dumb, announced itself in awful language.

The room was very dark, too dark to be observed with any accuracy, though Scrooge glanced round it in obedience to a secret impulse, anxious to know what kind of room it was. A pale light, rising in the outer air, fell straight upon the bed; and on it, plundered and bereft, unwatched, unwept, uncared for, was the body of this man.

Scrooge glanced towards the Phantom. Its steady hand was pointed to the head. The cover was so carelessly adjusted that the slightest raising of it, the motion of a finger upon Scrooge's part, would have disclosed the face. He thought of it, felt how easy it would be to do, and longed to do it; but had no more power to withdraw the veil than to dismiss the spectre at his side.

Oh cold, cold, rigid, dreadful Death, set up thine altar here, and dress it with such terrors as thou hast at thy command: for this is thy dominion!

But of the loved, revered, and honored head, thou canst not turn one hair to thy dread purposes, or make one feature odious. It is not that the hand is heavy and will fall down when released; it is not that the heart and pulse are still; but that the hand was open, generous, and true; the heart brave, warm, and tender; and the pulse a man's. Strike, Shadow, strike! And see his good deeds springing from the wound, to sow the world with life immortal!

No voice pronounced these words in Scrooge's ears, and yet he heard them when he looked upon the bed. He thought, if this man could be raised up now, what would be his foremost thoughts? Avarice, hard-dealing, griping cares? They have brought him to a rich end, truly!

He lay, in the dark empty house, with not a man, a woman, or a child, to say that he was kind to me in this or that, and for the memory of one kind word I will be kind to him. A cat was tearing at the door, and there was a sound of gnawing rats beneath the hearth-stone. What they wanted in the room of death, and why they were so restless and disturbed, Scrooge did not dare to think.

"Spirit!" he said, "this is a fearful place. In leaving it, I shall not leave its lesson, trust me. Let us go!"

Still the Ghost pointed with an unmoved finger to the head.

"I understand you," Scrooge returned, "and I would do it, if I could. But I have not the power, Spirit. I have not the power."

Again it seemed to look upon him.

"If there is any person in the town, who feels emotion caused by this man's death," said Scrooge quite agonised, "show that person to me, Spirit, I beseech you!"

The Phantom spread its dark robe before him for a moment, like a wing; and withdrawing it, revealed a room by daylight, where a mother and her children were.

She was expecting some one, and with anxious eagerness; for she walked up and down the room; started at every sound; looked out from the window; glanced at the clock; tried, but in vain, to work with her needle;

and could hardly bear the voices of the children in their play.

At length the long-expected knock was heard. She hurried to the door, and met her husband; a man whose face was careworn and depressed, though he was young. There was a remarkable expression in it now; a kind of serious delight of which he felt ashamed, and which he struggled to repress.

He sat down to the dinner that had been hoarding for him by the fire; and when she asked him faintly what news (which was not until after a long silence), he appeared embarrassed how to answer.

"Is it good?" she said, "or bad?" — to help him.

"Bad," he answered.

"We are quite ruined?"

"No. There is hope yet, Caroline."

"If he relents," she said, amazed, "there is! Nothing is past hope, if such a miracle has happened."

"He is past relenting," said her husband. "He is dead."

She was a mild and patient creature if her face spoke truth; but she was thankful in her soul to hear it, and she said so, with clasped hands. She prayed forgiveness the next moment, and was sorry; but the first was the emotion of her heart.

"What the half-drunken woman whom I told you of last night, said to me, when I tried to see him and obtain a week's delay; and what I thought was a mere excuse to avoid me; turns out to have been quite true. He was not only very ill, but dying, then."

"To whom will our debt be transferred?"

"I don't know. But before that time we shall be ready with the money; and even though we were not, it would be a bad fortune indeed to find so merciless a creditor in his successor. We may sleep to-night with light hearts, Caroline!"

Yes. Soften it as they would, their hearts were lighter. The children's faces, hushed and clustered round to hear what they so little understood, were brighter; and it was a happier house for this man's death! The only emotion that the Ghost could show him, caused by the event, was one of pleasure.

"Let me see some tenderness connected with a death," said Scrooge; "or that dark chamber, Spirit, which we left just now, will be forever present to me."

The Ghost conducted him through several streets familiar to his feet; and as they went along, Scrooge looked here and there to find himself, but nowhere was he to be seen. They entered poor Bob Cratchit's house; the dwelling he had visited before; and found the mother and the children seated round the fire.

Quiet. Very quiet. The noisy little Cratchits were as still as statues in one corner, and sat looking up at Peter, who had a book before him. The mother and her daughters were engaged in sewing. But surely they were very quiet!

" 'And He took a child, and set him in the midst of them.' "

Where had Scrooge heard those words? He had not dreamed them. The boy must have read them out, as he and the Spirit crossed the threshold. Why did he not go on?

The mother laid her work upon the table, and put her hand up to her face. "The color hurts my eyes," she said.

The color? Ah, poor Tiny Tim!

"They're better now again," said Cratchit's wife. "It makes them weak by candle-light; and I wouldn't show weak eyes to your father when he comes home, for the world. It must be near his time."

"Past it rather," Peter answered, shutting up his book. "But I think he has walked a little slower than he used, these few last evenings, mother."

They were very quiet again. At last she said, and in a steady, cheerful voice, that only faltered once:

"I have known him walk with — I have known him walk with Tiny Tim upon his shoulder, very fast indeed."

"And so have I," cried Peter. "Often."

"And so have I," exclaimed another. So had all.

"But he was very light to carry," she resumed, intent upon her work, "and his father loved him so, that it was no trouble: no trouble. And there is your father at the door!"

She hurried out to meet him; and little Bob in his comforter — he had need of it, poor fellow — came in. His tea was ready for him on the hob, and they all tried who should help him to it most. Then the two young Cratchits got upon his knees and laid, each child a little cheek, against his face, as if they said, "Don't mind it, father. Don't be grieved!"

Bob was very cheerful with them, and spoke pleasantly to all the family. He looked at the work upon the table, and praised the industry and speed of Mrs. Cratchit and the girls. They would be done long before Sunday, he said.

"Sunday! You went today, then, Robert?" said his wife.

"Yes, my dear," returned Bob. "I wish you could have gone. It would have done you good to see how green a place it is. But you'll see it often. I promised him that I would walk there on a Sunday. My little, little child!" cried Bob. "My little child!"

He broke down all at once. He couldn't help it. If he could have helped it, he and his child would have been farther apart perhaps than they were. He left the room, and went up-stairs into the room above, which was lighted cheerfully, and hung with Christmas. There was a chair set close beside the child, and there were signs of some one having been there, lately. Poor Bob sat down in it, and when he had thought a little and composed himself, he kissed the little face. He was reconciled to what had happened, and went down again quite happy.

They drew about the fire, and talked; the girls and mother working still. Bob told them of the extraordinary kindness of Mr. Scrooge's nephew, whom he had scarcely seen but once, and who, meeting him in the street that day, and seeing that he looked a little — "just a little down you know," said Bob, inquired what had happened to distress him. "On which," said Bob, "for he is the pleasantest-spoken gentleman you ever heard, I told him. 'I am heartily sorry for it, Mr. Cratchit,' he said, 'and heartily sorry for your good wife.' By the bye, how he ever knew that, I don't know."

"Knew what, my dear?"

"Why, that you were a good wife," replied Bob.

"Everybody knows that!" said Peter.

"Very well observed, my boy!" cried Bob. "I hope they do. 'Heartily sorry,' he said, 'for your good wife. If I can be of service to you in any way,' he said, giving me his card, 'that's where I live. Pray come to me.' Now, it wasn't," cried Bob, "for the sake of anything he might be able to do for us, so much as for his kind way, that this was quite delightful. It really seemed as if he had known our Tiny Tim, and felt with us."

"I'm sure he's a good soul!" said Mrs. Cratchit.

"You would be surer of it, my dear," returned Bob, "if you saw and spoke to him. I shouldn't be at all surprised — mark what I say! — if he got Peter a better situation."

"Only hear that, Peter," said Mrs. Cratchit.

"And then," cried one of the girls, "Peter will be keeping company with someone, and setting up for himself."

"Get along with you!" retorted Peter, grinning.

"It's just as likely as not," said Bob, "one of these days; though there's plenty of time for that, my dear. But however and whenever we part from one another, I am sure we shall none of us forget poor Tiny Tim — shall we — or this first parting that there was among us?"

"Never, father!" cried they all.

"And I know," said Bob, "I know, my dears, that when we recollect how patient and how mild he was; although he was a little, little child; we shall not quarrel easily among ourselves, and forget poor Tiny Tim in doing it."

"No, never, father!" they all cried again.

"I am very happy," said little Bob, "I am very happy!"

Mrs. Cratchit kissed him, his daughters kissed him, the two young Cratchits kissed him, and Peter and himself shook hands. Spirit of Tiny

Tim, thy childish essence was from God!

"Spectre," said Scrooge, "something informs me that our parting moment is at hand. I know it, but I know not how. Tell me what man that was whom we saw lying dead?"

The Ghost of Christmas Yet To Come conveyed him, as before — though at a different time, he thought: indeed, there seemed no order in these latter visions, save that they were in the Future — into the resorts of business men, but showed him not himself. Indeed, the Spirit did not stay for anything, but went straight on, as to the end just now desired, until besought by Scrooge to tarry for a moment.

"This court," said Scrooge, "through which we hurry now, is where my place of occupation is, and has been for a length of time. I see the house. Let me behold what I shall be, in days to come!"

The Spirit stopped; the hand was pointed elsewhere.

"The house is yonder," Scrooge exclaimed. "Why do you point away?"

The inexorable finger underwent no change.

Scrooge hastened to the window of his office, and looked in. It was an office still, but not his. The furniture was not the same, and the figure in the chair was not himself. The Phantom pointed as before.

He joined it once again, and wondering why and whither he had gone, accompanied it until they reached an iron gate. He paused to look round before entering.

A churchyard. Here, then; the wretched man whose name he had now to learn, lay underneath the ground. It was a worthy place. Walled in by houses; overrun by grass and weeds, the growth of vegetation's death, not life; choked up with too much burying; fat with repleted appetite. A worthy place!

The Spirit stood among the graves, and pointed down to One. He advanced towards it trembling. The Phantom was exactly as it had been, but he dreaded that he saw new meaning in its solemn shape.

"Before I draw nearer to that stone to which you point," said Scrooge, "answer me one question. Are these the shadows of the things that Will be, or are they shadows of things that May be, only?"

Still the Ghost pointed downward to the grave by which it stood.

"Men's courses will foreshadow certain ends, to which, if persevered in, they must lead," said Scrooge. "But if the courses be departed from, the ends will change. Say it is thus with what you show me!"

The Spirit was immovable as ever.

Scrooge crept towards it, trembling as he went; and following the finger, read upon the stone of the neglected grave his own name, Ebenezer Scrooge.

"Am I that man who lay upon the bed?" he cried, upon his knees.

The finger pointed from the grave to him, and back again.

"No, Spirit! Oh no, no!"

The finger still was there.

"Spirit!" he cried, tight clutching at its robe, "hear me! I am not the man I was. I will not be the man I must have been but for this intercourse. Why show me this, if I am past all hope!"

For the first time the hand appeared to shake.

"Good Spirit," he pursued, as down upon the ground he fell before it: "Your nature intercedes for me, and pities me. Assure me that I yet may change these shadows you have shown me, by an altered life!"

The kind hand trembled.

"I will honor Christmas in my heart, and try to keep it all the year. I will live in the Past, the Present, and the Future. The Spirits of all Three shall strive within me. I will not shut out the lessons that they teach. Oh, tell me I may sponge away the writing on this stone!"

In his agony, he caught the spectral hand. It sought to free itself, but he was strong in his entreaty, and detained it. The Spirit, stronger yet, repulsed him.

Holding up his hands in a last prayer to have his fate reversed, he saw an alteration in the Phantom's hood and dress. It shrunk, collapsed, and dwindled down into a bedpost.

 THE END OF IT

Yes! And the bedpost was his own. The bed was his own, the room was his own. Best and happiest of all, the Time before him was his own, to make amends in!

"I will live in the Past, the Present, and the Future!" Scrooge repeated, as he scrambled out of bed. "The Spirits of all Three shall strive within me. Oh Jacob Marley! Heaven, and the Christmas Time be praised for this! I say it on my knees, old Jacob; on my knees!"

He was so fluttered and so glowing with his good intentions, that his broken voice would scarcely answer to his call. He had been sobbing violently in his conflict with the Spirit, and his face was wet with tears.

"They are not torn down," cried Scrooge, folding one of his bed-curtains in his arms, "they are not torn down, rings and all. They are here — I am here — the shadows of the things that would have been, may be dispelled. They will be. I know they will!"

His hands were busy with his garments all this time; turning them inside out, putting them on upside down, tearing them, mislaying them, making them parties to every kind of extravagance.

"I don't know what to do!" cried Scrooge, laughing and crying in the same breath; and making a perfect Laocoön of himself with his stockings. "I am as light as a feather, I am as happy as an angel, I am as merry as a schoolboy. I am as giddy as a drunken man. A merry Christmas to everybody! A happy New Year to all the world. Hallo here! Whoop! Hallo!"

He had frisked into the sitting-room, and was now standing there: perfectly winded.

"There's the saucepan that the gruel was in!" cried Scrooge, starting off again, and going round the fireplace. "There's the door, by which the Ghost of Jacob Marley entered! There's the corner where the Ghost of Christmas Present, sat! There's the window where I saw the wandering Spirits! It's all right, it's all true, it all happened. Ha ha ha!"

338

Really, for a man who had been out of practice for so many years, it was a splendid laugh, a most illustrious laugh. The father of a long, long line of brilliant laughs!

"I don't know what day of the month it is!" said Scrooge. "I don't know how long I've been among the Spirits. I don't know anything. I'm quite a baby. Never mind. I don't care. I'd rather be a baby. Hallo! Whoop! Hallo here!"

He was checked in his transports by the churches ringing out the lustiest peals he had ever heard. Clash, clang, hammer; ding, dong, bell. Bell, dong, ding; hammer, clang, clash! Oh, glorious, glorious!

Running to the window, he opened it, and put out his head. No fog, no mist; clear, bright, jovial, stirring, cold; cold, piping for the blood to dance to; Golden sunlight; Heavenly sky; sweet fresh air; merry bells. Oh, glorious! Glorious!

"What's today!" cried Scrooge, calling downward to a boy in Sunday clothes, who perhaps had loitered in to look about him.

"Eh?" returned the boy, with all his might of wonder.

"What's today, my fine fellow?" said Scrooge.

"Today!" replied the boy. "Why, Christmas Day."

"It's Christmas Day!" said Scrooge to himself. "I haven't missed it. The Spirits have done it all in one night. They can do anything they like. Of course they can. Of course they can. Hallo, my fine fellow!"

"Hallo!" returned the boy.

"Do you know the Poulterer's, in the next street but one, at the corner?" Scrooge inquired.

"I should hope I did," replied the lad.

"An intelligent boy!" said Scrooge. "A remarkable boy! Do you know whether they've sold the prize Turkey that was hanging up there? — Not the little prize Turkey: the big one?"

"What, the one as big as me?" returned the boy.

"What a delightful boy!" said Scrooge. "It's a pleasure to talk to him. Yes, my buck!"

"It's hanging there now," replied the boy.

"Is it?" said Scrooge. "Go and buy it."

"Walk-er!" exclaimed the boy.

"No, no," said Scrooge, "I am in earnest. Go and buy it, and tell 'em to bring it here, that I may give them the direction where to take it. Come back with the man, and I'll give you a shilling. Come back with him in less than five minutes and I'll give you half-a-crown!"

The boy was off like a shot. He must have had a steady hand at a trigger who could have got a shot off half so fast.

"I'll send it to Bob Cratchit's!" whispered Scrooge, rubbing his hands, and splitting with a laugh. "He sha'n't know who sends it. It's twice the size of Tiny Tim. Joe Miller never made such a joke as sending it to Bob's will be!"

The hand in which he wrote the address was not a steady one, but write it he did, somehow, and went down-stairs to open the street door, ready for the coming of the poulterer's man. As he stood there, waiting his arrival, the knocker caught his eye.

"I shall love it, as long as I live!" cried Scrooge, patting it with his hand. "I scarcely ever looked at it before. What an honest expression it has in its face! It's a wonderful knocker! — Here's the Turkey! Hallo! Whoop! How are you! Merry Christmas!"

It was a Turkey! He never could have stood upon his legs, that bird. He would have snapped 'em short off in a minute, like sticks of sealing-wax.

"Why, it's impossible to carry that to Camden Town," said Scrooge. "You must have a cab."

The chuckle with which he said this, and the chuckle with which he paid for the Turkey, and the chuckle with which he paid for the cab, and the chuckle with which he recompensed the boy, were only to be exceeded by the chuckle with which he sat down breathless in his chair again, and chuckled till he cried.

Shaving was not an easy task, for his hand continued to shake very much; and shaving requires attention, even when you don't dance while you are at it. But if he had cut the end of his nose off, he would have put a piece of sticking-plaister over it, and been quite satisfied.

He dressed himself "all in his best," and at last got out into the streets. The people were by this time pouring forth, as he had seen them with the Ghost of Christmas Present; and walking with his hands behind him, Scrooge regarded every one with a delighted smile. He looked so irresistibly pleasant, in a word, that three or four good-humored fellows said, "Good morning, sir! A merry Christmas to you!" And Scrooge said often afterwards, that of all the blithe sounds he had ever heard, those were the blithest in his ears.

He had not gone far, when coming on towards him he beheld the portly gentleman, who had walked into his counting-house the day before, and said, "Scrooge and Marley's, I believe?" It sent a pang across his heart to think how this old gentleman would look upon him when they met; but he knew what path lay straight before him, and he took it.

"My dear sir," said Scrooge, quickening his pace, and taking the old gentleman by both his hands.

"How do you do? I hope you succeeded yesterday. It was very kind of you. A merry Christmas to you, sir!"

"Mr. Scrooge?"

"Yes," said Scrooge. "That is my name, and I fear it may not be pleasant to you. Allow me to ask your pardon. And will you have the goodness" — here Scrooge whispered in his ear.

"Lord bless me!" cried the gentleman, as if his breath were taken away. "My dear Mr. Scrooge, are you serious?"

"If you please," said Scrooge. "Not a farthing less. A great many back-payments are included in it, I assure you. Will you do me that favor?"

"My dear sir," said the other, shaking hands with him. "I don't know what to say to such munifi —"

"Don't say anything, please," retorted Scrooge. "Come and see me. Will you come and see me?"

"I will!" cried the old gentleman. And it was clear he meant to do it.

"Thank'ee," said Scrooge. "I am much obliged to you. I thank you fifty times. Bless you!"

He went to church, and walked about the streets, and watched the people hurrying to and fro, and patted children on the head, and questioned beggars, and looked down into the kitchens of houses, and up to the windows, and found that everything could yield him pleasure. He had never dreamed that any walk — that anything — could give him so much happiness. In the afternoon he turned his steps towards his nephew's house.

He passed the door a dozen times, before he had the courage to go up and knock. But he made a dash, and did it:

"Is your master at home, my dear?" said Scrooge to the girl. Nice girl! Very.

"Yes, sir."

"Where is he, my love?" said Scrooge.

"He's in the dining-room, sir, along with mistress. I'll show you up-stairs, if you please."

"Thank'ee. He knows me," said Scrooge, with his hand already on the dining-room lock. "I'll go in here, my dear."

He turned it gently, and sidled his face in, round the door. They were looking at the table (which was spread out in great array); for these young housekeepers are always nervous on such points, and like to see that everything is right.

"Fred!" said Scrooge.

Dear heart alive, how his niece by marriage started! Scrooge had forgotten, for the moment, about her sitting in the corner with the footstool, or he wouldn't have done it, on any account.

"Why bless my soul!" cried Fred, "who's that?"

"It's I. Your uncle Scrooge. I have come to dinner. Will you let me in, Fred?"

Let him in! It is a mercy he didn't shake his arm off. He was at home in five minutes. Nothing could be heartier. His niece looked just the same.

So did Topper when he came. So did the plump sister when she came. So did every one when they came. Wonderful party, wonderful games, wonderful unanimity, won-der-ful happiness!

But he was early at the office next morning. Oh, he was early there. If he could only be there first, and catch Bob Cratchit coming late! That was the thing he had set his heart upon.

And he did it; yes, he did! The clock struck nine. No Bob. A quarter past. No Bob. He was full eighteen minutes and a half behind his time. Scrooge sat with his door wide open, that he might see him come into the Tank.

His hat was off, before he opened the door; his comforter too. He was on his stool in a jiffy; driving away with his pen, as if he were trying to overtake nine o'clock.

"Hallo!" growled Scrooge, in his accustomed voice, as near as he could feign it. "What do you mean by coming here at this time of day?"

"I am very sorry, sir," said Bob. "I am behind my time."

"You are?" repeated Scrooge. "Yes. I think you are. Step this way, sir, if you please."

"It's only once a year, sir," pleaded Bob, appearing from the Tank. "It shall not be repeated. I was making rather merry yesterday, sir."

"Now, I'll tell you what, my friend," said Scrooge, "I am not going to stand this sort of thing any longer. And therefore," he continued, leaping from his stool, and giving Bob such a dig in the waistcoat that he staggered back into the Tank again; "and therefore I am about to raise your salary!"

Bob trembled, and got a little nearer to the ruler. He had a momentary idea of knocking Scrooge down with it, holding him, and calling to the people in the court for help and a strait-waistcoat.

"A merry Christmas, Bob!" said Scrooge, with an earnestness that could not be mistaken, as he clapped him on the back. "A merrier Christmas, Bob, my good fellow, than I have given you, for many a year! I'll raise your salary, and endeavor to assist your struggling family, and we will discuss your affairs this very afternoon, over a Christmas bowl of smoking bishop, Bob! Make up the fires, and buy another coal-scuttle before you dot another i, Bob Cratchit!"

Scrooge was better than his word. He did it all, and infinitely more; and to Tiny Tim, who did not die, he was a second father. He became as good a friend, as good a master, and as good a man, as the good old city knew, or any other good old city, town, or borough, in the good old world. Some people laughed to see the alteration in him, but he let them laugh, and little heeded them; for he was wise enough to know that nothing ever happened on this globe, for good, at which some people did not have their fill of laughter in the outset; and knowing that such as these would be blind anyway, he thought it quite as well that they should wrinkle up their eyes in grins, as have the malady in less attractive forms. His own heart laughed: and that was quite enough for him.

He had no further intercourse with Spirits, but lived upon the Total Abstinence Principle, ever afterwards; and it was always said of him, that he knew how to keep Christmas well, if any man alive possessed the knowledge. May that be truly said of us, and all of us! And so, as Tiny Tim observed, God bless Us, Every One!